Liam Cleris 2017

MW00629074

Praise for *The Midas Paradox*

"Scott Sumner is one of the most original economists around. Having been a pioneer in making the case for nominal GDP targeting, he has now turned his insightful talents to economic history, providing an important and fresh reexamination of the causes of the Great Depression and the halting recovery thereafter. Provocative, well argued and well written, *The Midas Paradox* is an important contribution to our understanding of the roots of the worst economic period in the nation's history."

> —**Robert E. Litan**, former Senior Fellow and Vice President for Economic Studies, The Brookings Institution

"*The Midas Paradox* is a must read to understand the complexities of monetary management under the international gold standards of the 1930s. Scott Sumner importantly focuses his research on the critical role of market expectations and labor policy failures that compounded central bank mistakes and led to tragic consequences for the global economy."

> —**Manuel H. Johnson II**, former Vice Chairman, Federal Reserve System

"Scott Sumner is one of the preeminent monetary thinkers today. *The Midas Paradox* represents his twenty years' study of the Great Depression, one of the most important economic events of the twentieth century. Highly recommended."

> —**Tyler Cowen**, Holbert C. Harris Chair of Economics and Director of the Mercatus Center, George Mason University

"In *The Midas Paradox*, Scott Sumner provides a fascinating account of how monetary policy under the gold standard got us into the Great Depression and how wage policies under the New Deal slowed the subsequent recovery. The book is deep and rich and has important lessons for today—a must-read for anyone interested in monetary policy and history and the errors of government policy."

> —**Douglas A. Irwin**, Robert E. Maxwell '23 Professor of Arts and Sciences, Department of Economics, Dartmouth College

"Explaining the Great Depression is the 'holy grail' of macroeconomics, in the words of none other than Ben Bernanke. By combining economic theory with economic history and the history of economic thought, Scott Sumner shows how it is possible to make substantial progress on this ambitious project. Sumner may not explain everything, but he explains a lot. *The Midas Paradox* deserves a place on that short shelf of essential books on the Depression."

—**Barry Eichengreen**, George C. Pardee and Helen N. Pardee Professor of Economics and Political Science, University of California, Berkeley

"Having done some recent research myself on the causes of the Great Depression, I have found Scott Sumner's book *The Midas Paradox* a source of new insights on that subject. In particular, he sheds light on why deflation proved to be such an important factor in disrupting economic activity after the 1929 Crash. He makes a properly global appraisal of monetary policy and concludes that central banks, on balance, were actually tightening the money supply when they should have been easing to offset the loss of liquidity in the financial sector from the 1929 crash. *The Midas Paradox* is an important contribution to the study of the Great Depression, because it adds another explanation to such known factors as ill-timed protectionism or why producer prices dropped so sharply from 1929 to 1933, causing much distress in a heavily agrarian economy."

—**George Melloan**, former Deputy Editor, *The Wall Street Journal*; author, *The Great Money Binge: Spending Our Way to Socialism*

"In *The Midas Paradox*, Scott Sumner adopts an ideal method (for my taste) of writing economic history. He presents plenty of details on episodes, including pending and enacted legislation, and on contemporary consensus or disagreement on explanations and recommendations. Sumner also presents judicious amounts of statistical and econometric evidence. I find all this a gripping story."

—**Leland B. Yeager**, Ludwig von Mises Professor of Economics, Emeritus, Auburn University

"*The Midas Paradox* fills a gap in our understanding of the Great Depression. The author continues the work of a long and distinguished line of scholarship that goes back to Rueff and Mundell in pinpointing the role of the gold market and the price of gold as a key factor in some of the salient episodes of the period."

　　　—**Michael D. Bordo**, Professor of Economics and Director of the
　　　　Center for Monetary and Financial History, Rutgers University

"With special attention to gold and labor market legislation, Sumner's book *The Midas Paradox* provides an enlightening blend of detailed, warm-bodied financial and economic history of the 1930s with its broad-based statistical counterpart, using both national income accounts and financial data. His perspective will be seen as a unique contribution to the large and still growing literature on the Great Depression."

　　　—**Roger W. Garrison**, Professor Emeritus of Economics, Auburn
　　　　University

"Scott Sumner's wonderful book *The Midas Paradox* provides a thought-provoking reinterpretation of the Great Depression: it combines a monetary approach based on shocks to the gold market with a supply-side approach based on legislated real-wage shocks that fits the evidence for the entire interwar period. Sumner's insights into the Great Depression are also highly relevant to the global financial crisis. *The Midas Paradox* is a major contribution both to economic history and to contemporary economic policy issues."

　　　—**Kevin Dowd**, Professor of Finance and Economics at Durham
　　　　University and Professor Emeritus of Financial Risk Management
　　　　at the University of Nottingham, England

"Scott Sumner offers a unified view of the Great Depression as seen through the lens of how financial markets' expectations of future monetary policy appeared in the price of gold especially but also in other asset markets like the stock market. In addition, the detailed, rich, historical narrative is full of insights about the causal nature of policy (monetary, fiscal, and regulatory) not captured in a single, abstract model. Unlike the gold standard at the time, *The Midas Paradox* is not orthodox, but it certainly forces the reader to examine critically his or her prior views about the Depression."

　　　—**Robert L. Hetzel**, Senior Economist and Research Advisor,
　　　　Research Department, Federal Reserve Bank of Richmond

"*The Midas Paradox* is a fascinating, very clearly written and very important book. It sheds a new light on the root causes of the Great Depression. And, it encourages the rethinking of the fundamentals of the macroeconomic theory and policy."

> —**Leszek Balcerowicz**, Professor of Economics, Department of
> International Comparative Studies, Warsaw School of Economics;
> former President, National Bank of Poland; and Former Deputy
> Prime Minister and Finance Minister, Republic of Poland

"The Great Depression is the biggest puzzle in the history of modern capitalism. How could millions of people be prospering one year, then out of work the next? Building on the work of previous scholars and adding fresh insights, Scott Sumner's book *The Midas Paradox* offers perhaps the most ambitious analysis of the Depression yet, which seeks to explain its major ups and downs as well as how it got started. Sumner's book has important (and worrying) implications for today. He argues that the Great Recession of 2008–09 was so severe because economists and central banks still have not fully learned the lessons of the Depression."

> —**Kurt Schuler**, Senior Fellow, Center for Financial Stability;
> Economist, Office of International Affairs, US Department
> of the Treasury

"Think you know what caused the Great Depression? If so, be prepared to think again: *The Midas Paradox* bristles with well-mounted challenges to orthodox— and to many *un*orthodox—accounts of history's most notorious economic crisis. Whether it manages to change your most confidently held beliefs or not, Scott Sumner's painstaking book is bound to improve your understanding of the deepest and longest-lasting business downturn of them all."

> —**George A. Selgin**, Senior Fellow and Director, Center for
> Monetary and Financial Alternatives, Cato Institute; Professor
> Emeritus of Economics at the University of Georgia

"*The Midas Paradox* succeeds in shedding new light on the Great Depression, and the gold market approach provides an effective unifying thread as the author navigates through the many shocks and policy shifts occurring over this key period. The integration of international events over this period is also the best I have seen, and the connection between the 1930s policy dilemmas and those of today could not be more relevant."

> —**Richard C. K. Burdekin**, Jonathan B. Lovelace Professor of Economics, Claremont McKenna College

"Scott Sumner provides a very thought-provoking and unique perspective on the causes of the Great Depression and the implications for current monetary and fiscal policy. Whether or not you agree with Sumner's analysis, *The Midas Paradox* will challenge some of your beliefs and make you think."

> —**John A. Allison IV**, Retired President and CEO, Cato Institute; Retired Chairman and CEO, BB&T Corporation

"Just over 50 years ago the publication of *A Monetary History of the United States*, by Milton Friedman and Anna Schwartz, was a crucial episode in the monetarist counterrevolution that overturned the Keynesian dominance over postwar macroeconomics, gradually persuading most of the economics profession that the Great Depression was largely caused by the monumental ineptitude of the Federal Reserve. However, the account of the Great Depression provided by *A Monetary History*, its many virtues notwithstanding, was defective in a number of respects, the most important of which being that its strictly quantity-theoretic focus on the behavior of the monetary aggregates was inconsistent with the workings of the international gold standard that was in operation for much of the Great Depression. A number of subsequent researchers have since pointed out that the gold standard was a critical factor in causing and propagating the Great Depression. Now in *The Midas Paradox*, Scott Sumner has, with great theoretical and empirical insight and ingenuity, provided a masterly narrative account of the onset and propagation of the Great Depression and of its decade-long duration, buttressed by striking quantitative and statistical evidence of the pivotal role played by the international gold standard in the Great Depression. It is no exaggeration to say that *The Midas Paradox* has completely eclipsed all previous accounts of the Great Depression, and I have little doubt that a half century from now *The Midas Paradox* will remain the definitive account of that catastrophe."

> —**David Glasner**, author, *Free Banking and Monetary Reform*

"Scott Sumner offers readers of *The Midas Paradox* a bountiful harvest of new nuggets about the 'gold standard view' of the Great Depression. This rewarding read begins with Sumner's excellent preface—an important element that allows the author to review his own book, a privilege usually denied by journals."

> —**Steve H. Hanke**, Professor of Applied Economics and Co-Director of the Institute for Applied Economics, Global Health, and the Study of Business Enterprise, Johns Hopkins University

"Whatever you know, or think you know, about the Great Depression, *The Midas Paradox* will teach you something new. And as Scott Sumner points out, properly understanding what happened in the 1930s matters a great deal for getting policy right in our own time."

> —**Ramesh Ponnuru**, Senior Editor, *National Review*

"Scott Sumner has provided a tour de force of the Great Depression in *The Midas Paradox*. He convincingly shows in this accessible but thorough retelling of the Great Depression that policy errors were behind the long economic slump. In particular, Sumner demonstrates that the combination of contractionary monetary policy working through the gold market and supply-side disruptions arising from New Deal policies created a large drag on economic activity. This is a must read for anyone wanting to better understand the Great Depression and its implications for policy today."

> —**David Beckworth**, Assistant Professor of Economics, Western Kentucky University; Editor, *Boom and Bust Banking: The Causes and Consequences of the Great Recession*

"Where Scott Sumner's *The Midas Paradox* is most useful is in its short-interval narrative of monetary, labor market, and sometimes political factors that drove U.S. financial markets from the 1929 stock market crash through the 1937–1938 depression. His view of the impact of many New Deal initiatives is controversial, and often harsh, but well-documented. His discussion of the role of non-official hoarding and dis-hoarding of gold as a driver of liquidity conditions is original. The book will be an indispensable source for anyone on the economic dynamics of the period."

> —**H. Clark Johnson**, author, *Gold, France, and the Great Depression, 1919–1932*; former Senior Economist, U.S. Department of Defense

THE
MIDAS
PARADOX

INDEPENDENT INSTITUTE

INDEPENDENT INSTITUTE is a non-profit, non-partisan, public-policy research and educational organization that shapes ideas into profound and lasting impact. The mission of Independent is to boldly advance peaceful, prosperous, and free societies grounded in a commitment to human worth and dignity. Applying independent thinking to issues that matter, we create transformational ideas for today's most pressing social and economic challenges. The results of this work are published as books, our quarterly journal, *The Independent Review*, and other publications and form the basis for numerous conference and media programs. By connecting these ideas with organizations and networks, we seek to inspire action that can unleash an era of unparalleled human flourishing at home and around the globe.

FOUNDER & PRESIDENT
David J. Theroux

RESEARCH DIRECTOR
William F. Shughart II

SENIOR FELLOWS
Bruce L. Benson
Ivan Eland
John C. Goodman
John R. Graham
Robert Higgs
Lawrence J. McQuillan
Robert H. Nelson
Charles V. Peña
Benjamin Powell
William F. Shughart II
Randy T. Simmons
Alexander Tabarrok
Alvaro Vargas Llosa
Richard K. Vedder

ACADEMIC ADVISORS
Leszek Balcerowicz
WARSAW SCHOOL OF ECONOMICS

Herman Belz
UNIVERSITY OF MARYLAND

Thomas E. Borcherding
CLAREMONT GRADUATE SCHOOL

Boudewijn Bouckaert
UNIVERSITY OF GHENT, BELGIUM

Allan C. Carlson
HOWARD CENTER

Robert D. Cooter
UNIVERSITY OF CALIFORNIA, BERKELEY

Robert W. Crandall
BROOKINGS INSTITUTION

Richard A. Epstein
NEW YORK UNIVERSITY

B. Delworth Gardner
BRIGHAM YOUNG UNIVERSITY

George Gilder
DISCOVERY INSTITUTE

Nathan Glazer
HARVARD UNIVERSITY

Steve H. Hanke
JOHNS HOPKINS UNIVERSITY

James J. Heckman
UNIVERSITY OF CHICAGO

H. Robert Heller
SONIC AUTOMOTIVE

Deirdre N. McCloskey
UNIVERSITY OF ILLINOIS,
CHICAGO

J. Huston McCulloch
OHIO STATE UNIVERSITY

Forrest McDonald
UNIVERSITY OF ALABAMA

Thomas Gale Moore
HOOVER INSTITUTION

Charles Murray
AMERICAN ENTERPRISE
INSTITUTE

Michael J. Novak, Jr.
AMERICAN ENTERPRISE
INSTITUTE

June E. O'Neill
BARUCH COLLEGE

Charles E. Phelps
UNIVERSITY OF ROCHESTER

Nathan Rosenberg
STANFORD UNIVERSITY

Paul H. Rubin
EMORY UNIVERSITY

Bruce M. Russett
YALE UNIVERSITY

Pascal Salin
UNIVERSITY OF PARIS,
FRANCE

Vernon L. Smith
CHAPMAN UNIVERSITY

Pablo T. Spiller
UNIVERSITY OF CALIFORNIA,
BERKELEY

Joel H. Spring
STATE UNIVERSITY OF
NEW YORK, OLD WESTBURY

Richard L. Stroup
NORTH CAROLINA STATE
UNIVERSITY

Robert D. Tollison
CLEMSON UNIVERSITY

Arnold S. Trebach
AMERICAN UNIVERSITY

Richard E. Wagner
GEORGE MASON UNIVERSITY

Walter E. Williams
GEORGE MASON UNIVERSITY

Charles Wolf, Jr.
RAND CORPORATION

100 Swan Way, Oakland, California 94621-1428, U.S.A.
Telephone: 510-632-1366 • Facsimile: 510-568-6040 • Email: info@independent.org • www.independent.org

THE
MIDAS
PARADX

Financial Markets, Government Policy Shocks, and the Great Depression

SCOTT SUMNER

INDEPENDENT
INSTITUTE

OAKLAND, CALIFORNIA

Copyright © 2015 by the Independent Institute

All Rights Reserved. No part of this book may be reproduced or transmitted in any form by electronic or mechanical means now known or to be invented, including photocopying, recording, or information storage and retrieval systems, without permission in writing from the publisher, except by a reviewer who may quote brief passages in a review. Nothing herein should be construed as necessarily reflecting the views of the Institute or as an attempt to aid or hinder the passage of any bill before Congress.

Independent Institute
100 Swan Way, Oakland, CA 94621-1428
Telephone: 510-632-1366
Fax: 510-568-6040
Email: info@independent.org
Website: www.independent.org

Cover Design: Denise Tsui
Cover Image: © 1935 / AP Photo

Library of Congress Cataloging-in-Publication Data

Sumner, Scott

The Midas paradox : financial markets, government policy shocks, and the Great Depression / Scott Sumner.

528 pages cm

Includes bibliographical references and index.

ISBN 978-1-59813-150-5 (hardcover : alk. paper) -- ISBN 978-1-59813-151-2 (pbk. : alk. paper)

1. Depressions--1929--United States. 2. Monetary policy--United States--History--20th century. 3. United States--Economic policy--20th century. I. Title.

HB37171929 .S86 2015

330.973'0917--dc23

2013043553

For my mother

Contents

PART V Conclusion

Preface

I FIRST STUDIED macroeconomics during the highly inflationary 1970s. Like many students of that era, I was greatly influenced by
monetarist ideas, particularly *A Monetary History of the United States*, written
by Milton Friedman and Anna Schwartz. By the mid 1980s, I began to discover a new approach to monetary history, one that focused on the constraints
of the international gold standard, not the quantity of money in a particular
country. Because I had found the views of Friedman and Schwartz to be quite
persuasive, but also saw merit in the new "gold standard view" of the Depression, I was forced to try to reconcile these two perspectives.

This book represents the fruits of two decades of research on the role of
gold in the Great Depression. I began by trying to think through the concept
of monetary policy under a gold standard. If interest rates and commodity
prices were determined internationally via arbitrage, in what sense could a
country be said to have an independent monetary policy? Ultimately, I decided that the *gold reserve ratio* was the most sensible way of thinking about
the stance of monetary policy under a gold standard. When I worked out the
numbers, I was surprised to find that world monetary policy tightened sharply
between October 1929 and October 1930, a policy shift that had been missed
by previous researchers.

Next, I discovered that the gold ratio wasn't the only important way in
which the gold standard impacted macroeconomic conditions during the
1930s. Private gold hoarding increased sharply on four occasions; each of
which was associated with falling output and falling asset prices in the U.S.
Changes in the price of gold were extremely important during 1933–34, as
rising gold prices led to rising asset prices and economic recovery. I also

discovered interesting links between government policies that impacted the global gold market, asset market prices, and the broader macroeconomy. In particular, markets seemed to anticipate the effects of policy shifts, and there were even cases where the *effects* of policy seemed to precede the *causes*.

Obviously, "effect" cannot precede "cause"; what was actually happening was that markets were anticipating that gold market disturbances would impact future monetary policy, and this caused asset prices to respond immediately to the expected change in policy. Broader price indices and even industrial production also responded surprisingly quickly—not the long and variable lags often assumed by macroeconomists.

Much of this work was done in the 1980s and 1990s, and I was quite pleased that three of these papers were cited by Gauti Eggertsson in 2008, in an important article in the *American Economic Review*. Eggertsson applied cutting edge "new Keynesian" models to the gold standard era, which suggested that anticipations of future monetary policy would often have a much more powerful impact on current conditions than the current stance of monetary policy. I had stumbled on some ideas that had important implications for theoretical macroeconomics.

By the early 1990s, I was beginning to think in terms of a comprehensive narrative of the Great Depression. The idea was to do something roughly analogous to Friedman and Schwartz's seminal work, but from a gold standard perspective. Instead of focusing on the famous MV=PY equation as the organizing principle, I developed some identities relating the gold market to the macroeconomy, and then collected the relevant data.

When I reached the middle of 1933, however, I noticed that the monetary approach to the Great Depression seemed to suddenly break down. That's when I turned my attention to the role of wages, which were raised by over 20 percent in just two months, from July to September 1933. This would be the first of five "wage shocks," each of which set back a promising recovery. At that point, I did some research with Stephen Silver on the issue of wage cyclicality during the Great Depression.

When I combined the two approaches, a monetary approach based on the gold market, with a supply-side approach based on legislated wage shocks, I had a model that provided an excellent fit for the entire period from 1929 to 1940, indeed, in some respects, for the entire interwar period. Unfortunately, the project kept getting delayed (once a year's worth of work was simply lost), and hence this book is coming out many years after the original research was done.

However, this delay may have been a blessing in disguise, as the research turned out to have very important implications for the economic crisis of 2008. At that point, I began advocating a new monetary policy, as I concluded that most of the profession had misdiagnosed the crisis. And more surprisingly, the profession misinterpreted the 2008 crisis in almost exactly the same way that the Great Depression was originally misdiagnosed. See if any of the following sounds familiar:

1. In the Depression most people assumed monetary policy was ineffective, as interest rates fell close to zero and the monetary base increased sharply (i.e., "QE.").
2. Most assumed the Depression was caused by financial distress, not tight money.
3. Most assumed that monetary policy was too expansionary during the 1920s, and that the Depression was a relapse from an overheated boom.

Sound familiar? In 1963 Friedman and Schwartz showed that those views were mistaken, yet economists made precisely the same errors this time around. My hope is that by gaining a better understanding of what happened in the 1930s, we will be able to better understand our current policy dilemma, and develop more effective solutions.

My original manuscript included two theory chapters after the introduction, which would have proved intimidating for the average reader. This material has been moved back to Chapter 13. Specialists should read Chapter 13 after the intro, and before the nine narrative chapters. It will make it easier to follow the theory that is used to evaluate policy shocks. Nonetheless, the basic message is easy enough for even non-specialists to follow. Gold hoarding led to deflation and the Great Contraction of 1929–1933, and also the depression of 1937–1938, and five attempts to artificially raise wages during the New Deal slowed the recovery.

I have worked on this project for so long that I won't be able to recall all of those who assisted me, but a few names stand out. Stephen Silver coauthored the paper that provided the template for the analysis of interwar wage shocks. Michael Bordo and George Selgin encouraged me to turn my academic papers into a unified narrative of the Depression years. Tyler Cowen and Alex Tabarrok encouraged me to persevere after an initial setback. Clark Johnson provided a great deal of useful feedback over the years, as did my colleagues at Bentley University. A portion of the research was funded by the National Science Foundation. And I'd like to thank my wife and daughter, who put up with huge stacks of paper swamping our home office.

PART I

Gold, Wages, and the Great Depression

Real monetary equilibrium in any single country requires the price level to be in harmony with the wage level, so that the margin of profit is sufficient, but not more than sufficient, to induce full activity and full employment.
    —R.G. Hawtrey (1947, p. 45)

1

Introduction

OVER THE PAST fifty years economic historians have made great progress in explaining the causes of the Great Depression. Many economists now see the initial contraction as being caused, or at least exacerbated, by monetary policy errors and/or defects in the international gold standard. Some argue that New Deal policies delayed recovery from the Depression. But we still lack a convincing narrative of the many twists and turns in the economy between 1929 and 1940. This book attempts to provide such a narrative.

In this book I use an unorthodox approach to monetary economics: one that focuses not on changes in the money supply or interest rates, but rather on disturbances in the world gold market. Others have looked at how the gold standard constrained policy during the Great Depression, and/or how the undervaluation of gold after World War I put deflationary pressure on the world economy. These studies gave insights into the structural inadequacies of the interwar monetary system, but they didn't tell us why a major depression began in America in late 1929, and they certainly didn't explain the seventeen high-frequency changes in the growth rate of U.S. industrial production shown in Table 1.1.

I will show that if we take the gold market seriously we can explain much more about the Great Depression than anyone had thought possible. Three types of gold market shocks generated much of the variation shown in Table 1.1: changes in central bank demand for gold, private sector gold hoarding, and changes in the price of gold. The remaining output shocks are linked to five wage shocks that resulted from the New Deal. This is the first study to provide a comprehensive and detailed look at all high frequency macro shocks during the Great Depression.

3

Table 1.1 Seasonally Adjusted Changes in Industrial Production

Period	Change in IP	Period	Change in IP
9/29 to 12/30	−29.3%	5/35 to 1/37	+38.8%
12/30 to 4/31	+2.5%	1/37 to 9/37	−0.9%
4/31 to 7/32	−34.8%	9/37 to 5/38	−29.1%
7/32 to 10/32	+13.3%	5/38 to 11/38	+23.0%
10/32 to 3/33	−9.2%	11/38 to 5/39	+1.5%
3/33 to 7/33	+57.4%	5/39 to 11/39	+22.4%
7/33 to 11/33	−18.8%	11/39 to 5/40	−2.0%
11/33 to 5/34	+15.9%	5/40 to 12/41	+39.8%
5/34 to 5/35	+3.1%		

Note: These are actual changes, not annualized rates of change.

See Appendix 2.a for sources of data.

In order to be useful, economic history must be more than mere story-telling. Because asset prices in auction-style markets respond immediately to policy news, they can be much more informative about policy than econometric studies relying on estimated "long and variable lags." Throughout the narrative we will see that financial market responses to the policy shocks of the 1930s were consistent with a gold market approach, but inconsistent with many preceding narratives of the Depression.

This model of the Great Depression has radical implications for monetary theory and policy, and particularly for the current economic crisis. Just as in the early 1930s, policymakers in 2008 missed important warning signs that monetary policy was disastrously off course. Later, we'll see important similarities between the slumps that began in 1929, 1937, and 2008.

In 1963, Friedman and Schwartz's *Monetary History of the United States* seemed to provide the definitive account of the role of monetary policy in the Great Depression. Over the past few decades, however, a number of economic historians have suggested that Friedman and Schwartz paid too little attention to the worldwide nature of the Depression, especially the role of the international gold standard. Here are just a few of the revisionist studies that influenced my own research:[1]

1. Deirdre [Donald] N. McCloskey and J. Richard Zecher (1984) on monetary policy endogeniety.
2. David Glasner (1989) on the impact of changes in the demand for gold.
3. Peter Temin (1989) on how devaluation impacts policy expectations.
4. Barry Eichengreen (1992) on the importance of policy coordination.
5. Ben Bernanke (1995) on multiple monetary equilibria.
6. Clark Johnson (1997) on the undervaluation of gold and French hoarding.

Why, then, is there a need for an additional narrative of the Depression, which also focuses on the role of monetary policy and the gold standard?

The analytical framework used in this book differs in important ways from preceding gold standard oriented monetary analyses of the Depression. For instance, although others have pointed to the deflationary consequences of an increased demand for gold, it has generally been viewed more as a secular problem—that is, as a factor tending to depress prices throughout the late 1920s and the 1930s. This is the first study to examine the impact of *high frequency gold demand shocks* on short-term fluctuations in U.S. output.

In addition, most previous studies have focused on central bank gold hoarding, paying relatively little attention to private gold hoarding. Where central bank hoarding has been examined, it has often been in an ad hoc context, without a framework capable of providing a quantitative estimate of the impact of each central bank on the world price level. And those who did look at the role of gold often focused on the period before the United States and France left the gold standard, and thus missed the severe instability in the world gold market during 1936–1938.

The book concludes with a chapter that describes a gold and labor market model of the Depression, and specialists may wish to examine this chapter first. However, the most important contributions of this study show up not in the formal models, but rather in the narrative provided in Chapters 2 through 10.

---

1. Unless otherwise specified, all subsequent references to McCloskey and Zecher, Glasner, Temin, Eichengreen, and Johnson will refer to the works cited in the following list.

These chapters offer the first comprehensive examination of the complex inter-relationship between gold, wages, and financial markets during the 1930s. We'll see repeated examples of how policy shocks that influenced gold demand and/or wages also impacted financial markets, which will give us a better understanding of how macroeconomic policy impacts the broader economy. This narrative is followed by a brief essay where I show how a misreading of the events of 1932–1933 profoundly influenced the development of twentieth-century macroeconomics.

As with much of economic history, the goal of this exercise is not simply to fill in blank spots in our understanding of the Depression, but also to develop a better understanding of macroeconomics as a whole. To take just one example, I believe this account provides the first convincing explanation for why the Depression began (in the United States) during the fall of 1929. If other researchers have not been able to provide a convincing explanation for the onset of the Depression, then how can they claim to have explained the cause of the Depression? Indeed, this timing issue calls into question all sorts of standard assumptions about policy exogeniety, the identification of shocks, transmission mechanisms, and policy lags. Thus, I see this study as offering both a narrative of the Depression and a critique of modern monetary analysis.

The manuscript was basically completed in 2006, but revisions were made after the severe crisis of late 2008. During this period I was shocked to see so many misconceptions from the Great Depression repeated in the current crisis:

1. Assuming causality runs from financial panic to falling aggregate demand (rather than vice versa).

2. Assuming that sharply falling short-term interest rates and a sharply rising monetary base meant "easy money."

3. Assuming that monetary policy became ineffective once rates hit zero.

I had thought that Friedman and Schwartz had disposed of these misconceptions, and was surprised to see so many economists making these assumptions during the current crisis. Indeed, the view that Fed policy was "easy" during late 2008 was almost universal. How could we have so quickly forgotten the lessons of the Great Depression? The reaction of economists to the current crisis suggests that much of macroeconomic theory is built on a foundation of sand. We think we have advanced far beyond the prejudices of the 1930s, but when a crisis hits we reflexively exhibit the same atavistic impulses as our ancestors. Even worse, we congratulate the Fed for avoiding the mistakes of the 1930s, even as it repeats many of those mistakes.

The next section lists a few key findings from each chapter, many of which are new, and some of which directly challenge previous accounts of the Depression. In other cases, I develop explanations for events that most economic historians have overlooked.

Key Findings

Chapter 1

Because financial markets respond immediately to new information, they can be especially useful in resolving questions of *causality*—arguably the most difficult problem faced by economic historians. Between 1929 and 1938, U.S. stock prices were unusually volatile. And between 1931 and 1938, there was an especially close correlation between news stories related to gold and/or wage legislation and financial market prices. A simple aggregate supply and demand (AS/AD) framework can explain most of the output volatility of the 1930s. The demand shocks were triggered by gold hoarding (or changes in the price of gold), and the supply shocks were caused by policy-driven changes in hourly wage rates.

Chapter 2

U.S. monetary policy tightened in mid-1928, but there is little evidence to support the view that the events of October 1929 were a lagged response to this action. *World* monetary policy (as measured by changes in the gold reserve ratio) was stable between June 1928 and October 1929, and then tightened sharply over the following twelve months. It was this policy switch, perhaps combined with bearish sentiment from the reduced prospects for international monetary coordination, which triggered a sharp decline in aggregate demand.

Chapter 3

The German economic crisis of 1931 was a key turning point in the Depression. It led to substantial private gold hoarding, and between mid-1931 and late 1932 strongly impacted U.S. equity markets. The two October 1931 discount rate increases by the Federal Reserve (Fed) had little or no impact. Instead, gold hoarding triggered by the British devaluation was the most important factor depressing aggregate demand during the fall of 1931.

Chapter 4

Keynes suggested that the Fed's spring 1932 open market purchases might have been ineffective due to the existence of a "liquidity trap." Friedman and Schwartz suggested that the modest upswing in late 1932 was a lagged response to the Fed's efforts. Neither view is supported by the evidence. The open market purchases were associated with extensive gold hoarding, and this prevented any significant increase in the money supply. Stock prices, commodity prices, and economic output only began rising when renewed investor confidence in the dollar curtailed the hoarding of gold.

Chapter 5

President Roosevelt instituted a dollar depreciation program in April 1933 with the avowed goal of raising the price level back to its 1926 level. This program was unique in U.S. history and was the primary factor behind both the 57 percent surge in industrial production between March and July 1933 and the 22 percent rise in the wholesale price level in the twelve months after March 1933. The initial recovery was triggered not by a preceding monetary expansion, but rather by expectations of future monetary expansion.

Chapter 6

The National Recovery Administration (NRA) adopted a high wage policy in July 1933, which sharply increased hourly wage rates. This policy aborted the recovery, led to a major stock market crash, and helped lengthen the Depression by six to seven years. In a sense, one depression ended and a second "Great Depression" began in late July 1933, unrelated to the contraction of 1929–1933.

Chapter 7

The gold-buying program of late 1933 is a little known and widely misunderstood part of the New Deal. The program was a variant of Irving Fisher's "Compensated Dollar Plan," and was essentially a monetary feedback rule aimed at returning prices to pre-Depression levels. Although the program helped promote economic recovery, it eventually became a major political issue and led key economic advisors to resign from the Roosevelt Administration. This program exposed the deep structure of the monetary transmission mechanism, a structure hypothesized by modern new Keynesians, but normally almost entirely hidden from view.

Chapter 8

Although the conventional view is that Franklin D. Roosevelt took America off the gold standard, U.S. monetary policy became even more strongly linked to gold after 1934 than it had been before 1933. A recovery in the United States finally got underway when the Supreme Court declared the NIRA to be unconstitutional in mid-1935. Because the demise of the gold bloc in 1936 reduced devaluation fears, its impact on gold demand and the broader macroeconomy was exactly the opposite of the British devaluation of 1931.

Chapter 9

Actual and prospective gold dishoarding led to high inflation during late 1936 and early 1937. Expectations of future gold supplies were so high that tight monetary policies lacked credibility. Rapid inflation led to a "gold panic" in the spring of 1937 as investors became concerned that the buying price of gold would be reduced. During 1937, the expansionary impact of gold dishoarding began to be offset by wage increases, which reflected the resurgence of unions after the Wagner Act and Roosevelt's landslide reelection.

Chapter 10

Many economic historians have argued that the 1937–1938 depression was caused by restrictive fiscal policy and/or increases in reserve requirements. Neither view is persuasive. Instead, the rapid wage inflation (combined with the end of gold panic–induced price inflation) modestly slowed the economy during the spring and summer of 1937. This slowdown led to renewed expectations of dollar devaluation during the fall, and as gold was again hoarded on a massive scale, expectations of future U.S. monetary growth declined sharply. It was this shift in expectations that triggered the precipitous declines in stock prices, commodity prices, and industrial production during late 1937.

Chapter 11

A misinterpretation of two key policy initiatives, the open market purchases of 1932 and the NIRA, had a profound impact on macroeconomic theory during the twentieth century. Because early Keynesian theory was based on a misreading of these policies, it could not survive the radically altered policy environment of the postwar period. By the 1980s, the original Keynesian model had been largely replaced by a (quasi-monetarist) "new Keynesianism," featuring highly effective monetary policy and a self-correcting economy. This era may have ended in 2008.

Chapter 12

Economic historians continue to debate whether the international gold standard was an important constraint for interwar central banks. It seems unlikely that this issue can ever be resolved, and the debate may have diverted attention from the much more important issue of how the world gold market impacted contemporaneous policy expectations. At the deepest level, the causes of the Great Depression and World War II are very similar—both events were generated by policymakers moving unpredictably between passivity and interventionism.

Chapter 13

If one defines real wages as the ratio of nominal wages to wholesale prices, then high frequency fluctuations in real wages during the 1930s were tightly correlated with movements in industrial production. Understanding real wage cyclicality is the key to understanding the Great Depression. This requires separate analysis of nominal wage and price level shocks.

New Deal legislation led to five separate nominal wage shocks, which repeatedly aborted promising economic recoveries. The gold market approach can help us understand price-level volatility between October 1929 and March 1933, and, surprisingly, is *even more useful* during the first five years after the United States departed from the gold standard. Under an international gold standard, the domestic money supply, the interest rate, and gold flows are not reliable indicators of domestic monetary policy. Rather, changes in the gold reserve ratio, and the dollar price of gold, are the key monetary policy instruments.

Methodological Issues

The problem of causality is a central issue in both macroeconomics and history. Yet, despite impressive improvements in econometric techniques, no consensus has been reached on how to model the monetary transmission mechanism. Economists often look for leads and lags as a way of establishing causality, but as we will see, these attempts have foundered on the problem of identification. Put simply, 250 years after David Hume elegantly described the quantity theory of money, we still don't know how to identify monetary "shocks."

From a methodological perspective, the most notable aspect of this study is its use of financial and commodity market responses to disturbances in the gold market (and to a lesser extent, the labor market) as a way of establishing causality. Indeed, the "efficient market hypothesis" suggests that if we wish to think of causality pragmatically, say as a guide to policy, then we probably cannot go beyond financial market reactions to economic shocks. Any factors that were invisible to financial markets, even root causes that seem blindingly obvious to historians, do not provide a realistic guide to policymakers. (A modern example of this conundrum occurred when many pundits blamed the Fed for missing a housing bubble that was also missed by the financial markets.)

Deirdre McCloskey has been critical of what she regards as the excessively narrow and rigid methodology of much of modern economics.[2] She advocates the more eclectic approach employed by what she calls the "good old Chicago School." For our purposes, the most relevant example would be Friedman and Schwartz's *Monetary History*. Their work combined an extremely detailed narrative, insightful theoretical analysis, and a wealth of descriptive statistics. In a later paper they argued that it was important to "examine a wide variety of evidence, quantitative and non-quantitative, bearing on the question under study."[3] Despite its reliance on some very basic statistical techniques, the *Monetary History* remains the single most influential empirical analysis of monetary policy. It is worth examining the reasons why.

The extensive historical narrative in the *Monetary History* is not provided merely to add color to an otherwise dry subject. Their narrative helps give the reader a feel for *why* monetary policy changes occurred when they did. In other words, the narrative gives a sense of whether policy changes were *exogenous*, which is essential for making any statements about causality. A number of readers have attributed the persuasiveness of Friedman and Schwartz's analysis to their ability to show that money supply changes occurring over widely separated periods of time, and under widely different policy regimes, had similar macroeconomic effects.[4]

This study differs from the *Monetary History* in its much heavier focus on market responses to policy-related news events. There are obvious risks with this type of "event study." In the worst case, one could search for news stories occurring in close proximity to major stock price movements and then simply assume that those news events caused the change in stock prices. There is no way that I can respond to this concern on a purely theoretical level. In a sense, the long narrative at the center of this book represents both an analysis

2. See McCloskey (1994).

3. Friedman and Schwartz (1991), 39.

4. See Miron (1994) and Rockoff (2001).

of the Great Depression and a defense of my method. Nevertheless, it will be useful if we first examine a few of the practical problems associated with the use of event studies.

Clinton Greene (2000) refutes some common misconceptions about "data mining," calling it a necessary and inevitable part of the process of formulating theoretical models. In my case, I began doing gold market research with an assumption that central bank gold hoarding and currency devaluation were probably the two most important gold market variables affecting aggregate demand. Only after seeing how strongly markets reacted to private gold hoarding did I begin to pay serious attention to that issue.

How much confidence can we attach to hypotheses generated by data mining? At a minimum, the new hypothesis should be logically consistent with basic economic principles. This is why many are skeptical of ad hoc theories of "market anomalies" generated by scanning massive data sets, especially when there is often no good theoretical justification for the correlation. In contrast, the observed (negative) response of stock and commodity markets to private gold hoarding is consistent with the predictions of commodity money models of aggregate demand. More demand for gold *should* raise the real value of gold. If gold is the numeraire, then this *should* be deflationary. This hypothesis is not ad hoc; it is an application of the most fundamental economic theory of all, supply and demand.

In Chapters 2 through 10, I develop a narrative of the Great Depression that relies heavily on the relationship between policy news and the financial markets. It is easy to imagine finding a spurious correlation for a single observation; it is less obvious that it would be easy to do so for many dozens of observations that all exhibit a common causal relationship. Indeed, Cutler, Poterba, and Summers (1989) were unable to find *any* significant news events associated with most of the largest (daily) movements in U.S. stock market indices in the postwar period.

In one respect, the event study approach used in this book makes it more difficult to find statistical significance where none exists. A researcher looking for market anomalies can use regression analysis to quickly examine thousands of different relationships over numerous time periods, and just as quickly discard those that don't produce statistical significance. In contrast, I have only one Great Depression to examine. It has been my good fortune that stock prices

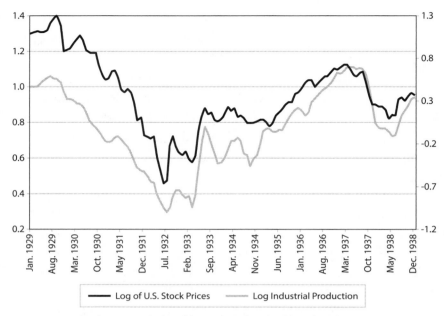

Notes: Stock prices are the log of the Cowles Index, monthly (right scale).
Industrial production (also logs) are from the Federal Reserve Board (left scale).

Figure 1.1. U.S. Stock Prices and Industrial Production, 1929–1938

during the Depression were unusually volatile, and unusually closely related to policy-oriented news events linked to the world gold market and also to federal labor market policies. This is especially fortunate because in the 1930s those gold and wage shocks were also linked tightly to fluctuations in industrial production—that is, the Great Depression itself.

Previous studies of the Great Depression, notably Friedman and Schwartz's *Monetary History*, have not been able to closely link policy changes with movements in industrial production. As a result, they are often forced to rely on dubious assumptions of "long and variable lags." Although policy may affect aggregate output with a lag, it should affect asset prices almost instantaneously. And as Figure 1.1 shows, stock prices were highly correlated with industrial production during the Depression. This is important, as it suggests that whatever shocks drove industrial production were either hard to spot, or else took effect with almost no lag. One purpose of this study is to show that monetary policy lags are much shorter than many researchers have assumed, and that both stock prices and industrial output often responded quickly to monetary shocks.

During the 1930s the standard deviation of daily changes in the Dow Jones Industrial Average (Dow) was 1.9 percent, which is more than double the volatility of most other decades.[5] At first glance, this suggests that any stock market movements up or down of more than 3.8 percent could be considered "significant." Yet this cutoff is either too generous or too restrictive, depending on the context. It is obviously too generous if we have restricted our analysis only to days with large stock price innovations, and then adopt 95 percent confidence intervals for the hypothesis that a particular contemporaneous news story had had a causal impact on the Dow. But it may be too restrictive if we have access to other information as well.

Relatively small market changes can be significant if the timing can be pinned down with some precision. Although most interwar stock market data is available only at daily frequencies, the contemporaneous financial press often reported stories such as "stocks traded lower in the morning, but shot upward after the market received a wire report that the President would propose a tax cut." Because interwar financial reporters observed market reactions in "real time," those reports can be far more significant that modern data sets with daily returns.

A recent study of the U.S. Treasury bond market showed that if one divides the trading day into five-minute intervals, virtually all of the largest price changes occur during those five-minute intervals that immediately follow government data announcements.[6] There is simply no plausible explanation for this empirical regularity other than that these events are related, and that the causation runs from the data announcement to the market response.

---

5. Regarding the "significance" of stock market fluctuations cited in this paper, Schwert (1990) showed that the stock market was unusually volatile throughout the Great Depression. He found the standard deviation of daily stock returns to be 1.9 percent during 1928–1937, but only 0.8 percent during 1917–1927 and 1938–1987. Thus, a daily movement in the Dow of 1.6 percent would be twice the standard deviation of the market during "normal" periods and a 3.8 percent movement would be large, even relative to the highly volatile 1928–1937 period. On the other hand, there is some evidence that the distribution of daily stock price fluctuations shows kurtosis, i.e., extreme changes are more common than what one would expect if the distribution was normal.

6. See Fleming and Remolona (1997).

Observation of near-instantaneous market responses to significant news events can increase the significance of a given market reaction by several orders of magnitude.

There are other more subtle advantages offered by contemporaneous press accounts. Many news events do not speak for themselves. The most obvious example is where a policy announcement might be either more or less aggressive than expected. Press accounts often indicate when and how financial markets were surprised by a particular policy announcement. A less obvious advantage is that interwar financial markets can help us to better understand how investors viewed the broader policy environment. A wide variety of political, economic, or military events might have been expected to indirectly impact policy, but in ways that are exceedingly difficult to discern after eighty years have elapsed. And the impact of events often depended on the circumstances in which they occurred.

Although we need to look at qualitative news stories, this does not mean that we should dogmatically reject the tools of modern statistical analysis.[7] This book includes regressions involving gold stocks, spot exchange rates, forward exchange rates, stock prices, commodity prices, bond prices, yield spreads, industrial production, real wages, and wholesale prices, among other variables. Because the economic shocks of the 1930s were so heterogeneous, it would be difficult to develop a VAR (vector autoregression) analysis of one overarching model of the Depression. Indeed, one of my goals is to show that the surprising heterogeneity of political and economic shocks during the interwar years virtually requires an eclectic research method. Solow offered a similar defense of methodological flexibility:

> To my way of thinking, the true functions of analytical economics are best described informally: to organize our necessarily incomplete

---

7. As already noted, Depression-era data obviously had some influence on the construction of the models employed in this book. Thus, I don't want to make any grand claims about the statistical results providing any kind of conclusive "tests" of the models. The statistical results that are reported are best viewed as providing the reader with a sense of the extent to which the various correlations are consistent with the underlying models. With regard to causality, I put much more weight on the analysis of market responses to a wide range of political and economic shocks, many of which are unique and therefore not susceptible to ordinary statistical tests of "significance."

perceptions about the economy, to see connections that the untutored eye would miss, to tell plausible—sometimes even convincing—causal stories with the help of a few central principles, and to make rough quantitative judgments about the consequences of economic policy and other exogenous events. In this scheme of things, the end product of economic analysis is likely to be a collection of models contingent on society's circumstances—on the historical context, you might say— and not a single monolithic model for all seasons. (1985, p. 329)

We will see numerous examples where news events impacted expectations of future monetary policy, which then impacted the prices in auction-style stock and commodity markets. In those cases the impact is virtually instantaneous, and Granger causality tests would be inappropriate. This supports new Keynesian models in which changes in the current setting of the policy instrument are much less important than changes in the future expected path of monetary policy. Indeed, the subsequent narrative provides examples where the "effect" (higher prices) occurs before the "cause" (increased growth in the money supply).[8]

Finally, the reader needs to be patient with the news analysis/financial market response analytical approach. This method is probably least effective during the first part of the Depression, when it is often difficult to see what sort of news events traders were responding to, and only reaches a high level of effectiveness during the period from mid-1931 to mid-1938. Fortunately, the analysis of the impact of policy news on financial markets represents merely one aspect of a three-pronged research method. Ideally, each policy shock that we identify should pass all three of the following tests:

1. Is the predicted impact consistent with economic theory?
2. Do the broader macroeconomic aggregates respond as predicted?
3. Do prices in auction-style markets respond appropriately to news relating to these policy shocks?

---

8. Obviously, in this case there would be a deeper causal factor that occurred before even the price level increase. The point is that these root causes may come from a wide range of (often subtle) political and economic shocks that are hard to measure and especially hard to model in a VAR setup.

The Plan of the Book

Establishing causality in macroeconomic history is something like peeling an onion, or opening a Russian doll. As each layer is removed, there always seems to be another layer inside. In the next section, I show how the Great Depression can be explained using the aggregate supply/aggregate demand (AS/AD) framework. We will see that the observed pattern of interwar wage and price cyclicality suggests that aggregate demand and autonomous wage shocks can explain much of the Great Depression. I then show how the real wage fluctuations represent a combination of supply and demand side factors. On the supply side, there were five autonomous wage shocks during the New Deal, each of which led to higher nominal wage rates. On the demand side, a series of gold market shocks produced a highly unstable price level, which then impacted real wage rates. The mixture of gold market and labor market shocks can explain the high frequency changes in industrial production, and indeed can explain the Great Depression itself.

The following nine chapters peel back two more layers of causation: first, by considering what kind of policy shocks could have disturbed the world gold market during the 1930s, and then, by looking for political and economic factors that might have generated those policy shocks. In Part II (Chapters 2–4), I focus on the Great Contraction of 1929–1932. Because others have already examined the role of banking panics, I concentrate most of the analysis on how a lack of policy cooperation led to central bank gold hoarding and how devaluation fears triggered private gold hoarding. Eichengreen entitled his study *Golden Fetters* to emphasize the policy constraints imposed by the international gold standard. If I were to choose a metaphor for the approach taken in Part II, it might be something like "the Midas curse"—that is, a world impoverished by an excessive demand for gold.

In Part III (Chapters 5–7), I examine two of the most important policy shocks in U.S. history, which occurred in close proximity during 1933. Because the expansionary impact of dollar depreciation was largely offset by the contractionary impact of the NIRA wage codes, economic historians have greatly underestimated the importance of each shock considered in isolation. After April 1933, daily changes in the free market price of gold become an excellent proxy for exogenous monetary shocks. I show that the various market responses to dollar depreciation call into question many traditional theories of the monetary policy transmission mechanism.

In Part IV (Chapters 8–10), I focus primarily on one gold market variable, the level of private gold hoarding. The major focus of this section is the bubble in commodity prices during 1936 and 1937. I show that the commodity price boom was caused by instability in the world gold market, and was the mirror image of a more fundamental change—a sharp dip in the value of gold. Previous economic historians have missed the way that gold market instability triggered the boom and bust of 1936–1938 and have mistakenly blamed the recession on tighter fiscal policy or higher reserve requirements. As with 1933, a complete understanding of economy's path during 1937 requires a subtle analysis of the interrelationship between gold market and labor market disturbances.

In Part V (Chapters 11–13), I show that the gold market approach can help us understand how the Great Depression impacted macroeconomic thought, particularly Keynesian thought. I argue that the original Keynesian model is not really a "depression model"; rather, it is a model based on two assumptions, the ineffectiveness of monetary policy and the lack of a self-correcting mechanism in the economy. The first assumption confuses the two (unrelated) concepts of gold standard policy constraints and absolute liquidity preference. And Keynes's stagnation hypothesis falsely attributes problems caused by government labor market regulations to inherent defects in free-market capitalism.

Chapter 12 discusses how this study sheds light on those aspects of the Great Depression that have divided economic historians, as well as macroeconomic theorists. If the monetary model in this book is correct, then we have fundamentally misdiagnosed the stock and commodities market crashes of late 2008, which share some interesting parallels with the crashes of late 1929 and 1937. Unfortunately, just as contemporaneous observers misdiagnosed those earlier crashes, our modern policymakers attributed the current recession to financial market instability, rather than to the deeper problem of falling nominal expenditures caused by excessively tight monetary policy.

In Chapter 13, I develop a more detailed model of the gold market, and also discuss some of the thorny issues involved in analyzing real wage cyclicality. This material would be primarily of interest to specialists.

A Simple AS/AD Framework

It would be an understatement to suggest that the AS/AD model works well for the contraction of 1929–1933; *it is the event the model was built to explain.* Nominal income fell by half, as both prices and output declined by roughly 30 percent. It was the greatest adverse demand shock in modern history. The rest of the Depression is more problematic, as both output and price did recover after 1933, but the recovery was quite uneven. So much so that even as late as the spring of 1940 the U.S. economy was still quite depressed. I'll argue that this uneven path reflects the impact of a series of supply and demand shocks.

There are many versions of the AS/AD model, but in some respects the "sticky-wage" variant of it seems to best fit the interwar period. Figure 1.2 shows the relationship between real wages and industrial production (both detrended) from 1929 through 1939.

The real wage series is average hourly earnings in manufacturing deflated by the wholesale price index (WPI). The actual correlation is strongly negative, as real wages tend to rise when industrial production declines. In Figure 1.2 I have *inverted* the real wage series to make it easier to see the very strong *countercyclical* pattern of real wages during the Depression.

If I were asked to give a talk on the Great Depression and allowed just one slide, it would undoubtedly be Figure 1.2. There is much to be said about this graph, but let's start with the observation that modern macroeconomic theory would predict essentially no correlation between real wages and output. We would expect to see no pattern at all. Since World War II, real wages haven't shown any consistent cyclical pattern. On the other hand, an interwar economist like Ralph Hawtrey would not have been at all surprised by Figure 1.2:

> Real monetary equilibrium in any single country requires the price level to be in harmony with the wage level, so that the margin of profit is sufficient, but not more than sufficient, to induce full activity and full employment. (1947, p. 45)

So a sharp fall in output could be caused by either a rise in nominal wages or a fall in the price level. It so happens that both factors played an important

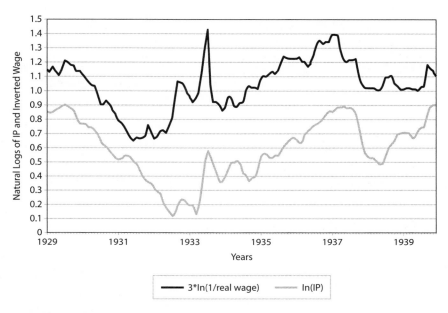

Figure 1.2. The Relationship between Detrended Industrial Production and Detrended (Inverted) Real Wages, 1929–1939, Monthly

role in the Great Depression. Before explaining how and why, however, we need to ask why real wages have not been countercyclical since World War II.

Let's return to the AS/AD model. During the 1930s, the biggest supply shocks were New Deal programs aimed at artificially raising nominal wages. There were five big wage shocks, each of which tended to abort otherwise promising recoveries in industrial production. These wage shocks thus tended to make real wages more countercyclical—higher wages led to lower output. In contrast, the postwar supply shocks tended to make wages more *procyclical*. A good example is the famous oil shocks of the 1970s. They caused prices to rise much faster than the relatively sticky nominal wages; thus, workers experienced declines in their real wages. Because the oil shocks also reduced output, we saw real wages fall at the same time as output, making wages very procyclical during the 1970s.

To summarize, it just so happens that the supply shocks of the 1930s were of the type that made real wages very countercyclical. But what about the demand shocks, which were the major cause of the Great Contraction? Recall that the real wage rate is the nominal wage divided by the price level. The most comprehensive price index of the 1930s was the WPI, which was quite volatile and very procyclical. Wholesale prices fell sharply during the 1929–1933 and 1937–1938 contractions and rose sharply after the dollar was devalued in April 1933. Because nominal wages tend to be sticky, or slow to adjust, sudden changes in the WPI tend to show up inversely as changes in the real wage rate. That is what Hawtrey's quote is all about. If prices fall much faster than wages, then profits decline and companies lay off workers. Real wages actually rose sharply during the early 1930s for those lucky enough to maintain full-time jobs.

Because the WPI plays a big role in Depression research, it is important to consider its possible biases. For instance, the WPI tends to oversample commodity prices, which are especially volatile. For this reason the WPI fluctuated more than the broader indices, which explains a small part of the strong counter-cyclicality of real wages during the Depression. But not all—real wages were only slightly less countercyclical if deflated with the crude "cost of living" indices of 1930s. Although the WPI is biased toward commodities, it's also important to note that the interwar economy really was much more commodity intensive than our twenty-first-century economy. In the narrative chapters we'll see that daily indices of commodity prices often responded strongly to monetary shocks and can provide a timely indicator of deflationary shocks hitting the interwar economy.

In Chapter 13, there is a much more detailed examination of interwar wage and price cyclicality. One important finding is that prices were highly procyclical throughout the interwar years, which suggests that demand shocks were the primary driver of changes in the price level. (Recall that most supply shocks cause prices to rise as output falls.) In contrast, nominal wages were roughly acyclical during the 1920s, and then became strongly procyclical after July 1933. Later we will see how various New Deal policies created these wage shocks. All that remains is to model the interwar price level. Once we've modeled wage and price level fluctuations, we will have gone a long way toward explaining the path of output described in Figure 1.2.

Figure 1.3 shows how we can work backward from our wage cyclicality findings to the deeper "root causes" of the Great Depression.

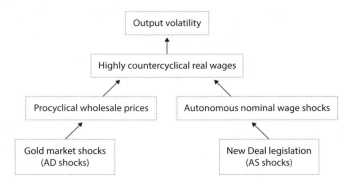

Figure 1.3. Causal Factors in the Great Depression

Demand shocks explain the earliest and most important phase of the Depression, the contraction of 1929–1933, and the initial recovery from March to July 1933. Thus, most of this study will focus on the left side of Figure 1.3, and we will defer consideration of supply-side factors until Chapter 6. This does not mean that aggregate supply shocks played no role in the initial contraction; President Hoover's high wage, high tariff, and high tax policies almost certainly aggravated the initial downturn. But the sharp increase in the real demand for gold explains why (nominal) national income fell by half between 1929 and early 1933. Even if Hoover had avoided his counterproductive "remedies" for the Depression, a fall in nominal income of that magnitude would have generated a major depression. Indeed, we don't observe large declines in nominal GDP that are not associated with major contractions, and we don't know of any "real" factors that were even close to being powerful enough to produce a depression after 1929.

A Gold Standard Model of the Interwar Price Level

At least as far back as David Hume, economists have been aware of the effect of a sharp fall in nominal spending. But what should we call that type of shock? It could be called a contractionary monetary shock, except that it need not involve any decline in money—reductions in velocity ($MV = PY$) would do just as well. Or it might be termed a deflationary shock, except that deflation can also result from an increase in aggregate supply and need not be contractionary at all. It could be called a demand shock, but in some new Keynesian models, a supply shock can reduce both prices and output. Unfortunately, we lack a simple term for one of the most important concepts in macroeconomics, changes in nominal GDP.

To be clear, I strongly believe that nominal GDP is a better indicator of demand shocks than the price level. Unfortunately, we lack good high frequency data for nominal GDP during the interwar period. In contrast, we have lots of monthly and even weekly data for prices and output, indices such as the WPI and industrial production. Even better, the two variables are highly correlated during the Depression, with a few notable exceptions. For pragmatic reasons, I have decided to take a linguistic short cut. Whenever I use the term "deflationary shock," it should be understood as referring to deflation that is caused by falling nominal GDP. I will use this term synonymously with falling aggregate demand, to refer to episodes where both prices and output are declining. You should think of it as representing falling nominal GDP. An "inflationary shock" will refer to a price-level increase caused by rising nominal GDP, and will be used synonymously with rising aggregate demand. The term 'inflationary shock' will describe periods where both prices and output (and hence, nominal GDP) are rising. In those rare cases where prices and output move in opposite directions (a few months in 1933 and 1934), I will clearly emphasize that a supply shock is occurring, and hence that the price level gives a misleading indication of demand conditions. The other advantage of using the language of inflation and deflation is that it links up with the strong real wage/output correlation seen in Figure 1.2. It is an ad hoc model, but one that works surprisingly well for the 1930s.

In this section I'll sketch out a simple gold market model of the price level to explain demand shocks. But why gold? At the risk of oversimplification, one might identify three basic approaches to monetary economics: an interest rate (or Keynesian) approach, a quantity theoretic (or monetarist) approach, and a commodity money (or gold market) approach. According to the Keynesian view, prices are "sticky" in the short run and the single best indicator of monetary policy's stance is the interest rate. Policy-induced changes in interest rates affect investment spending, aggregate demand, the output gap and, in the long run, prices.

The monetarist approach puts much less emphasis on the interest rate transmission mechanism. Instead, the quantity of money is the key policy indicator and the real demand for money is assumed to be relatively stable. In the long run the price level will rise in proportion to any exogenous change in the money supply. The short-run transmission mechanism is more complex (or ambiguous) than under the Keynesian approach, with the relative prices of many different financial and real assets being impacted by monetary shocks.

Under a gold standard we can employ a third approach to monetary economics; the price level (or aggregate demand) can be modeled in terms of shifts in the supply and demand for gold. Either a decrease in the supply of gold or an increase in the demand for gold will raise money's real value, or purchasing power. If the nominal price of gold is fixed, as under a gold standard, then by definition a higher purchasing power for gold means a lower price level.

Money is generally the medium of account, or the good in which other prices are measured.[9] Because all prices are measured in terms of money, changes in its real value, or purchasing power, are inversely proportional to changes in the overall price level. A large crop of apples can be easily accommodated by a fall in the nominal price of apples. Similarly, a huge gold discovery reduces the value of gold. But under a gold standard, the nominal price of gold cannot change, and thus a fall in the value of gold can only occur through a rise in the price of all other goods. That's what makes gold special. Or perhaps I should say that's what makes gold and money special. There were actually two media of account under a gold standard, currency and gold. Between 1879 and 1933, the U.S. dollar was both a dollar bill and $1/20.67$ ounces of gold. And, during times of crisis, there was often tension resulting from this dual system, as investors might begin to fear a change in the price at which currency was pegged to gold.

In principle, the price level could be modeled by looking at the supply and demand for money, or the supply and demand for gold. Although most previous researchers have focused on money, we will see that the evidence points to gold as being the more important "market"; that is, the factor that destabilized aggregate demand during the 1930s. And this isn't just my view; later we will see that the financial markets seemed to share this view, reacting

---

9. A medium of account is an asset whose nominal price is fixed by law or convention.

strongly to gold market shocks, but often remaining impassive in the face of seemingly important changes in the traditional levers of monetary policy.

Other advantages exist in looking at the world gold market. The Depression was an international phenomenon, but generally most severe in countries with currencies linked to gold. During the early 1930s prices fell sharply in gold terms all over the world. It makes no sense to explain that sort of phenomenon solely by looking at the money supply of a single country. Under the gold standard the money supply of an individual country is partly endogenous, reflecting changes in the world price level.

It will be useful to begin with a simple commodity money model applicable to either a closed economy or an international gold standard regime. Bits and pieces of this model have been developed by others: Benanke's "multiple monetary equilibria," Eichengreen's analysis of the asymmetrical response to gold flows, Temin and Wigmore's analysis of the impact of devaluation on expectations, Romer's analysis of the impact of European war scares on gold flows, and Mundell and Johnson's gold undervaluation hypothesis all play roles in this story.[10] But no previous account of the Depression has combined all of these perspectives into a coherent model capable of showing how gold market disturbances generated high frequency fluctuations in aggregate demand during the 1930s.

Let's begin with a simple barter economy where prices are denominated in terms of other goods. Now assume the community agrees that, henceforth, all prices will be quoted in terms of a specified quantity of a designated good. For instance, suppose that $\frac{1}{35}$ ounce of gold is defined as one dollar. In that case, the community has shifted from barter to a monetary economy, with ($\frac{1}{35}$ ounce of) gold serving as the medium of account toward the term "dollar" becoming the unit of account. Now the price level will be inversely proportional to the real value of gold, where the term "value" refers to purchasing power, not international exchange rate value. Basic economic principles[11] suggest that we can use supply and demand theory to model the real value of gold (and hence the price level) in any gold standard economy.

---

10. See Eichengreen (1992, 2004); Bernanke (1995); Johnson (1997); Romer (1992); Temin and Wigmore (1990); and Mundell (2000).

11. Barro (1979) provides a good example of a monetary model based on these principles.

Monetary theory often begins with a simple identity. In equilibrium, the price level is equal to the ratio of the nominal supply of money (the policy variable) and the real demand for money (which is the focus of the modeling process). Under the gold market approach a similar identity is used, but it is interpreted somewhat differently. The nominal supply of money is replaced with the (nominal) gold stock, and monetary policy now generally impacts the *demand* side of the market:

$$P = G_s/g \tag{1.1}$$

where P is the price level, G_s is the nominal monetary gold stock, and g is the real demand for monetary gold.[12]

From Equation 1.1 we can see that price stability would occur if the gold stock increased at the same rate as the real demand for gold. These conditions were approximated (in the very long run) under the nineteenth-century gold standard, as price levels showed relatively little long-run variation. Even the classical gold standard, however, exhibited substantial short-run price-level volatility. During the 1920s, prices were well above pre–World War I levels, and there was concern about a looming "shortage" of gold; that is, future increases in the world gold supply would not be sufficient to prevent deflation. (The term "shortage" is misleading; "scarcity" better describes the problem.) Several experts claimed the world gold stock needed to rise by about 3 percent per year in order to maintain stable prices.[13]

---

12. On theoretical grounds, nominal GDP would represent a better proxy for aggregate demand than the price level. (Recall that for any given level of nominal spending, higher prices mean lower output.) Prices will only work as a proxy for aggregate demand during periods dominated by demand shocks (i.e., during periods where prices and output are moving in the same direction). But because we lack high frequency data for changes in nominal spending, and because the (wholesale) price level was highly procyclical during the Depression, the changes in the WPI and industrial production will often prove to be useful proxies for demand shocks.

13. In a 1930 report commissioned by the League of Nations, Gustav Cassel pointed out that the ratio of (annual) gold output to the existing stock of gold had fallen from over 3 percent prior to World War I to just over 2 percent by the late 1920s. (Because very little gold is lost, this is roughly the rate of increase in gold stocks.) Cassel expressed concern that future gold supplies might be inadequate. On the other hand, he also acknowledged many uncertainties on both the supply side and the demand side of the gold market, and he certainly did

Equation 1.1 is an identity whether we are referring to the supply and demand for all gold, or just the supply and demand for monetary gold.[14] If we focus on monetary gold stocks, then flows in and out of private gold hoards show up as changes in the *supply* of monetary gold. This is a bit awkward since one normally thinks of the term "private gold hoarding" as applying to the demand for gold. There are several reasons, however, why it makes more sense to model the supply of monetary gold, rather than the total gold stock. First, we have relatively good monthly data on monetary gold stocks, particularly during the late 1920s and early 1930s. More importantly, it simplifies the process of modeling the key determinants of the price level.

Now let's segment real monetary gold demand into two components, the gold reserve ratio (r) and the real demand for currency (m_d). The gold reserve ratio is defined as the ratio of the monetary gold stock and the currency stock:[15]

$$P = G_s^*(1/r)^*(1/m_d) \qquad (1.2)$$

Thus, an increase in the price level can be generated by one of three factors: an increase in the monetary gold stock, a decrease in the gold reserve ratio, and/or a decrease in the real demand for currency. The rate of inflation is the percentage increase in the monetary gold stock, minus the percentage increase in the gold reserve ratio, minus the percentage increase in the real demand for currency. At this level of abstraction the term "gold standard" simply refers to a monetary regime where the nominal price of gold is fixed. As long as the nominal price of gold is constant and the real value of gold is set in free markets, then we can apply the gold standard model without making any further assumptions about policymakers following "the rules of the

---

not predict the catastrophic deflation that we now know was already underway. As we will see, while the supply side was an aggravating factor, the demand side of the gold market holds the key to understanding the Great Contraction.

14. During the 1920s and 1930s, most gold was used for monetary purposes. (Had most gold been used in filling teeth, then market conditions in the dental industry might have been the most important determinant of the price level.)

15. This approach was first developed in Sumner (1991). Bernanke and Mihov (2000) use slightly different ratios to model changes in M1. (M1 = Cash held by the public plus demand deposits at banks.)

game"; that is, we do not need to assume a stable gold reserve ratio, or in fact any relationship between the monetary gold stock and the currency stock.

Under the so-called rules of the game, countries were supposed to adjust their currency[16] stock in proportion to changes in their monetary gold stock. Although most countries did not adhere to this set of rules, we will see that it is a useful policy benchmark. Variations in the gold reserve ratio can be seen as an indicator of discretionary monetary policy. In the appendix to this chapter I provide some data on changes in these variables during the early 1930s.

When we apply the gold market approach to U.S. monetary policy during the Depression we are confronted with a nine-month period where the price of gold was not fixed. If we wish to generalize the model to allow for changes in the price of gold (i.e., currency depreciation) we can modify the previous identity by separating the nominal gold stock into the nominal price of gold (P_g) and the physical gold stock (g_s):

$$P = (P_g)^*(g_s)^*(1/r)^*(1/m_d) \tag{1.3}$$

The right-hand side of Equation 1.3 features the four primary variables that will be used in the gold market model of aggregate demand and the price level. Interestingly, all four of these variables played a key role in the Great Contraction and initial recovery. Of course, Equation 1.3 is merely an identity, and as such plays roughly[17] the same role in gold market analysis as the equation of exchange plays in monetarist analysis. Critics of the equation of exchange often point out that merely because a change in M or V is correlated with a change in nominal spending, this does not prove that the equation is a useful way to think about causal relationships. To construct a useful gold market *model* we need to identify the factors that cause variations in these four variables. These causal factors are discussed in Chapter 13 and also the narrative chapters, but it will be helpful to make a few brief comments here.

---

16. It might have been better to use the monetary base, which also includes bank deposits at the central bank. However, I found it easier to find currency data for many of the smaller countries, and my qualitative findings don't seem to be particularly sensitive to whether currency or base money is used, at least for the larger countries where I did find monetary base data.

17. The comparison would be even closer if P were replaced with nominal GDP, and ($1/m_d$) were replaced with velocity.

The world monetary gold stock tended to grow at about 2 percent per year during normal times, mostly due to the output of gold mines. After mid-1931 a series of economic crises materialized that led investors to fear currency devaluation, and private gold hoarding increased significantly on several occasions. This reduced the growth rate of the monetary gold stock, which was deflationary.

The gold reserve ratio was the only truly exogenous policy lever available to central banks. This ratio increased sharply after October 1929, and that contractionary policy seems to have triggered the Great Contraction. The real demand for currency tended to rise when the cost of holding currency (i.e., the interest rate) was low, and when there were fears of bank failures. Currency hoarding was also deflationary. And finally, President Roosevelt increased the dollar price of gold between April 1933 and February 1934, which was very inflationary. These were the four primary factors driving the price level and aggregate demand in America during the Great Depression.

Why Was the Depression Initially Misdiagnosed?

What is misleadingly termed "classical economic theory" suggests that an autonomous fall in nominal spending should result in an equal fall in wages and prices, leaving output unchanged. Of course, the classical economists knew that things weren't that simple. Even before the Great Depression they had noticed that rapid deflation was usually associated with falling output. The actual "classical theory" used by economists at least as far back as David Hume was surprisingly similar to modern business cycle theories; nominal shocks have real effects in the short run (due to sticky wages), but affect only prices in the long run.

Another common misconception is that the classical economists had an oversimplified view of what caused nominal shocks, focusing solely on changes in the money supply, and assuming the "velocity of circulation" was constant. But again, at least as far back as Hume, economists knew that a decline in the velocity of circulation could depress prices and output just as easily as a decline in the money supply:

If the coin be locked up in chests, it is the same thing with regard to prices, as if it were annihilated.[18]

Classical economists did not just focus on demand shocks; they also understood that adverse supply shocks such as a higher minimum wage could depress output. Indeed, by 1929 economists had all the intellectual tools necessary to understand the Great Depression, and even to prevent it. But if the classical economic theory can provide a satisfactory account of the Depression, then where are those explanations? And why didn't they prevent the Depression? And what explains the Keynesian revolution?

At least some economists were able to account for the Great Depression using classical ideas. Indeed, in many respects this book follows in the footsteps of the prewar analysis of Irving Fisher, Gustav Cassel, and Ralph Hawtrey. But the very complexity of the Depression tended to obscure causal factors, and this opened the door to non-classical models, most notably the Keynesian models. Complexity is a theme I will return to again and again. At one level of generality the Depression looks quite simple; aggregate demand (AD) was allowed to fall sharply after 1929. But at another level it was very complex, as the forces that drove AD lower were confusing and liable to be misinterpreted.

I would argue that the same could be said of the 2008–2009 recession. Between mid-2008 and mid-2009, U.S. nominal GDP fell roughly 4 percent, or about 9 percent below trend. All our mainstream macro theories tell us that this sort of AD shock would be quite damaging to both the real economy and the financial system. And yet our policymakers allowed it to happen. Some would argue that there is nothing the Federal Reserve could have done, but that's not what Fed officials claim. Ben Bernanke has repeatedly emphasized that the Fed is never "out of ammunition."

At the time the disaster was unfolding in late 2008, almost no one pointed to a lack of monetary stimulus as being the problem. And that's because it didn't look like it was the problem. But looks can be deceiving. In the 1930s, very few thought the Depression was caused by excessively tight monetary

18. David Hume. 1752. "Of Money" in *David Hume Writings on Economics*. Edited by Eugene Rotwein (1970), Madison Wisconsin: The University of Wisconsin Press, 42.

policy by the Federal Reserve, as it seemed like a series of financial crises were the main problem. Today, exactly the reverse is true; macroeconomists tend to blame the Fed and other central banks for the Great Depression and view the financial crisis as a symptom of falling nominal income. The events of the past five years should make us all a bit more forgiving of those interwar policy experts who failed to correctly diagnose the problem in real time. When aggregate demand collapses, it looks to almost everyone as if the *symptoms* of the fall in aggregate demand are the *causes*. That was true in the 1930s and it is equally true today.

PART II

The Great Contraction

2

From the Wall Street Crash
to the First Banking Panic

*Partly, no doubt, the stock market crash was a symptom
of the underlying forces making for a severe contraction
in economic activity. But partly also, its occurrence must
have helped to deepen the contraction.*
  —M. Friedman and A. Schwartz, 1963a, p. 306

in mid-**1929** the performance of the U.S. macroeconomy seemed close to ideal. Growth in output was strong, prices were stable, unemployment was low, the federal budget had a surplus, as did trade, and the stock market was booming.[1] Then after September 1929, both prices and output began a precipitous decline that would continue for nearly three years. It is now widely agreed that the 1929–1932 contraction was caused by a decline in aggregate demand. But no one has yet explained why demand fell so sharply in the year after the market crash.

Over the next nine chapters we will be looking at the response of financial markets, and especially the U.S. stock market, to economic policy-related news. An obvious place to begin is with the famous stock market crash of 1929, which might have been linked to the subsequent Depression in one of two

---

1. Of course, it is natural to compare the U.S. economy of the late 1920s with the late 1990s, which featured many of the same characteristics. But even with that comparison the 1920s would probably come out ahead. In retrospect, it is obvious that in the late 1990s there was overinvestment in information technology (IT) and telecommunications, even assuming there had been no recession in 2001. Although overinvestment may have occurred in the 1920s as well, it is not at all obvious that booming industries such as automobile manufacturing would have been overextended had the U.S. economy continued to grow at a healthy rate during the early 1930s.

ways. Most historical accounts have assumed that the crash helped trigger the Depression. Alternatively, the stock market crash could have been caused by (expectations of) an oncoming Depression. The latter interpretation is most compatible with the efficient markets hypothesis.

Let's begin by briefly comparing the 1929 crash with a strikingly similar market decline that occurred in 1987. In 1929, the Dow peaked in early September, fell at an increasing rate during late September and early October, and finally plunged 23 percent on October 28 and 29. The total eight-week decline was 39.7 percent. In 1987, the Dow peaked in late August, fell at an increasing rate during September and early October, and then plunged 22.6 percent[2] on October 19. The total eight-week decline was 36.1 percent. And both crashes occurred after the U.S. economy had experienced a sustained period of economic growth under conservative Republican tax-cutting administrations. One difference is that further sharp declines occurred over the weeks following "Black Tuesday," and thus the total market decline in 1929 was nearly 48 percent. The more important differences, however, relate to macroeconomic events that occurred after each crash.

The 1987 stock market crash was followed by three more years of a strong economy and healthy corporate profits. Because of the lack of significant news at the time of the 1987 crash, it was widely viewed as an example of investor irrationality, a violation of the efficient markets hypothesis. Popular historical accounts also tend to portray the 1929 crash as an episode of mass hysteria, which is odd, given that the 1929 crash was followed by the most severe depression in U.S. history. The 1929 crash might just as well be viewed as a striking confirmation of the extraordinary sophistication of market expectations—as investors were able to perceive the onset of a depression, even as many so-called experts remained optimistic about the economy. To make sense of 1929, we first need to take a closer look at the relationship between the stock market and the business cycle.

Schwert (1990b, p. 1237) showed that between 1889 and 1988, "future [industrial] production growth rates explain a large fraction of the variation in stock returns." Dwyer and Robotti (2004, p. 11) observed that the "stock market does not necessarily decline before a recession, but the onset of a reces-

---

2. This was by far the largest single-day decline in U.S. stock market history.

sion is invariably associated with a substantial decline in stock prices." And McQueen and Roley (1993, p. 705) noted that "news of higher-than-expected real activity when the economy is already strong results in lower stock prices, whereas the same surprise in a weak economy is associated with higher stock prices," a result of particular relevance to this study. In the following nine chapters I will show that during the Depression stock prices responded positively to news of policy initiatives that were expected to boost output, and vice versa.

It seems unlikely that the stock market crash and the Great Depression were entirely unrelated. But is it plausible that the 1929 crash could have been triggered by policy-related news? The crash might have merely been a reaction to signs that the economy was slowing in the autumn of 1929; industrial production had already peaked in late summer. Yet, why would a relatively modest decline in production over a period of just a few weeks reduce equity values by 48 percent? On the other hand, if bad policy was the cause, then, what were those policies?

If the Depression did cause the stock market crash then the very scale of the crash suggests that any plausible explanation must involve a forward-looking mechanism whereby investors foresaw at least a part of the economic calamity to come. Did the stock market receive such bearish information in October 1929? It is unlikely that we will ever find an answer that is completely consistent with the efficient market hypothesis. But, if the scale of the 1929 crash is destined to remain something of a mystery, we will at least find some tantalizing hints that can be developed much further in subsequent chapters.

This chapter focuses on two key questions: Did an increase in the world gold reserve ratio begin reducing aggregate demand in late 1929? And if so, did it also contribute to the 1929 stock market crash? Before applying the gold market approach to the onset of the Depression, however, let's first review some explanations for the 1929 crash.

Previous Explanations of the 1929 Stock Market Crash

The monetarist view of the Depression generally begins with the Federal Reserve's (Fed's) move toward a tighter monetary policy in mid-1928, a policy switch that also shows up clearly in the U.S. gold reserve ratio, but not in the world gold reserve ratio.[3] Despite the quotation that opens this chapter, in Friedman and Schwartz's account the "underlying forces" behind the October 1929 stock market crash are never really explained. Instead, they basically treat the crash as an aggravating factor that depressed velocity. The problem with this omission is that the monetarists' "long and variable lags" might explain why the Depression began more than a year after the Fed adopted a tight money policy, but it cannot account for the strong performance of U.S. equity markets during the intervening period. Although monetarists tend to believe in market efficiency, their policy narratives often overlook market responses to monetary policy actions, or even imply highly irrational behavior by investors. They are not alone in this regard.

In the Austrian view, inflationary monetary policies during the 1920s led to an unsustainable investment boom in higher order goods. Both the stock market crash and the ensuing Depression were a consequence of those policy errors.[4] The assumption of market inefficiency is even more central to the Austrian view; as rational investors presumably would not have bid stock prices up to such lofty levels in mid-1929 if they understood that Fed policy would inevitably produce a bust. And whereas monetarists can at least point to the fact that monetary tightening has often been followed by economic downturns, the Austrian view is hard to reconcile with postwar U.S. monetary policy. Several postwar decades saw far more inflationary booms than those of the 1920s, and stock market booms of a nearly comparable magnitude. Yet, none were followed by major depressions. Thus, Austrians often distinguish between the initial downturn, representing an adjustment after the excesses of the 1920s, and what's called a "secondary deflation," which may be caused by deflationary monetary policies.

As with the monetarists, Keynesians viewed the 1929 crash as both an exogenous event and a causal factor in the ensuing contraction. Indeed, because the initial stages of the Depression are difficult to explain within a standard

---

3. Friedman and Schwartz focus more on the forces that worsened the slump after the onset of the banking panics, but Schwartz (1981) clearly attributes the initial downturn to a tight money policy adopted in 1928.

4. See Rothbard (1963) and Palyi (1972). For the Austrians, the term "inflation" often refers to growth in the money supply or nominal spending, not prices (which did not increase during the 1920s).

Keynesian (IS-LM) framework, the importance of the crash is typically even greater than in monetarist accounts of the Depression. And Keynesians are even more likely to view the spectacular 1928–1929 bull market as a bubble, the bursting of which depressed aggregate demand. For instance, Romer (1990) argued that the 1929 stock market crash sharply reduced consumer confidence, and that this was a major factor depressing aggregate demand.[5] But the quite similar stock market crash in 1987 seemed to have no impact at all on economic growth, suggesting that the direct impact of stock prices on real output is almost certainly very small.[6] If Friedman and Schwartz had written their *Monetary History* twenty-five years later, they probably wouldn't have even mentioned the crash as a causal factor.

Romer suggested that the 1929 crash may have had a greater impact on consumer confidence than the 1987 crash because the earlier crash was followed by a higher level of stock market instability, but this hypothesis has two serious flaws. First, the fact that the stock market was modestly more unstable in 1930 than 1988 could explain a small difference in economic growth, but it can hardly explain the difference between a severe slump in 1930, and an economic *boom* in 1988. And even worse, the extra market volatility didn't begin until mid-April 1930, by which time the economy was already deep in recession. Indeed, the Dow actually performed much better in the six months after the 1929 crash than during the six months following the 1987 crash. Of course, the striking lack of impact from the 1987 crash might be an anomaly. But recent studies using both time series and cross-sectional data found little or no evidence of a significant wealth effect from changes in stock prices.[7] In

---

5. Temin (1976) also argued that the first year of the Depression could be explained by an autonomous drop in consumption, but was uncertain as to what caused consumption to fall.

6. It might be argued that the Fed eased policy much more aggressively after the 1987 crash, and that otherwise, that crash would also have been followed by a depression. Even if one accepts this argument (and recall that the Fed also cut rates after the 1929 crash), it seems more of an argument for the importance of *monetary policy* as a determinant of business cycles, rather than stock prices.

7. Case, Quigley, and Shiller (2005, p. 26) find "at best weak evidence of a stock market wealth effect." Dwyer and Robotti (2004) also find little evidence of a "wealth effect." And note that measured correlations probably overstate the impact of stocks on consumption, as both variables will, at least to some extent, respond to (unobservable) changes in expectations of future economic conditions.

fairness, even most Keynesians don't see the crash as the cause of the Great Depression, but rather as simply one of many contributing factors.[8]

What evidence do we have that stocks were overpriced in the late 1920s? Some finance models suggest that stocks were grossly undervalued throughout most of the twentieth century.[9] If the investment community expected economic growth to continue right on into the 1930s, then would investor expectations really have been so irrational? Perhaps. Economists are split on this issue.[10] Alexander Field (2003) showed that the 1930s were "the most technologically progressive decade of the century," so there really were a lot of new developments for investors to get excited about. Before we throw up our hands and accept the "bubble" explanation, we should first see whether there is an alternative explanation that allows for sensible investors to have been highly optimistic in September 1929 and much more pessimistic in November 1929.

Gold Market Indicators at the Onset of the Depression

It is not surprising that many observers would blame the stock market crash for the sharp decline in aggregate demand after October 1929; there were no other obvious culprits. For instance, there was no dramatic break in the growth rate of U.S. monetary aggregates in the year following the crash. But domestic monetary aggregates may not be a reliable indicator of monetary policy under an international gold standard. Rather, it is the world gold reserve ratio that is the theoretically appropriate indicator of central bank policy.

Table 2.1 uses Equation 1.2 to decompose changes in the price level into changes in the stock of monetary gold (G) and changes in the real demand

---

8. Temin (1989, p. 44) argues that the crash was not a major independent shock and also cites the 1987 crash.

9. During the twentieth century, long-term rates of return on U.S. stocks have been much higher than on risk-free Treasury securities. The undervaluation hypothesis is based on the view that this differential is much too large to be explained by any plausible risk premium on equity investments.

10. During the Great Depression Irving Fisher was widely ridiculed for having called the stock market undervalued in October 1929. And studies by DeLong and Schleifer (1991) and Rappoport and White (1993) provide indirect evidence of bubble-like behavior. But McGrattan and Prescott (2004) suggest that "Irving Fisher was right" about stocks being undervalued in 1929 if one accounts for the value of intangible corporate assets.

Table 2.1. The Impact of Changes in the World Gold Reserve Ratio, Real Demand for Currency, Real Demand for Gold, and Monetary Gold Stock, on the World Price Level, 1926–1932

	Time Period					
	Dec 1926 to Jun 1928	Jun 1928 to Oct 1929	Oct 1929 to Oct 1930	Oct 1930 to Aug 1931	Aug 1931 to Dec 1932	Dec 1926 to Dec 1932
Gold ratio	−2.65	−2.38	−9.62	+1.86	−4.35	−3.64
Cash/P	−2.70	−2.21	−4.97	−19.42	−10.17	−6.80
Real gold	−5.35	−4.59	−14.59	−17.56	−14.52	−10.44
Gold stock	+3.88	+4.06	+5.25	+4.72	+3.88	+4.27
Price level	−1.47	−0.53	−9.34	−12.84	−10.64	−6.18

Gold ratio = change in the log of (the inverse of) the gold reserve ratio

Cash/P = change in the log of (the inverse of) real currency demand

Real gold = change in the log of (the inverse of) the real demand for monetary gold

Gold stock = change in the log of the world monetary gold stock

Price level = change in the log of the world price level

(The percentage changes represent *annualized* first differences of logs.)

Notes: Outside the United States, the currency stock was used as a proxy for the monetary base. The change in the real demand for monetary gold is equal to the sum of the changes in the gold reserve ratio and the real demand for currency. The change in P reflects changes in the monetary gold stock and the (inverse of the) real demand for monetary gold. The changes are not seasonally adjusted.

for monetary gold (g). The changes in gold demand are then further separated into changes in the gold reserve ratio (r) and changes in the real demand for currency (m). Equation 1.2 can be rewritten as the first difference of logs, to express percentage changes:

$$\Delta \ln P = \Delta \ln G + \Delta \ln(^1/_g) = \Delta \ln G + \Delta \ln(^1/_r) + \Delta \ln(^1/_m) \qquad (2.1)$$

The latter three variables are inverted to make it easier to see the impact on the world price level. Thus, an increase in gold demand is deflationary, whether caused by the hoarding of currency or a higher gold reserve ratio. Because all the changes are expressed as first differences of logs, they add up to the change in the global price level. This decomposition of the world gold market plays roughly the same role in the gold market approach to monetary economics as the equation of exchange plays in monetarism. In Chapter 13, I discuss the difficult issue of causality in much more detail.

Notice that prices were fairly stable in the late 1920s and then fell sharply after October 1929. Because the gold stock grew throughout this period, the proximate cause of the massive deflation was a large increase in real gold demand. The world monetary gold stock grew by over a quarter between 1926 and 1932, so the Great Depression was not caused by a shortage of gold. Instead, the "problem" was a huge increase in the real demand for gold. Roughly half of the increase occurred in France and another 20 percent in America.

Both currency hoarding and central bank gold hoarding contributed to the increase in gold demand. The public held much larger real cash balances (due to low interest rates and fear of bank failures) and the world's central banks raised the gold backing of their currency stocks—that is, the gold reserve ratio increased. However, the timing of these changes differed in a highly significant way. The world gold reserve ratio soared by 9.62 percent in the twelve months after the Wall Street crash, consistent with an extraordinarily tight global monetary policy. There was another increase in the gold reserve ratio in late 1931 and early 1932, but after October 1930 the biggest problem was currency hoarding. In contrast to the gold ratio, the U.S. monetary base fell in 1930, and then rose rapidly over the next few years.

To explain the collapse in aggregate demand after September 1929 we need to disaggregate the data in Table 2.1 by country. This is a rather complicated process, explained in Chapter 13. Table 2b.1 in Appendix 2.b summarizes the results. If we focus on the gold reserve ratio there is one country that really stands out. Between December 1926[11] and December 1932 the French gold reserve ratio increased by enough to reduce the entire *world price level* by 17.3 percent! If the gold reserve ratio is a useful policy indicator, then we ought to be able to see links between changes in that ratio and policy actions by major central banks.

The data in Table 2b.1 support studies by Johnson and Eichengreen that showed the deflationary impact of French policy.[12] Eichengreen (1986) cites

---

11. Although the French franc was fixed to gold in December 1926, France did not officially return to the gold standard until June 1928.

12. By 1932, France held almost twice as large a proportion of the world's monetary gold stock as during 1914. This led Nurske (1944), Hawtrey (1947), and Cassel (1936) to assert that

France's Monetary Law, which prohibited purchases of foreign exchange, as an important constraint on the Bank of France. This law mandated 100 percent gold backing for any increase in the currency stock. Press reports noted that almost all of the increased circulation was occurring in the larger denomination notes, and attributed this increase to widespread currency hoarding by French peasants.[13]

The French gold reserve ratio increased at a fairly steady rate, at least until uncertainty surrounding the devaluation of the British pound in September 1931 led France to sharply accelerate the rate at which it substituted foreign exchange reserves with gold. Thus, while French policy may have contributed to the worldwide deflation that occurred between 1926 and 1932, it doesn't tell us anything about why the U.S. price level was stable in the late 1920s and then suddenly plummeted after October 1929.

Because Friedman and Schwartz focused on the U.S. monetary aggregates, they had difficulty identifying any significant policy shift in the fall of 1929. They argued that U.S. monetary policy became highly contractionary after the first banking panic began in late 1930. If the gold market approach is to provide an explanation for the onset of the Depression in late 1929, and by implication, the stock market crash, it must identify a monetary shock in late 1929. Figure 2.1 shows the relationship between the twelve-month change in the (inverted) gold reserve ratio and U.S. industrial production. In Chapter 13, there is a similar graph (Figure 13.4) showing a close correlation between the gold ratio and the U.S. wholesale price index. The higher gold reserve ratio meant a tighter monetary policy and this tended to depress AD in all gold standard countries. This reduced both prices and output in the United States during late 1929 and 1930.

The spike in the gold ratio in the last two months of 1930 represents a decline in the ratio of gold to currency after the onset of the first U.S. banking crisis in November 1930. The Fed partially (but not completely) accommodated the currency hoarding by increasing the monetary base and reducing the gold reserve ratio.

French policies resulted in a "maldistribution" of gold stocks, which contributed to the 1929–1932 deflation.

13. See the *Commercial and Financial Chronicle* (*CFC*; 5/3/30, p. 3089).

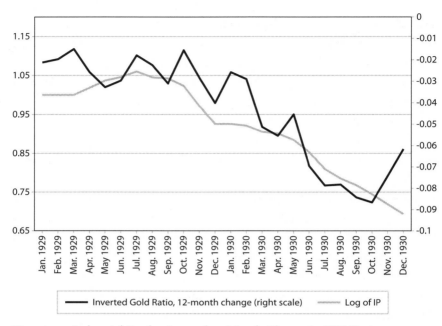

Figure 2.1. Industrial Production and 12-Month Change in C/G Ratio

Although French policy was undoubtedly important throughout the late 1920s and early 1930s, if one looks at shorter time periods, then shifts in U.S. and British policies take on greater significance.[14] Table 2b.1 shows that between December 1926 and June 1928 expansionary monetary policy in the United States helped offset the contractionary effects of French policy. Note that the terms "expansionary" and "contractionary" refer to the gold reserve ratio, not the money supply, which is endogenous under an international gold standard. The U.S. currency stock actually *declined* slightly over this period. The expansionary monetary policy reflected the (activist) views of New York Fed Governor Benjamin Strong, who was supporting his friend Montegu Norman at the Bank

---

14. Of course, the concept of causation is difficult to define when the actions of several countries are independently affecting the world price level. For instance, if policies in England, France, and the United States each tend to reduce the world price level by 2 percent, and if the monetary gold stock rises by 4 percent, then the price level will decrease 2 percent. In this case, each of the three countries independently, or all three jointly, could be said to have "caused" the 2 percent deflation.

of England. The pound was greatly overvalued in the late 1920s because Britain had returned to gold at the prewar parity, despite a much higher price level. In contrast, France had sharply depreciated its currency during the mid-1920s.[15] Strong's decision to adopt an expansionary policy during 1927 allowed Britain to attract gold without being forced to adopt highly deflationary policies.

Governor Strong's policy was criticized at the time for being highly inflationary. This characterization may seem puzzling given that the U.S. currency stock and price level actually declined during this period. Yet, the decrease in the gold reserve ratio confirms the expansionary nature of the policy. By mid-1928, the United States had exported almost $500 million in gold and there was a growing perception of excessive speculation in the stock market. At this time, the Fed switched to a contractionary policy aimed at restraining Wall Street's "irrational exuberance."

This shift in U.S. policy was partially offset by a move toward a more expansionary policy in England. After the death of Governor Strong in 1928, the Bank of England was the only major central bank that saw the need for international cooperation to maintain price stability. However, England's resources were severely limited. Between July 1928 and October 1929, its monetary gold stock fell by nearly a fourth. By the summer of 1929, Britain's gold stock had fallen below the £150 million level recommended in the Cunliffe Committee report, and thus, on September 26, 1929, the Bank of England was forced to raise its discount rate. By late October, the pound had risen to the gold import point and Britain's gold reserve ratio began to increase rapidly.

In retrospect, the period from October 1929 to October 1930 was decisive. U.S. monetary policy became even more restrictive than during the previous sixteen months. During 1930 Fed officials continued to emphasize the need to liquidate the excessive debts accumulated during the previous boom. Proposals that monetary policy be eased were rejected on the grounds that such

---

15. The fact that the French franc was undervalued does not explain the huge inflows of gold into France. Hawtrey (1947) noted that France's creditor position and favorable balance of payments could only affect her demand for gold by affecting the demand for currency notes. Instead, the undervaluation of the franc explains why, in returning to the gold standard, France did not have to deflate its price level by as much as England.

a policy would simply repeat the mistakes that resulted in the crash.[16] At the same time, France continued to increase the gold backing of its currency. The simultaneous adoption of tight money policies in the United States, France, and Britain made worldwide deflation almost inevitable. The world gold reserve ratio, which had increased at an annual rate of 2.53 percent from December 1926 to October 1929, soared by 9.62 percent over the next twelve months. Despite a slight acceleration in the growth rate of the monetary gold stock, the price level fell almost as sharply.

The sudden upward surge in the world gold reserve ratio after October 1929 refutes the Keynesian view that monetary policy is unable to explain the first year of the Depression. Even previous researchers who focused on the contractionary role of the gold standard, such as Temin and Eichengreen, were not able to find the sort of dramatic shift in world monetary policy that could have plausibly caused both stocks and output to fall sharply in the fall of 1929. The next step is to see what specific policy actions might have contributed to the increase in central bank gold reserve ratios, and how markets reacted to those policy shifts. As we do so, we need to continually think about investor perceptions of monetary policy from a "what did they know, and when did they know it" perspective.

Monetary Policy and Stock Prices during 1928–1929

The post-October 1929 rise in the world gold reserve ratio provides an explanation for the onset of the Depression that is broadly consistent with the gold market approach to aggregate demand. This increase seems to have begun after the stock market crash of October 1929, however, which was well after the cyclical peak in output was reached in August 1929. How then could it have triggered the Depression? To answer this question we first need to take a closer look at the events leading up to the 1929 crash.

After the Fed switched to a tight money policy in mid-1928 the gold out-flow from the United States reversed and the gold reserve ratio began to in-crease. In the absence of offsetting actions elsewhere, this increase was sizable enough to push the world toward deflation. Was this policy reversal then a root cause of the subsequent depression, or were the financial markets correct

---

16. See Nelson (1991).

in essentially shrugging off the Fed's tightening? One place to begin is with the stock market reaction to Fed policy announcements during the late 1920s.

Under the leadership of Governor Strong the Fed had focused on macroeconomic stabilization. Strong was skeptical of the view that the Fed could restrain stock market speculation without hurting the overall economy:

> Must we accept parenthood for every economic development in the country? That is a hard thing for us to do. We would have a large family of children. Every time one of them misbehaved, we might have to spank them all. (Ahamed, 2009, p. 277)

But when Strong's health declined in 1928, the Fed did begin trying to restrain the stock market boom.

On June 4, 1928, the *New York Times* (p. 4) reported "Credit Curb Hinted by Reserve Board." The market actually rose slightly on June 5, but then, over the following week, the Dow plunged 7 percent. Policy news ought to be incorporated into securities prices almost immediately, and thus, it is unclear whether the Fed's announcement had any impact on the markets. The June 13 *New York Times* attributed the previous week's stock plunge to "disappointment . . . at the turn of politics in Kansas City, with the evident elimination of President Coolidge and the substitution of Hoover as a candidate" and also to "determination of the Federal Reserve . . . to liquidate broker's loans." This was the first of several stock market crashes that the press would at least partially attribute to Herbert Hoover.[17]

On July 10 the Fed raised the discount rate by one-half percent, and the next day the Dow fell 3.0 percent. But once again, it is not clear that we can attribute the decline to tight money. The July 12 *New York Times* (p. 1) indicated that the market actually opened "rather firm" and that the price break didn't occur until late in the session. This is not to deny that the Fed's tightening might have had some impact on securities prices—one can find many instances of rumors about tight money coinciding with sharp stock price declines during late 1928 and early 1929. But these declines were merely brief interludes in a powerful bull market, with the Dow nearly doubling between

---

17. Five days earlier the *NYT* (p. 38) had predicted that Wall Street would be disappointed if Coolidge wasn't drafted at the Republican convention.

June 1928 and September 1929. There is no evidence that investors thought that the Fed tightening in mid-1928 was likely to trigger a major depression. To understand why both the stock market and the economy performed so well during 1928–1929 we need to examine the pivotal role played by the Bank of England during this period.

The June 2, 1928, *New York Times* predicted "another large movement of gold from here to London" as Strong's easy money policy allowed Britain to rebuild its monetary gold stock (p. 21). Only a few days later, however, that perception began to change rapidly as interest rates rose in the United States on rumors of Fed tightening. By June 8 the *New York Times* was suggesting (p. 32) that high money rates in New York might lead to a reversal in gold flows back toward the United States. Britain would go on to lose 22.8 percent of its gold reserve during the period from June 1928 to October 1929. This is the price the Bank of England paid for delaying the onset of the Great Depression by one year with a highly expansionary monetary policy.

The famous bull market of 1928–1929 was punctuated by a series of sharp price breaks followed by rapid recoveries. For instance, between December 5 and December 8, 1928, the Dow plunged 11.5 percent over worries about a discount rate increase. Then, between February 5 and February 8, stocks plunged another 6.4 percent, and a February 8 *New York Times* headline reported "RESERVE BOARD WARNING SENDS STOCKS TUMBLING; LONDON RAISES BANK RATE." The article attributed the market decline to both a Fed warning that "drastic action might be taken unless the funds going into speculative channels were curtailed" and "the advance of the discount rate of the Bank of England from 4½ per cent to 5½ per cent." The next day the *New York Times* (p. 24) suggested (wrongly) that, "the prospect of further gold shipments from London to New York has definitely been disposed of by the advance of the discount rate of the Bank of England." The "correction" seemed to have ended on February 11, when the Dow rose by nearly 3 percent. On the following day a front-page *New York Times* story attributed the rally to the fact that the Fed had failed to raise rates as had been anticipated. But, just a few days later, the market again fell sharply on renewed warnings of monetary tightening by the Fed.

In some respects, the world monetary situation in the late 1920s was similar to that of the late 1990s. There was great optimism about the prospects for the

U.S. economy. Unfortunately, the sort of monetary policy that allowed for strong, noninflationary growth in the United States tended to exert deflationary pressure on many weaker nations whose currencies were tied to the dollar.[18] By March 1929 pundits were complaining that the Fed's antispeculation policy was hurting the European economies, particularly Britain. There was even concern that the Fed's policy might eventually force Britain off the gold standard.[19] Stocks again broke sharply during late March on "fear of a drastic advance in the rediscount rates by the Federal Reserve."[20] As with the previous setbacks, stocks resumed their upward march once it became apparent that the Fed's threats were not slowing the economy. The final two weeks of May saw the last mini-crash, once again attributed primarily to fear of a discount rate increase.[21]

During the summer of 1929, concern over the monetary situation eased as the peak in the seasonal demand for credit passed and the Fed failed to boost the discount rate. The *New York Times* even predicted (wrongly) that increased gold flows to the United States would eventually force the Fed to expand credit.[22] On August 9, the summer bull market in stocks was temporarily derailed by the Fed's decision (the previous evening) to boost its discount rate from 5 percent to 6 percent, as the Dow fell 4.0 percent in a slump the *New York Times* called the "Most Severe Since 1911." And this time stocks plunged right from the opening bell.

In retrospect, the Fed's decision to raise rates may have been a mistake. Only a few days earlier the *New York Times* had reported that the Bank of England had seen its gold holdings fall £8,000,000 below the minimum level recommended by the Cunliffe Committee.[23] They speculated that the Bank of England might be forced to raise its discount rate, an action that was seen as

---

18. In the late 1920s, it was European powers such as Britain that were under pressure from a strong dollar; in the late 1990s, it was been developing nations such as Argentina.

19. See the *NYT*, 3/25/29, p. 42.

20. *NYT*, 3/26/29, p. 1.

21. See the *NYT*, 5/23/29, p. 38 and 5/28/29, p. 1.

22. In fact, the Fed responded to the gold inflow with a contractionary policy during 1930. (See the *NYT*, 6/30/29, p. N7.)

23. The committee recommended that Britain maintain a minimum gold reserve of £150 million. It should be noted that when testifying at the Macmillan Commission of 1931, Governor Norman denied that the Bank of England felt constrained by that benchmark.

likely to depress the British economy and disturb financial markets throughout the world. Ironically, the day before the Fed's discount rate increase had sent U.S. stock prices tumbling, Wall Street had rallied on the reassuring news that the Bank of England had refrained from an increase in its discount rate.[24]

Despite what we now know about its ultimate effects, it is hard to be too critical of the Fed's action, given that the markets seem to have made the same miscalculation. After dropping to 337.99 on August 9, the Dow soared to its prewar peak of 381.17 on September 3. The sharp price break on August 9 suggests that Wall Street was concerned about the discount rate increase, but the subsequent rally also suggests that it wasn't seen as likely to trigger a severe slump. U.S./British policy coordination had been effective during the 1920s, and this may have lulled investors into believing that central bankers would again be able to cooperate enough to handle the monetary difficulties that might lie ahead.

Although the cyclical peak in output occurred in August 1929, it probably makes more sense to view October 1929 as the actual beginning of the Great Depression. Industrial production did decline slightly in August and September 1929, but this sort of modest drop in monthly output was not unusual; similar declines had occurred during May, June, and September 1925, a year when no recession occurred. The *New York Times* weekly business index suggests that output only began falling rapidly during the final week of October. And it wasn't until November and December that we observe sharp declines in the monthly industrial production index. In addition, the fact that stock prices rose rapidly during the late summer of 1929 suggests that it is very unlikely that investors anticipated even a mild recession until at least late September.[25] Almost all of the stock market crash occurred between late September and early November 1929. It is during this period that the market would have gradually become aware of any adverse shocks that might have triggered the Depression.

---

24. *NYT,* 8/9/29, p. 23.

25. These perceptions changed rapidly after mid-September. The September 21 *NYT* (p. 38) predicted a strong economy during the fall and winter. By October 17, they noted (p. 38) that stocks had been following a business slowdown since mid-September. And by November 11, 1929, the *NYT* (p. 35) suggested that many were now forecasting a severe recession in the United States.

In retrospect, the September 26 decision by the Bank of England to boost its bank rate from 5.5 percent to 6.5 percent appears to have been the decisive step that led to a reversal in Britain's gold outflow and thus helped trigger the dramatic increase in the world gold reserve ratio. But the market response to this action was not quite what one might have expected. To see why, we need to first consider exactly what type of information is conveyed by a change in central bank lending rates.

Although all indicators of monetary policy, including the money supply, exchange rates, and even the world gold reserve ratio, are susceptible to the identification problem, nominal interest rates are especially problematic. While an unanticipated increase in the central bank's target interest rate can be viewed as being contractionary *on the day it is announced*, over longer periods of time the nominal interest rate is an especially unreliable indicator of the stance of monetary policy. Whether a given discount rate will have an expansionary or contractionary impact depends on a complex set of economic factors, including expectations of inflation and real economic growth.[26]

Recent monetary theory[27] has revived the Wicksellian notion that monetary authorities implement policy by moving their target rate above or below the "natural rate of interest." Because investors do not directly observe the natural rate, they have difficulty judging the current stance of monetary policy. Often, it is only in retrospect (after discount rates changes have impacted other variables such as the gold reserve ratio), that investors are able to see whether a particular policy action has altered a country's monetary policy. In addition, markets often seem undisturbed by discount rate increases that are consistent with a given central bank's underlying operating procedures, but react very adversely to gold flows and/or other economic shocks that are expected to lead to undesirable changes in monetary policy. We will see this dynamic at work in the British policy changes of September 1929, and again in the Fed policy actions of October 1931.

As late as September 19, 1929, the Dow had declined only slightly from its previous peak. A 2.1 percent stock price break on September 20 was attributed

---

26. This point has been emphasized by monetarists such as Friedman and Schwartz, and Meltzer (2003). Also see Hawtrey (1947, p. 120).

27. See Woodford (2003).

to fears of an imminent decision by the Bank of England to raise its discount rate.[28] Just four days later an "unprecedented withdrawal of gold from the Bank of England" had been reported and another 1.8 percent decline in the market was linked to expectations that the Bank would raise the discount rate on September 26 as a way of averting a financial crisis.[29] The actual increase was somewhat anticlimactic, and there was no adverse impact on U.S. stock prices. But the next day stocks fell by another 3.1 percent, a decline attributed to concerns that the discount rate increase would fail to provide the needed boost to sterling.

Unfortunately, there is no smoking gun linking monetary policy to the October stock market crash. One possibility is that during the month of October, the market gradually became aware of the fact that discount rates in the United States and Britain were set at levels that would soon lead to a large increase in the world gold reserve ratio. For instance, as late as October 19 the *New York Times* (p. 26) was continuing to report that "experts" doubted that gold flows from the United States to Britain were likely to resume before year end and that the Bank of England would be forced to take further steps to attract gold. In fact, although Britain's contractionary monetary policy appeared to lack credibility, the bank rate increase to 6.5 percent would prove to be so effective that a *reduction* in the bank rate occurred a mere twelve days after the *New York Times* prediction. What changed, of course, was the economic environment. The U.S. stock market crash so reduced the demand for credit that existing discount rates throughout the world, and even somewhat lower rates, now represented highly contractionary policies capable of dramatically increasing the world gold reserve ratio. As output began to fall sharply in late 1929 and into 1930, the natural rate of interest fell even further, and discount rate reductions in the United States and elsewhere were not large enough to prevent a sharp rise in the world gold reserve ratio.[30]

---

28. *NYT*, 9/21/29, p. 25.

29. *NYT*, 9/25/29, p. 1.

30. Glasner (1989, p. 123) also suggests that excessive demand for monetary gold by the major central banks contributed to the Depression and blames the October crash on investor disappointment that the Fed didn't reverse course in late 1929. This is similar to my own view, although, because Glasner does not look at world gold reserve ratios, he is unable to provide an explanation for the timing of the crash. He credits Earl Thompson with the basic idea.

By October 28, 1929, the *New York Times* (p. 34) was reporting that London expected to receive gold imports from the United States and South America, and on November 1 the *New York Times* (p. 24) predicted that, "we have already seen the end of the crumbling-away of the Bank of England's gold reserve." This shift in British policy need not have had a major impact if other countries had simultaneously shifted to a more expansionary policy. In practice, "other countries" meant primarily the United States and France, which between them held over one-half of the world's monetary gold stock. However, because of the French Monetary Law, investors had little reason to believe that France would reduce its demand for gold. Prior to October 1929, France had been receiving much of its gold from England. After England tightened its monetary policy the French had to go elsewhere for gold. On October 29, the *New York Times* (p. 52) reported that France had just received its first shipment of gold from the United States since the Armistice.

At the time of the crash, the U.S. monetary gold stock was well in excess of legal requirements and thus the Fed could have easily accommodated the Bank of England, as it had during 1927. Had it done so, the world gold reserve ratio would have only increased by 3 or 4 percent, and the economy would have held up much better during 1930. On October 31, the Federal Reserve Bank of New York, in coordination with the Bank of England, did cut its discount rate to reassure the markets. The same day the Dow rose by 5.8 percent. Statements by Fed officials, however, gave the market little reason to believe that any significant accommodation was forthcoming. The Fed was particularly anxious to avoid a repeat of its expansionary policy during 1927, which was perceived as causing a large gold outflow and excessive stock market speculation.

Other Factors Contributing to the 1929 Crash

In addition to the highly uncertain monetary situation, several political developments may have played a supporting role in the stock market crash. On the evening of October 25, 1929, Attorney General William Mitchell gave a speech advocating much more aggressive enforcement of antitrust laws. Bittlingmayer (1996) showed that throughout the early 1900s, both the stock market and the overall economy reacted adversely to aggressive enforcement of antitrust laws and tended to do well when enforcement was lax (as under

President Coolidge). Although stocks did not fall on October 26, Bittlingmayer (p. 399) suggested that the speech's "contents or fundamental message could have reached Wall Street a day or two earlier, in the middle of the week-long October 1929 stock market decline that started on October 23."

Concern over the worsening political situation in Europe, and especially Germany, may have also played a modest role in the crash. Although in retrospect the interwar years are often seen as a period of almost unending political crises, in the late 1920s there was a brief window of optimism about the prospects for both continued prosperity (the so-called New Era), and international cooperation. At the time, even the conservative business press tended to view developments such as the League of Nations, the World Court, and the Kellogg-Briand Pact (which outlawed war) as effective devices for reducing hostilities. There was also a perception that progress was being made at the London Naval Disarmament Conference, at the Hague Conference on war reparations, and in the talks aimed at creating the Bank of International Settlements (BIS).

On the economic front, the Young Plan (which rescheduled war debts and reparations) and the BIS were viewed as being particularly important. Supporters of the BIS argued that the bank could play an important role in coordinating monetary policy among the major central banks. The *Economist* (7/6/30, p. 6) suggested that the BIS might be able to "stabilize the value of gold" and also noted that Wall Street was hopeful that the U.S. government would support the BIS. After the BIS began operating in 1930, it did try to encourage central bank policy coordination. In order for the BIS to play an important role, however, it was seen as essential that there be cooperation on the question of reparations and war debts, especially between Germany and France. Because German Foreign Minister Stresemann and French Premier Briand were highly respected internationalists who had played a key role in the rapprochement between France and Germany during the late 1920s, there was optimism that a solution could be reached.

Stocks stabilized during the first half of October, with the only sharp price break occurring on October 3. Early on the morning of October 3, there occurred an event which can be seen in retrospect as signaling the end of the cooperative spirit of the late 1920s, and the beginning of the much more contentious 1930s. The *Economist* called the death of German Foreign Minister Stresemann a "calamity . . . overhanging Europe for months, years" and the *New York Times* termed it a "political catastrophe."[31] Carr reported that, "almost at the same moment a panic occurred on the New York Stock Exchange."[32] Carr probably exaggerated the importance of this event on U.S. stock prices, Stresemann's death occurred before the market even opened. In retrospect, however, it seems just as clear that such a market reaction *would have been appropriate.* The ominous fears of the *Economist* concerning the impact of Stresemann's death seem mild when compared with subsequent events. The situation in Germany began deteriorating almost immediately, and by mid-1931, turmoil in Germany had become *the single most important influence on the U.S. stock market.*

The most severe phase of the 1929 crash began on October 16, when the Dow fell by 3.2 percent. Coincidentally, this was the same day that the German nationalists began a petition drive to stop the Young Plan. If the nationalists could register at least 10 percent of the electorate within two weeks, then a plebiscite would have to have been held on the proposal. Even if this were to occur, it was considered highly unlikely that the effort would be ultimately successful, since rejection of the Young Plan would require 50 percent of all *eligible* voters. Nevertheless, the petition drive was viewed as an irritant to the delicate negotiations underway at the time. In commenting on the petition drive, the October 26 *Economist* (p 752) lamented the passing of Dr. Stresemann whom they regarded as having been a key factor in restraining nationalist sentiment.

The same issue of the *Economist* (p. 766) described the collapse of the Briand government in France, which occurred on the evening of October 22, as a "bolt from the blue" and suggested that it had occurred at the worst possible moment because of "the delicate situation with the German plebiscite, the Saar Conference, and the evacuation." The *New York Times* noted concern that the collapse could undermine German support for the Young

---

31. See the *Economist* (10/5/29, p. 610) and the *NYT* (10/3/29, p. 1).

32. See Carr (1947, p. 129). The *NYT* did attribute the weak opening of the Berlin börse to Stresemann's death, and also suggested that it may have depressed French stock prices. But the London market was mixed on October 3 and it seems unlikely that this event could, by itself, have pushed the Dow lower by 4.3 percent.

Plan, and thus delay its adoption. On October 23 the Dow dropped 6.3 percent, although the financial press could not find any reason for the decline.[33]

In late October, it appeared unlikely that the German petition would be successful, and thus it is unlikely to have been a significant contributor to the October crash. An October 29 *New York Times* headline prematurely called the "Anti-Young Plan Vote a Nationalist Rout," and then six days later had to backtrack with a report that the nationalists had surprised everyone by collecting the 4 million signatures necessary to force a referendum on the Young Plan. At the same time, the Briand government was replaced by a more hawkish regime headed by Tardieu. The weak opening on the German Börse on Monday, November 4, was attributed to both the German referendum and to the gains made by reactionaries in France. And the U.S. market, which had been widely expected to open higher, instead plunged by 5.8 percent.

If European political troubles contributed in any way to the October crash, the most likely mechanism would have involved a change in expectations regarding international monetary cooperation. An October 29 *New York Times* headline stated that, "Europe Is Disturbed by American Action on Occupation Debt." The reports that the United States would take a unilateral approach to German war debts created concern that "German nationalists can make further use of [the] American action as showing that Washington thinks little of the Young Plan or the International Bank." And an October 28 *New York Times* headline noted that the "Young Plan [is] endangered by deadlock over BIS."

Although these European disturbances occurred at roughly the same time as the October crash, there is little evidence linking specific news stories with important stock market movements. In addition, these events received less coverage in the U.S. press during late October than did the fight over the Smoot-Hawley tariff bill. A number of economists[34] have suggested that the Smoot-Hawley tariff contributed to the Great Depression, and Jude Wanniski (1978) even argued that it triggered the October stock market crash. The tariff may have had an impact, but probably not for the reasons suggested in previous accounts. Indeed, the mechanism by which Smoot-Hawley impacted the market appears to have changed over time, and thus it will be

---

33. The October 30 *NYT* declared that uncertainty regarding the political situation in France had depressed stock prices in Paris.

34. See Meltzer (1976), Gordon and Wilcox (1981), and Saint-Etienne (1984).

useful to separate the impact of the tariff fight of 1929 from the impact of its enactment in 1930.

Wanniski argued that the tariff began affecting the market in December 1928 when word got out that the Republicans planned hearings on a bill that would include more than the agricultural protection promised in Hoover's presidential campaign. He also noted that stocks dropped sharply on March 25 and the morning of March 26, 1929, on news that pressure was building for tariff protection on many industrial goods. Wanniski missed several other news stories that support his interpretation. The March 5 *New York Times* (p. 40) observed that stocks fell sharply "during yesterday's inauguration" but could find no explanation. The only significant economic news contained in the speech, however, was Hoover's announcement that he planned to call a special session of Congress for tariff legislation. And the May 8 *New York Times* (p. 30) reported that the proposed tariff increases reported out of the House Ways and Means Committee on the previous day "go far beyond what the President had led the country to expect." The *Commercial and Financial Chronicle* called the proposals "a great shock to the community." The Dow dropped 1.3 percent on May 7.

The first big tariff fight occurred in the U.S. Senate during late October and early November of 1929. One of the key votes cited by Wanniski was a procedural vote on the afternoon of October 23 over the issue of the tariff rate on calcium carbide. A split on this issue within the coalition of Democrats and progressive Republicans that had opposed higher industrial tariffs was treated as a major news story in the October 24 *New York Times*. The Dow fell 6.3 percent on October 23, with most of the decline occurring in the last hour of trading, following the Senate vote.

Despite the preceding evidence, there is a serious problem with Wanniski's account of how Smoot-Hawley contributed to the October 1929 stock market crash. After the October 23 vote, the anti-tariff coalition grew progressively *stronger*, just as the crash entered its most severe phase. The November 1 *New York Times* (p. 1) reported, "Republicans Admit Coalition Control." By November 10, the protectionist Republicans had been completely routed and there were predictions that the coalition might force *reductions* in tariffs on manufactured goods. Contemporaneous observers also believed the news favored the low tariff bloc. Bankers Trust director Fred Kent argued that a contributing factor in the crash was the *success* of the coalition in blocking the tariff.[35] Even if one does not accept Kent's analysis of the market reaction, it is hard to reconcile Wanniski's view with the widespread contemporaneous interpretation that in the weeks following October 23, 1929, the protectionist wing of the Republican Party had suffered a major setback.

There is another way that the tariff dispute could have affected the markets. The tariff fight was unquestionably the major news story during the October crash (after the crash itself) and *New York Times* headlines indicated that the Senate battle had created a serious split in the Republican Party. An October 26 *New York Times* headline reported that Kahn had been appointed chair of the Republican election committee as a slap at Republican members of the antitariff coalition. Only days later, however, an angry reaction from the anti-tariff Republicans forced Kahn to decline the position. An October 30 *New York Times* headline stated that an outraged Joseph Grundy (the principal lobbyist for eastern manufacturers) had suggested that small (i.e., agricultural) states should be denied equal representation in the Senate.

In November the situation grew even worse for the Republicans. The November 1 *New York Times* reported: "it is a long time since such utter confusion prevailed in Congress as was revealed today." On November 10, the *New York Times* reported that even Smoot's total capitulation to the coalition, which included an offer to let the coalition write its own bill, had been rejected. And the next day the *New York Times* headline read, "Republican Revolt Seen, Following Senate Split and Chaos in Leadership . . . Call Party Disorganized." The same issue (p. 1) argued that the public was upset with the apparent inability of the Republicans to govern and (correctly) predicted major Democratic gains in the next Congress. This view was reinforced by recent Democratic gains in certain state and local contests. It was the sort of crisis that could have brought down a parliamentary government.

Roger Babson called the Senate's actions on the tariff the "most important" factor in the crash.[36] By explicitly blaming both sides of the tariff issue, Babson

---

35. *NYT*, 11/12/29, p. 3.

36. See the *CFC* (11/23/29, p. 3257). Babson was respected on Wall Street because of his September 1929 forecast of a stock market crash. Interestingly, although in November he blamed the crash on the tariff fight, his earlier forecast was based on the Fed's "tight money"

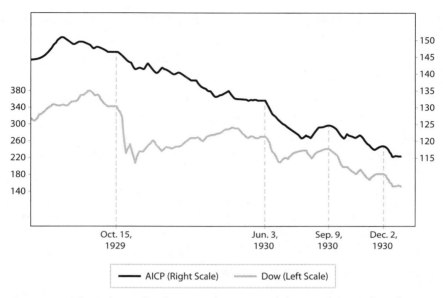

Figure 2.2. The Relationship between the Dow and the Annualist Index of Commodity Prices, 1929–1930

suggested that the problem had more to do with the spectacle of government ineptitude than with the specifics of the legislation.[37] In general, however, observers were much less likely to connect the October crash to the tariff bill than would be the case during the June 1930 market plunge.

The attractiveness of the political paralysis explanation is enhanced by the fact that these events would not necessarily have had a deflationary impact on the economy. Although commodity prices during late October and early November 1929 (see Figure 2.2) decreased significantly, the drop was smaller than one would expect if a deflationary monetary shock had caused the nearly 50 percent stock crash. And the fact that the crash was more severe in the United States than in Europe also points to the likelihood that some specific American factors were involved.

---

policy. He may simply have been lucky, however, as many of his other predictions were much less accurate.

37. A comparable example might be the adverse stock market reaction to the disarray in the Republican Party during the summer of 1990 after President Bush abandoned his no new taxes pledge.

Additional support for the hypothesis that political turmoil contributed to the October crash comes from its dramatic denouement. The November 12 and 13 issues of the *New York Times* reported that there was no explanation for the continual slide in the stock market. The next issue, however, had a very different tone. The income tax cut announced by the Hoover Administration on the evening of November 13 was treated as the major news story. Equal importance was given to the promise of cooperation from House and Senate leaders. The news led to widespread speculation that the market had hit bottom and would rally the following day (November 14).

The next day the *New York Times* was even more optimistic. The 9.4 percent increase in the Dow was one of its sharpest gains ever. Front page articles were entitled "Congress to Rush Tax Cut," "Leaders Are Enthusiastic," and "Officials Confident Will Suffer No Severe Depression Now." The financial page (p. 38) noted "there has not been a day in many weeks in which such an aggregation of good news descended on Wall Street." One of those pieces of "good news," the final approval for the BIS, was not entirely unexpected. Nevertheless, the *New York Times* argued that the French signature was "significant" because it showed that "the Tardieu Cabinet is as conciliatory as its predecessor." The Fed also contributed to the government's effort by cutting the discount rate.

While the plethora of good news makes it difficult to attribute market gains to any one factor, the tax cut was treated as the major news story of the day. And although its effect on the market was undoubtedly partly due to an anticipation of its expansionary impact, the *New York Times* (p. 26) also suggested a political interpretation; "What will make an unquestionably good impression [to Wall Street] in the Treasury's present move is the promptness with which Congressmen dismissed political differences in their ready assent to the government's proposal."

What Do We Know about the 1929 Stock Market Crash?

At the beginning of this chapter, I suggested that in order to understand the October crash, one needed to explain why it would have been sensible for investors to be highly optimistic in September 1929, and somewhat pessimistic in November 1929. Is there an explanation for such a dramatic change in sentiment?

We know that between 1922 and 1929 the United States experienced strong economic growth accompanied by stable prices, as well as budget and trade surpluses. Government was widely viewed as being competent and pro-business. Of course, the international situation was never really completely satisfactory during the interwar years, but 1929 saw distinct signs of progress. In September 1929 there really were good reasons to anticipate a "New Era."

If we were to list some of the underlying causes of not just the downturn in late 1929, but also the Depression itself, the list might include the simultaneous adoption of tight money in the major economies, international political discord and lack of policy coordination, ineffectual leadership from President Hoover, and widespread banking panics. It is rather striking that three of these four problems suddenly appeared on the horizon in October and early November 1929. Nevertheless, it is unlikely that a "Great Depression" was anticipated by investors in the immediate aftermath of the October crash. The Dow fluctuated between 200 and 260 during the first six months after the crash, levels comparable to those of highly prosperous 1928, or for that matter, the early 1950s. By contrast, during the summer of 1932, the Dow would fall into the low 40s. In order to explain the crash, it is only necessary to show how investors moved from the giddy optimism of mid-1929 to a much more circumspect mood during the final three months of the year.

The decision by the Bank of England to raise interest rates in September 1929 may have triggered a dramatic tightening in world monetary policy, but we only know this in retrospect. Contemporaneous observers find it difficult to ascertain even the *current* stance of monetary policy. And what matters to most investors is not so much what a central bank or a group of central banks is doing at a point in time, but rather the policy they are expected to adopt over an extended period of time. This makes it almost impossible to establish a clear link between monetary policy and the 1929 crash.

If moves toward a tighter monetary policy did contribute to the crash, one might also have expected a decline in commodity prices. A significant decline did occur in October; however, a major stock market crash might reduce commodity prices even in the absence of tight money, and so this correlation doesn't really provide independent confirmation that tight money triggered the stock market crash. All we can say is that if markets did begin to perceive a worldwide move toward higher gold reserve ratios after October 1929, then that perception was accurate.

A tightening of monetary policy that leads to lower equity prices and a slowdown in the economy is also likely to reduce the natural rate of interest. Unless central bankers understand this and reduce the discount rate sufficiently, policy will become steadily more contractionary over time. And this doesn't even account for the deflationary effects of banking panics. At the most fundamental level, the New Era optimism was predicated on confidence in government policy, especially monetary policy. If markets had expected the macroeconomic environment of the 1920s to continue into the 1930s, that belief was presumably predicated on the assumption that Fed policy would continue on the path set by Governor Strong.[38]

The instability of domestic monetary policy would be even worse in the absence of international policy coordination. In particular, if the world's central banks began competing for the limited supply of monetary gold then it would be harder for any individual central bank to stabilize domestic prices. France was accumulating gold throughout the late 1920s and early 1930s. Once investors became convinced that Britain and the United States had raised interest rates enough so that their gold reserve ratios would also start increasing, it is likely that expectations turned sharply bearish, and this could explain why prices and output began falling rapidly.

When viewed in isolation, the political events of late 1929 don't seem all that significant. But the fact that the turning point in monetary policy occurred in the midst of a tumultuous period in both domestic and international political affairs would have naturally led to doubts about whether a "New Era" had actually arrived. Investors may have begun to (correctly) perceive that governments would not be up to the task of effectively responding to the

---

38. There is some dispute as to whether the Fed's underlying policy regime policy actually changed after the death of Governor Strong. Meltzer (2003) argues that it did not. Yet several prominent contemporaneous observers, including Irving Fisher and R.G Hawtrey, argued that Strong's death left the system without leadership, and that this contributed to the Fed's passivity during the early 1930s. While either interpretation is plausible, Strong's activist policy bent and forceful personality were certainly needed in the early 1930s.

weaknesses of the international monetary system. Further support for this view comes from the fact that several of the subsequent crashes during the early 1930s were clearly linked to bearish economic or political news, especially to news stories that first appeared in the October 1929. The first such example is the June 1930 stock market crash.

The June 1930 Stock Market Crash

We have already seen that the 1929 tariff debate may have had an adverse impact on stock prices. In 1930, the tariff debate reemerged with even greater intensity, and this time the impact on stock and commodity markets was unmistakable. By mid-1930, fears of political paralysis in Washington were replaced with worries about the international repercussions of the enactment of a higher tariff. And now there was evidence that investors were concerned about—not just the potential impact of Smoot-Hawley on trade —but also on the prospects for monetary cooperation.

The stock market rose throughout early 1930, and on April 17, it peaked at a level 48.0 percent above its post-crash low. Then, between April 17 and June 4, the market fell 7.4 percent. After June 4, the decline in the market accelerated sharply with the Dow falling 19.7 percent June 4 to June 18. And, as shown in Figure 2.2, commodity prices, which had been stable in the spring of 1930, also broke sharply after June 4.

Many in the financial community attributed these declines to the enactment of the Smoot-Hawley tariff in mid-June. But why would stock prices have been adversely affected by a tariff that was designed to aid big business? And why would commodity prices decline if tariffs have the effect of reducing aggregate supply? One possibility is that the tariff was viewed as a factor reducing the likelihood of international cooperation on monetary issues. The *Commercial and Financial Chronicle* warned that the tariff might overturn peace policies, and predicted, "there may be a general tariff war as a prelude to a military war."[39] News stories discussing the possibility of a European war increased dramatically during 1930, reflecting an environment where monetary policy coordination would be much more difficult.

---

39. See the *CFC*, 4/5/30, p. 2297. They issued a similar warning as early as 11/30/29, p. 3379.

As with the October 1929 crash, the June 1930 stock market decline was associated with a major tariff fight in the U.S. Congress. To a far greater extent than during the 1929 crash, however, the press (rightly, in my view) attributed the June 1930 stock market decline to the tariff bill. And compared with the October crash, during June 1930 the press focused less on the tariff's domestic political impact, and more on its international repercussions.

As the seriousness of the Depression became more apparent during 1930, opposition to the tariff spread among the public, the press, and even many business groups. The May 10 *Commercial and Financial Chronicle* (p. 3247) reported that 1,028 economists had signed a "document without parallel in American history" urging that Hoover not sign the tariff bill. The document concluded with a warning that a "tariff war does not furnish good soil for the growth of world peace." In the weeks preceding the passage of Smoot-Hawley, opposition poured in from numerous trade associations—including bankers, retailers, and textile producers—as well as from major exporters such as Ford and General Motors.

Hoover had shown great skill in leading the American aid efforts in Europe after the First World War and Europeans viewed Hoover as the "one big man in American public life who is sufficiently acquainted with the European mentality to anticipate the dangers which the new tariff holds for American trade abroad."[40] Thus, European opinion initially may have underestimated the likelihood of the tariff becoming law. As passage became more likely during early June, the press noted a sharp escalation in threats of trade reprisals from overseas.

The June 12 *New York Times* (p. 24) reported that European opinion was having some effect on protectionists such as Senator Reed (who was attending the London Naval Conference). But Reed decided to support the tariff, and next day, the *New York Times* headline read, "Stocks Break and Rally throughout the Day; Traders Lay Declines to Reed Tariff Stand." Two days later, the *Times* headlined the market reaction to the bill's passage: "Stock Prices Sag on Passage of Tariff; Viewed as Wall Street's Disapproval of Bill." The vote was so close that (arch-protectionist) Senator Grundy was not able to vote against the bill in protest of its not being even more protectionist. They

---

40. *CFC*, 5/17/30, p. 3467.

also noted (p. 9N) that both the tariff and falling commodity prices were adversely affecting the stock market.

Although it was considered likely that the President would in fact sign the bill, there was definitely some doubt regarding Hoover's intentions. His reputation as an internationalist, the opposition of Treasury Secretary Mellon, and his own statements that he would take a fresh look at the issue all served to create some uncertainty. In a controversial decision, he had pointedly refused to get involved in the drafting of what was clearly the most important legislation of the 71st Congress.

On Sunday, June 15, Hoover announced his intention to sign the tariff bill. The next day, commodity prices plunged and the Dow fell by 5.8 percent, the largest single-day decline of 1930. The *New York Times* described the mood on Wall Street:

> There was a feeling of discouragement that extended to all of the speculative markets. Everywhere the disposition was to lay the blame at the doors of Congress. Loud lamentations against the tariff bill were heard throughout the financial district. Traders, gathered in the customers' rooms of brokerage houses, berated the administration and Congress. One disgruntled person posted a placard in a brokerage house reading, "A Business Administration—the Only Party Fit to Rule?" (6/17/30, p. 1)

Although one should be cautious in accepting the views of traders, these stories suggest that at the very least, there had been some uncertainty regarding Hoover's intentions. Furthermore, the view that the tariff had adversely impacted Wall Street was not restricted to the *New York Times*.

The June 21 issue of the *Economist* (p. 1378) called the signing a "tragicomic finale to one of the most amazing chapters in world tariff history" and suggested that "fear of its economic consequences at home and abroad was mainly responsible for the heaviest slump of the year in Wall Street." Passage of the tariff was also associated with declines in foreign markets, including German bonds that had recently been issued to finance war reparations. Over the next several years, these bonds would play an increasing role in the U.S. stock market. A June 18 *New York Times* headline reported that "Peril to War Debts Seen in Our Tariff."

To summarize, we know that political battles over the tariff were *the* major news story during both the October 1929 and the June 1930 stock market declines. During the 1929 crash, the probability of passage decreased and the political discord in the Republican Party increased throughout late October and early November. During the June 1930 decline, these two factors were almost exactly reversed. The probability of passage increased steadily and the bill ceased to be a source of domestic political turmoil after receiving Hoover's signature. Between 1929 and 1930 Smoot-Hawley metamorphosed from a domestic political problem to an international macroeconomic problem.

Smoot-Hawley demonstrates the difficulty of quantifying the impact of a political event on the stock market. Even were it possible to estimate the changing subjective probability of passage over time, these probabilities will not fully capture the way in which perceptions of the *meaning* of the event change over time. For instance, Kindleberger (1973) argued that adverse market reactions to the signing of the tariff bill in June 1930 reflected perceptions that Hoover had not shown leadership. It could be argued that a similar lack of leadership was demonstrated in 1929 by Hoover's failure to mobilize Republican insurgents in support of the bill.

The German Elections and the 1930 Banking Panic

In the three months after the Smoot-Hawley crash, the Dow rose by nearly 10 percent and then plunged 19.7 percent between September 13 and October 11, 1930. Commodity prices followed a similar pattern. After rising 2.9 percent between July 29 and September 16, the Annualist Index of Commodity Prices (AICP) declined by an equal amount over the last two weeks of September. These declines coincided with political disturbances in Brazil, and more importantly, in Germany. Wigmore (1985) suggested that gains by extremist parties in the German elections might have contributed to the decline in the U.S. stock market.

During 1930, the German economy had been particularly hard hit by the worldwide depression. In the September 14 elections the communists gained 22 additional seats while the number of fascist (Nazi) seats soared from 12 to 107. Since the fascists had campaigned against the concept of German war guilt in general and, more specifically, against the Young Plan, the surprisingly large gains made by Hitler's party were viewed with alarm, particularly in Paris.[41] These gains weakened the position of moderates such as Foreign Minister Briand (who had negotiated the French withdrawal from the Rhineland).

The response of the stock market to the election itself was fairly mild, with the Dow declining by 1.5 percent. In the September 16 *New York Times* (p. 3) it is possible to find both pessimistic assessments: "League Is Uneasy over German Vote," as well as more optimistic reports: "Bankers Minimize Reich Fascist Gain—See Reparation Agreement Safe." Many observers expected Hitler to become more responsible as he got closer to power. The *New York Times* (p. 34) admitted that the German elections "had some conceivable financial implications" and that the drop in reparations bonds was to be expected, but also suggested that such a drop "can scarcely be imagined to reflect [the] belief of serious people that the reparations treaties and contracts are forthwith to be torn up."

Hopes that Hitler would moderate his views were dashed during late September as he made one inflammatory statement after another. The September 20 *New York Times* (p. 7) reported that German stock and war bond prices fell on "disquieting rumors of political disturbances in Germany." The September 26 *New York Times* (p. 11) noted that "Hitler's Outburst Stirs British Press," and in the following issue they observed that

> Herr Hitler's speech was a keen disappointment to thousands of French liberals who had hoped the Fascist chief would come rapidly to realize that the economic prosperity and international relations of his adopted country depended foremost upon the confidence of other nations. His extreme utterances of yesterday, however, have destroyed these hopes and increased the fears for the future. (9/27/30, p. 6)

By October 1 the *New York Times* front page was dominated by ominous news headlines; "Hindenburg Backs Dictatorship Plans for Fiscal Reform" . . . "Hitler Warns President . . . Hints That Revolt Would Follow Indefinite Closing of German Parliament" . . . "Briand Hits at Foes Trying to Oust Him . . . Answers Appeal for German Moderation—Reich Fears Loss of Briand" . . . "Stock Prices Break." Although many contemporaneous press reports linked

---

41. The *Economist* (9/20/30, p. 511) called the results a "surprise."

declines in German financial markets, and to a lesser extent other European markets,[42] to the political turmoil in Germany, relatively few stories linked these disturbances to the U.S. stock market. Fortunately, movements in the price of German war reparations bonds, the so-called Young Plan bonds, offer an excellent proxy for German political problems.

There can be little doubt that the sharp declines in the Young Plan bonds in the weeks following the German elections were caused by the fear of a repudiation of the Young Plan. These declines were *not* associated with any general decline in government bond markets (the prices of U.S. and French government bonds did not decline) and thus, the decline was presumably attributable to market perceptions of an increased default risk. Between September 13 and September 30, 1930, the price of Young Plan bonds declined 8.1 percent, with most of the decline occurring on the four news days discussed above.[43] During this period the Dow increased on three of the four days that the price of Young Plan bonds increased and declined on nine of the ten days that the price of Young Plan bonds declined. A regression of the (first difference of the log of the) Dow on the (first difference of the log of the) price of Young Plan bonds (DLYPB), during the period from September 13 to September 30, shows a positive and significant relationship:

$$\text{Dow} = -.008 + .549 * \text{YoungBondPrice} \quad R^2 = .225 \quad DW = 2.69 \qquad (2.1)$$
$$(2.18)$$

And, since these markets closed at different times, the R^2 statistic would be expected to understate the actual correlation.

The increased probability of default on the Young Plan bonds could have affected the market for a variety of reasons. For instance, the September 27 *Commercial and Financial Chronicle* (p. 1982) reported "Hoover Counts on Funds—Allies Interest Payments Needed to Permit Continuance of Reduction in Tax Rate." The fact that the Dow would soar after Hoover's debt moratorium proposal of 1931, however, suggests that the impact of German political difficulties on the U.S. markets owed more to their perceived effect on the prospects for international cooperation, than any impact they might have

---

42. See, for example, the *Economist* (9/27/30, p. 583; 10/4/30, p. 612); and the *NYT* (9/29/30, p. 33).

43. September 15, 19, 25, and 30.

had on U.S. fiscal policy. And the concurrent decline in commodity prices indicates that this anticipated lack of cooperation might have had monetary implications. By October 24, the *New York Times* (p. 33) was warning that the "singular change in the international gold movement that came with Germany's 'Fascist' scare has postponed the check to the French bank's acquisition [of gold reserves], which was thought a month ago to be near at hand."

The crisis in Germany seemed to precipitate a general worsening of the political situation in Europe during the last three months of 1930. As prices and output continued to fall throughout the world, there was increasing discussion of the need to address the "maldistribution of gold" through policy coordination by the major central banks. Unfortunately, the banking panics that began in November 1930 led to increased currency hoarding, which neutralized the effect of slightly more expansionary policies initiated by key central banks. This marks a key turning point in this narrative. The first year of the Depression, like the 1920–1921 depression, was a pure monetary policy shock. After October 1930, the worsening economy led to increased private hoarding of cash and then, later, gold. These factors also tended to raise the value of gold, which meant that the fundamental nature of the problem remained the same—a shortfall of nominal spending, or aggregate demand. But the root causes became much more complex.

As early as September 1930 some economists were already blaming the Depression on French gold hoarding.[44] After the closure in early November of the important Oustric Bank, as well as several other French banks, the French demand for currency increased and large quantities of gold began flowing from England to France. U.S. stock and commodity prices declined on October 31 when news of the impending failure of the Oustric Bank was first made public.[45]

During November banking problems spread to the United States, and the Dow fell 3.3 percent on Monday, November 17, following the failure of more than fifty southern banks. Temin (1989, p. 51) called the first banking panic of the Depression a "minor event," because it was somewhat localized in nature.

---

44. See the *NYT*, 9/16/30, p. 38.

45. Although the Oustric Bank actually failed on November 6, the failure was expected after the suspension on October 31 of trading in stocks of groups that it controlled. The Dow fell 2.5 percent on October 31, and corn, wheat, and commodity prices also fell.

But there can be no doubt that currency hoarding increased dramatically in November and December 1930. (In the United States, as in France, this increase was entirely concentrated in large denomination notes.) Because of the high gold backing of the U.S. dollar and French franc, this increase in currency demand translated into a large increase in the demand for gold.[46] Thus, the bank failures also impacted foreign stock markets and commodity prices. The AICP, which had risen slightly between September 30 and October 28, fell 3.5 percent between October 28 and November 18.

The United States suffered an even more serious set of bank failures during December 1930. Rumors of problems at the Bank of the United States began circulating on Monday, December 8, as last-minute attempts were made to rescue the bank. The bank finally failed on December 11 and the December 13 *Commercial and Financial Chronicle* (p. 3748) blamed the failure for the 4.5 percent drop in the Dow during the first four days of the week. The AICP, which had been stable for several weeks, fell 2.9 percent between December 2 and December 16 and then leveled off. Although the Dow reached its lowest level of the year on December 16, sharp price breaks continued to occur on news of major bank failures. For instance, the Dow dropped 4.3 percent on December 22 on news of the failure of the Bankers' Trust Co. in Philadelphia. And two days later the *New York Times* (p. 21) noted that the market broke early on December 23 on news of the failure of the Chelsea Bank and Trust, before recovering on news of a cut in the discount rate.

Because many of the U.S. bank failures occurred when the markets were open, contemporaneous observers were able to easily ascertain their (adverse) impact on U.S. stock and commodity prices. Friedman and Schwartz have already extensively documented the impact of the failures on U.S. monetary aggregates, and Bernanke (1983) argued that bank failures might have depressed output by reducing the efficiency of financial intermediation. The evidence that European bank failures impacted U.S. markets, and vice versa, is of special interest because the gold market approach suggests that bank

---

46. Recall that because the French Monetary Law of 1928 encouraged the Bank of France to provide 100 percent gold backing to new currency injections, increases in French currency hoarding led to a higher French gold reserve ratio. Eichengreen (1992, p. 254) suggested that "Gold inflows led to the growth of currency in the hands of the [French] public." But in this case causality presumably went in the opposite direction.

failures anywhere in the world should have led to increased currency demand in the country affected, which would have increased the world demand for monetary gold and depressed world aggregate demand.

Deflation, the Gold Standard, and Policy Coordination

Despite their close correlation during most of the interwar period, there is no necessary relationship between stock and commodity prices. For instance, a severe drought in early August 1930 (a supply shock) moved stock and commodity prices in opposite directions. The August 9 *Commercial and Financial Chronicle* noted:

> The [stock] market now manifested weakness. It began to dawn upon the minds of traders that the grain speculation really betokened much damage to the corn crop, and thereby assumed the dimensions of a severe infliction in the agricultural world, and furthermore that a crop disaster was hardly a legitimate basis for a bull speculation in the stock market. (p. 831)

But this pattern was very atypical. Throughout most of the 1930s there was a positive correlation between stock and commodity prices, presumably because there was also a strong correlation between commodity prices and industrial production. The close correlation between stock and commodity prices in Figure 2.2 suggests the primacy of demand shocks, even during a year with a drought.

Interestingly, the financial press seemed to interpret the relationship between stocks and commodities differently in 1929 than in 1930. Because stock prices fell far more sharply than commodity prices in October 1929, many analysts viewed the concurrent commodity price decline as merely a symptom of the stock market crash. By mid-1930 the order of causality was usually reversed, with the commodity markets (i.e., "deflation") seen as exerting a "depressing" influence on stocks.[47]

Those reports that attributed the decline in commodity prices to nonmonetary factors such as overproduction saw these declines as reducing the incomes

---

47. See Wigmore (1985) for a similar interpretation.

and thus the purchasing power of farmers and other producers of primary products. This interpretation often led to awkward theories of falling production being caused by overproduction. More sophisticated observers held that declines in both markets could be attributed to monetary factors:

> The drop in wheat cannot, of course be blamed entirely on the decline in stocks, anymore than the latter can be explained by the break in wheat; but each reacted on the other, and was caused largely by tightening credit. (*Economist*, 6/15/29, p. 1342)

Those who attributed commodity price declines to monetary factors stressed the need for cooperation among central banks. Early in 1930 Keynes already saw that "the current decline in wholesale prices for raw materials had taken on the character of a worldwide disaster" and as a "remedy for these conditions he [Keynes] sees cessation of the internecine struggle for gold stocks . . . co-operation of the Central Banks."[48] Military analogies were often employed. Irving Fisher argued that, "gold disarmament is just as difficult of attainment as is military disarmament. No greater problem exists today than a possible gold shortage."[49] Although Fisher's preferred solution involved an increase in the price of gold, he knew that such a radical policy was politically unacceptable and also recommended that, "if we are attended by deflation, the first step would be to decrease the gold reserve ratio." The crucial importance of the gold reserve ratio may not be obvious to modern readers who have lived their whole life in a fiat money world, but it was very apparent to interwar economists like Fisher, Keynes and Hawtrey.

The BIS was often seen as a mechanism for achieving central bank cooperation. The April 12 *Commercial and Financial Chronicle* (p. 2502) reported "Sir Charles Addis of Bank of England, Urges Co-operation to Stabilize Gold on Scale Contemplated through Bank for International Settlements." And in the June 14 *Commercial and Financial Chronicle* (p. 4161) Josiah Stamp suggested that "the Bank for International Settlements is the beginning of an institution that can develop into a machine for co-ordinated and thoroughgoing control of these capricious matters," and, "one of the first requirements

---

48. *CFC*, 2/8/30, p. 903.
49. *CFC*, 1/11/30, p. 219.

toward such co-ordination and control, Sir Josiah said, is the demilitarization of finance by the scrapping of belligerent terms."

Those in favor of monetary policy coordination included many economists and financial market participants. By November 1930 there was active consideration of a stabilization plan run by the BIS:

> World Gold Parley Considered in Paris—English Sources Report Dozen of More Nations May Take Up Distribution Problem—Berlin Said to Favor Plan—New York Banks Believed to Support It, but Solution Depends on France—Suggest Control at Basle [BIS]—Proponents Want Each Country to Contribute a Certain Proportion of Its Precious Metal. (*NYT,* 11/18/30, p. 11)

The strongest support for international cooperation came from England and Germany. The position of the United States, which was hit hard by the Depression but also in possession of the world's largest gold stock, was less clear-cut. President Hoover argued, "This is not an occasion for analysis of the many theories such as too little gold or the inflexible use of it."[50] Important congressmen including Rep. McFadden, as well as many of the Federal Reserve members, were also opposed to monetary cooperation. The French had a strong economy throughout much of 1930 as well as rapidly growing gold stocks and thus saw little need for policy coordination.

A November 1930 visit to Europe by New York Fed Governor Harrison (an advocate of both monetary ease and greater international cooperation) was followed with great interest by the financial markets. The November 11 *New York Times* (p. 9) noted that (Governor of the Bank of England) Montagu Norman was so anxious to continue his talks with Harrison that he boarded the liner Bremen on which Harrison was returning to New York and then in the English Channel "the 59-year-old banker climbed down the swaying ladder to a launch bobbing up and down in a choppy sea" and returned to England.

Table 2b.1 shows that in late 1930 and early 1931, the gold reserve ratios of the United States, England, and the "Rest of World" showed modest declines, suggesting that monetary policies did become more expansionary. Unfortunately,

---

50. *CFC,* 10/4/30, p. 2105.

the movement toward greater ease was completely offset by the large increases in real currency demand associated with banking panics, particularly in the United States. While the Bank of England clearly did move toward monetary ease during late 1930, it is difficult to know whether the Fed was attempting a similar policy shift or whether its lower gold reserve ratio merely represented a passive response to currency injections associated with banking instability.

An additional factor inhibiting recovery was the rising political discord in Europe. In commenting on the possibility of Harrison's talks leading to a coordinated policy of easing by the major central banks, the *New York Times* reported that "the big stumbling-block in the path of such a policy, however, is the present unsettled political position of Europe."[51] There would be a brief period of stability in early 1931 (accompanied by a hiatus in the ongoing economic contraction), but by the spring of 1931 the European political situation had again begun to deteriorate.

Eichengreen (p. 263) argued that the BIS was unable to coordinate monetary policy because key central banks lacked a "common conceptual framework." If so, then the various political disturbances considered in this chapter may not have been as significant as they seemed at the time. But even if policy coordination was doomed to failure from the beginning, the public may have only gradually become aware of this fact. The prices of commodities and equities would have been lower in the late 1920s had investors known that monetary policy would be so dysfunctional during the 1930s. The political and economic crises of the 1930s were important because they gradually convinced the public that there was no "wizard behind the curtain" of international finance. And, as investors began to understand that fact, expectations of future monetary growth declined, as did aggregate demand.[52]

---

51. See the *NYT*, 12/25/30, p. 16.

52. Note that to argue that policy coordination would have been helpful, or even essential, in 1929, is not at all equivalent to arguing that it was an important aspect of the classical gold standard. Thus I take no position of the debate between Flandreau (1997) and Eichengreen on this issue.

What Caused the Depression of 1930?

In this chapter we have seen that the first year of the Depression was associated with a sharp rise in the world gold reserve ratio. As theory would predict, this depressed aggregate demand and produced deflation throughout much of the world. Surprisingly, despite the fact that the slump was already considerably worse than the 2008–2009 recession, no significant problems arose with the banking system. Banks were conservatively managed in the 1920s, at least relative to the banking system of the early twenty-first century, as there was no government deposit insurance and no policy of "too big to fail."

Of course, correlation doesn't prove causation, so we also need to consider other evidence that a gold reserve ratio triggered the contraction. If we were to look at the entire twentieth century, the contraction that most resembled 1929–1930 was the depression of 1920–1921. In both cases the monthly indices for both wholesale prices and industrial production showed extremely sharp declines. Does our explanation of the onset of the Great Contraction shed any light on that earlier depression?

The Fed began raising interest rates in early 1920 in order to stop inflation, and between October 1920 and October 1921 the U.S. gold reserve ratio soared by more than 53 percent. With the United States then holding more than one-third of the world monetary gold stock, this would have been sufficient, *ceteris paribus*, to reduce the world price level by at least 18 percent. The actual U.S. GNP deflator declined by 16 percent between late 1920 and late 1921, and wholesale prices and industrial production fell even more sharply. The contractionary Fed policy also induced a large inflow of gold to the United States. But because the increase in the U.S. gold stock was roughly equal to the world increase, foreign gold stocks remained relatively stable. Even so, the sharp deflation (which was even greater in many European countries) can be plausibly attributed to U.S. policy. Although most European powers were not on the gold standard at that time, they intended to eventually return to the standard and were reluctant to allow their currencies to depreciate against the dollar (i.e., gold). They were also reluctant to see a reduction in their gold stocks, which had already been depleted during the war. To prevent gold outflows they were forced to follow the deflationary policies of the Fed.

If the preceding story can explain the similarities between 1929–1930 and 1920–1921, can it also explain the differences? In particular, why did 1920–1921 not see anything comparable to the 1929 stock market crash, and why wasn't the 1920–1921 downturn followed by a "great depression"? The answer to the first question is fairly clear. The immediate post–World War I situation was highly unstable, both domestically and internationally. In 1920, there was as yet no reason to anticipate a New Era where central banks would be able to deliver macroeconomic stability, and thus stock prices never approached the lofty levels of 1929. Also, recall that in 1930, stock prices had only fallen to the levels of the relatively prosperous mid-1920s; it wasn't until late 1931 that the Great Depression was fully priced into the U.S. equity markets. It would have been reasonable for investors to view 1921 as a painful but brief transition toward "normalcy." In contrast, by 1929 investors (incorrectly) believed that after seven years of relative stability, all of the postwar adjustments had already occurred.

The instability of the early postwar period may also explain why the 1920–1921 depression was relatively brief. There were no exchange rate crises comparable to those of 1931, because in 1921 most of the major currencies were still floating. And because the United States did not experience a major banking panic during 1921, none of the major factors that deepened the Great Depression after late 1930 were at work during the 1920–1921 contraction. Conservatives often point to Hoover's high wage policy, which contrasts with Harding's more laissez-faire approach. This difference cannot account for the sharp fall in nominal GDP after 1929, but it may explain why the 1921 depression saw a bit more price deflation, whereas in 1930 a larger share of the decline in nominal GDP was comprised of falling output.

Another difference between 1920–1921 and 1929–1930 is that in the latter period the causes of the monetary policy shift were much more international in scope. Previous narratives of the Depression often focus on problems in one country being transmitted to the rest of the world through gold flows. In contrast, the gold market approach used here is not reliant on Hume's price-specie-flow transmission mechanism. Simultaneous increases in central bank demand for monetary gold in many different countries caused the real value of gold to rise sharply during 1930. This was equivalent to a change in the terms of trade between gold and other commodities traded in international markets—that is, deflation of tradable goods' prices in all countries adhering to the gold standard. And this deflation occurred *immediately* in the commodity markets, even before exchange rate pressures had time to impact domestic money supplies.

Of course, the Great Depression did not begin at precisely the same time in every country. In France, the undervaluation of the franc led to rising prices for non-tradable goods, and for a time this offset the effect of deflation in the international commodity markets. But, in a more fundamental sense, both the causes and the consequences of the tight money policy during 1929–1930 were international in scope from the very beginning. Even in France, the wholesale price index was already falling by late 1929.

Eichengreen placed great emphasis on the fact that the Depression began earlier in some countries on the periphery of the world economy. He argued (p. 392) that the tight U.S. monetary policy of 1928 forced those countries experiencing balance of payment deficits to also tighten their monetary policies. But I don't think it makes sense to see this as the beginning of the Depression. Rather, the strong supply side of the U.S. economy raised the real exchange rate for the dollar, which forced mild deflation on those less robust economies that also had tied their currencies to gold. Wall Street had no particular reason to be concerned about this pattern, which was quite similar to the problems faced by countries with currencies tied to the dollar in the late 1990s, when there was another supply-side boom in the United States. Some countries slumped before the United States, and some after, but Table 2.1 shows that the *world* price level broke sharply in late 1929.

The use of gold *flows* to interpret monetary policy has two major drawbacks. While the inflow of gold into a country suggests that that country is following a contractionary policy (relative to the rest of the world), it does not provide a way of *quantifying* that policy's impact. Furthermore, if all major countries simultaneously conduct a contractionary policy (as during 1929–1930) then gold flows may be unable to detect the policy shift. The deflationary nature of this policy shift would, however, be evident from the sharp increase in the world's gold reserve ratio.

Friedman and Schwartz cited the large gold flows into the United States during 1929–1931 as evidence that contractionary monetary policies in the United States helped transmit the Great Depression to the rest of the world.

Fremling (1985) disputed this contention, noting that the U.S. gold inflows, while substantial, were smaller than the net increase in the world's gold stocks and did not lead to a decrease in foreign gold stocks; therefore, U.S. policy did not force foreign central banks to contract their money supplies. Both of these views oversimplify a complex phenomenon. U.S. policy had the largest (deflationary) impact on the world price level during 1929–1930; French policy had the greatest impact over a longer time horizon; and British policy was most responsible for the sudden tightening of world monetary policy in late 1929 (although Britain had little choice because of its low gold reserves).

How one partitions "blame," depends on how seriously one takes the concept of the "rules of the game" (i.e., a stable gold reserve ratio). In my view, the system was fundamentally flawed, which makes it difficult to assign blame. Nevertheless, during the 1920s there was an understanding that a shortage of gold posed a deflationary threat to the world economy. Given the risk of deflation, I think it is fair to say that the large increase in U.S. and French gold ratios during 1930 was quite unhelpful.

Although I have argued that monetary tightening was the proximate cause of the onset of the Great Contraction and may also have contributed to the 1929 stock market crash, I do not believe that the Depression had any single root cause, in the sense of a cause deeply embedded in preceding events. Of course, there are many difficult philosophical problems associated with establishing causation, some of which will be discussed in Chapter 12. For the moment, consider the following five policy counterfactuals:

1. Through deflation or currency devaluation, policymakers avoided undervaluing gold in the immediate aftermath of World War I. (The Mundell–Johnson solution)

2. Policymakers allowed the purchasing power of gold to rise gradually during the 1920s, through a policy of mild deflation. (The Austrian solution)

3. Beginning in 1929, the major central banks cooperated to economize on the holding of gold reserves. (The Bretton Woods solution)

4. Beginning in 1929, the Fed adopted a 3 percent money supply (M2) growth target. (The monetarist solution)

5. Beginning in 1929, the United States switched to a fiat money regime and began targeting the inflation rate at 2 percent. (The new Keynesian solution)

It is quite plausible that any of these policy counterfactuals would have prevented the sharp decline in aggregate demand after 1929. In that sense, the *failure* to adopt any one of these policies could be viewed as a root cause of the Depression. The root causes approach, however, is hard to reconcile with modern finance theory. By 1929, investors presumably knew that these policy counterfactuals had not occurred, or were not likely to occur. If the root causes of the Depression were already in place by September 1929, then stock prices should never have risen to such lofty levels. Either the Great Depression was not forecastable in September 1929, or financial markets are not efficient.

Viewed from an efficient markets perspective, a true causal factor would be an event that would generate unanticipated movements in stock and commodity prices. One might view the 1929 macroeconomy as a highly complex and potentially unstable system that was impacted by a perfect storm of unforecastable events. Even worse, those political and economic shocks may have been at least partially interrelated—raising the prospect of small shocks having enormous repercussions—the so-called butterfly effect.[53] Events such as the Great Contraction don't happen very often—indeed only once in modern world history—so it's not hard to see why investors in prosperous 1929 would have had difficulty foreseeing this complex oncoming disaster.

If we look at Mundell and Johnson's gold undervaluation hypothesis we can see some of the conceptual difficulties associated with determining causality. They argued that World War I (which roughly doubled the U.S. price level) had left gold severely undervalued. Even after the deflation of 1921, wholesale prices in the United States were about 50 percent above their prewar level. And because the interwar gold exchange standard economized on the monetary

---

53. The Depression might never have been "Great" without the ripple effects flowing from the banking panics, which began in late 1930. And these panics might have been avoided had the economy been a bit stronger in the summer and fall of 1930. Thus, events such as the death of Governor Strong, or Hoover's decision to sign Smoot-Hawley, could well have been pivotal turning points, even if their direct effects were quite modest.

use of gold, prices remained far above the prewar level for the remainder of the 1920s. According to Mundell and Johnson, the Great Deflation of 1929–1932 was caused by the preceding (unsustainable) undervaluation of gold. It was almost inevitable that the value of gold would eventually return to its long-run equilibrium value, and when that happened price levels would fall in terms of any currency tied to gold. This hypothesis (which does use the gold market approach to monetary economics) has the virtue of being correct about the weaknesses in the interwar gold standard. After 1929, the gold exchange standard did gradually evolve into something closer to the prewar system, as central banks replaced foreign exchange with gold reserves. And prices did fall to roughly their prewar levels.

If we take a closer look at the Mundell–Johnson hypothesis, however, a key issue is whether or not the gold undervaluation was *sustainable*. Prior to the crash, investors might have believed that central banks would be able to continue the policies that had successfully stabilized the U.S. price level during 1922–1929; that is, would continue to economize on gold reserves with a "gold exchange standard." In retrospect they would have been wrong, but their expectations were not obviously unreasonable—the U.S. economy had continued to boom during 1927–1929 even as the French were hoarding large quantities of gold. It wasn't obvious that this process could not continue. Indeed, Bordo and Eichengreen (1998) showed that with more enlightened monetary policies the world monetary gold stocks were sufficient to underpin the international gold standard for several more decades. From this perspective, one could just as easily argue that the root cause of the Great Depression was not the undervaluation of gold, but rather the failure of central banks to maintain the policies they had so effectively pursued during the late 1920s.

Nor is it obvious that a series of well-timed currency devaluations in the early 1920s could have solved the gold undervaluation problem. It wasn't so much that gold was undervalued in 1920 (the market was in short-run equilibrium) but rather that one might reasonably have expected the value of gold to have gradually risen during the 1920s and 1930s, as the gold standard was restored and monetary gold demand increased. Thus, a policy of coordinated devaluations in 1920 would have had to have been accompanied by massive gold sterilization, in order to prevent a burst of inflation from again undervaluing gold in the short run. If this were done, then gold would have needed to have been gradually desterilized as countries like France built up their gold stocks. But if policymakers were capable of that sort of sophisticated inflation targeting in 1920, why couldn't they have done the same in 1929? I will consider one answer to this question in Chapter 4 when I examine liquidity traps, which imply an asymmetry in the gold standard that supports the Mundell-Johnson view.

Similar objections could be raised regarding any of the other four policy counterfactuals. Nevertheless, one can combine all five policy counterfactuals into a plausible composite hypothesis: where the Depression was caused by the failure to set postwar exchange rates at appropriate levels, and given that decision, the failure of the Fed to allow a gradual deflation after 1921 (as the Austrians preferred), and given that they had already rejected these two policy options, the failure of the Fed (and other central banks) to maintain high prices after 1929. Then the policy switch that led to high gold reserve ratios after late 1929 (and that also surprised investors) becomes the *proximate* cause of the Depression, and the deeper root causes depend on one's views of which policy alternatives would have been both effective and politically feasible.

Summary

Many economists have argued that monetary policy was too tight during 1928–1929, and that the slump that began in late 1929 was a lagged response to the tightening. Others argued that policy was too loose, feeding a stock market bubble that would inevitably burst. As far as I know this is the only study to argue that there were *no significant policy failures* in the period preceding the Wall Street crash of 1929.[54] Rather, policy only began to depress aggregate demand in late 1929.[55] A switch toward tighter monetary policy in Britain and the United States led to a sudden increase in the world gold ratio,

---

54. Schuker (2003) takes a partial exception to this generalization. He argues that the gold exchange standard of the 1920s was not fundamentally flawed, and that the subsequent problems reflected "contingent political outcomes."

55. This is not to say that *given what happened later*, a different policy in 1928–1929 would not have been preferable. I will consider some other counterfactuals in Chapter 12. Austrian economists can make a good argument that policy was too expansionary in the 1920s, given the actual path of policy in the 1930s.

which was the proximate cause of the subsequent (worldwide) deflation. The key U.S. policy error was the failure to accommodate Britain's need to rebuild gold reserves in 1930, as they had in 1927. French policy also continued to exert deflationary pressure on the world economy. There are at least five pieces of evidence for this interpretation:

1. Only the gold reserve ratio changed sharply after October 1929; there were no major changes in the other two factors influencing the international gold market; growth in real currency demand increased by less than 3 percent and growth in the supply of monetary gold actually accelerated slightly (which is inflationary). Indeed, these other two factors essentially neutralized each other.

2. Economic theory predicts that a sharp increase in the real demand for gold will increase the value of gold, which is deflationary for any country using gold as a medium of account.

3. Between 1920 and 1921 there was an (even sharper) increase in the world gold gold reserve ratio, and there was even greater worldwide deflation.

4. Stock markets in many countries fell sharply about the time this policy switch occurred.

5. We found some evidence that, throughout 1929 and 1930, the U.S. stock market reacted adversely to signs that Hoover would not be an effective leader and also responded negatively to signs that international cooperation would not be forthcoming.

The last point is obviously very tentative, and we need much more evidence to have any confidence in the hypothesis that a lack of international policy coordination affected monetary policy expectations in the United States. Fortunately, the year 1931 will provide a mountain of such evidence.

Appendix 2.a
Data Sources

The monthly wage data came from two different sources. The 1930s data were taken from the Bureau of Labor Statistics (BLS) production-worker average hourly earnings series. This data are found in *Employment, Hours, and Earnings, United States, 1909–84*, Vol. 1, U.S. Dept. of Labor, Bureau of Labor Statistics, March 1985, p. 57. The 1920s data were taken from the National Industrial Conference Board (NICB) average hourly earnings in manufacturing series reported in Beney (1936, pp. 44–47), and *Survey of Current Business*, 1936–40, various issues. (There is a six-month gap in the NICB series from January to June 1922.)

The Wholesale Price Index series are BLS data taken from various issues of the *Federal Reserve Bulletin*. The industrial production series is from *Industrial Production: 1976 Revision*, a 1977 publication by the Board of Governors of the Federal Reserve System. The monetary gold stock and foreign currency stock data are from the *Federal Reserve Bulletin*, various issues. The U.S. monetary base data are from Friedman and Schwartz (1963a.)

Appendix 2.b

Table 2b.1 (on the next page) provides the same data as Table 2.1, as well as gold demand data for some of the more important individual central banks. All percentage changes are expressed as first differences of logs. Unlike Table 2.1, the changes are not annualized. This allows each change to be added across both time and space. Note that roughly one-half of the world increase in real gold demand between 1926 and 1932 occurred in France, and another 20 percent occurred in the United States. Chapter 13 contains a detailed explanation of how the table was constructed.

Table 2b.1. The Impact of Changes in the Gold Reserve Ratio, the Real Demand for Currency, the Real Demand for Gold, and the Total Monetary Gold Stock on the World Price Level, 1926–1932

		Time Period					
		Dec 1926 to Jun 1928	Jun 1928 to Oct 1929	Oct 1929 to Oct 1930	Oct 1930 to Aug 1931	Aug 1931 to Dec 1932	Dec 1926 to Dec 1932
United States	1. r	+1.24	−2.59	−4.69	+1.55	+9.46	+5.15
	2. m	+1.55	−0.58	−0.46	−9.85	−9.66	−19.01
	3. g	+2.79	−3.17	−5.15	−8.30	−0.20	−13.86
England	4. r	−1.07	+1.52	−1.38	+1.05	1.37*	−1.19
	5. m	−0.13	+0.30	−0.55	−0.59	+1.19	+0.29
	6. g	−1.20	+1.82	−1.93	+0.46	−0.18	−0.90
France	7. r	−3.23	−2.73	−2.49	−1.80	−6.53	−17.27
	8. m	−1.47	−1.68	−3.08	−3.02	−5.17	−13.99
	9. g	−4.70	−4.41	−5.57	−4.82	−11.70	−31.26
Rest of World	10. r	−0.92	+0.62	−1.06	+0.75	−7.36	−8.55
	11. m	−4.01	−0.98	−0.89	−2.73	+0.08	−8.09
	12. g	−4.93	−0.36	−1.95	−1.98	−7.28	−16.64
World	13. r	−3.98	−3.18	−9.62	+1.55	−5.80	−21.86
	14. m	−4.05	−2.94	−4.97	−16.18	−13.56	−40.80
	15. g	−8.03	−6.12	−14.59	−14.63	−19.36	−62.66
	16. G	+5.82	+5.42	+5.25	+3.93	+5.18	+25.61
	17. P	−2.21	−0.70	−9.34	−10.70	−14.18	−37.06

r = direct impact of changes in gold reserve ratio on price level
m = direct impact of changes in real currency demand on price level
g = direct impact of changes in real demand for gold on price level
G = change in the total world monetary gold stock
P = change in the world price level

Note: All numbers represent the first difference in the log of P (times 100); the numbers are not annualized. The sum of the impact of changes in r and m should equal the impact of changes in g. For the world as a whole, the change in P reflects changes in G and g. For more information on rest of world (ROW), see appendix.

*The decomposition of the British demand for gold has little significance after Britain left the gold standard in September 1931.

The German Crisis of 1931

*The collapse of demand is another name for the appreciation
of gold. It means the offer of less gold in exchange for commodities. And we may regard the responsibility of the Central
Banks as arising from their control over the market for gold.*
—R.G. Hawtrey, 1947, p. 140

THE FIRST THREE months of 1931 was a period of relative calm.
There were no banking panics to cause currency hoarding and no devaluation
fears to cause private gold hoarding. Even growth in the world gold reserve ratio slowed somewhat. Thus far the Depression had looked a lot like 1920–1921,
with industrial production falling 31 percent, and then beginning to rise. If
the Federal Reserve (Fed) had pursued an expansionary policy (a lower gold
ratio), then a vigorous recovery might have occurred. Even without help from
the Fed, industrial production rose 3.2 percent between January and April
and there were numerous signs that the Depression might be ending. Then,
between mid-1931 and mid-1932, an extraordinary series of events turned a
major recession into the Great Contraction.

The renewed downturn was accompanied by some fundamental changes
in the nature of the international gold standard. Contrary to popular belief,
1931 did not mark the end of the international gold standard; if it had, the Depression might have ended much more quickly. Instead, it marked the end of
a *stable* international gold standard. For the remainder of the 1930s, a hobbled
gold standard did far more damage than would have been possible from either a
pure gold standard or a pure fiat money regime. It was the worst of both worlds;
the gold standard continued to constrain monetary policymakers in many

countries, including the United States, but the panicky search for liquidity took away gold's greatest virtue, its stability of value.

In the next two chapters we will take a detailed look at how political and economic shocks impacted the international gold market, financial markets, and the overall economy during 1931–1932. First, let's look at how the gold market approach can provide a framework for explaining changes in aggregate demand during 1931 and 1932.

Gold Hoarding and Aggregate Demand during 1931

In the previous chapter we saw how a 9.6 percent increase in the world gold reserve ratio sharply lowered output and prices after October 1929. With the onset of banking crises in late 1930, however, increases in real currency demand (or lower currency velocity) also contributed to worldwide deflation. In fact, Tables 2.1 and 2b.1 suggest that currency hoarding can explain nearly all of the deflation after October 1930. Nominal currency demand actually rose by about 5 percent between October 1930 and the end of 1932, despite a 25 percent drop in the world price level. This means that real currency demand soared by roughly 30 percent over that twenty-six-month period. Even with no change in gold stocks or gold reserve ratios, such an increase in real currency demand would have had a severe deflationary impact.

To make matters even worse, private and central bank gold hoarding also put strong downward pressure on the world price level during the crucial period of June 1931 to June 1932. Net private gold demand, which had averaged about *negative* $50 million per year from the beginning of 1927 to mid-1931 (i.e., the stock of privately held gold was declining), soared to positive $355 million in the twelve months between June 1931 and June 1932. This swing of more than $400 million toward private gold holdings represented nearly 4 percent of total world monetary gold stocks—a most unwelcome development in a world economy already struggling with deflation. The world's gold reserve ratio also rose, mostly due to hoarding by European central banks.

The effect of public and private gold hoarding may have been even greater than suggested by the data in Tables 2.1 and 2b.1. In the decomposition of changes in the world price level, increases in real currency demand were essentially a residual, which picked up all factors other than private gold hoarding or central bank deviations from the "rules of the game." But the increase in currency hoarding *was itself a response to the Depression*, particularly low interest rates and fear of bank failures. In addition, Wicker (1996) found evidence that two of banking panics were aggravated by runs on the dollar, which were at least partly attributable to worries over the sufficiency of monetary gold reserves.[1]

Thus, gold hoarding by both private citizens and foreign central banks may have indirectly contributed to currency hoarding during the early 1930s. If so, then the impact of both private and central bank gold hoarding on the price level would have been far larger than suggested by the data in Tables 2.1 and 2b.1. In other words, the root cause of the currency hoarding of 1931–1932 was the Depression itself, which in turn was caused by contractionary central bank policies (higher gold reserve ratios) and then, later, by private gold hoarding.

Growth in the world monetary gold stock slowed only slightly after October 1930, from an annual rate of 4.3 percent between December 1926 to October 1930, to an annual rate of 4.2 percent between October 1930 and December 1932.[2] How, then, could private gold hoarding have played a role in the severe deflation of the latter period? If we look at shorter time periods, we see a much more complex pattern. During the first year of the Depression, growth in the world monetary gold stock actually accelerated to a rate of 5.2 percent per year. After the first banking panics began in late 1930, growth accelerated further to an annual rate of 5.9 percent between October 1930 and June 1931.

The initial acceleration in the growth rate of the world monetary gold stock is exactly what one would expect during a period of deflation. Recall that under a gold standard regime, deflation raises the real price of gold. Unless the deflation was caused by a leftward shift in the supply of gold (clearly not the case in the 1930s) one would expect an increase in the quantity of newly mined gold. In addition, a higher real price of gold would be expected to reduce the industrial demand for the metal (assuming that the ongoing

---

1. See also Wigmore (1987).

2. Bernanke (1995) and Sumner (1991) both argued that the continued growth in the world monetary gold stock after 1929 meant that the deflation must have come from other (demand side) factors.

deflation was not caused by increased industrial demand for the metal). And the fall in real incomes during the 1930s would have been expected to further reduce demand for a metal often used in luxury goods. It is also possible that a higher real price of gold led to some reduction in private demand for gold as an investment. In fact, there was an increase in the supply of newly mined gold during the early 1930s, and there was also substantial gold dishoarding from India after mid-1931,[3] which added several percentage points to the growth rate of the world monetary gold stock.

Between the growth in newly mined gold and the dishoarding from India, one might have expected the growth of monetary gold stocks to have accelerated to a rate well above 5.9 percent after mid-1931. Instead, after the German reichsmark came under attack, growth in the world monetary gold stock came to an abrupt halt, rising just 0.7 percent over the following twelve months. Rapid growth in world gold stocks briefly resumed after July 1932, before there was renewed hoarding in early 1933. Coincidentally, it was in July 1932 that U.S. industrial production (and the Dow) reached its lowest point of the Great Depression.

There is some evidence that investors may have been counting on the stabilizing properties of the gold standard. When the increased supply of gold was not forthcoming, the *New York Times* noted that during previous depressions an "increase in the world's gold supplies had a definite influence in bringing recovery" and then asked, "Why did not this process affect prices and prosperity" in 1932?[4]

To summarize, gold standard models suggest that the supply and demand for gold tends to adjust to shocks in a way that ensures rough stability in the long-run value of gold (and hence price level). To be sure, this process may take decades and was certainly too slow to prevent the Depression, but one would at least have expected some response in the supply of monetary gold to

---

3. The *NYT* noted:

    Last year [1932] the high premium paid for gold in England's depreciated currency drew out an estimated $50,000,000 from sale to the banks of British gold ornaments and hoarded coin, and had the much more remarkable effect of turning India, hitherto an immense absorbent of the world's new gold, into a huge exporter. Estimates vary as to the amount thus released, but they range from $300,000,000 to $400,000,000. (1/3/1933, p. 25)

4. *NYT*, 1/3/1933, p. 25.

the ongoing deflation. At first, that sort of supply response seemed to be occurring. That's why the subsequent gold hoarding during 1931–1932 takes on such importance. Investors may have anticipated (and the world economy certainly needed) continued acceleration in the growth rate of the world monetary gold stock. As we will see, the financial markets reacted extremely negatively to signs that that growth in monetary gold stocks was being disrupted.

At first glance, the data in Table 2.1 also seem to suggest that the world gold reserve ratio played only a modest role during the second stage of the Depression. The ratio actually fell slightly after October 1930, and even though it rose after mid-1931, the total increase between October 1930 and December 1932 was only about 4.2 percent. Once again, however, a closer look at the data shows that the gold reserve ratio played a significant deflationary role during 1931 and 1932.

In Chapter 1, I defined the "rules of the game" as a stable gold reserve ratio and suggested that it was a good benchmark for a neutral monetary policy. But it is not clear that a stable gold reserve ratio should be viewed as the baseline policy. If Bagehot's maxim that central banks should lend freely in response to internal drains is regarded as standard operating procedure under a gold standard regime, then gold reserve ratios should have *fallen* during banking panics. In that case, a stable gold reserve ratio would represent a *de facto* tightening of monetary policy. By using the gold reserve ratio as a policy indicator, we will tend to *overestimate* the importance of currency hoarding, and underestimate the failure of central bank monetary policies. As shown in Figure 3.1, there was indeed a tendency for the world gold reserve ratio to fall during banking panics. (The gold ratio was inverted in the graph, to make it easier to see the correlation.)

Consider, for example, the response of the Fed to the extensive currency hoarding that occurred in the United States after the banking panics. A policy of maintaining a stable gold reserve ratio would have forced the Fed to accumulate enormous quantities of gold during 1931–1932. Instead, it partially accommodated the currency hoarding by lowering the U.S. gold reserve ratio. In fact, the decrease in the U.S. gold reserve ratio was large enough, by itself, to reduce the *world* gold reserve ratio by roughly 11 percent between October 1930 and December 1932. Given that the United States held almost 40 percent of world monetary gold stocks, how then could the world gold reserve ratio

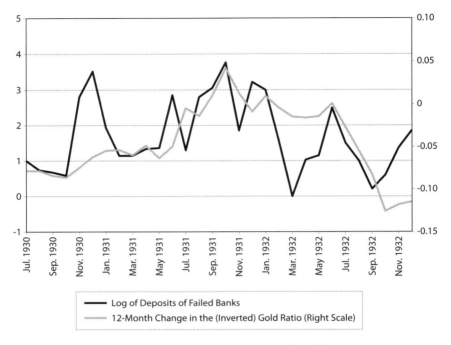

Figure 3.1. Deposits of Failed Banks and the Inverted Gold Ratio

have *risen* by 4.2 percent during the same period? As we will see, after mid-1931 there was extensive gold hoarding by central banks in the so-called gold bloc, especially France.[5]

In the next few sections we will see evidence that the financial markets were adversely affected by signs that central banks and private individuals intended to hoard gold. But the policy implications of this were not as obvious as one might imagine. An expansionary policy that reduced the gold reserve ratio could trigger devaluation fears, which would then lead to more private gold hoarding. Was the way out of this policy dilemma, then, to abandon the gold standard and inflate? Perhaps, but actual devaluations in one country often triggered devaluation fears in other countries, again leading to more gold

---

5. This is not to exonerate the Fed; most of the world's currency hoarding occurred in the United States, and with its massive gold stocks, the Fed arguably had both the ability and duty to be much more accommodative of the increased currency demand.

hoarding. The interconnections are complex and difficult to disentangle, but the proximate causes of the second stage of the Depression seem to have been:[6]

1. Currency hoarding (primarily in the United States)
2. Central bank gold hoarding (primarily in the gold bloc)
3. Private gold hoarding (especially between mid-1931 and mid-1932)

The Problem of the "Maldistribution" of Gold

As prices continued to fall during 1931, increasing concern materialized that the demand for gold was outstripping the supply. There was little explicit discussion of the world gold reserve ratio; instead, many commentators saw the problem as being caused by a maldistribution of gold among the major central banks. At the time France returned (de facto) to the gold standard in December 1926, they held less than 8 percent of the world's monetary gold stock. After four years of steady gold inflows, France began 1931 with nearly 20 percent of the world monetary gold stock. Although the U.S. share dipped slightly over this period, it still held almost 39 percent of the world total at the beginning of 1931.

Eichengreen argued that the maldistribution of gold was symptomatic of a lack of policy coordination among the major central banks. Temin (1989, p. 87) countered, "the only kind of cooperation possible was under the gold-standard orthodoxy. More of this kind of cooperation would have been dysfunctional." No doubt Temin is right that a joint devaluation in 1931 would have been preferable to continued adherence to the gold standard, but given the political impossibility of devaluation in America and France, some sort of coordinated move to reduce central-bank gold hoarding would have been welcomed by the financial markets.

In the last two months of 1930 the British gold stock had resumed its decline and the pound was under renewed pressure. Not surprisingly, much of the criticism of U.S. and French gold policies came from Britain. The French and

---

6. Hamilton (1988, p. 81) also emphasizes the deflationary impact of private and central bank gold hoarding during 1931–1932. Appendix 13a presents evidence that increased private and central bank gold hoarding tended to be correlated with declines in aggregate demand.

British met in Paris on January 2, 1931, to develop a plan to curb the persistent flow of gold from London to Paris. The same day the Dow opened the year up 3.2 percent. On January 3, the Bank of France cut its discount rate by a half point, and the following day's *New York Times* (p. N11) cited this move as one reason for an additional 1.3 percent increase in the Dow.

During the early months of 1931 there were encouraging signs that the gold agreement was having some success. Beginning in late January 1931 the French monetary gold stock leveled off for a period of four months, during which time the British were able to add to their gold stocks. Gold flows mean little in and of themselves, but in this case gold was being redirected toward countries with lower gold reserve ratios than France, and thus the net impact of this accord was to lower the world's gold reserve ratio. On February 10, 1931, the *New York Times* was able to report that Europe was becoming more optimistic as the pound strengthened in value, and by February 23 (p. 26) it was reporting that confidence was returning to Europe. The very next day, the Dow hit its 1931 high, up 18.1 percent from the beginning of the year. Stocks then moved sideways for the next four weeks, before beginning a severe decline that would continue over the following fifteen months.

Although we now know that the relative stability in early 1931 was merely a pause in the Great Contraction, there are a number of reasons why investors might have felt optimistic. The British–French monetary accord had improved international monetary conditions and worldwide commodity price deflation had moderated. In Germany, the Nazi party seemed to have been marginalized by the government. And in the United States, the banking situation was improving after the wave of failures during late 1930. Between July 1929 and July 1932, there was only one period where monthly industrial production figures increased, January to April 1931. During this period, many financial commentators expressed the view that the Depression had bottomed out and a recovery was already underway.

Unfortunately, the Fed began hoarding gold again during early 1931. On May 7, the Fed cut the discount rate in an attempt to stem the gold inflow, and the next day investors responded enthusiastically with a 4 percent increase in the Dow. But this move would prove to be too little, too late, as growing financial instability in Europe made American investments seem relatively attractive. The U.S. gold stock continued to increase right up until September

1931, when Britain departed from the gold standard. Indeed the U.S. gold stock during this period grew faster than the world stock, which meant that countries in a precarious reserve position were forced to adopt contractionary monetary policies.

The Price of Young Plan Bonds and the U.S. Stock Market

During the early 1930s, the U.S. financial press paid far more attention to international monetary and financial news than do postwar American newspapers (at least, until the 2011 Greek crisis). Of course, this change in emphasis might have merely reflected stylistic differences, perhaps owing to a change in readership. Of even greater significance, however, was the extraordinary extent to which movements in the U.S. stock market paralleled those news headlines. We have already seen evidence that the German election of 1930 had a modest impact on the U.S. stock market. Now we will see that, beginning in mid-1931, the Dow was heavily influenced by German financial and monetary news. And this influence appears to have been far stronger than what could plausibly result from "real" channels such as the U.S.–German trade relationship.

It was during mid-1931 that the international monetary system began to unravel, and Germany was at the center of the crisis. The price of the German war reparations bonds, dubbed "Young Plan bonds" (YPBs), were a good indicator of political turmoil in Germany during late 1930 and proved to be an even better indicator during 1931 and 1932. The bonds originally had been issued in June 1930 at a price of 90, began 1931 trading at 69.25, and remained in the 68 to 84 range throughout the first five months of the year. One indication of the severity of the German economic crisis is that by year end their price had fallen to 23.5.

Table 3.1 shows the correlation between the price of YPBs and the Dow for selected periods during 1930, 1931, and 1932. Perhaps the most striking finding is that whereas there was little or no correlation between the first difference of the log of the Dow (DOW) and the first difference of the log of the price of YPBs (YPB) during the first half of 1931, the two variables were highly correlated during the final six months of the year, and also the first half of 1932. To make sense out of these correlations we need to take a closer look at the economic and political developments that influenced markets during 1931.

Table 3.1. The Relationship between Variations in the Dow Jones Industrial
Average (DOW), and the Price of Young Plan Bonds (YPB),
Sept. 1930–Dec. 1931, Selected Periods, Daily

	Dependent Variable—DOW				
Sample Period	Number of Obser-vations	Coefficient on YPB	T-Statistic	Adjusted R²	Durbin Watson
1. 9/14/30–9/30/30	14	.5492	2.18	.225	2.69
2. 12/31/30–3/20/31	65	.1202	0.71	.000	2.19
3. 3/20/31–5/1/31	35	.5714	2.12	.094	2.59
4. 5/1/31–6/19/31	41	−.1084	−0.54	.000	1.94
5. 6/19/31–7/30/31	34	.4559	5.05	.426	1.96
6. 7/30/31–9/17/31	40	.3554	3.78	.254	2.39
7. 9/17/31–11/6/31	41	.2888	3.85	.257	2.40
8. 11/6/31–12/30/31	43	.2801	3.72	.234	2.33
9. 12/30/31–3/31/32	75	.2617	4.03	.171	1.80
10. 3/31/32–6/30/32	77	.3152	3.75	.147	2.30
11. 6/30/32–9/30/32	76	.0799	0.66	.000	1.92

Note: The regressions use first differences of logs.

The German Economic Crisis of 1931

In retrospect, the March 21 announcement that Germany and Austria had
agreed to form a customs union appears as the first of a long series of events that
disrupted European affairs. The Austro-German Customs Union was viewed
by many as a violation of the Versailles Treaty provision that guaranteed the
sovereignty of Austria, and the French, in particular, were concerned that
the union was merely the first step toward an "Anschluss," or political union.
The dispute became a complicating factor several months later when Austria
and Germany required financial assistance from their international creditors.

The Dow reached its March peak on the day before the announcement of
the customs union, and then began a long steady decline that extended into

early June. Equation 3 in Table 3.1 shows the result of regressing movements in the Dow on YPBs during the period from March 20 to May 1. Although, in contrast to the January 1 to March 20 period (Equation 2), the coefficient on the YPB price is significant at the 5 percent level, the relatively low correlation (adjusted R^2) provides little evidence that German problems were a major factor in the ongoing decline in the Dow.

During the period from May 1 to June 19, 1931, it is surprising that we do not see a stronger link between Germany and Wall Street. Historians consider the failure of Austria's Kreditanstalt in mid-May to be the event that triggered the subsequent international monetary crises. The Dow did decline continuously for eight straight trading days from May 11 and May 20, and the YPBs also declined almost continuously during this period. Yet, as Equation 4 clearly indicates, there was no significant relationship between changes in the Dow and the price of YPBs during the period from May 1 to June 19.

There was plenty of news relating to problems in Central Europe during mid-May 1931. On May 11, the *New York Times* reported that uncertainty over the customs union was slowing investment in Germany and Austria and on May 13 they reported that the Kreditanstalt crisis was depressing German stock prices. French Premier Briand favored closer policy coordination, and according to the May 15 *New York Times,* his unexpected defeat in the French presidential election of May 14 was likely to increase political tensions in Europe. Briand's conciliatory position toward Germany had been undermined by the German government's decision to form a customs union with Austria.

On June 1, the Dow declined by 4.4 percent, and the next day the *New York Times* noted that the German situation had deteriorated rapidly in the previous few days. It also reported that a bailout of the Kreditanstalt was expected soon, but that the customs union had injected politics into the negotiations. By this time, the banking crisis had spread from Austria to Germany, and there was growing speculation that the Young Plan would have to be revised. In early June, the British and German leaders conferred on the debt issue at Chequers, England, where German Prime Minister Breuning argued that the German economy was in dire straits and that some form of debt relief was essential. Unfortunately, the entire war debts/reparations crisis was complicated by the fact that Germany's biggest reparations creditors (Britain and France) had also incurred large war debts with the United States. Thus, any debt relief for Germany would require leadership from the leading creditor nation, the United States.

June 3 saw the largest increase in the Dow (7.1 percent) since the rebound in November 1929. The following day's *New York Times* (p. 39) found no explanation in the news and suggested, "that [startling news] may conceivably come later, and speculative Wall Street's reversal of position may have had in mind its possibility." Startling news *did* arrive on June 19 in the form of a debt moratorium, but it is difficult to say whether the June 3 rally anticipated this development. We do know that it was announced on June 3 that Secretary of State Stimson would depart soon for Europe, and that in a secret meeting on the evening of June 2, President Hoover had communicated his intentions to the U.S. ambassadors to Britain and Germany.

The June 7 announcement that Secretary of State Mellon would also be departing soon for Europe and rumors of a moratorium began affecting the financial markets. The June 8 *New York Times* headline suggested a "Change Seen In Our Attitude On Debts" and also (p. 26) enigmatically referred to the "sudden appearance of a few unpredicted reassuring developments in the news, which the stock market [on June 3] may or may not have foreseen."

There is one glaring weakness with the preceding hypothesis: the correlation between the price of YPBs and the Dow turning negative during the weeks immediately preceding the moratorium (see Figure 3.2). The interests of Young Plan bondholders and U.S. stockholders did not exactly coincide, and thus, it is conceivable the bondholders could have (erroneously) believed that the deteriorating economic situation in Germany would lead to a moratorium that included the YPBs, while U.S. stockholders focused on the widely held expectation that a moratorium would improve the prospects for international monetary cooperation. Even before the moratorium was announced, some contemporary observers were making exactly that argument—that is, that holders of YPBs had misunderstood the likely impact of a moratorium:

> In any case, the postponement of transfers contemplated in the Young Plan has, of course, nothing whatever in common with a moratorium in the ordinary sense, and would involve no suspension of payments in connection with Germany's private or public loan obligations. Nobody

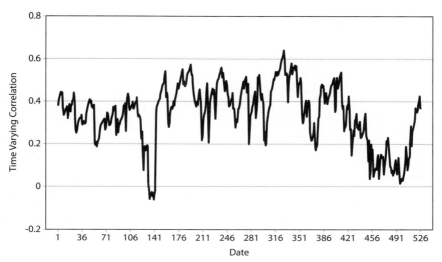

Note: The moratorium occurred on date 142.

Figure 3.2. Time Varying Correlation between the DOW and the Price of
Young Plan Bonds, January 1, 1931 to September 30, 1932, Daily

in Germany has thought of such a thing for a moment, but misunderstanding on this question seems to have had an unfortunate effect,
especially in America. (*Economist*, 6/20/31, p. 1326)

Of course, this hypothesis is a bit ad hoc, and also seemingly at odds with
the efficient markets hypothesis that I use throughout this narrative. But
rational expectations do not imply perfect foresight, and subsequent events
strongly support the *Economist*'s view that Americans initially misjudged
the effect of the moratorium on YPBs. U.S. stock and German (Young Plan)
bond prices became closely synchronized immediately following President
Hoover's June 19 announcement (at 6:00 p.m.) of his intention to put forward
a plan for international debt relief.[7] The following day the Dow jumped 6.6
percent, and the YPBs soared by 7.9 percent. After the stock market closed on
Saturday, June 20, the details of the plan were revealed to show an even more
far-reaching moratorium than had been anticipated. The following Monday,

---

7. Apparently the rapid deterioration in the German economy led Hoover to move forward the announcement of the moratorium. Eichengreen (1992, p. 161) notes that Hoover had
proposed a war debt moratorium as far back as 1922.

the Dow rose another 4.9 percent and the price of YPBs advanced another 4.2 percent. And the extraordinary (worldwide) stock market rally[8] was also accompanied by large increases in the prices of major commodities such as corn, wheat, and cotton.

The correlation between changes in the Dow and the prices of YPBs jumped from 0.0 percent in the period from May 1 to June 19, to an astounding 42.6 percent in the period from June 19 to July 30 (Table 3.1, Equation 5). The increased correlation between the Dow and the price of YPBs is certainly consistent with the hypothesis that Wall Street became concerned about Germany when the German crisis threatened to disrupt the entire international monetary system. Nevertheless, no level of correlation between changes in the Dow and the price of YPBs is able to establish causality. Thus, it is essential to examine contemporaneous news coverage.

One of the most striking aspects of this period is the intensive coverage of the German crisis provided by the *New York Times*. For thirty-six consecutive days, at least one *New York Times* headline discussed the German debt and/or exchange rate crisis, and almost all were the dominant headline. This certainly indicates a level of interest in European financial affairs that would be unimaginable in post–World War II America, even during the recent euro crisis. Even more striking is that fact that, throughout this period, movements in Dow were frequently linked to these news stories.

The heterogeneous nature of news makes it difficult to quantify. Therefore, I provide the *New York Times* headlines from June 20 to July 24, 1931 in Appendix 3.a, along with some clarifying excerpts and market reactions for the Dow and the price of YPBs. The column width of each headline is also given, which serves as a proxy for the importance that the editors of the *New York Times* gave to each story. (A typical lead headline would be two or three columns across.) The headlines are accompanied by data showing the market response of the Dow and the price of YPBs from the closing prior to the news event, to the subsequent closing. European news reported in the *New York*

---

8. The *NYT* (6/28/31, p. 10N) noted that except for the recoil from the 1929 crash, the rally in the week following Hoover's announcement was the "swiftest advance during any corresponding period in a generation."

Times on a given day was usually received by U.S. financial markets before the markets closed on the previous day.

Enthusiasm for Hoover's proposal was not confined to the *New York Times*. The June 27 issue of the *Commercial and Financial Chronicle* (p. 4635) enthused, "President Hoover has electrified the whole world and possibly turned the tide of business depression." A "Hooverstrasse" was proposed for Berlin. The British compared the proposal to a new armistice and suggested that the move ranked in importance with the U.S. entry into World War I. Of course, Hoover's debt moratorium was subsequently shown to be ineffective in arresting the ongoing depression. Nevertheless, the financial community had great hope for the plan, which indicates they saw the debt crisis as inhibiting recovery.

Between June 2 and June 27, the Dow soared by almost 29 percent, and the next day's *New York Times* (p. 7N) suggested that "War Debt Plan Aids Commodity Prices . . . Sharpest Advance Since Last Summer Shown in Most Groups in Fortnight." Although the reaction of financial markets to the moratorium was unquestionably enthusiastic, the reasons are unclear. Perhaps it was felt that the moratorium would reduce gold flows to countries with high propensities to hoard (i.e., the United States and France). The June 27 *Commercial and Financial Chronicle* (p. 4653) suggested that Hoover's goals were limited and that it was hoped that the agreement could lead to a climate of "international good will."

On June 30 the *New York Times* (p. 1) quoted a bank official as indicating that, "it would be a mistake to over-emphasize the proposed debt adjustment as an economic factor in itself." Unfortunately, Hoover strongly opposed two initiatives that might have provided meaningful help for Germany: a coordinated international policy of tariff reduction and a coordinated attempt to lower the world gold ratio through expansionary monetary policies.[9] Those who have followed the recent events in Europe will see an obvious parallel. The Europeans have worked hard to develop a debt relief plan for countries on the periphery but have failed to take the one step that could actually make a

---

9. Hoover criticized the theory that deflation was resulting from a "maldistribution" of monetary gold stocks.

big difference, a European Central Bank (ECB) policy aimed at faster nominal growth in the eurozone.

After June 27, U.S. stock prices seesawed for several days as the French raised objections to various aspects of the agreement. Because the size of Germany's debts to France greatly exceeded the French war debts to America, the French were naturally less enthusiastic about the moratorium than the British, who had a less favorable net creditor position at the governmental level covered by the moratorium, but who were also important commercial lenders to Germany. Although a preliminary agreement was finally hammered out in early July, the contentious negotiations made it clear that future cooperation on international monetary and financial issues would be exceedingly difficult. Meanwhile, the German financial system continued to deteriorate rapidly and the *Commercial and Financial Chronicle* noted that "it was also realized that the delay of two weeks [in the agreement] had somewhat vitiated the good effects."[10]

The July 18 issue of the *Commercial and Financial Chronicle* (p. 335) ominously reported that "the world the present week has been confronted with one of the greatest and gravest financial crises of which history furnishes any record." Both the Dow and the price of YPBs declined steadily in the week leading up to Germany's establishment of strict exchange controls on July 15. Although historians sometimes view July 15, 1931 as the date that Germany "departed from the gold standard," the contemporaneous view was different. Maintenance of the exchange rate at its par value was viewed as the sine qua non of being on the gold standard. Germany did not devalue the reichsmark, and was viewed as having partially surmounted the crisis (albeit with a much weakened link to gold). The 6.2 percent drop in the Dow between July 10 and July 15 was made up over the next five trading days as Hoover organized an international loan to assist the Reichsbank.

Unfortunately, political discord continued to complicate efforts to aid Germany. French opposition prevented anything more that a temporary aid package, and the markets fell back in late July as it became apparent that a permanent solution to the German financial crisis had not been achieved. The largest movement in the Dow during August 1931 occurred on the eleventh,

---

10. *CFC*, 7/11/31, p. 174.

when the Dow jumped 4.4 percent. The next day's *New York Times* (p. 27) commented that "suddenly reversing its trend, the stock market advanced spiritedly yesterday, simultaneously with the announcement that agreement had finally been reached on all points involved in the debt suspension proposal."

Temin argued that the short-term victory associated with the maintenance of the reichsmark at par merely ensured that Germany's financial crisis would continue to intensify. In contrast, by devaluing the pound in September 1931, Britain was able to swiftly end its financial crisis, although it did not take full advantage of its new position. German leaders were prevented from devaluing the reichsmark by treaty obligations associated with the reparations agreement, and by the public's still fresh memories of the 1920–1923 hyperinflation.

The temporary nature of the moratorium also ensured that the war debts/reparations issue would reappear later. Only three months into the one-year moratorium, the international crisis associated with the British devaluation intensified the worldwide deflation, and it became abundantly clear that Germany would be in no better position to pay its debts in mid-1932 than it had been in mid-1931. Financial markets faced additional months of bitter recriminations and debate over these issues. The parallels with recent events in Europe are obvious.

The Devaluation of the British Pound

In light of subsequent events, it is interesting to read the minutes of the summer 1931 MacMillan hearings. The committee (which included Keynes) had a sophisticated understanding of how the Depression was caused by an imbalance between a price level determined in the gold market and the costs of industry, especially wages (which are the two themes of this book):

> The first set of difficulties has been caused by the fact that the various gold parities established by the countries returning to the gold standard did not bear by any means the same relation in each case to the existing levels of incomes and costs in terms of the national currency. For example, Great Britain established a gold parity which meant that her existing level of sterling incomes and costs was relatively too high in terms of gold, so that, failing a downward adjustment, those of

her industries which are subject to foreign competition were put at an artificial disadvantage. France and Belgium, on the other hand, somewhat later established a gold parity which, pending an upward adjustment of their wages and other costs in terms of francs, gave an artificial advantage to their export industries. Other countries provide examples of an intermediate character. Thus the distribution of foreign trade, which would correspond to the relative efficiencies of different countries for different purposes, has been seriously disturbed from the equilibrium position corresponding to the normal relations between their costs in terms of gold. This, however, has been a consequence of the manner in which the postwar world groped its way to back to gold, rather than of the permanent characteristics of the gold standard itself once the equilibrium of relative costs has been re-established, though, even after six years, this is not yet the case." (Macmillan Committee Report, p. 245)

Despite this awareness of their precarious macroeconomic situation, they argued that because of Britain's position as a major creditor nation, leaving the gold standard would be impractical.

Notwithstanding the extended crisis of July 1931, the price of YPBs, which began the year at 69¼, had only declined to 56¼ by the end of July. They would finish 1931 trading under 24. Similarly, the Dow, which began 1931 at 164.58, ended July at 135.39, and then plunged to 77.90 at year-end. During September the Dow declined almost continuously, ending the month down over 30 percent. Although it would be natural to attribute this decline to the developing crisis in Britain, there is actually very little evidence until September 18 (in the forward exchange rate market) that Wall Street had been affected by fears of a British devaluation. The devaluation of the pound was unquestionably the dominant economic event of the autumn of 1931, yet it appears to have had only a modest *direct* effect on U.S. financial markets. Its indirect effects, however, were profound.

The British crisis actually began in July 1931 as the run on the reichsmark reduced confidence in the entire international gold standard. On July 26 (the first time in 36 days that the German debt problems failed to earn a *New York Times* headline), a *Times* headline reported, "British Gold Loss Totals

$145,500,000 in the Last 13 Days." The three-month forward discount on the pound (against the dollar) rose from less than ½ cent during the first half of 1931 to just over 2 cents in early August and then remained at that level until the eve of the devaluation. By the fall of 1931 the actual spot exchange rate had declined by well over *one hundred* cents. Thus, although some concern about the pound was evident in the forward markets, there is no indication that a significant devaluation was considered imminent during the two months leading up to Britain's departure from the gold standard.

There are good reasons why the markets would not have anticipated the devaluation. First, only six years earlier, the British had undergone a prolonged period of austerity in restoring the gold standard. Second, the British financial position was clearly stronger than that of Germany, and Germany had been able to avoid devaluing during the July crisis. Third, a new National (coalition) government was formed in August, and this government agreed to balance the budget by cutting government salaries and unemployment benefits.

Nevertheless, the increased forward discount shows that currency traders were a bit more apprehensive about the pound during August and the first half of September, probably owing to uncertainty regarding the government's willingness to reduce the deficit through painful budget cuts. An imminent election created further uncertainty. On September 16, a *New York Times* headline reported "Disorders in British Navy Follow Economy Pay Cut." Withdrawals of gold from Britain accelerated sharply, with $25 million leaving on September 16, $50 million on September 17, and $90 million on September 18.

This Navy "mutiny," or "strike" (depending on one's perspective), touched off a series of events that led to the devaluation. What appears to have been decisive was not the disturbance itself, but rather the government's willingness to listen to the sailors' demands, and their promise of no reprisals. The press coverage of the event provides a fascinating study in contrasts. While the British Government was trying to downplay the importance of the sailors' action, the foreign press expressed astonishment at the willingness of the once-proud British Navy to cave in to the demands of mutinous sailors.[11] In

---

11. The September 17 *NYT* (p. 1) reported "as startling as was the incipient mutiny in the British fleet, without precedent in modern times, the actions of the government in making terms with those who have broken discipline is regarded as even more startling."

the House of Commons, Labour party members taunted, "You've surrendered once, and you'll keep on surrendering,"[12] a reference to escalating demands that proposed cuts in the pay of teachers, police, and other members of the military be rescinded.

Although the suspension of convertibility occurred on September 20, word that the government was considering devaluation appeared to have leaked out several days earlier. The price of British government bonds (5½ percent coupon), which had traded in the 104¾ to 105⅝ range throughout the first seventeen days of September, fell to 101¼ on September 18, then plunged to 93 on September 19. Thus, data from the British bond market complements the forward market evidence that devaluation was not considered likely until the last moment. What then caused the sharp decline in U.S. stock prices during the first part of September 1931?

Whereas the value of British government bonds remained stable during early September, the price of YPBs fell from 58⅜ at the beginning of the month to 46¾ on September 17, before dropping to 40 on September 18, and 38 on September 19th. Similarly, the Dow declined from 139.41 at the beginning of the month, to 121.76 on September 17, and then plunged 5.5 percent on the eighteenth, and an additional 2.9 percent on the nineteenth. And, although during September 1931, German events were not dominating U.S. news coverage to the extent that they had in June and July, the *New York Times* continued to link movements in U.S. stock prices to problems in Germany.[13] Equation 6 in Table 3.1 shows that movements in the price of YPBs remained highly correlated with the Dow throughout the interval between the German and British exchange crises.

The First Dollar Panic

It is not particularly surprising that the Dow declined by less than one percent on September 21; the averages had already declined by 8.2 percent over

---

12. The *NYT*, ibid.

13. For instance, the September 4 *NYT* blamed the previous day's 3.1 percent decline on the unexpectedly severe collapse in German stock prices following the reopening of the German Bourse.

the previous two days in apparent anticipation of the devaluation.[14] What *was* surprising, however, was the 25.4 percent plunge in the Dow between September 23 and October 5, 1931. Although theory suggests that asset prices should respond immediately to news, the extraordinary rapidity of this decline, and its close proximity to the British devaluation, makes it unlikely that the two events were completely unrelated. Figure 3.3 shows the relationship between U.S. stock prices and important policy news during 1931–32.

The 7.1 percent drop in the Dow on September 24, 1931 was the tenth largest decline in history, and on the following day the *New York Times* headline announced "Sales of Gold Upset Money Market Here; Stock Prices Break." Is there a plausible link between the gold outflow and the decline in the Dow? We have already seen that gold flows, by themselves, provide no information regarding the stance of world monetary policy under an international gold standard. A gold flow from the United States to France could be caused either by a reduction in the U.S. gold ratio (i.e., an expansionary policy in the United States), or an increase in France's gold ratio (a contractionary policy in France).

We now know that the late 1931 gold flows were associated with sharp increases in the gold ratios of the gold bloc countries, as world monetary policy tightened sharply after the British devaluation. The subsequent increases in the U.S. discount rate were merely the symptom of this tightening. If one views the behavior of (the gold bloc) central banks in terms of a profit-maximizing model where low nominal interest rates and fears of subsequent devaluations lead central banks to sell foreign assets for gold, then the dollar crisis should have been fully discounted by September 21. Alternatively, if the markets viewed the interwar central banks as having *some* ability to cooperate in the pursuance of other goals such as macroeconomic stability, then it is not surprising that Wall Street apparently failed to immediately anticipate all of the repercussions associated with the British decision to devalue the pound.

The growing maldistribution of gold (i.e., rising gold reserve ratios) was not the only fallout from the German and British crises. A number of other countries followed Britain's lead in leaving the gold standard, and during the fall of 1931 it was feared that the United States might do the same. This climate

---

14. This decline was presumably due to the perception that the British devaluation would force countries remaining on the gold standard to adopt more contractionary monetary policies.

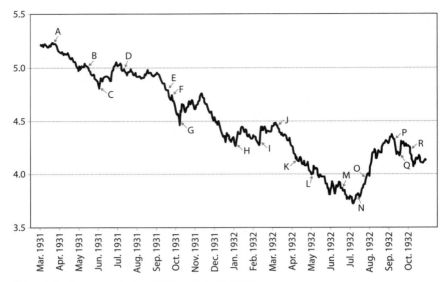

Notes: A. March 21, 1931—Austrian/German Customs Union
B. May 11, 1931—Kreditanstalt crisis
C. June 19, 1931—Hoover proposes debt moratorium
D. July 8–15, 1931—German monetary crisis
E. September 19, 1931—Britain leaves gold standard
F. September 24, 1931—Run on dollar begins
G. October 7, 1931—Hoover proposes National Credit Corporation
H. January 6–9, 1932—Hopes for debt accord
I. February 11, 1932—Hoover proposes Glass-Steagall
J. March 10, 1932—Budget fight begins
K. April 13, 1932—Fed accelerates open market purchases
L. May 6, 1932—Progress on budget
M. June 22, 1932—Midwest bank panic
N. July 14, 1932—Fed slows open market purchases
O. July 29, 1932—United States resumes gold imports, dollar rallies
P. September 13, 1932—Democrats gain in Maine election
Q. September 21, 1932—Republicans gain in Wisconsin election
R. October 4–7, 1932—Hoover gaffe spooks markets

Figure 3.3. The Log of the Dow Jones Industrial Average, 1931–1932

of uncertainty led to an increase in the private hoarding of gold, and the world monetary gold stock declined in July, September, and October 1931.[15] Private gold hoarding provides a second mechanism by which the German and British currency crises depressed aggregate demand throughout the world.

---

15. There had been no monthly declines during 1930 or during the first half of 1931.

Table 3.2. Annualized Changes in World (Physical) Monetary Gold Stock and Related Crises, 1929–1939

Time Period	Gold Stock	Event
Dec. 1929–June 1931	6.0 percent	
June 1931–Oct. 1931	–3.4 percent	German/UK crises
Oct. 1931–Apr. 1932	6.7 percent	
Apr. 1932–June 1932	–8.7 percent	Deficit fears, Fed OMPs
June 1932–Jan. 1933	8.4 percent	
Jan. 1933–Feb. 1933	–18.8 percent	Third run on the dollar
Feb. 1933–Apr. 1933	11.8 percent	
Apr. 1933–Jan. 1934	–0.1 percent	Dollar depreciation
Jan. 1934–Mar. 1935	7.6 percent	
Mar. 1935–May 1935	–15.8 percent	Belgian crisis
May 1935–Mar. 1936	5.3 percent	
Mar. 1936–Sep. 1936	0.4 percent	French crisis
Sep. 1936–June 1937	11.3 percent	Gold panic (revaluation fears)
June 1937–Mar. 1938	0.0 percent	Dollar panic (devaluation fears)
Mar. 1938–Dec. 1939	9.8 percent	

Gold Stock is the (annualized) first difference of the log of the world monetary gold stock.

Table 3.2 summarizes the (annualized) growth rate of the world monetary gold stock over selected periods during the 1930s.

This table clearly shows that growth in the world monetary gold stock slowed sharply during periods when currencies were perceived to be at risk. Gold stocks grew especially fast when fears of devaluation receded, or when there were fears of currency revaluation, as in early 1937. And because monetary gold stock data excludes U.S. gold coins, Table 3.2 understates the amount of private gold hoarding that occurred during currency crises.[16]

16. For the same reason, Table 2.2 slightly overstates the role of currency hoarding in the Depression. Brown (1940) indicates that Europeans hoarded large quantities of U.S gold coins during the currency crises of the early 1930s. At that time, the United States was one of the few countries to still mint gold coins, and the stock of those coins was roughly 1/30 the size of the world monetary gold stock.

Paul Einzig (1937a) reports weekly forward exchange rate data for six currencies. The dollar/pound exchange rate shows the dollar slipping from a premium to a discount against the pound during October 1931. Unfortunately, Einzig does not report forward data for the U.S. dollar price of gold. However, there was no realistic prospect of a *revaluation* in the gold bloc currencies, and thus we can use the forward premium on the French franc (and three-way arbitrage) to estimate a lower bound for the discount of the forward dollar against gold. Using this procedure, the U.S. dollar sold at a forward discount against the franc throughout October 1931, with the three-month forward discount peaking at close to 2 percent on October 17. Chapter 13 (Table 13.4) includes several regression equations showing a positive and highly significant correlation between forward currency discounts and private gold hoarding.

One problem with forward exchange rate data is that it provides no information regarding fears of a devaluation occurring more than three months into the future. Long-term bond prices can provide some indication of investor perceptions about the long-run soundness of the dollar. Friedman and Schwartz (p. 319) note that the prices of long-term U.S. Treasury bonds declined sharply during the final quarter of 1931. They indicate that some observers attributed this decline to fears of huge budget deficits produced by radical congressional spending bills, but then argue that a more likely explanation is that financial market and regulatory difficulties led banks to sell bonds in order to accumulate excess reserves. One problem with Friedman and Schwartz's hypothesis is that the price of French government bonds (also payable in gold) did not decline substantially during this period. Thus, their hypothesis requires the existence of some degree of market segmentation.

An alternative hypothesis is that devaluation fears led to an increase either in the inflation premium or the default risk on U.S. Treasury bonds.[17] We don't know if investors did draw this distinction between U.S. and French government bonds, but subsequent events show that it would have been sensible for them to have done so. Less than two years later the U.S. dollar was devalued, the gold clause was abrogated, and U.S. inflation did accelerate vis-à-vis French

---

17. This would be viewed as an increase in default risk if one viewed U.S. Treasury bonds as being payable in gold, and an increase in inflation risk if one viewed the bonds as being payable in dollars. Hamilton (1988) looks at short term T-bill yields and comes to a similar conclusion. Also see Wigmore (1985, pp. 215–16).

inflation. It is also significant that the price of U.S. Treasury bonds (3 percent coupon, due 1951–1955, henceforth "T-bonds") remained remarkably stable throughout the turbulent period from September 15 through September 23, never varying by more than 2/32 of a point on any given day. Then on September 24, the very day the heavy gold outflows began, the prices of these bonds dropped from 99 15/32 to 99 3/32, the beginning of a decline that would take bond prices below 90 by October 19, 1931.

One of the most interesting aspects of the October bear market in Treasury bonds was the contrasting reactions of the U.S. and (continental) European press. The U.S. financial press was perplexed by the sharp decline in T-bond prices. During earlier stages of the Depression, T-bonds had often rallied when stock, corporate bond, and commodity prices were declining. Thus, the October 17 issue of the *New York Times* (p. 23) noted that, "the fluctuations [in T-bond prices] were as confusing as they were incomprehensible to the rational mind." The decline in T-bond prices could conceivably have been due to the unusual circumstance of a discount rate increase during a period of economic weakness. But the press knew that that explanation was inadequate. The fact that French bond prices were stable during this period indicated that there was a decline in investor perceptions of the soundness of U.S. Treasury obligations. Rather than confront this issue head on, an October 11 *New York Times* headline argued that a French "Campaign of Insinuation Leads Public to Believe We Plan Wholesale Inflation."

These rumors were attributed to a lack of understanding on the part of Europeans of the American banking system in general, and, in particular, to a lack of understanding of a recent policy initiative of the Hoover administration. On October 6, 1931, President Hoover had proposed the creation of a "National Credit Corporation" to provide up to $500,000,000 in loans to ailing banks, and the Dow soared 14.9 percent on the news, which was second only in size to the 15.3 percent rise after the 1933 bank holiday. On October 8, the Dow jumped another 8.3 percent and on the following day the *New York Times* headline reported "Further Moves Considered by Hoover, Including Federal Reserve Revision." Commodity prices also increased sharply during this period.[18]

---

18. In the absence of any supply-side news, these commodity price increases were also attributed to Hoover's announcement. French stock prices fell sharply. This presumably reflects the fact that a major devaluation has an adverse effect on those nations remaining on the gold standard.

Hoover's initiative was prompted by the unprecedented amount of U.S. currency hoarding associated with the British devaluation and the subsequent banking panic. In just the five weeks, from September 16 to October 21, the U.S. currency stock rose by nearly 10 percent. During a period of declining prices and output, an increase of this magnitude meant a significant slow-down in currency velocity and the money multiplier. The situation was so tense that weekly changes in the currency stock became front-page news in the *New York Times*![19] European rumors regarding the dollar appear to have been motivated both by the Hoover banking initiative and by massive gold outflows coinciding with a huge increase in the currency stock.

As with the debt moratorium, the National Credit Corporation proved to be ineffective, probably because of the mistaken assumption that the banking crises merely reflected a lack of liquidity. Nevertheless, the Wall Street reaction suggests that investors understood the deflationary impact of currency hoarding, and that a proposal offering even a hope of reflation could have a major impact on real stock values.

The two discount rates increases of October 1931 are widely viewed as a major policy error by the Federal Reserve. Hamilton (1988, p. 83) called their impact on the economy "devastating," and Temin (1989, p. 29) also thought that the rate increases depressed the economy. Friedman and Schwartz (p. 317) argued that the increase "contributed to a spectacular increase in bank failures." Yet, in contrast to the other major monetary shocks of 1931, the reaction of the stock market to the two discount rate increases was, if anything, slightly positive.[20]

One explanation for this nonreaction is that investors did not view the discount rate as an important policy indicator. Yet, the two previous increases in the discount rate (on July 11, 1928, and August 8, 1929) were associated with major stock market declines. Another possible explanation is that the increases in the discount rate were anticipated, particularly in light of the ongoing gold

---

19. The October 30 *NYT* headline read "Currency Is Abated; Gold Drain Wanes."

20. The first discount rate increase (from 1.5 to 2.5 percent) was announced at 3:30 p.m. on October 8, and the Dow decreased just over one percent the next day. A week later, the Dow actually increased 3.8 percent after an additional one percentage point increase in the discount rate.

outflow.[21] The October 16 *New York Times* (p. 1) did indicate that investors were anticipating a discount rate increase, but also indicated that, although the stock exchange was closed, in the over-the-counter market "bank stocks went soaring after the news was flashed at 3:30," a clear indication that the increase was at least partially unexpected and/or larger that anticipated. And the yields on short-term T-bills and T-notes jumped sharply on the day after each of the discount rate increases, another indication that the increases were partially unexpected.[22]

When viewed from the perspective of the gold market approach, market reaction to the discount rate increases is not surprising. Investors may have realized that during this tense period the expansionary impact (on the gold ratio) of a low discount rate would be more than offset by the contractionary effects stemming from a loss of confidence in the dollar, which could have led to more gold hoarding. This is Ben Bernanke's "multiple monetary equilibria" hypothesis.[23] In any event, the higher discount rates were successful in restoring confidence in the dollar and, after October 1931, there was a modest reduction in currency and gold hoarding. Stock prices rose significantly during early November.[24]

The various market responses to different types of monetary policy news suggest that investors focused on areas where policy discretion could make a meaningful difference. Although Hoover's banking initiative was not successful, the subsequent impact of the Federal Deposit Insurance Corporation shows that it wasn't unreasonable for investors to believe that banking reforms could influence the level of currency hoarding. And the sharp increase in the gold reserve ratio within the gold bloc represented a discretionary policy

---

21. French officials pressured the United States into taking steps to restore confidence in the dollar. In return, the French agreed to repatriate their gold holdings at a measured pace.

22. The yield on T-notes with a maturity of three to nine months rose from a range of 0.76 to 1.15 percent on October 8, to between 1.66 and 2.08 percent on October 9. The yields then increased from a range of 1.86 to 2.23 percent on October 15 to between 2.26 and 2.81 percent on October 16.

23. See Bernanke (1995).

24. Wigmore (1985, p. 217) is one of the few to dissent from the standard view, arguing that monetary policy was loose during this period. Despite the large gain in stock prices, I wouldn't go that far. The Fed had two options (tight money or a run on the dollar); neither option was very appealing and neither would have meant policy was expansionary.

choice for these gold-rich nations. Conversely, proposals that the Fed engage in modest open market purchases were viewed as being even less feasible than had been the case prior to the British devaluation.[25]

Along with the various international monetary crises, the political situation during October 1931 was disturbed by the onset of the Sino-Japanese war and by Nazi agitation in Germany. In addition, currency realignments were leading many nations to impose retaliatory tariffs, further reducing the prospects for international monetary cooperation.[26] Even proponents of cooperation, such as Gustav Cassel, felt that it was now too late for an institution such as the Bank of International Settlements (BIS) to coordinate an expansionary monetary policy.[27] Paul Einzig argued that following the international monetary crisis of 1931, central bankers had not acted as autonomous economic policymakers, but rather had substituted gold for foreign exchange reserves much as "ignorant and illiterate depositors do in times of panic."[28]

More Problems in Germany

Equations 7 and 8 from Table 3.1 show that movements in the prices of YPBs continued to be strongly correlated with the Dow during the final three months of 1931. The October 17 *Commercial and Financial Chronicle* noted that problems in Germany were depressing U.S. stock prices on October 13, 14, and 15. But what was the mechanism linking these two markets? The financial press claimed that Wall Street was concerned about the large quantity of short-term credits that U.S. banks had extended for German firms and municipalities. Many of these credits were frozen by a "standstill agreement" in the wake of the German exchange crisis of July 1931. Because these credits were dollar-denominated, a major German devaluation would have greatly increased

---

25. The November 7, 1931, issue of the *CFC* (p. 3029) discusses a proposal by Irving Fisher for more open market purchases to boost the economy.

26. Those who would argue that the higher tariffs, rather than monetary shocks, can explain the 1931 stock market decline must contend with the fact British stock prices rose sharply following the devaluation, despite the fact that Britain now faced higher tariff barriers on the continent.

27. Cassel (1936) blamed the depression on the hoarding of gold by the United States and France.

28. Einzig (1933, p. 14). Hawtrey expressed similar views.

the debts in mark terms, and almost certainly would have led to widespread defaults. This may explain why the prices of YPBs declined so sharply during the British exchange crisis of September 18–19. Many European nations immediately followed Britain off the gold standard, and investors were naturally concerned that Germany would be the next domino to fall.

By November 7, 1931, the YPBs had regained all of the ground lost between September 23 and October 6, and two days later, the Dow also regained its September 23 peak. Then, between November 9 and December 17 the Dow fell by nearly 37 percent, and from November 7 to December 17 the price of YPBs plunged by more than 48 percent, both reaching their yearly low on the same day. During mid-November a number of *New York Times* reports indicated that Wall Street was continuing to be affected by the reparations dilemma and/or the deteriorating situation in Germany. The new British tariffs were hurting German exports, and Germany was again requesting a reduction in its war debts. On November 27, the prices of YPBs fell 3.9 percent in reaction to an uncompromising speech by French Premier Pierre Laval.[29] The Dow fell 2.8 percent.

During December 1931, *five months* after the German exchange crisis began, German news was still dominating the front page of the *New York Times*. On December 4, the prices of YPBs declined 8.5 percent and the Dow dropped 3.3 percent. The following day the *New York Times* (p. 8) reported, "Bank Stocks Break on German Rumor" (meaning that the gold standard would be abandoned). On December 5, the prices of YPBs jumped 17.6 percent, the Dow rose 3.9 percent, and the next day's *New York Times* (p. 14N) noted that "traders took heart on the news that the slogan of the Hitler party will be: 'private debts—yes; reparations—no!'"

Several December 11 headlines in the *New York Times* reported another major initiative by President Hoover: "Hoover Wants War Debt Board Revived" and "Hoover Debt Stand Hailed in Europe." Unfortunately, a great deal of hostility to the plan surfaced in Congress, and in contrast to previous Hoover initiatives, this plan failed to boost stock prices. The next day the *New*

---

29. He indicated that France would not allow private German debts to take precedence over war reparations.

York Times (p. 11N) noted that "it was pointed out yesterday that several news developments which formed the bases for substantial upturns during the last year were regarded as of paramount importance when they first made their appearance, although subsequent events showed that their significance had been greatly exaggerated." That is quite an understatement.

During mid-December, stocks and YPBs continued to fall as Congressional hostility to further debt relief dominated the headlines. Finally, on December 18, the Dow rebounded 8.9 percent and the prices of YPBs jumped 14.2 percent. The financial press attributed the dramatic (midday) rally to concurrent Congressional testimony by banking expert Thomas W. Lamont. He suggested that the German debt situation was not as serious as had been rumored, and bank stocks experienced especially impressive increases. Of more importance, however, was the dramatic rise in the prices of industrial and railroad stocks, as well as commodities. These increases suggest that the debt problems were perceived as affecting not just bank earnings, but more broadly, the entire monetary sector and thus, total aggregate demand.

Summary

After a modest upturn in early 1931, the final eight months of the year saw a major recession turn into the Great Contraction. During this period, foreign monetary and financial shocks dominated the news headlines in the *New York Times*.[30] Relative to the postwar era, stock prices were much more volatile, and their movements were much more likely to be obviously linked to headline news stories. Although the British decision to leave the gold standard received extensive press coverage in the United States, and undoubtedly impacted U.S. markets, the German crisis received even greater news coverage and appears to have had a much longer lasting impact on U.S. securities markets. These findings provide circumstantial evidence that foreign monetary shocks were having an important impact on real stock values and, by implication, the real economy.

---

30. This is not just my view. In its year-end review of U.S. stock markets, the *NYT* did not mention German problems in any of the first five monthly reports but then cited them as a market influence in all of the final seven months of 1931.

Four primary mechanisms by which foreign monetary crises impacted the U.S. economy can be identified. First, these crises led to a sharp increase in private gold hoarding, which then lowered expectations of future money supply growth. These bearish expectations immediately showed up in falling commodity and equity prices. It is especially interesting to note that the period of close correlation between the prices of YPBs and the Dow (mid-1931 to mid-1932) almost exactly coincides with the period of massive private gold hoarding. In principle, the major central banks held enough gold to offset the impact of private hoarding. But there was also an increasing maldistribution of monetary gold, as fear of further devaluations led central banks within the European gold bloc[31] to sharply increase their gold reserve ratios. This increase in central bank gold hoarding provides a second mechanism by which exchange rate uncertainty impacted the world price level.

Both the German and the British policy actions were resented by many other countries, which made policy coordination more difficult. Thus, not only did these exchange crises result in a near-term increase in the world's gold reserve ratio, they also reduced the prospects for international agreements that might have allowed for greater monetary ease in the future. The enthusiastic market response to Hoover's debt proposal shows that American investors were paying close attention to the issue of policy cooperation. And one can find numerous other examples, such as when the Dow rose on news of the French/British monetary agreement of early 1931. In the end, hopes for policy coordination were dashed, but markets clearly reacted as though it might happen, and that it would be very important if it did.

In discussing the failures of the Kreditanstalt and the German banking crisis, Friedman and Schwartz noted that

> The failure of world-famous financial institutions and the widespread closing of banks in a great country could not but render depositors throughout the world uneasy and enhance the desire of bankers everywhere to strengthen their positions. (1963a, p. 314)

---

31. The exact definition of the gold bloc varies, but France, Switzerland, and the Netherlands were certainly members. Belgium and Poland are also usually included, and Italy is occasionally included in this group.

Their suggestion that the German financial crisis led to an increased demand for currency and bank reserves provides a fourth transmission mechanism, as more demand for base money also has a deflationary impact on the economy. The U.S. banking crises of June and August to October occurred in close proximity to the European financial crisis, and it is unlikely that these events were unrelated.

It was Britain's aversion to deflation that led it to abandon the gold standard in September 1931. Because many countries held sterling or dollar assets in addition to their gold reserves, the devaluation of the pound resulted in large capital losses in countries holding sterling assets. Not surprisingly, fear that the United States would also abandon the gold standard led many of the gold bloc countries to exchange their dollar assets for gold. The exchange of paper assets for gold by European central banks, like the hoarding of currency by the public, represented a preference for greater liquidity. Even so, there is no necessary correlation between a central bank reducing its holdings of foreign assets, and increasing its gold reserve ratio. Gold bloc countries could have prevented their gold reserve ratios from increasing if they had exchanged their dollar and sterling assets for domestic assets, rather than gold. Had they done so, prices in the gold bloc would not have been so depressed during 1932.

Temin (1989, p. 75) argued that the British action did not lower the world price level, because [commodity] "prices fell before Britain went off gold. They did not fall faster afterward." This betrays a misunderstanding of auction-style commodity markets. Price changes are not serially correlated in efficient markets. The Great Contraction was not one event, requiring one explanation, but a series of distinct, and unexpected, shocks that continually drove prices and output lower between 1929 and 1932 (excepting early 1931). Under a gold standard the expected inflation rate for commodities is roughly zero, not the change that occurred in preceding months.

Nevertheless, I do agree with Temin's broader point that Britain should not receive condemnation for its actions. Temin is surely right that the greater tragedy is that others did not follow Britain off the gold standard. Britain can hardly be blamed for being among the first to recognize that gold was merely a "barbarous relic," a view that is now widely held. Britain might deserve some condemnation if other countries had played by the rules of the game. But the primary victims of the British decision (the United States and France) were the countries that most flagrantly violated those rules and hence did the most to put Britain into an untenable position.

With hindsight, the unfortunate events of 1931 may seem almost inevitable. But Ferguson and Temin (2001) showed that Bruening's sharp turn to the right in March 1931 was not preordained. They also noted (p. 41) that Bruening's "reckless pursuit of 'Mitteleuropa' destroyed the possibility of French financing for Germany. Stabilizing Germany by this means was clearly Briand's policy, and he came heartbreakingly close to bringing it off." The behavior of U.S. markets during 1931 certainly supports this view. Equity markets were relatively optimistic during early 1931, but then declined sharply as the German crisis became more severe. More importantly, these declines were closely correlated with changes in the prices of YPBs. Of course, we don't know for certain that German debt problems impacted the United States by increasing the demand for gold, but once the United States left the gold standard, the German debt problem no longer had a major impact on the U.S. stock market.

The sharp decline in stock prices amidst the September–October run on the dollar can be interpreted in several different ways. It might have reflected a fear that the gold outflows would cause the Fed to tighten policy. But there are two reasons to believe that it represented more than just a near-term fear of discount rate increases. First, when those increases did occur the market reacted positively. And second, we will later see several other examples of the stock market reacting negatively to gold outflows. And in some of those cases (such as late 1937) there was no realistic prospect of a near-term discount rate hikes. Instead, the most plausible explanation is that the run on the dollar increased the demand for gold (from both private citizens and central banks) and that this directly increased the real value of gold, and reduced the price level.

This does not mean that the critics of the Fed's actions were completely off base. The United States had massive gold reserves in the early 1930s, and an ambitious attempt to reflate the economy might have worked. But the market understood that the Fed was not likely to take such a big risk. A more cautious attempt at reflation, such as no discount rate increase and modest open market purchases, was more politically feasible, but might easily have been counterproductive if such policies led to a loss of confidence and a large gold outflow. In the next chapter we will see an example of just such a policy failure.

Appendix 3.a
German News and U.S. Stock Prices

The following quotations are from various issues of the *New York Times* (dated June 20, 1931, through July 25, 1931. Also indicated are the columns spanned by the headlines, selected quotes, and the corresponding movements in the first differences of the logs of the Dow Jones Industrial Average (DLDOW) and the prices of Young Plan bonds (DLYPBs).

---

1. **6/20** "HOOVER MOVES FOR RELIEF OF GERMANY" (4 columns)
   (announced after the stock market closed on 6/19)
   6/20 DLDOW = +6.4 percent DLYPB = +7.6 percent

---

2. **6/21** "HOOVER PROPOSES YEAR WAR DEBT SUSPENSION"
   (5 columns) (announced after the stock market closed on 6/20)
   6/22 "BERLIN OFFICIALLY ACCEPTS HOOVER PLAN" (4 columns)
   6/23 "DEBT PLAN WINS FRENCH POPULAR FAVOR" (4 columns)
   6/22 DLDOW = +4.9 percent DLYPB = +4.1 percent

---

3. **6/24** "FRANCE AGAINST ANY DELAY IN YOUNG PLAN PAYMENTS"
   (2 columns)
   6/23 DLDOW = −1.3 percent DLYPB = −1.3

---

4. **6/25** "FRENCH REPLY TO HOOVER ACCEPTS AID FOR GERMANY,
   BUT WITHIN THE YOUNG PLAN" (2 columns)
   6/24 DLDOW = +5.2 percent DLYPB = +1.0 percent

---

5. **6/26** "MELLON STARTS DEBT PARLEYS IN PARIS WITH
   WASHINGTON CONFIDENT OF ACCORD" (3 columns)
   6/25 DLDOW = −0.8 percent DLYPB = +0.3 percent

---

6. **6/27** "FRANCE'S REPLY IS UNACCEPTABLE TO U.S." (3 columns)
   Stocks declined on "France's reaction to the debt moratorium," then rose in the last hour on signs that "Paris was more tractable." (p. 23)
   6/26 DLDOW = +2.4 percent DLYPB = +0.0 percent

---

7. 6/28 "FRENCH TO CONSULT GERMANS ON DEBTS AS MELLON
WINS LAVAL TO DISCUSSION OF PARIS RESERVATION
ON HOOVER PLAN" (3 columns)
"War Debt Plan Aids Commodity Prices"

6/27 DLDOW = +1.9 percent DLYPB = +0.0 percent

---

8. 6/29 "POLES AND CZECHS ACCEPT HOOVER'S WAR DEBT PLAN;
PARIS TALKS TO CONTINUE" (2 columns)

6/30 "DEBT ACCORD DELAYED BY FRENCH STAND" (3 columns)

6/29 DLDOW = –2.8 percent DLYPB = –1.7 percent

---

9. 7/1 "[FRENCH] SENATE SUPPORTS LAVAL, SCORES OUR DEBT
ATTITUDE" (2 columns)

6/30 DLDOW = –1.6 percent DLYPB = –2.1 percent

---

10. 7/2 "HOOVER DEBT NOTE OFFERS CONCESSION TO FRANCE"
(2 columns)

7/1 DLDOW = +1.7 percent DLYPB = +0.3 percent

---

11. 7/3 "AGREEMENT WITH FRANCE ON DEBTS NEAR" (3 columns)

7/2 DLDOW = –0.8 percent DLYPB = +0.3 percent

---

12. 7/4 "WAR DEBT ACCORD REACHED IN PARIS, ONLY MINOR
DETAILS TO BE ADJUSTED" (4 columns)

7/3 DLDOW = +2.5 percent DLYPB = +3.0 percent

---

13. 7/5 "'BASIS OF ACCORD' ANNOUNCED IN PARIS ON FINAL
DETAILS OF DEBT HOLIDAY" (4 columns)

7/6 "WASHINGTON SEES DEBT ACCORD DELAY, BUT PARIS
EXPECTS AGREEMENT TODAY" (3 columns)

7/6 DLDOW = –1.6 percent DLYPB = +0.3 percent

---

14. 7/7 "FINAL AGREEMENT ON DEBTS IS SIGNED IN PARIS" (5 columns)

7/8 "LONDON SUMMONS YOUNG PLAN POWERS TO SETTLE
DETAILS OF THE DEBT ACCORD" (3 columns)
"Long Wrangle Predicted"

7/7 DLDOW = –4.6 percent DLYPB = –2.7 percent

15. **7/9**   "REICH TO SEEK LARGE LOAN" (2 columns)
   7/8   DLDOW = −1.4 percent DLYPB = −0.5 percent

16. **7/10** "LOAN OF $400,000,000 IS SOUGHT BY LUTHER IN LONDON
   AND PARIS" (1 column)
   7/9   DLDOW = +0.7 percent DLYPB = −3.3 percent

17. **7/11** "FRANCE ASKS REICH FOR POLICY PLEDGES IN RETURN
   FOR LOAN" (1 column)
   7/10 DLDOW = +1.4 percent DLYPB = +1.1 percent

18. **7/12** "BERLIN EXPECTS NEW YORK AND LONDON WILL HELP
   THE REICHSBANK TOMORROW TO PREVENT GERMAN
   FINANCIAL CRASH" (4 columns)
   "Gold Dictatorship Near"
   7/11 DLDOW = −2.1 percent DLYPB = −3.8 percent

19. **7/13** "FEDERAL RESERVE LIKELY TO AID REICH IN COOPERATION
   WITH EUROPEAN BANKS; BIG [GERMAN] BANK FAILS"
   (4 columns)
   7/14 "CENTRAL BANKS AGREE TO HELP REICH; ACT AFTER ALL
   DAY MEETING AT BASLE; GERMAN BANK RUNS BRING
   2-DAY CLOSING" (4 columns)
   7/13 DLDOW = −1.0 percent DLYPB = −8.1 percent

20. **7/15** "GERMANS TURN TO SELF AID TO END CRISIS" (3 columns)
   7/14 DLDOW = −1.1 percent DLYPB = −7.4 percent

21. **7/16** "GERMANY CURBS EXCHANGE" (2 columns)
   7/15 DLDOW = −2.1 percent DLYPB = −1.7 percent

22. **7/17** "WASHINGTON JOINS DEBT CONFERENCE, TAKING NEW
   ROLE IN WORLD POLITICS; PARIS AND LONDON MOVE TO
   AID REICH" (4 columns)
   "Debt Parley Sends Stock and Bonds Up Here"
   7/16 DLDOW = +3.0 percent DLYPB = +10.3 percent

23. 7/18   "PARLEYS ON REICH START IN PARIS TODAY" (3 columns)

    7/17   DLDOW = +0.4 percent DLYPB = +0.8 percent

24. 7/19   "PROGRESS MADE IN FRANCO-GERMAN TALK" (3 columns)

    7/18   DLDOW = −0.1 percent DLYPB = +1.9 percent

25. 7/20   "FRANCE AGREES TO BEFRIEND GERMANY" (4 columns)

    7/21   "NEW HOOVER PLAN TO HELP GERMANY" (3 columns)

    7/20   DLDOW = +1.4 percent DLYPB = −1.1 percent

26. 7/22   "POWERS AGREE TO BASE AID TO REICH ON HOOVER'S NEW CREDIT PROPOSAL" (4 columns)

    7/21   DLDOW = +1.5 percent DLYPB = +0.2 percent

27. 7/23   "POWERS TO VOTE AID TO REICH TODAY, TAKING ONLY TEMPORARY STEPS NOW; WALL STREET DOUBTS SUCCESS OF PLAN" (3 columns)

        "Markets Here Drop on London Reports"

        "German Radicals Gloating over 'Failure' of the London Parley"

    7/22   DLDOW = −2.9 percent DLYPB = −7.8 percent

28. 7/24   "HOOVER PLAN VOTED BY LONDON PARLEY" (4 columns)

        "French Stand Condemned" "Germans Are Pessimistic"

    7/23   DLDOW = +0.1 percent DLYPB = −3.8 percent

4

The Liquidity Trap of 1932

DURING 1932 AND 1933 the United States embarked on two important policy experiments that would have a profound impact on the future course of macroeconomic theory and policy. In Chapter 11 we will see that Keynesian macroeconomics was partially based on a misreading of the impact of these two policies. In this chapter we will focus on the first of these experiments, the open market purchase program of 1932. Then in Chapter 6, we will consider an even more dramatic policy experiment, the National Industrial Recovery Act of 1933.

We saw that 1931 began with some promising signs of international monetary cooperation, but ended in a climate of bitter recriminations over war debts, currency depreciation, and tariff policies. In some ways 1932 was the reverse, with the U.S. economy doing very poorly until July, when both stock prices and industrial production hit their depression lows, and then experiencing a mild recovery in the late summer. But that recovery fizzled out after a few months, as Hoover election gaffes and uncertainty created by the presidential interregnum triggered a severe dollar crisis. In some ways, it makes more sense to view May 1931 to July 1932 as a single *annus horribilis*, which essentially represented the second and decisive phase of the Great Contraction.

The dollar crisis that began in late September 1931 resumed in spring 1932, and reached its greatest intensity in early 1933. A debate is ongoing about whether this crisis significantly constrained Federal Reserve (Fed) policy. Temin and Eichengreen challenged Friedman and Schwartz's claim that the gold standard was not a binding constraint on Fed policy, particularly after February 1932 when the Glass-Steagall Act greatly augmented the amount of

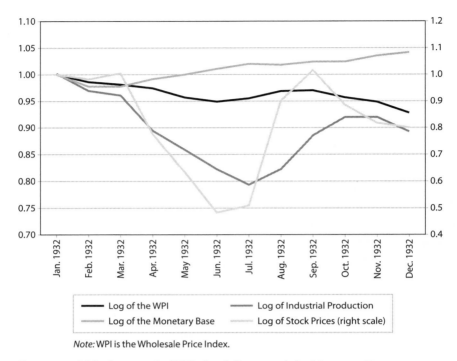

Note: WPI is the Wholesale Price Index.

Figure 4.1. U.S. Output, the WPI, Stock Prices and the Monetary Base

"free gold." They argued that it was fear of a run on the dollar that prevented the Fed from moving toward a more expansionary policy after Britain left the gold standard.

Much of the debate centers on how to interpret the open market purchase (OMP) program of 1932, which, in retrospect can be seen as a key turning point in American monetary history. Today, we'd call this sort of policy "quantitative easing." During the peak period of April to June 1932 the Fed purchased government securities at the rate of between 50 and 100 million dollars per week, and yet the monetary base increased only slightly and the broader monetary aggregates continued to decline. Furthermore, the program was accompanied by sharp declines in stock prices, commodity prices, and industrial production. Its perceived failure led to widespread doubts about the efficacy of monetary policy.

From a closing value of 88.78 on March 8, the Dow fell almost continuously to its Depression nadir of 41.22 on July 8, 1932. The most controversial question from this period is whether the Fed's bond purchases helped mitigate an otherwise disastrous set of exogenous shocks, had no impact on the economy, or actually worsened conditions by reducing confidence and increasing hoarding. Temin and Eichengreen argued that the OMPs did reduce confidence and that the resulting outflow of gold prevented the program from having an expansionary impact.

Bernanke's (1995) "multiple monetary equilibria" approach suggests that the spring OMPs might even have had a *contractionary* impact if they led to fears of dollar devaluation, and if this caused private and foreign central bank gold hoarding to rise by more than the decrease in the Fed's demand for gold fell. Before considering this episode, we need to look at how financial markets responded to some of the major nonmonetary policy shocks of 1932.

Congressional Initiatives and the Run on the Dollar

The German reparations issue continued to dominate the financial news during the first part of 1932. There was concern that even solvent German institutions would be unable to make scheduled debt payments if the Reichsbank imposed exchange controls to facilitate reparations payments. On January 6, the Dow jumped 7.1 percent and the prices of Young Plan bonds (YPBs) rose 10.7 percent on rumors that France would acquiesce to a cancellation of reparations. A January 10 *New York Times* headline read, "Stocks Up $3,000,000,000 in Four-Day Rally; Debt Outlook Held a Factor in Market's Rise." The story noted that "several factors have given new hope to the financial community, among the most prominent of which were the meetings of Adolf Hitler with Chancellor Bruening in Germany, out of which came the feeling that the international debt situation would be clarified." Commodity prices also rose sharply during that period. Table 3.1 shows that movements in the Dow and the prices of YPBs remained strongly correlated throughout the first half of 1932.

Banking panics resurfaced during December 1931 and January 1932, and in February, the financial press became concerned that currency hoarding was impeding Federal Reserve attempts to adopt a more expansionary policy. The

Hoover administration used everything from moral suasion to the issuance of small denomination Treasury securities[1] in a futile attempt to dislodge private currency hoards.

Monetary policy in the United States was complicated by the legal requirement that Federal Reserve notes be backed with either gold or eligible paper reserves. With insufficient holdings of eligible paper, the Fed was forced to maintain a gold ratio far above the legal minimum. On February 10, 1932, President Hoover met with congressional leaders and worked out a plan to give greater flexibility to the Federal Reserve. As embodied in the first Glass-Steagall Act (1932), the legislation also allowed the Fed to use government bonds as collateral, thereby greatly augmenting its holdings of free gold.

The response of the financial markets was wildly enthusiastic, with the Dow advancing by 9.5 percent on February 11. The next day, the plan was made public and the *New York Times* headlines clearly indicate that the proposed legislation was perceived as an expansionary move: "Congress Gets Credit Expansion Bill; Hailed as Marking End of Deflation; Stock Prices Up $3,000,000,000 Here." Although financial markets were closed on the twelfth, the bill sailed through both the House and the Senate banking committees, and on the thirteenth the Dow jumped another 9.2 percent, completing the largest two-day rally in modern stock market history.[2] The February 14 *New York Times* headline noted "Stocks and Bonds Rise in the World's Markets; Commodities Also Gain," and a few signs that the economy might be stabilizing were observed in March.

The positive response of stocks and commodities to Glass-Steagall was not surprising. The rally in Treasury bonds (T-bonds) after the announcement was attributed to the perception that Washington was engaging in a

---

1. These securities, dubbed "Baby Bonds," were issued in denominations of $50, $100, and $500 and carried a coupon rate of 2 percent. The bonds were sold door to door by volunteers in Hoover's antihoarding program. In late March 1932, demand for the notes all but dried up, and the program was discontinued after the issuance of only $28 million worth of bonds. This episode would seem to contradict the "legal-restrictions theory" of money.

2. It is worth recalling that real business cycle theory would predict no response of real stock prices to the Hoover announcement. It could be argued that real stock values rose because investors perceived that inflation would redistribute wealth from bondholders to stockholders, but corporate bonds also rallied strongly on the announcement.

carefully *controlled* inflation,[3] meaning that it would not lead to the dollar being devalued. But then why, after stabilizing for four weeks, did the stock and commodities markets decline sharply after mid-March?

Our basic gold market model suggests that a decline in aggregate demand can result from increased currency demand (due to bank panics), an increase in the gold ratio (at the discretion of central banks), or a decline in the world monetary gold stock (due to fears of devaluation). There was a banking panic in the Midwest during late June and early July, but most of the stock market decline had already occurred by this time. Instead, private and central bank gold hoarding seem the likeliest culprits for the spring downturn. After increasing briskly during the period from October 1931 to March 1932, the world monetary gold stock leveled off in April, and then declined by $167 million during the next two months. Yet, in the face of this surge in private gold hoarding, gold bloc central banks continued to import large quantities of gold. Table 2a.1 showed that the gold reserve ratio in the gold bloc increased sharply enough to reduce the *world* price level by roughly 14 percent between mid-1931 and late 1932.[4]

After the British devalued in September 1931, many members of the gold bloc began shifting their reserve holdings from paper assets to gold. Some historical accounts imply that this decision was almost inevitable. Immediately before the spring 1932 bear market was about to begin, however, Wall Street was still uncertain as to whether European central banks would ultimately convert their dollar-denominated assets into domestic assets, or gold:

> Under existing conditions it would be simpler and cheaper for the French bank of issue to recall its dollar balances through the exchange market by selling dollars for francs in Paris. Whether it will pursue this course or insist on adding to its already large gold stocks in the face of an unfavorable exchange position remains to be seen. If future sailings of French ships continue to carry consignments of gold to France, it will be concluded that the Bank of France is not merely desirous of

---

3. See the February 17 *NYT.* Press accounts often used a less pejorative term such as "reflation."

4. This figure actually applies to France plus Rest of the World, but almost all of that increase occurred in the gold bloc.

recalling its foreign balances but wants in addition to obtain more gold. (*NYT* 3/9/32, p. 29)

The U.S. Congress provided another source of uncertainty for the markets. The amicable, nonpartisan climate that greeted Glass-Steagall in February turned increasingly contentious as Congress attempted to close a huge budget deficit. A March 10 *New York Times* headline reported the first signs of growing opposition to the painful steps required to balance the budget: "Committee's Report Defends Sales Tax; Opposition Growing." On March 9, the Dow had declined 2.1 percent, the beginning of a major bear market. Although many of the declines accompanying congressional disputes were modest is size, the pattern was clear enough that by early April, Wall Street traders were referring to a "congressional market."

Over the next several weeks the political climate continued to worsen. On March 16, the Dow dropped 2.4 percent and the next day's *New York Times* headline read, "Fifty Democrats in Bloc to Defeat the Sales Tax." On March 18, the Dow fell another 2.5 percent and the following day's *New York Times* reflected the worsening situation: "Democratic Leaders Deplore Tax Revolt," "Leaders Are Bewildered," and "Long Step toward Disorganization Is Seen." By March 25, the *New York Times* was reporting that, "for the time being the financial community is absorbed—to the exclusion of almost everything else—in the fiscal problems of the Federal Government."

The tax dispute could have affected the stock market in many ways. The most straightforward explanations would involve the traditional channels by which taxes impact aggregate supply and/or demand. But traditional supply or demand-side models cannot explain the stock market's apparent support for (marginal income) tax increases to balance the budget. Nor can this reaction simply be attributed to Wall Street's blind acceptance of orthodox financial dogma. In 1933, the stock market greeted the devaluation of the dollar with great enthusiasm, despite the fact that most leading financiers viewed devaluation as an even greater abomination than an unbalanced budget.

By late March, it had become clear that with ongoing budget battles, "mischievous inferences are likely to be drawn in foreign financial centers."[5] On March 26, the Dow fell 2.9 percent and the following day's *New York Times*

---

5. *NYT,* 3/26/32, p. 21.

blamed the tax fight—not only for the stock market decline—but also for declines in government bonds and the dollar. From March 23 to 28, T-Bonds fell nearly two points, their largest decline since the first week of January. Finally, on March 29 and 30, the markets rallied modestly on signs of progress toward a balanced budget.[6]

Because the tax bill was so complex, there are numerous ways of interpreting the financial market's reactions to congressional deliberations. For instance, April 1 *New York Times* headlines noted both that "Market Off Sharply on Stock Tax Vote" and that "Bonus Advocates in House Ready to Pass Bill; Undaunted by President's Threat of Veto." Replacing the sales tax with a stock transfer tax and/or higher marginal income tax rates could reduce aggregate supply and thus, could depress stock prices without significantly affecting the level of aggregate demand, or the dollar. In contrast, the financial press viewed the Bonus bill, which would have financed $2 billion in accelerated veteran's bonuses by printing fiat currency, as a reckless example of "greenbackism" that would trigger a loss of confidence in the dollar.

The dollar came under increasing pressure in April. Although the French franc had risen to the gold export point by April 5, and U.S. gold exports were now expected, it was still "doubted that [gold] movement can obtain large proportions."[7] The April 8 *New York Times* (p. 31) noted that "the foreign attack on the dollar began just before Easter [March 27], when the defeat of the sales tax in Congress led to the widespread belief in Europe that the United States budget would not be balanced." The weakening dollar and renewed fears of a gold outflow were accompanied by an 11.6 percent decline in the Dow between April 4 and 8. By April 12, the *New York Times* was reporting that

> The experience of recent gold movements has shown that the exports of gold are slow to have their normal depressing effect upon the exchanges of the countries to which the metal is shipped. Presumably the reason is because the recent gold transfers have had nothing to do with normal capital movements. As the product of disturbed confidence, they have had to run their course until the effects of whatever particular shock had set a gold flow in motion had worn off. (p. 27)

---

6. "Garner Gets Pledge to Balance Budget" (*NYT*, 3/30/32); and "293,500,000 in New Taxes Quickly Voted by House" (*NYT*, 3/31/32).

7. *NYT*, 4/7/32, p. 33.

In other words, these gold flows did not represent the normal sorts of adjustments one sees in response to trade imbalances, but rather reflected a decision by some countries to increase their gold reserve ratios out of fear that paper assets could be devalued.

One puzzle presented by the spring 1932 dollar crisis is the failure of T-bond prices to decline sharply, as they had during the October 1931 crisis. After late March's decline, long-term T-bond prices recovered slightly and traded at six to twelve points below par during April, May, and June, before rallying to 97 in late July, when the dollar crisis ended. There are several possible explanations for the strength of T-bond prices. The spring of 1932 was a period of severe depression and deflation, corporate default risk was soaring, and a highly aggressive open market purchase operation was driving T-bill yields to below ½ percent. This is exactly the sort of period when one would expect T-bond prices to rally. Thus, the fact that they continued to trade at well below par could be viewed as a sign that other (hidden) factors were putting upward pressure on long-term yields. One of those hidden factors was presumably fear of devaluation.[8]

Investors may have also taken a more benign view of the inflationary consequences of devaluation than they had during the October 1931 crisis. Immediately after Britain left the gold standard, the financial press looked back on the inflationary European devaluations of the early and mid-1920s. By the spring of 1932, however, it was evident that (after rising modestly during late 1931), prices in Britain were again trending downwards.

The Spring Open Market Purchases and the Run on the Dollar

Several plausible alternatives to the hypothesis that congressional turmoil sparked the dollar crisis were suggested. Temin argued that the spring 1932 OMPs led to the gold outflow, noting that the outflow ended in July when the pace of open-market purchases slowed dramatically. In contrast, Friedman and Schwartz argued that the gold bloc nations converted their dollar assets into gold for domestic political reasons unrelated to Fed policy.

---

8. Ferderer and Zalewski (1994) argue that during mid-1932 policy uncertainty also increased the risk premium in interest rates.

Unfortunately, it is difficult to know exactly when the financial markets received information regarding shifts in Fed policy. We do know that the day after the key April 12 meeting of the Open Market Policy Conference, the *New York Times* accurately predicted a sharp acceleration in the Fed's weekly purchases of securities. And neither that meeting nor any of the other key meetings in early 1932 were accompanied by unusual stock price movements. Yet T-bond prices did increase during this period, and the April 14th *New York Times* suggested that the bond market rally over the previous five days was triggered by expectations of an acceleration in the open-market purchases of securities. This picture is still further clouded by the fact that the *New York Times* also attributed sizable stock (and bond) market rallies on April 14 and 21 to greater than expected open market purchases.[9]

Both the British devaluation of 1931 and the American devaluation of 1933 provide overwhelming evidence that, during the Great Depression, currency devaluations increased real (domestic) stock values.[10] Short of actual devaluation, however, it is difficult to ascertain the impact of expansionary monetary policies that might raise the probability of devaluation, and even more difficult to decipher the market response to uncertainty over legislative proposals to force a more expansionary monetary policy. The financial markets seemed to welcome expansionary policies, but only so long as they did not trigger a crisis of confidence that neutralized the impact:

> The financial community is in general strongly opposed to the [Bonus bill] scheme, but it is a curiously sympathetic opposition in many quarters. The professed object of proponents of the plan, which is to bring about an advance in the price level, is viewed widely as commendable, but the method by which it is sought to achieve this end is felt to be unsound. It would result, in the opinion of most bankers, in great disturbance to confidence here and abroad and would, despite this sacrifice, *fail of achieving its purpose.* (*NYT*, 4/12/32, p. 27, emphasis added)

9. See the *NYT* (4/15/32, p. 27; and 4/22/32, p. 28). The Dow rose 3.4 percent on April 14 and 4.3 percent on April 21, 1932.

10. This evidence is not restricted to the time of the initial devaluation. Real U.S. stock prices were highly correlated with the price of gold throughout the April 1933 through February 1934 dollar devaluation.

This is a puzzle that economists have still not fully resolved. Devaluation is strongly bullish for equity markets. Fear of devaluation is bearish. At what point does expectation of devaluation become so strong that the bullish effects outweigh the bearish?

In addition to the Bonus bill, Wall Street also faced uncertainty over the Goldsborough bill, which would have instructed the Fed to raise prices back to the average level of the mid-1920s. The May 7 *Commercial and Financial Chronicle* argued that this bill would force a devaluation of the dollar and suggested that the bill was contributing to the U.S. gold outflow. The April 27 *New York Times* (p. 25) noted that a few Wall Street analysts supported the Goldsborough bill because they were afraid that without congressional pressure the Fed would abandon its policy of purchasing government securities, but later suggested that the majority view was more complex:

> Wall Street as a whole is strongly in sympathy with the idea behind the Goldsborough bill, which imposes a mandate upon the Treasury and the Federal Reserve System to lower the purchasing power of the dollar, but is opposed ever more strongly to the bill on practical grounds. (*NYT*, 5/3/32, p. 29)

The financial press attributed sharp declines in the dollar and T-bonds on May 3 and 4 to a positive House vote on the Goldsborough bill (and European misunderstanding of the U.S. political system).[11] On May 5, the *New York Times* (p. 29) referred to a "flight of funds from this market, set in motion by the action of the House of Representatives on Monday in passing the Goldsborough bill." Wall Street's response, however, was ambiguous. Although the May 4 *New York Times* (p. 29) noted that the Goldsborough bill "may have depressed stocks" (the Dow declined 2.2 percent on May 3), the stock market rose on May 4, despite an even sharper break in government bond prices and an even weaker dollar. The ambivalent reaction to the Goldsborough bill may have reflected investor support for a more expansionary monetary policy, but apprehension over the possibility of a dollar crisis.

---

11. Foreign currencies rose sharply against the dollar on May 3, and on May 4 several European currencies reached their highest levels since October 1931. T-bonds fell $^{19}\!/_{32}$ on May 4 and $1\,^{13}\!/_{32}$ on May 14. Although the bill passed the House by an (unexpectedly) overwhelming margin, the *NYT* (5/4/32, p. 29) gave the bill little chance of being enacted by the Senate.

The political climate in Washington, DC, changed abruptly on the evening of May 5: "Hoover Sends Congress Sharp Message, Saying Its Inaction Disturbs the Nation; Demands Quick Balancing of Budget."[12] The next day the Dow soared by 9.1 percent,[13] and the following day the *New York Times* headlines reported "Tax Bill Completed" and "Bonus Bill Buried in House's Red Tape." Although the budget fight would drag on for several more months, it was becoming apparent that even as the probability that Congress would approve the more radical legislation diminished, the stock market remained mired far below its mid-March levels. When the dollar again declined on May 9, the *New York Times* suggested that:

> There was the usual disposition in Wall Street to ascribe this movement solely to the vagaries of Congress. That explanation possibly lost some force from the fact, which other markets than foreign exchange have appeared to reflect, that the Congressional situation has in the last few days taken a distinct turn for the better. What apparently has been happening is that the foreign central banks, notably that of Holland, have been pursuing somewhat aggressively the policy of turning their foreign exchange reserves into gold. (5/10/32, p. 29)

The *New York Times* blamed inflation concerns partly on the fear that the Goldsborough bill would force the United States off the gold standard, but also on the fact that (due to gold outflows) the Fed had now been forced to invoke the provisions of Glass-Steagall, which allowed eligible paper to be augmented with government securities. They also noted that:

> The contrast presented by these fears of inflation and the unremitting fall in the prices of stocks and commodities is one of the curious aspects of the current situation. Obviously if there was any genuine belief in the likelihood of inflation, the attempt of capital to escape depreciation by conversion into some tangible form of wealth would be reflected at once in a demand for commodities and common stocks. (5/14/32, p. 23)

---

12. *NYT*, 5/6/32, p. 1.

13. The 15 percent wage cut announced by U.S. Steel may have also contributed to the strong rally in stock prices.

This would be true if dollar depreciation was thought to be imminent, but the opposite can occur if an immediate devaluation is considered unlikely. Under a fiat money system, fears of future inflation will reduce the demand for money, thereby causing an immediate increase in prices. Under a gold standard, however, fears of future devaluation can be deflationary. After a currency is devalued, nominal prices continue to be quoted in terms of the medium of exchange (money), and the nominal price of the medium of account (gold) will increase. Thus, under a gold standard, fears of devaluation will increase the demand for the gold, whereas under a fiat money system, fears of future inflation will reduce the demand for currency.

In principle, the problem of gold hoarding could have been neutralized by the expansionary effects of the Fed's open market purchases. But the effect of these purchases was already being more than offset by contractionary policies in Europe. The problem was not so much the U.S. gold outflow (a fall in the U.S. gold ratio is the expected consequence of an expansionary policy), but rather, the fact that the gold bloc central banks sterilized their gold inflows by sharply increasing their gold ratios. They weren't playing by the rules of the game.

As it became apparent that the budget situation wasn't the only factor affecting the dollar, investors began to view the gold outflows as an *independent* disturbance to the foreign exchange market. Commenting on European views that the outflow was depressing the dollar, the *New York Times* noted ironically that:

> It resembles the reasoning which attained much popularity in this country a year or more ago; which began by declaring that the stock market decline was the result of unfavorable trade [i.e., business] conditions, and ended by insisting still more vigorously that the trade situation was the direct result of the decline in stocks. (5/22/32, p. N7)

If the gold outflow had been due solely to the actions of private agents, then it would be natural to consider the flows as simply an endogenous response to economic shocks. But given the wide discretion practiced by the gold bloc central banks, it is not unreasonable to view the flows as being at least partially exogenous, and as being an independent factor contributing to the weakness of the dollar.

During the latter part of May, the U.S. gold outflow accelerated, the dollar became very weak, and stock prices continued to decline. The situation was worsened by political developments in Germany and France that increased tensions and reduced expectations for the upcoming Lausanne Conference. On May 31, Hoover made another surprise appearance before the Senate to press for quick passage of the budget. His dire warnings that the situation had deteriorated sharply in the previous few days, however, did not inspire as much confidence among investors as did his May 5 speech.[14]

Later, we will see that Hoover's penchant for overdramatizing economic crises actually hurt the markets, and perhaps the economy, during the fall of 1932. Nevertheless, Congress did begin to move more aggressively, and the Dow rose by 13.7 percent during the first four days of June, an increase that the June 5 *New York Times* attributed to congressional progress on the budget. A June 15 *New York Times* headline reported that "France Withdraws Her Last Gold Here; Dollar Value Rises," "Our Bankers Are Elated," and "Dollar Is Dominant Again." Yet, the crisis was not quite over. The markets faced one more banking panic, an additional month of congressional budget battles, and completion of the Lausanne Conference, before a sustained recovery could begin in mid-July.

From June 15 to July 8, the Dow declined steadily and the June 26 *New York Times* (p. F1) argued that the end of the gold outflow had put critics of the Fed OMPs in an "awkward position." The *New York Times* did concede that the slowdown in the rate at which the Fed was buying securities may have helped to stem the outflow, but argued that the Fed could now reach its excess reserve target with smaller weekly purchases. Unfortunately, because the Fed's excess reserve targeting procedure automatically synchronized these events, it is not possible to know whether cessation of the gold outflow slowed the open market purchases, or vice versa. As less gold flowed out, the Fed didn't need to purchase as many securities to hit its reserve target. Fortunately, the recovery that began in the summer of 1932 provides independent evidence that gold hoarding was a problem for the markets, and for the broader economy.

Given that German developments were the dominant factor influencing the U.S. stock market during 1931, it is surprising how little market reaction

---

14. Stock prices declined immediately after the speech.

there was to the Lausanne Conference. The *New York Times* did report that stock prices rallied after 2:00 p.m. on July 6 on rumors of a Lausanne agreement. And the market opened strongly on July 8, following the announcement of an agreement that essentially ended German reparations. But despite the agreement, the Dow closed at its lowest level of the Depression on July 8, and the July 9 *New York Times* (p. 19) noted that "stocks moved up and down with a strange indifference to the overshadowing reparations agreement." The next day the *New York Times* argued that Wall Street pessimism was due to the perception that a broader agreement for (allied) war debt rescheduling was also needed, but unlikely to occur because of opposition in Congress, and in the Democratic Party platform.

On July 11, the *New York Times* reported that the Conference produced a secret "Gentlemen's Agreement" that made the reparations cancellation conditional on the United States forgiving the allied war debts. The United States immediately disavowed any involvement in this "understanding," which dissipated some of the goodwill that might have resulted from the treaty. Nevertheless, it is unlikely that anticipation of these problems could fully explain the stock market's weakness during the first week of July, particularly in light of the fact that the prices of YPBs soared by 45.6 percent between June 29 and July 9.

An alternative explanation for the weak stock market was the renewal of banking difficulties in the Midwest. During late June and early July, Midwestern banking problems, centered in Chicago, led to an upsurge in currency hoarding, and as early as June 25 the *New York Times* was suggesting that the Chicago bank failures were depressing stock prices. Lastrapes and Selgin (1995) provided evidence that a tax on bank checks, which took effect on June 21 may have substantially increased the currency/deposit ratio. If so, then this tax could have contributed to the ongoing banking difficulties in the Midwest. The banking problems may have also helped to delay the rally in the dollar until mid-July.

As late as July 11, *New York Times* headlines continued to show little evidence that a dramatic reversal in the dollar's position was imminent: "Possibility of [Gold] Shipments to America Discussed, but Doubted." Although radical legislation was now considered unlikely, congressional deliberations continued to overhang the market. The July 12 *New York Times* noted that a late rally in the stock market was due to rumors of congressional adjournment on the following day, and argued that adjournment was necessary before confidence in the dollar could be restored.

During the final days of the 72nd Congress, deliberations continued on one last issue with important monetary implications. Carter Glass had proposed legislation that would allow banks to substantially increase their issuance of national bank notes, as a way of forestalling even more radical legislation. And in early June the Glass bill did displace the Goldsborough bill. Although the Glass bill theoretically allowed the issue of over $1 billion in new currency, some doubted that it would have much impact. The actual increase in national bank notes over the next twelve months was slightly more than $200 million (roughly 4 percent of the total currency stock).

The July 17 issue of the *New York Times* (p. F1) attributed a decline in the T-bond market to the (apparent) rejection of the Glass bill on the eve of congressional adjournment. The bill actually *was* adopted by Congress late in the evening on the 16th, and therefore, the subsequent market reaction provides a useful confirmation of the *New York Times'* analytical skills. On Monday, July 18, the price of T-bonds rose $1^5/_{32}$, the largest daily movement during the entire month of July. Four weeks later T-bonds prices fell $1^8/_{32}$ on Attorney General Mitchell's ruling that national bank notes could only be issued for a three-year period (ending in 1935).

Signs of Recovery

The period from July 8 to September 7 saw one of the largest stock market rallies during any two-month period in American history. The Dow nearly doubled, and other indices showed considerably larger gains on very heavy volume. As late as July 19, however, the market had risen only slightly from its Depression lows. And since by that date Congress had already adjourned, the Midwest banking panic had ended, and the press was already predicting the imminent termination of the Fed's open market purchases, it is difficult to account for the subsequent boom in stock prices.

The analysis in the preceding section suggests that the dollar crisis contributed to the spring 1932 stock market crash. If so, then a turnaround in the dollar's position would be expected to boost stock prices. A July 29 *New York*

Times headline reported that "Stocks Rise Again in Year's Heaviest Trading," and in addition to rising commodity prices, attributed the gain to a "spectacular rise of the dollar in terms of foreign currencies which reflected the further reinforcement of the gold position of the United States." Another story noted the "discovery that the United States is securely anchored to the gold standard" and then asserted that

> Certainly the financial community does not relish the return of the bulk of the gold shipped from New York to Europe a few months ago, in view of the fact that many other nations need the metal far more than the United States, but at least there is a distinct feeling of satisfaction that there is a movement in this direction and that the ill-starred raids on the dollar are over. (7/29/32, p. 23)

The *New York Times* may actually have understated the gains from the gold inflow. Most of the previous outflows had gone to nations with less need for the gold than the United States, such as Britain, France, Holland, and Switzerland, rather than to nations in a precarious financial positions, such as Germany. And news that private gold hoarding ceased in July was even more unambiguously positive, as dishoarding pushed the world monetary gold stock up by $143 million in August and another $131 million in September.

France was easily the largest gold hoarder during the Great Depression. Her monetary gold stock rose almost continually from $711 million in late 1926 to over $3.2 billion at the end of June 1932 (nearly 30 percent of the world total). After June, French gold imports slowed to a trickle, and on August 5 the *New York Times* (p. 21) cited the "new [French] situation" as one of the factors that contributed to the return flow of gold. The *Times* also suggested these flows were leading to inflation expectations, which were being reflected in soaring stock and commodity prices. This supports the view of Clark Johnson, and others[15], that French gold hoarding played a significant role in the Depression. On August 11 the *New York Times* reported that, in a significant policy shift, foreign central banks were now buying dollar assets with gold. By this time, the Dow had already risen 68.3 percent from its July low.

---

15. See Irwin (2012).

During August, confidence in the international monetary system returned. The August 19 *New York Times* (p. 23) argued that Britain was moving inexorably toward resumption of gold payments "without asking the permission of the Keyneses and the Cassels." The Dow reached a peak on September 7, and the next day the *New York Times* (p. 29) reported that the Dutch guilder and Swiss franc declined as confidence returned and investors pulled funds out of "neutral" countries.

Along with the rise in stock and commodity prices, industrial production rose 2.9 percent in August, 6.5 percent in September, and 3.5 percent in October. It looked like the Depression was ending. But then, industrial production leveled off in November, and declined 2.6 percent in December. By March 1933 output had almost fallen back to the July lows. Although it is unclear exactly what caused the recovery to abort, there is strong evidence that the looming presidential election had a dramatic impact on the stock market from mid-September onward.

The Election of 1932

On September 2, a serious intra-party fight erupted among Democrats in New York and the following day's *New York Times* headline reported "Roosevelt Chance Hurt" and "Carrying of State Held in Doubt, Endangering Hope of Presidency." The Dow rose 4.2 percent on the day the story broke, and commodity prices also increased. Given the subsequent Roosevelt landslide, it may seem odd that the markets would have viewed the outcome as uncertain, but there are several reasons why the situation in September was less clear-cut than it appears in hindsight. First, although the economic situation was still very poor, it did look much more promising in mid-September than it did on November 8. And despite the subsequent deterioration in the economy, Hoover actually carried important industrial states such as Pennsylvania and Connecticut and came close in several others. The popular vote landslide was partly due to Roosevelt margins of up to 50 to 1 in states such as South Carolina, but Hoover did not need any southern states to win the election.

On September 12, there was an important set of state elections in Maine and that day, the Dow fell 5.5 percent (commodity prices also declined). The next day, the *New York Times* reported, "All Eyes on Maine," and although they were unaware of the outcome, noted a "fear of Democratic success, or near-success." The Dow fell another 3.4 percent on September 13, although the election of a new Democratic governor was not assured until well after the markets closed. The Dow dropped another 5.7 percent on September 14 and that day's *New York Times* called the election an upset of "vast significance." The *CFC* noted that this Democratic victory in a traditionally Republican state did not bode well for the Hoover campaign:

> The overshadowing event of the week has been the Maine election on Monday and portents which it is supposed to carry. On the Stock Exchange the outcome has been viewed with no little concern, and both stock and bond prices have suffered serious declines as the result, though there have been other contributing causes for the weakness. (9/17/32, p. 1859)

Immediately after the election, Hoover changed his strategy and took to the stump.

The following Tuesday saw another key state election in Wisconsin, but this time conservative Republicans upset LaFollette's Progressives. The Dow rose 3.7 percent during the afternoon of the 20th (election day), and then soared 11.4 percent the next day (although other economic news contributed to this extraordinary gain). A September 22 *New York Times* headline reported, "Republicans Hail LaFollette Defeat as Trend to Hoover."

Given how poorly stocks had done under the Hoover administration, it might seem odd that the market apparently rooted for his reelection. As we will see, however, his defeat triggered five months of additional uncertainty about the dollar, which further depressed the economy. Some of Franklin D. Roosevelt's (FDR's) policies, such as dollar devaluation, would eventually boost stock prices. But in October 1932 there was no guarantee that Roosevelt would devalue the dollar and many of his other policies would prove to have a negative impact on stock prices. And finally, it can be argued that, while deflationary monetary policies had been the biggest mistake of the Hoover administration, the market understood that the real value of gold had already exceeded its prewar levels, and that prices were unlikely to fall much lower regardless of who was elected in November.

A set of news stories during early October provides a fascinating picture of how the "news" to which markets respond consists not simply of events, but also of changing perceptions of those events. In a speech given on the evening of October 4, Hoover mentioned the fact that at one time during the previous winter the United States had been only two weeks away from being forced to abandon the gold standard. The implication was that his adroit leadership had prevented this "disaster." Of course, during this period, the administration had consistently assured both the public and foreign investors that there was no possibility of the United States leaving the gold standard. Although the Dow plunged 7.2 percent the day after the speech,[16] there is no indication in the financial press, or in the movements of other markets, that the drop was attributable to Hoover's statement. Instead, the decline was attributed to investor disappointment in a lack of "fresh proposals" for economic recovery.[17]

On October 7, Carter Glass publicly contradicted Hoover's statement (his rebuttal was apparently delayed by illness), and on the same day the Dow declined an additional 5.4 percent as the dollar fell sharply against the gold bloc currencies. The next day, the (pro-Hoover) *New York Times* (p. 25) reluctantly reported that "in some quarters the movement was ascribed to a misunderstanding of Mr. Hoover's recent statement that at one time this country had been within two weeks of going off the gold standard unless remedial measures were taken" and indicated that there was a "belated reaction abroad" to the statement.

On October 8, the Dow fell another 2.4 percent and the following day the tempest was headline news in the *New York Times*: "No Danger to Dollar from Foreign Raids Seen Now in Capital," "Hoover Blamed in Paris," and "Papers Lay Decline to His Speech—The Dollar Takes Sharp Drop, Along with Sterling." The *New York Times* also quoted some of the foreign reaction:

> What evils can result from an election! . . . Now President Hoover, to recover votes which seemed on the point of escaping, is willing to sacrifice the dollar. For the dollar again has become feeble and delicate . . . following the declarations of President Hoover, who in order to get

---

16. The ninth largest drop in modern times.

17. See *Business Week*, 10/19/32, p. 34.

business started again, has indicated the possibility of inflation. (*La Liberté*)

Everyone is saying that if the dollar is vulnerable, so must be most European moneys. (*Agence Economique et Financière*)

The President, seeking to restore confidence, seems somehow to accomplish the opposite result. (*Paris Midi*)

On the same issue's financial page (F1), the *New York Times* indicated that the continued decline in the dollar and the stock market on the morning of the 8th was widely assumed to be due to the President's remarks and that "business men are reported now to be apprehensive of the effects of a falling stock market on trade."

The next day, the *New York Times* carried several more stories on the negative impact of Hoover's statement on the European markets and observed "that stocks should fall and foreign exchange should move against New York because it has been disclosed that the 'gold position' was difficult, six months or a year ago, is in its way an odd incident of finance."[18] Hoover's gaffe had to be seen as a serious blow to his only campaign strengths, experience, and competence, and with his chances of reelection slipping away, it is not surprising that the Dow declined another 4.4 percent on Monday, October 10, despite the fact that the dollar had steadied.[19]

As the likelihood of a Roosevelt victory increased, the markets focused more heavily on Roosevelt's policy statements. On October 14, the Dow rose

---

18. There is an interesting parallel in Brown's (1940, p. 1232–34) attribution of the June/July currency hoarding to three factors; large gold outflows, banking difficulties, and the lingering effects of an April 1932 speech where Hoover bragged (discussing an earlier run on the dollar): "It had to be fought in silence . . . Happily we won this battle. There is no longer any danger from disclosure." Brown argued (p. 1234) that the speech made the public aware that "the suspension of the gold standard had only a few months before been a distinct possibility."

19. Einzig (1933, p. 64) even suggested that Hoover's statement may have contributed to future crises:

It was one of the biggest blunders made during the crisis. Many people remembered that at the time referred to by President Hoover's remark, official quarters were as emphatic as ever in their denials of any danger whatsoever. President Hoover's admission went a long way, therefore, towards discrediting the authorities in the eyes of the public. When, some months later, the dollar once more became vulnerable, no official reassuring statement was able to restore confidence.

6.8 percent, and the following day the *New York Times* (p. 23) reported that, "no one on Wall Street pretended that the advance was based on anything but the expectation of a positive [i.e., 'responsible'] declaration by Governor Roosevelt on the bonus issue." By November 8, there was a strong likelihood that Roosevelt would win, and the stock market showed little reaction to the actual election results.[20]

If the stock market performance leading up to the election was based on expectations of a difficult interregnum, then the market was remarkably prescient. Hoover received little cooperation from Roosevelt, who preferred to preserve a free hand and remain unencumbered by Hoover's failures. This meant that Hoover had little credibility in dealing with difficult issues, such as the war debts controversy that flared up in December. And when fears of dollar devaluation resurfaced during the winter (partly due to Roosevelt's refusal to precommit on policy questions), the Fed again tightened monetary policy in order to preserve the gold standard.

There was a brief period of optimism just after the election. Although the prospect of a Hoover loss seemed to worry Wall Street in September, by early November Hoover was so discredited that FDR found "moral and vocal support [among] some of the respected financial and industrial chieftains."[21] Furthermore, investors were beginning to focus on prospects for the repeal of Prohibition under a Democratic administration, an event that "would be interpreted as bullish, because it would imply the gradual reduction of corporation taxes, individual income taxes and inheritance taxes."[22] Stocks fell 4.5 percent on the day after the election but actually traded higher during the morning. Then, over the following several days, stocks and commodities rose strongly in what was termed a "Roosevelt market." The financial press reported expectations of political cooperation, particularly in the prickly war debts issue. The pound also rallied on expectations of a debt moratorium.

---

20. Just prior to the election, the betting odds suggested that Roosevelt was heavily favored to win (about 6 to 1), but it also seems likely that he did even better than anticipated. Oddsmakers had New Jersey even and Hoover was actually favored in Massachusetts. Roosevelt won both states.

21. *NYT*, 11/5/32, p. 25.

22. *NYT*, 11/2/32, p. 27.

The war debts issue was clearly the dominant financial story from mid-November to the end of 1932 and is the most plausible explanation for the 17.2 percent decline in the Dow between November 12 and the end of the month. The first price break (on November 14) seems to have been triggered by debt moratorium letters from France and the UK, as well as from growing indications of a possible congressional fight on the issue. The *New York Times* suggested a potential explanation for the market's concerns:

> In so far as the "Street" has any apprehension over the impending discussions of the debt question, it relates to the possible attitude of Congress. Obviously a protracted and acrimonious debate, holding out the imminent threat of a forced default by the greatest creditor nation, next to ourselves, in the world, would put to a severe test the reviving confidence in business and financial circles upon which the recovery from the depression rests. (11/16/32, p. 25)

When Hoover failed to get FDR's support for a debt revision proposal, both stock and commodity prices fell sharply on November 23.

On November 27, the *New York Times* noted falling commodity prices: "About 90% of the Recovery Made Up to Sept. 6 Has Now Been Wiped Out. . . . War-Debt Situation with the Drop in Sterling among General Causes" and, over the next several weeks, stock prices zigzagged up and down in sympathy with the prospects for a war debts settlement. On December 15, Britain made its $95.55 million payment by earmarking gold at the Bank of England. Britain could have saved several million dollars by paying with Liberty bonds purchased at a discount from par; by paying in gold it lodged a (implied) protest over the unfairness to debtors of the deflationary environment produced by the gold standard.[23]

Just as during the previous interregnum between presidents of different political parties (1920–1921), the long wait for FDR's inauguration proved extremely damaging to the economy. Indeed, the problems caused by the lack of effective presidential leadership were so obvious that they led to a constitutional amendment allowing the new president to take office in January,

---

23. And according to Eichengreen (1992, p. 320) it was also a "veiled threat that if the United States attempted to repatriate that gold, the Bank of England would liquidate its dollar balances."

Table 4.1. Economic Indicators during 1932, Monthly

Month	Output	WPI	Dow	Gold	MB	M1
Jan.	12.9	67.3	85.88	11,374	7,704	21,507
Feb.	12.5	66.3	82.18	11,454	7,537	21,310
Mar.	12.4	66.0	81.02	11,535	7,539	21,110
Apr.	11.6	65.5	64.49	11,551	7,644	20,882
May	11.2	64.4	53.96	11,452	7,710	20,531
June	10.8	63.9	50.62	11,384	7,788	20,449
July	10.5	64.5	45.47	11,456	7,858	20,152
Aug.	10.8	65.2	66.51	11,599	7,850	20,189
Sept.	11.5	65.3	67.94	11,730	7,897	20,211
Oct.	11.9	64.4	64.22	11,825	7,896	20,256
Nov.	11.9	63.9	65.26	11,897	7,978	20,555
Dec.	11.6	62.6	61.16	11,933	8,028	20,341

Note: Output is industrial production, the Dow represents mid-month closing prices, and gold is the world monetary gold stock in millions of U.S. dollars. The U.S. monetary base and M1 are taken from Friedman and Schwartz (1963a) and are also measured in millions of U.S. dollars.

rather than March. However, the change came too late to prevent a very grim winter during 1932–1933.

Was There a Liquidity Trap in 1932?

At the time, the spring 1932 OMPs were widely seen as being almost completely ineffective. To understand why, consider some of the macroeconomic data shown in Table 4.1. In many respects, the period from April to July 1932 represented the worst three months of the entire Depression. Commodity prices continued to fall, and both stock prices and industrial production reached their Depression lows in July. Even the M1 money supply declined, despite the massive OMPs. It would be many decades before monetary policy was again viewed as an effective stabilization tool.

I have not mentioned the term "liquidity trap" in this chapter, nor have I provided any evidence for the existence of such a phenomenon. Indeed, under the gold market approach to aggregate demand, it makes no sense to argue that a country is stuck in a liquidity trap. Either policy is constrained by a loss of gold reserves (which is a quite different concept) or the entire world is stuck in a liquidity trap, as would occur if large reductions in the world demand for gold had no impact on the purchasing power of gold.

Regardless of whether the United States was actually in a liquidity trap during the early 1930s, it appears that the Keynesian concept of monetary policy ineffectiveness was at least partly based on the perception that the Fed's spring 1932 open market purchases had failed to revive the economy. Scholars often cite Keynes' remark that "I know of no example of [absolute liquidity preference] hitherto." Less well known is that just a few lines later he provides the only real-world example of a liquidity trap in the entire *General Theory*:

> The most striking examples of a complete breakdown of stability in the rate of interest, due to the liquidity function flattening out in one direction or the other, have occurred in very abnormal circumstances. . . . [I]n the United States at certain dates in 1932 there was a . . . financial crisis or crisis of liquidation, when scarcely anyone could be induced to part with holdings of money on any reasonable terms. (1936 [1964], pp. 207–08)

Keynes developed much of the *General Theory* in 1932 and 1933, and thus, it would not be surprising if the failed 1932 OMPs were on his mind when he lost confidence in the efficacy of monetary policy during depressions. Nor was Keynes alone. Conservatives within the powerful financial community saw this as showing the folly of monetary cranks who thought the Depression could be cured by printing money.[24] Even Irving Fisher, who was to the left of Keynes on monetary issues, temporarily lost faith in the efficacy of

---

24. The almost universal perception that the spring 1932 OMPs had been a failure did not imply that all forms of monetary policy were viewed as being ineffective in a depression. Few doubted that unorthodox monetary solutions involving fiat money were capable of generating high rates of inflation, but there was little support for this type of experimentation. Eichengreen (1992, p. 315) suggests that the 1932 OMPs led conservative American policymakers to view expansionary monetary policy as "conducive not to economic recovery but to inflation." But this is based on his (mistaken) view that prices rose during the spring of 1932. In fact, prices fell, and conservatives looked at the liquidity trap issue pretty much the same way as Keynes did—that is, as a problem of "pushing on a string."

Fed policy.[25] Whether or not one sees the policy as having been a failure, it is clear that this event played an important role in shaping the public's views on monetary policy efficacy for the remainder of the 1930s.[26]

Friedman and Schwartz (1963a, p. 324) rejected the standard Keynesian view that monetary policy was ineffective during the early 1930s. They argued that the business upswing in the late summer of 1932 was a delayed reaction to the spring OMPs, and that the Fed had prematurely abandoned the OMPs. It should be clear from the analysis in this chapter that I have some problems with this view. Monetary policy may impact macroeconomic aggregates with a lag, but it is difficult to reconcile the behavior of stock and commodity prices with the Friedman-Schwartz view. Indeed, one might have expected stock and commodity prices to have risen during the spring OMPs, and then fallen back later in the year when the Fed reverted to a more contractionary policy. Instead, stocks and commodities moved in tandem with shifts in the *demand for gold*; plunging in the spring when public and private gold hoarding was intense, and then rising when the dollar panic ended and gold demand declined.

If the evidence is not entirely supportive of Friedman and Schwartz's views on monetary policy effectiveness, the same could be said for the Keynesian view of this episode. "Liquidity trap" generally refers to a scenario where increases in the money supply fail to boost aggregate demand. But that is not quite what happened in the spring of 1932, as the impact of the open market purchases was mostly negated by gold outflows. During this period, the monetary base rose by only about $300,000,000, despite the open market purchases totaling roughly a billion dollars, and M1 and M2 actually declined.[27] Thus the 1932 OMPs provide little support for the view that large increases in the money supply might fail to boost a depressed economy. It is ironic that the only real-world example of a liquidity trap in the entire *General Theory* actually shows something very different, the constraints imposed on policymakers by the international gold standard.[28]

---

25. Fisher favored switching to a pure fiat money regime. Keynes was unwilling to support such a radical step.

26. Laidler (1999, p. 259n) calls the perceived policy failure "one of the key 'stylized facts' underlying the evolution of monetary economics in the 1930s and 1940s."

27. M1 is cash held by the public plus demand deposits. M2 is M1 plus time deposits.

28. Currie (1934 [1935]) was one of the few interwar commentators who understood this.

It is not surprising that Keynes would have confused absolute liquidity preference with the constraints of the gold standard. Both concepts ultimately rest on policy instruments constrained by a zero lower bound (nominal interest rates in a liquidity trap and the gold reserve ratio under a gold standard regime). In contrast, if under a fiat money regime the central bank uses either a "quantity of money" or a "price of money" instrument (i.e., exchange-rate targeting), then expansionary policy faces no meaningful barriers; there is no upward limit to either the money stock or the nominal price of foreign exchange.[29]

In Chapter 2 I argued that Johnson and Mundell's gold undervaluation hypothesis ultimately relies on a peculiar assumption—that policymakers would have been able to effectively manage gold demand in 1920, but not in 1929. Now we can see one justification for this seeming inconsistency. A coordinated set of devaluations in 1920 (aimed at price stability) would have required central banks to increase their gold demand in the short run in order to prevent inflation. In contrast, a managed gold standard after 1929 (also aimed at price stability) would have required central banks to lower their demand for gold. Only the latter (expansionary) policy risks running up against the zero lower bound constraint on gold reserve ratios.

Interpreting 1932

Even though Friedman and Schwartz viewed the 1932 OMPs as being modestly effective, they also saw the policy as being too little, too late. The more important question, and the issue that separates them from critics like Temin and Eichengreen, is whether monetary policymakers in 1932 were constrained by the international gold standard. Although I don't believe there is any way to definitively answer this question, Friedman and Schwartz's optimistic view is at least plausible.

The United States still held massive gold reserves in 1932, and there is no reason why those reserves shouldn't have been used more aggressively in an emergency such as the Great Depression. In fact, Timberlake (1993, p. 272)

---

29. Technically, this assertion only holds for the price of money. But it is exceedingly unlikely that a central bank could buy up all of the world's stock of eligible financial assets, without first triggering inflation, if not hyperinflation.

pointed out that, "in the true sense of Walter Bagehot's prescriptions, *all* the Fed banks' gold was excess." Meltzer (2003, p. 276) makes a similar point and also observes that the Fed was well aware of the techniques used by the Bank of England during the nineteenth century to protect its gold holdings during panics.[30] And it's hard to argue with Timberlake's maxim (p. 273) that "a proper central bank does not fail because it loses all its gold in a banking crisis. It only fails if it does not." It is difficult to imagine a more shocking indictment of U.S. monetary policy than the fact that on the day FDR took the United States off the gold standard it still held over 37 percent of the world's monetary gold stock.

But even if it can be shown that the Fed should have done more, the ultimate success or failure of an even more expansionary policy during 1932 would have hinged on the extent to which the expansionary impact of this policy would have been offset by central-bank gold hoarding, private gold hoarding, and currency hoarding. If, as seems likely, the gold bloc had essentially completed its replacement of paper assets with gold reserves by mid-1932, then the ability of the Fed to have further increased the U.S. monetary base would have depended upon the response of private gold hoarders. Although this response would be difficult to predict, there is no evidence that private hoarding ever reached large enough levels to exhaust U.S. monetary gold stocks. But even if the Fed successfully increased the monetary base, there is also the possibility that such a policy would have driven nominal interest rates close to zero, triggering the sort of massive increase in the demand for currency and bank reserves that occurred in the late 1930s, or more recently in Japan and the United States.[31]

Keynes viewed a liquidity trap as a situation in which further increases in the money supply would have no impact on aggregate demand, or prices. We have no real evidence that such a trap existed in 1932.[32] Instead, the problem

30. Meltzer (p. 276) points out that the Bank of England "had suspended the gold reserve requirement and relaxed restrictions on eligible paper for discount" during panics.

31. The U.S. situation after October 2008 was complicated by the Fed's decision to pay interest on reserves at a rate above T-bill yields, which may have inflated commercial bank demand for reserves.

32. Hanes (2006) showed that even when U.S. short-term interest rates had fallen close to zero during the mid-1930s, changes in reserve supply continued to impact longer-term interest rates.

was that the gold standard limited the amount by which central banks could increase the monetary base. More recently, a number of economists[33] have argued that monetary injections that are viewed as being *temporary* might fail to boost aggregate demand, even under a fiat money regime. This sort of "expectations trap" is even more likely to form under an international gold standard regime, where monetary injections can lead to gold outflows. The public may have understood this and thus been skeptical of any proposal to inflate within the confines of a gold standard regime.[34] (See Appendix 4.b for a fascinating example of how interwar policymakers also intuited the importance of this distinction.)

Friedman and Schwartz's central hypothesis is that the Federal Reserve should have, and could have, done much more to prevent the Great Contraction. Although the gold market model developed in this book is not capable of refuting this hypothesis, it does suggest that they may have placed too much emphasis on specific policy steps that might have been more effective under a fiat money regime, including the discount rate increases of October 1931, the OMPs of 1932, and the reserve requirement increases of 1936–1937. And more importantly, they placed too little emphasis on events that changed expectations of the future path of monetary policy, such as private and central bank gold hoarding, Glass-Steagall, and especially changes in the price of gold during 1933–1934.

A recent study from Hsieh and Romer (2006) supports Friedman and Schwartz's view that the Fed policy was not constrained by gold outflows during 1932. They argue that the 1932 OMPs did not lead to fears that the dollar would be devalued and thus did not cause a run on the dollar. Although I find this conclusion to be plausible, I don't think the evidence they produce is quite strong enough to refute the alternative view of Temin, Eichengreen, and Bernanke (which is that the gold standard constrained policymakers during 1932). And later I will suggest that both sides of the debate are asking the wrong question.

---

33. See Sumner (1993b); Krugman (1998); and Eggertsson and Woodford (2003).

34. As noted in Chapter 6, "The NIRA and the Hidden Depression," one type of emergency currency injection during 1932 was explicitly ruled by the Attorney General to have a three-year limit.

The most important piece of evidence cited by Hsieh and Romer is that changes in the three-month forward discount on the dollar did not closely track changes in the open market purchase program. The forward discount against the French franc rose sharply after Britain left the gold standard but then quickly fell back after the Fed's discount rate increases temporarily restored faith in the dollar. During the first half of 1932 the forward discount on the dollar zigzagged up and down, while generally remaining well above its pre–September 1931 levels and, more importantly, well above its levels during the last half of 1932.

Hsieh and Romer (p. 153) focused on the fact that the forward discount fell sharply "following the passage of the Glass-Steagall Act and the first rounds of open market purchases in late February." Another way of looking at these same data would focus on the fact that the dollar's forward discount rose after the *announcement* of Glass-Steagall in early February (which was clearly when the news hit the stock market) and then fell back in late February and March when markets were reassured by the modest size of the early open market purchases. Then the forward discount began rising in April and eventually peaked in early June.

Hsieh and Romer are on firmer ground when they observe that the forward discount on the dollar fell briefly after the OMPs accelerated in mid-April and then again in mid-June before the end of the program had been announced. Even here one must be careful, however, as it is quite plausible that the market had some ability to anticipate these developments. While Hsieh and Romer rejected the hypothesis that OMPs had led to a run on the dollar, they gave some credence the contemporaneous press reports that agitation in Congress for deficit spending and especially the Goldsborough bill had contributed to the gold outflow.

It is probably true that fluctuations in both the forward discount on the dollar and the stock market correlate more closely to congressional turmoil than to OMPs. But recall that the Goldsborough bill would have required the Fed to reflate the economy, presumably the sort of policy that modern day critics think the Fed should have adopted. It must give some pause to those critics that even a slight possibility that such a bill might pass apparently contributed to a speculative attack on the dollar.

The biggest problem with Hsieh and Romer's analysis is their conclusion (p. 172) that during the OMPs "virtually no sign of expectations of devaluation" surfaced. I would argue exactly the opposite. There were four major runs on the dollar during the Depression, the fall of 1931, the spring of 1932, the winter of 1933, and the fall of 1937. In all four cases the press was full of rumors of the dollar being under stress. In each case there was a large increase in private gold hoarding (which did not occur prior to mid-1931). Yes, the forward discounts on the dollar were never very large in any of these crises, but that simply reflects that fact that traders never viewed dollar devaluation as a particularly likely outcome, especially within the next three months.[35] Forward discounts were even low during early 1933, when almost everyone agrees there was a run on the dollar (and the imminent inauguration of FDR made a near term devaluation somewhat more likely than in mid-1932). And recall that with very low nominal interest rates even a small probability of devaluation could trigger hoarding.

The bigger question is, what does this all mean for the policy counterfactuals that are of such interest to economic historians? Bordo, Choudhri, and Schwartz (2002) run some policy simulations that suggest that the U.S. economy was large enough that the Fed had sufficient leeway to take major expansionary steps at key dates during the early 1930s. They specifically criticize Eichengreen for linking gold reserves with U.S. monetary aggregates such as M1 (i.e., implicitly ignoring the money multiplier).[36] While this is a valid point, taken at face value, it also seems to suggest that the monetary base is the relevant monetary policy tool. Of course the base rose substantially in 1932, with little discernible effect on the economy, and fell after March 1933, even as production soared.

---

35. Hsieh and Romer also fail to find much evidence for devaluation fears in long-term bond yield differentials. But given the uncertain political situation in Europe, one must be careful in making any assumptions about the relative risk of these assets. The United States did devalue before France, but the French monetary situation eventually became even more unstable.

36. Gold reserves were used to back the monetary base. Because M1 is several times larger than the base, policy counterfactuals that assume M1 is backed by gold would imply an implausibly large need for gold reserves. Bordo (1994) first raised this issue.

Bordo, Choudhri, and Schwartz might reasonably argue that the broader monetary aggregates, not the base, are the appropriate policy *indicators*, and that these aggregates fell in 1932. Of course, this reflected the extreme instability of the money multiplier during the early 1930s. If one is to have any confidence in the Bordo, Choudhri, and Schwartz simulations, however, one has to assume that more expansionary policies would not have led to substantially more private hoarding of either cash or gold. But like Hsieh and Romer, they overlook evidence of massive private gold hoarding during 1932 (and 1931) and thus, end up doubting whether there really was a run on the dollar.

Bordo, Choudhri, and Schwartz also implicitly assumed that their policy counterfactuals would not have affected the money multiplier (i.e., would not have led to more cash hoarding). Maybe so, but one doesn't have to believe in absolute liquidity preference to note that during the early 1930s, runs on the dollar were often associated with banking panics and currency hoarding. I don't think we can simply assume that base money injections would have led to proportionate increases in the monetary aggregates. And finally, in their conclusion, Bordo, Choudhri, and Schwartz argue that adherence to the gold standard was a bar to recovery only in smaller nations. Although I think this is a defensible argument, in the next chapter we will see that an explosive increase in output occurred right after the United States abandoned the gold standard, even without much change in the money supply.

As with the Hsieh and Romer study, I find the Bordo, Choudhri, and Schwartz policy conclusions to be plausible. Well-timed monetary injections by the Fed might have been helpful in 1931 and 1932; given its massive gold holdings, it was certainly worth a try. But all of these policy counterfactuals may be asking the wrong question. If we assume interwar policymakers to have been well-intentioned proponents of fiscal and monetary stabilization, then surely they would have found a way to prevent the Depression. They probably could have done so without America being forced to devalue, but if not, they would have moved toward a fiat money regime.[37] But the more interesting

---

37. Meltzer (2003) noted that gold standard rules allowed gold reserve regulations to be adjusted in an emergency. And 1929–1932 would certainly seem to qualify as an emergency.

questions are: Were the actual OMPs of 1932 helpful? Did they account for the delayed economic bounce in the late summer? And what explains the severe economic downturn during the spring of 1932? Here I think the supporters of Friedman and Schwartz are on much shakier ground.

It is difficult to know what to make of the market reaction to the spring 1932 OMPs. There were some significant increases in stock prices in response to news of the OMPs, especially the announcement of Glass-Steagall. And yet, the stock and commodity markets' performances were abysmal during the period of rapid purchases, and then prices soared right after the policy was abandoned. Admittedly, a strict application of the efficient market view would favor the former evidence (that the OMPs helped). But it would be difficult to claim that the markets thought the OMPs would have a significant impact on the course of the Depression. And even if they had less direct impact on the gold outflows than did congressional agitation for expansionary policies, they might well have been a contributing factor to European fears that America would adopt inflationary policies. Brown saw these events firsthand and argued that

> The uninterrupted large scale purchases of government securities by the Federal Reserve's banks seemed in the eyes of foreigners to be evidence of approaching inflation in the United States. The gold outflow to the continental creditor countries was consequently sharply accelerated as this policy was vigorously pressed forward. (1940, p. 1233)

When the economic recovery began in late summer, it was accompanied by a sharp slowdown in OMPs. The recovery might conceivably have been a delayed response to the spring OMPs (although, in 1933, the economy responded *immediately* to an expansionary monetary policy) but policy lags can hardly account for the sharp fall in commodity and equity prices during the spring, and the equally powerful rally that began in late July. More importantly, the financial markets rallied at almost the exact moment that the private gold hoarding subsided and the dollar crisis ended. With regard to the issue of causality, Appendix 4.a provides strong evidence that private gold hoarding was far less correlated with the stock market during periods where there were no fears of dollar devaluation, and thus, causality almost

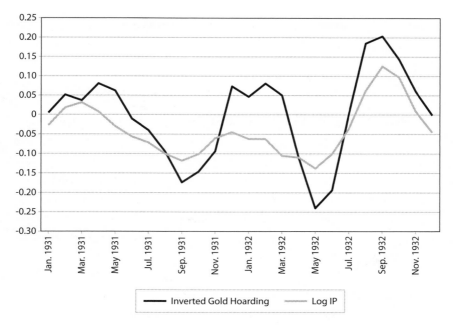

Figure 4.2. Private Gold Hoarding and Industrial Production,
3-Month Rates of Change

certainly ran from gold to stocks.[38] Private gold hoarding led to bearish policy expectations, which led to falling stock prices. When dishoarding began, stocks soared. It was exactly the same pattern that occurred in the fall of 1931, and it would happen again in 1937 and 1938.

In Figure 1.1 we saw that stock prices and industrial production were closely correlated throughout the Great Depression, and 1931–1932 was no different. As we can see from Figure 4.2, this meant that gold hoarding was not just associated with falling stock prices, but also falling output. (The private gold hoarding series is inverted, so that you are seeing its mirror image—the impact on central bank gold stocks.) And in this case, it is difficult to argue reverse causation, as the severe contraction of 1929–1930 (which was not accompanied by devaluation fears) did not cause private gold hoarding. So, devaluation fears led to private gold hoarding, which intensified the Depression not once, but

---

38. See Table 4.2.

twice, during 1931–1932. In Chapter 12 we will see another example of how devaluation fears and gold hoarding led to a severe recession in late 1937.

What about Real Interest Rates?

Thus far I have described the entire Great Contraction without any reference to interest rates playing a *causal* role. Temin (1976) suggested that because interest rates were declining during 1930, it is unlikely that the concurrent decline in output was caused by a tight monetary policy. He also argued that the deflation of 1930 was largely unanticipated, and hence, even *ex ante* real interest rates were probably declining during this period. I find Temin's assumption about low real interest rates to be plausible, but not his conclusions about the importance of monetary policy.

In August and September 1929 the United States and Britain raised interest rates to their cyclical peak just as the economy was about to contract, and then lowered rates throughout late 1929 and 1930. This pattern occurs frequently during U.S. business cycles. If it is evidence against money playing a causal role in the 1930 downturn, it is equally so for monetary policy playing *any* important cyclical role in the U.S. economy. The problem with Temin's argument is that interest rates (real or nominal) are simply not a very good indicator of the stance of monetary policy. During the Great Contraction it was central bank gold hoarding that best illustrated the contractionary stance of monetary policy.

In contrast to Temin, Cecchetti (1992) argued that investors were able to partially forecast deflation over three- to six-month horizons, and in a similar vein, Nelson (1991, p. 2) suggested that "while commodity prices fell very rapidly during 1929–1930, cost-of-living indices fell much more slowly. Commentators expected the cost of living to follow commodity prices downward." Once again, I accept the evidence but question the implication that real interest rates were high.

Barsky (1987) found little or no evidence that price level changes were forecastable under the classical gold standard, and in an earlier paper (1999) I argued that most economists began paying attention to the Fisher effect only after the world moved to the post–World War II fiat money regimes, when the *trend* rate of inflation moved from the near-zero levels of the classical gold standard to the positive and significant levels of the 1960s and 1970s. We need to be especially careful when looking at real interest rate movements over business cycle frequencies, where many prices are in disequilibrium. For instance, entrepreneurs considering investment projects are presumably interested in some sort of price level estimate showing expected market conditions for products that they plan to sell when their projects are completed. But when there is a sudden decrease in aggregate demand, the measured price level may not provide an accurate reading of those market conditions. As an example, measured rents are quite sticky, even during periods when housing prices are falling fast and new apartment buildings stand empty.

Consider the following example: aggregate demand falls unexpectedly by 10 percent. In the short run output falls 5 percent and the (somewhat sticky) price level also falls by 5 percent. Market sensitive commodity and asset prices immediately fall by roughly 10 percent. Investors (correctly) forecast an additional 5 percent fall in the general price level, as sticky prices gradually fall to their long run equilibrium. Assuming no further decrease in aggregate demand, output returns to its natural rate once these prices fully adjust. I would submit that the additional 5 percent by which the measured price level is expected to decline (as the economy moves from disequilibrium to equilibrium) is not a meaningful indicator of the expected change in *market conditions* facing sellers when the quantity of sales is restricted by a sticky price level.

In my scenario the (unexpected) fall in flexible asset prices may provide a better indicator of movements in the price level. Since commodity and asset price movements are generally regarded as being unanticipated, this might at first glance seem to deny any possibility of a Fisher effect under any scenario, i.e., higher inflation leading to higher nominal interest rates. But this is not the case; in the United States during the 1960s and 1970s, persistent inflation was so built into expectations that, even in auction-style markets, the trend rate at which prices changed was partly forcastable.

The preceding thought experiment finds some support in the research of Hamilton (1992), who found evidence from the commodity futures markets that the deflation of 1930 was unanticipated and, hence, that real interest rates were falling. In addition to finding that commodity prices were essentially unforecastable during the Great Depression, Hamilton also estimated that

> [K]nowledge of the actual course of commodity prices would have reduced the forecast variance for the CPI by 70% . . . and we would seem to have a solid basis for inferring that much of the overall deflation during 1929–1933 was unanticipated. (1987, p. 167)

Hamilton's conclusion seems to (at least implicitly) support the view that predictable changes in sticky prices (the CPI) are not economically meaningful for investors and should not be incorporated into estimates of real interest rates. Rather, what matters is the expected change in the equilibrium price level (as proxied by commodity prices).

Temin's (1976) view of real interest rates was consistent with the earlier Keynesian tradition, which viewed monetary policy as being less important than expenditure instability. The more recent new Keynesian view is that monetary policy is generally quite potent, and that real interest rates are the appropriate policy indicator. Papers in the new Keynesian tradition by Romer (1992) and Eggertsson (2006) have argued that *ex ante* real interest rates were quite high during the early 1930s, in the 10 percent to 20 percent range. I have already raised one objection to this view, and Bernanke and James (1991, p. 49) provide an even more persuasive reason to doubt that real interest rates were high during the early 1930s. They pointed out that those countries that left the gold standard early (such as Britain) were able to arrest the decline in prices but continued to offer the same sort of low nominal yields on safe assets as did countries remaining on the gold standard, such as the United States and France.

Given that the gold market approach to the Great Contraction is essentially monetary (broadly defined), the reader may wonder why I have not embraced the high real interest rate hypothesis, which provides a perfectly suitable transmission mechanism between gold hoarding and declining expenditure. In fact, I don't have any problem with either view of real interest rates during the Depression, as nothing in my gold market analysis hinges on this issue. This is one of those rare cases in economics where either of the opposing views can provide quite plausible monetary transmission mechanisms. If the deflation was anticipated, then high real interest rates depressed investment. If the deflation was unanticipated, then the sticky wage transmission channel provides a plausible link between gold, falling prices, and falling output. Instead, I would emphasize that gold hoarding will depress nominal spending and prices, regardless of what happens to real interest rates. There is *no gain from adding interest rates* to the story.

Summary

Given the unprecedented severity of the Depression, it seems implausible that any monocausal explanation is adequate. Even if the Great Contraction of 1929–1932 was essentially a monetary phenomenon, the preceding account suggests that it was monetary in the broad sense of a breakdown in the international monetary system (as emphasized by Temin and Eichengreen), rather than simply a result of inept Fed policy (the focus of Friedman and Schwartz).

But the gold market approach goes beyond previous accounts that emphasized the role of the gold standard by focusing on how shifts in the demand for gold impacted expectations of the future path of monetary policy, and not merely the fact that adherence to the gold standard constrained monetary policymakers. The large increases in the world gold reserve ratio during 1929–1930, and 1931–1932 did not reflect monetary policy being constrained by the gold standard. On the contrary, adherence to the rules of the game would have required far more expansionary monetary policies during these episodes. And although private gold hoarding cannot, by itself, explain the massive deflation of the early 1930s, the timing of these hoarding episodes played an important role in the latter stages of the Great Contraction, and (as we will see in Chapter 12) even more so in the depression of 1937–1938.

Although investors were focused on international monetary issues during 1931 and 1932, financial market responses need to be interpreted in the context of the contemporary institutional setting. Market responses to policy shocks merely show that the markets believed that the Fed was likely to act *as if it felt constrained* by potential gold outflows. The issue wasn't so much whether the quantity of "free gold" was actually a technical constraint on policy, but rather whether the markets thought the Fed viewed it as a constraint. As Eichengreen (1992, p. 316) observed: "Correctly anticipating that the Fed would draw back, producers and investors kept to the sidelines" (during the 1932 OMPs).

This does not mean that the Fed could not have safely adopted a somewhat more expansionary policy (as Friedman and Schwartz argued), and it does not necessarily even imply that the markets agreed with the Fed's cautious stance. But it does suggest that in the policy environment of 1932, gold hoarding reduced expectations of future monetary growth. And recent research suggests that what matters is not so much the current stance of monetary policy, but rather its expected future path.[39]

Perhaps the strongest support for the gold market approach comes from the period immediately following the British devaluation. The markets crashed on the onset of the dollar crisis in late September and the first few days of October as gold hoarding increased dramatically but remained strangely passive in the face of sharp increases in the discount rate during mid-October. Friedman and Schwartz might argue that the markets already knew that the gold outflow would require discount rate increases, but that sort of deterministic interpretation would be hard to reconcile with their often dramatic account of Fed policy, which emphasized the vast consequences resulting from the death of a single individual.[40]

During 1932, the monetary situation in the United States is especially difficult to decipher. We know that the markets welcomed Glass-Steagall, but this is consistent with the interpretations of Temin as well as Friedman and Schwartz. It also seems likely that markets were concerned that some of the more radical congressional proposals could lead to an outflow of gold, but there is a frustrating paucity of evidence on the impact of the much-debated spring 1932 open market purchase program. Although there were a few instances where the OMPs appeared to boost stock prices, the overall performance of the markets during this period suggests that the program was perceived as being largely ineffective.

The analysis becomes even more complex when we consider hypothetical alternatives. Given the fact that several switches in Fed policy were at least partly motivated by worries that Congress would adopt more radical mon-

---

39. See Sargent (1983) and Eggertsson and Woodford (2003).

40. New York Federal Reserve Bank President Benjamin Strong died in 1928. Less well known is the fact that Irving Fisher and R.G. Hawtrey shared Friedman and Schwartz's views regarding the significance of Strong's death.

etary proposals, it is unlikely that we will ever be able to know the precise extent to which a dollar crisis would have occurred with the congressional budget fight and without the OMPs or vice versa. But there is also a sense that it doesn't quite matter whether it was fiscal or monetary policy that caused this crisis. In either case the net effect of the crisis was to weaken the impact of countercyclical policy.

It should also be noted that the Temin/Eichengreen critique of Friedman and Schwartz doesn't really provide any comfort for (traditional) Keynesians. Keynes once warned that an expansionary *fiscal* policy aimed at boosting the economy might need to be curtailed if it led to a loss of confidence in the pound.[41] Ironically, Keynes later became famous for advocating fiscal policy precisely because monetary policy might be ineffective in a depressed economy. But the example of monetary ineffectiveness provided in his *General Theory* was a situation where, if monetary policy was ineffective, it was not for liquidity trap reasons but rather because it had led to a loss of confidence in the dollar. This sort of confidence trap is equally applicable to fiscal policy—indeed, perhaps more so—to judge by the market response to radical fiscal proposals during 1932. In Chapter 11 we will see how confusion over the constraints of the gold standard indirectly shaped Keynes' views of monetary policy ineffectiveness and subtly influenced his entire approach to macroeconomics.

The gold market approach emphasizes the international dimension of monetary policy under a gold standard. On one level, this study is certainly supportive of those (such as Johnson and, more recently, Douglas Irwin (2012)) who criticized the French policy of hoarding gold. Eichengreen suggested that the Bank of France's hands were tied by the French Stabilization Law of 1928, but there are two weaknesses with this argument. First, at this late date, surely what matters is not whether the Bank of France was to blame for hoarding gold, but instead, whether *France* was at fault. And second, Eichengreen's own account undercuts any attempt to exonerate the Bank of France:

January 1930 was the one occasion on which Emile Moreau, Governor of the Bank of France, proposed that the central bank buy or sell *Bons*

41. See Keynes (1982 [1933]), vol. 9, pp. 353–54.

de Caisse. Not only were the 2.5 billion francs of open market sales he proposed a mere 1.7 percent of the money supply, but they worked in the wrong direction. (1992, p. 197)

Moure (2002, p. 262) accepts Johnson's arguments that French gold accumulation contributed to the deflationary environment of the early 1930s, but then argues that "it is not French experience, but the broader systemic problems that French experience highlights, which are more worthy of note." Moure (p. 183) also cites a recent study by Bernanke and Mihov[42] that suggests France didn't so much violate the rules of the game as play a fundamentally flawed version of that game (which involved a gradual move from a gold exchange standard to a traditional gold standard).

It is possible to agree with Moure and still view France as having grossly departed from one common definition of the rules—a stable gold reserve ratio. This suggests that the whole "blame" issue is mostly a question of semantics. Are we accusing countries of violating well-agreed-upon ground rules (like a player cheating in a sports competition) or are we accusing countries of adopting ill-advised policies that hurt others and themselves? France is innocent of the first charge and guilty of the second. And to a greater or lesser extent the same judgment could be made with respect to all of the other major central banks.

Of course the gold market approach to the Great Contraction is equally supportive of the French criticism of the U.S. banking system, or the view that Britain made a serious mistake by not setting the pound at a more realistic level after World War I. The basic problem with assigning blame among countries is that there was no consensus as to what the rules of the game actually were. In a sense, the interwar gold standard was both too flexible and not flexible enough. A rigid adherence to a fixed gold reserve ratio would have greatly reduced central bank hoarding during the early 1930s. Alternatively, a much more flexible regime which completely disregarded the gold reserve ratio would have allowed central banks to more easily cooperate to economize on the demand for monetary gold during a deflationary crisis. Instead,

---

42. See Bernanke and Mihov (2000, pp. 148–50).

there was enough flexibility to do a lot of damage, but not enough to easily repair that damage.[43]

Friedman and Schwartz are probably correct that much more could have been done, even within the constraints of the gold standard regime. But policymakers had no simple roadmap for stabilizing the economy in a world where financial markets were very sensitive to any suggestion of policies that might put the dollar under a cloud of suspicion. And it's also important to recognize that some of the worst crises of the Depression occurred precisely because markets feared policies that would be expansionary enough to provoke a run on the dollar, but not expansionary enough to assure recovery.

Of course, both Keynes and Friedman opposed rigidly fixed exchange rates. When viewed from their perspective, it is difficult to avoid being contemptuous of the budget balancers and tight money advocates of the early 1930s. But the policymakers of that era (particularly in America) were living in a world where devaluation seemed almost inconceivable. The entrenchment of the gold standard regime in America helps explain why the financial markets placed such high hopes on the possibility of international monetary cooperation, despite the ultimate ineffectiveness of those initiatives. They saw it as the only game in town.

Postscript

The research for this book was completed well before the recent global crisis, which is the worst since the Depression. Given the similarities I am about to discuss, it is ironic that during 2008 the Fed was led by one of the leading scholars of the Great Depression, Ben Bernanke. Although my views on the Depression are quite close to Bernanke's in many respects, I believe that the Fed repeated many of the same mistakes made in the 1930s. (It is difficult to know exactly how Bernanke himself felt about these comparisons—at times he lobbied within the Fed for a more aggressive approach.)

---

43. George Selgin (2012) has an excellent survey of the gold standard in U.S. history, which distinguishes between problems that occurred under the gold standard, and those directly caused by the gold standard.

One of the most important lessons of Friedman and Schwartz's *Monetary History* is that neither interest rates nor the monetary base are reliable indicators of the stance of monetary policy. They did advocate use of the broader monetary aggregates, but after the early 1980s most of the profession rejected those indicators. Even our best-selling money textbooks emphasize the unreliability of interest rates as monetary policy indicators:

> It is dangerous always to associate the easing or the tightening of monetary policy with a fall or a rise in short-term nominal interest rates. (Mishkin, 2007, p. 606)

Unfortunately, despite the well-known problems associated with using nominal interest rates as indicators of the stance of monetary policy, most economists seem to have assumed that Fed policy during the current crisis was "easy," mostly on the basis of the low nominal rates. Even worse, unlike during the 1930s, we do know what happened to *ex ante* real rates on government bonds. Real rates on five-year indexed bonds soared from about 0.5 percent to 4.2 percent between July and November 2008, just when the recession intensified dramatically. Not so long ago, economists liked to make fun of statements such as Joan Robinson's claim that easy money couldn't have caused the German hyperinflation as (she argued) nominal interest rates weren't low. Yet, by late 2008 most of the economics profession seems to have made exactly the opposite error, assuming tight money couldn't have caused the sharp downturn in late 2008 because nominal rates were low.[44]

Even worse, in 2008 the Fed did not have the gold standard excuse to fall back on; they had virtually unlimited ability to ease monetary policy under a fiat money regime. Again, quoting from the best-selling money text:

> Policy can be highly effective in reviving a weak economy even if short-term interest rates are already near zero. (Mishkin, 2007, p. 607)

New Keynesian economists, including Ben Bernanke himself, had devised numerous "foolproof" strategies for implementing expansionary monetary policy once rates hit zero. And yet, the Fed did not adopt a single one of these

---

44. Hetzel (2009) was a notable exception.

strategies, not even replacing inflation targeting with price level targeting, a policy Bernanke had recommended the Japanese adopt in the late 1990s. In late 2008, the Fed did engage in "quantitative easing." However, the Fed sterilized the injections of new base money by paying banks interest on excess reserves. Later, we will see parallels between the Fed's recent interest on reserves policy and the infamous decision to double reserve requirements in 1936–1937.

At the time, few people understood that the Great Contraction was caused by a severe monetary shock. Instead, it was much easier to blame the Depression on the much more visible *symptoms* of sharply falling nominal spending, including the stock market crash, the banking crises and the exchange rate crises. This time around, economists fell into the same trap, although in this case their confusion was a bit more understandable. This time, there really was an exogenous financial shock (in 2007), a shock that was not caused by economic weakness. The subsequent fall in nominal spending did further weaken the banking system, but it wasn't the only problem.

Unfortunately, most economists seemed to miss the monetary nature of the second and more severe phase of the recent crisis, which began in mid-2008. Nominal GDP fell nearly 4 percent over the following twelve months, to a level more than 9 percent below trend. As in the 1930s, this fall in nominal GDP dramatically worsened bank balance sheets. With a more expansionary monetary policy that kept expected nominal GDP growth up around its 5 percent long-term average, banks would have done much better, and the recession would not have spread beyond construction to sectors such as manufacturing and services.

In retrospect, we now understand that falling nominal GDP was the root cause of the financial distress of the 1930s. We await a future Friedman and Schwartz to deconstruct the current crisis, and discover just how much was caused by the original sub-prime mortgage crisis, and how much was attributable to the Fed allowing nominal GDP growth expectations to plummet in late 2008. That policy error dramatically worsened the financial crisis, which in late 2008 spread to higher quality mortgages and commercial real estate loans.[45]

---

45. Hetzel (2012) has made an excellent start.

Perhaps the most important lesson of the Great Contraction is that it is possible for most pundits and policymakers to be almost completely in the dark about the causes of a crisis. To those closest to the problem, a severe fall in aggregate demand, or nominal GDP, *almost never looks like it was caused by monetary policy*. It is likely to be accompanied by very low nominal rates, and a bloated monetary base (as people and banks hoard currency). That looks like "easy money" to the untrained eye.

Instead, people are powerfully drawn to explanations that put the symptoms of falling nominal GDP, such as banking turmoil, front and center as the cause of the recession. This didn't just happen in the early 1930s, but in the late 1990s in Japan, and again in late 2008 in the United States. While this confusion is certainly understandable, it was nonetheless distressing to see history repeating itself as I concluded this study.

In the late 1990s, Milton Friedman also complained that modern economists had not really absorbed the lessons of the Great Depression:

> Low interest rates are generally a sign that money has been tight, as in Japan; high interest rates, that money has been easy. . . . After the U.S. experience during the Great Depression, and after inflation and rising interest rates in the 1970s and disinflation and falling interest rates in the 1980s, I thought the fallacy of identifying tight money with high interest rates and easy money with low interest rates was dead. Apparently, old fallacies never die. (Friedman, 1998.)

We need to always look beneath the surface, and keep in mind that no matter how severe a financial crisis is, under a fiat money regime the central bank has virtually unlimited ability to prop up nominal spending, even at zero rates. If they do so, the financial crisis will be much milder. In the next chapter, we will see how between March and July 1933 Roosevelt used monetary policy to boost aggregate demand at perhaps the fastest rate in American history, despite near-zero interest rates and despite a banking crisis much more severe than that faced by the Fed in 2008. It can be done, but it requires the courage to use unconventional monetary policy tools. In late 2008, the Fed wasn't willing to take the risk of using a radically different policy, such as level targeting. But in early 1933 the economy was in far worse shape than today, and FDR was willing to try almost anything.

Table 4.2. The Relationship between Variations in the Cowles Index of Stock Prices, the World Monetary Gold Stock, and the Deposits of Failed U.S. Banks, January 1927 to April 1933, Selected Periods, Monthly

	Dependent Variable—Stock Prices				
	Sample Periods				
	(1)	(2)	(3)	(4)	(5)
Coefficients on Independent Variables	1/27–4/33	1/27–6/31	6/31–4/33	1/27–6/31	
Gold Stocks	5.921	1.338	7.772	2.005	7.711
	(3.25)	(0.55)	(2.51)	(0.82)	(2.57)
Deposit Losses				−.0165	−.0284
				(−1.58)	(−1.52)
Adj R2	.115	.000	.201	.015	.250
Durbin-Watson	1.56	1.26	1.81	1.35	1.68

Notes: T-statistics are in parentheses. The regressions included a constant term (not shown).

Appendix 4.a

In Chapter 3, we saw that changes in the world monetary gold stock were positively correlated with changes in industrial production. But if production responds with a lag to monetary policy, then the contemporaneous correlations may prove misleading. Stock prices should respond immediately to policy shocks. If stocks responded positively to expectations of future economic growth (and during the 1930s it seems clear they did) and if private gold hoarding did reduce aggregate demand, then there should be a positive correlation between U.S. stock prices and the world monetary gold stock during periods when the United States was operating under a gold standard regime. The Cowles Index provides a nearly comprehensive monthly U.S. stock market index starting in 1871. In Table 4.2, the first difference of the log of real stock prices (Stock Prices)[46] is regressed on the first difference of the log of the world monetary gold stock (Gold Stock) and the log of deposits of failed U.S. banks.

46. Real stock prices were generated by deflating the Cowles Index by the National Industrial Conference Board's Cost of Living Index.

The regression for the entire period shows a positive correlation, but the Durbin-Watson statistic indicates some serial correlation in the residuals. Even if there was a significant correlation, one could argue that it would not prove that causality ran from gold hoarding to stock prices. Perhaps stock market declines led investors to hoard gold. This hypothesis can be tested by splitting the sample in two. The period from 1927 to June 1931 was devoid of devaluation crises, and the relatively minor fluctuations in the growth rate of gold stocks may have partially reflected endogenous responses to changes in the world price level. Although the coefficient on monthly changes in the gold stock was positive in regression 2, the adjusted $R2$ was zero and hence there was no significant correlation between real stock prices and the world monetary gold stock. Major stock market crashes in late 1929 and mid-1930 did not trigger substantial gold hoarding. This regression also shows evidence of serial correlation, which means that the already quite low t statistic is still overstated.

I have argued that between June 1931 and April 1933 changes in the world monetary gold stock were dominated by fluctuations in private hoarding associated with devaluation fears. After June 1931, the world monetary gold stock became much more volatile, falling during the first, second, and third runs on the dollar. Regression 3 shows that during this period, changes in real stock prices became strongly correlated with changes in the world monetary gold stock. Furthermore, this regression shows no evidence of serial correlation. This pattern supports the analysis in Appendix 13.a—that is, that a positive correlation between gold stocks and aggregate demand would be expected when changes in the world monetary gold stock are exogenous. It appears that after June 1931, devaluation fears caused hoarding, and hoarding reduced stock prices (and presumably aggregate demand as well). Regressions 4 and 5 repeat regressions 2 and 3, but with bank failures included as an explanatory variable. The qualitative results are similar to regressions 2 and 3.

Appendix 4.b

After this manuscript was completed I came across an outstanding analysis of the Great Depression by Robert Hetzel (2012), which anticipates some of the ideas discussed here. Hetzel provides excerpts from a congressional hearing that are too good not to quote. New York Fed President Harrison explains why the limits imposed by the gold standard made it more difficult for the Fed to reflate the economy to pre-Depression levels, while acknowledging that the Fed might have been a bit more aggressive. Representative Goldsborough argues for a bill requiring the Fed to do whatever it takes to reflate to pre-Depression levels. He also anticipates Paul Krugman's distinction between temporary and permanent currency injections, with only the latter being able to boost prices. We've seen echoes of this debate play out in 2012, this time involving Paul Krugman and Ben Bernanke.

> HARRISON: [T]hat pressure [excess reserves] does not work and will not work in a period where you have bank failures, where you have panicky depositors, where you have a threat of huge foreign withdrawals, and where you have other disconcerting factors such as you have now in various sorts of legislative proposals which, however wise, the bankers feel may not be wise. You then have, in spite of the excess reserve, a resistance to its use which the reserve system can not overcome.

> GOLDSBOROUGH: [I]n anything like normal times, specific directions to the Federal reserve system to use its power to maintain a given price level will tend to decrease very greatly these periods, or stop these periods of expansion and these periods of deflation which so destroy confidence and produce the very mental condition that you are talking about. . . . I do not think in the condition the country is in now we can rely upon the *action* of the Federal reserve system without the announcement of a *policy*. A banker may look at his bulletin on Saturday or on Monday morning and see that the Federal Reserve system has during the previous week purchased $25,000,000 worth of Government securities. But that does not restore his confidence under present conditions because he does not know what the board is going to do next week. . . . If this legislation . . . were passed, the Federal Reserve Board could call in the newspaper reporters and say that Congress has given us legislative directions to raise the price level to a certain point, and to use all our powers to that purpose, and we want you to announce to banks and public men at large that we propose to go into the market with the enormous reserves we now have available under

the Glass-Steagall Act and buy $25,000,000 of Governments every day until the price approaches the level of that of 1926. . . . [I]f the bankers and business men knew that was going to be the policy of the Federal reserve system, . . . it would restore confidence immediately. . . . and the wheels of business would turn [italics supplied].

HARRISON: [W]e have bought since the crash in the stock market approximately $800,000,000 to $850,000,000 of additional government securities . . . [H]owever, when after all the huge withdrawals of currency for hoarding purposes . . . we had in the system a relatively small proportion of free gold . . . [W]hile I would have liked to proceed further and faster last year, I was adverse to doing so till we had the protection of the Glass Steagall bill. . . . Perhaps we could have gone a little faster without clogging the banks by giving them too much excess reserve. If you give them too much excess reserve when they lack confidence it is just like flooding the carburetor of an automobile.

[D]iscounts in the system have gone down. . . . [I]n our experience in the Federal Reserve [S]ystem such a reduction is discounts or borrowings from the [R]eserve banks operates as a real relaxation in the attitude of lending banks. . . . Let us suppose we should go . . .

GOLDSBOROUGH: [interrupting] No; not whether you had determined to go so many millions further, but that you had announced a policy after the passage of this bill that you were going to raise the price level to a certain point and you were going to buy till that was done. That is a very different proposition.

HARRISON: Yes, I think so. I think it is a much more difficult proposition because I do not think there is any one power or authority in the world that can say they are going to raise the price level. There are so many factors to be taken into consideration; unless you have control of all of them (even human psychology), you cannot be assure you can raise it. . . . I think to make a statement of that character [raise the price level] to the public and to the world would be one of the most unfortunate things the system could do, because primarily they would not be able to deliver all by themselves.

(Hetzel, 2012, pp. 42–43)

PART III

Bold and Persistent Experimentation
Macroeconomic Policy during 1933

5

A Foolproof Plan for Reflation

THE YEAR 1933 saw the two most dramatic macroeconomic policy experiments ever undertaken by the U.S. Government. From April 1933 to February 1934, the Roosevelt administration took control of monetary policy away from the Federal Reserve (Fed) and pursued an avowedly inflationary policy directly out of the White House. Then, on July 19, 1933, President Franklin D. Roosevelt (FDR) issued an executive order that sharply boosted nominal wage rates. These two experiments were completely unprecedented—there is nothing comparable in American history either before or since. Although both policies had a powerful impact on the economy, their effects partially offset each other. Because most researchers have looked at these policies in isolation, their impact has been greatly underestimated.

Owing to the importance and the complexity of the events of 1933, three chapters are devoted to this period. In this chapter I examine the events leading up to Roosevelt's decision to leave the gold standard, as well as the initial impact of his dollar depreciation program. Chapter 6 focuses on the causes and consequences of the dramatic wage shock that occurred in mid-1933. And in Chapter 7 the fascinating gold-buying program of late 1933 is examined. I make two provocative claims in these three chapters. First, that in the absence of other policy initiatives, the devaluation of the dollar might have essentially ended the Depression by late 1934. And second, that Roosevelt's policy of increasing wages may have extended the Depression by nearly seven years and thus caused roughly half of all man-years of unemployment during the period from 1929 to 1941. In this chapter we will focus on one of Roosevelt's most successful initiatives, his policy of depreciating the dollar.

Table 5.1. Selected Monthly Indicators, 1933

Month	Industrial Production	Wholesale Price Index (WPI)	Cost of Living (COL)	Exchange Rate	Dow
1/33	106	101	103	100	99
2/33	106	99	101	100	91
3/33	100	100	100	100	100
4/33	107	100	100	100	101
5/33	125	104	101	115	128
6/33	144	108	102	118	143
7/33	157	114	105	140	171

Note: The exchange rate is the dollar price of French francs. Both the exchange rate and Dow are mid-month figures. The real wage is deflated by the WPI. The cost of living data is from Beney (1936).

The analysis will begin to shift away from the topics that dominated the first three narrative chapters. On the aggregate demand side, changes in the dollar price of gold completely dominated all other factors. And for the first time, aggregate supply shocks will also play an important role in the narrative. To be sure, some of Hoover's policies did reduce aggregate supply. But these policies did not dramatically impact the trend in output, and most of them would not even have occurred in the absence of the large fall in aggregate demand.[1]

Table 5.1 illustrates just how dramatically the economy was affected by the change in presidential administrations during early March 1933. It is important to bear in mind that in early 1933, over 25 percent of the workforce was unemployed and U.S. output was about as far below potential as it has ever been.

Note that despite the depressed state of the economy, the United States saw rapid inflation, particularly at the wholesale level. Output grew extremely

---

1. Hoover pressured firms to avoid wage cuts after 1929. But if deflation had not occurred, then this policy would not have had much impact on the aggregate real wage rate. And the sharp rise in income tax rates in 1932 would not have occurred in the absence of the dramatic decline in GDP.

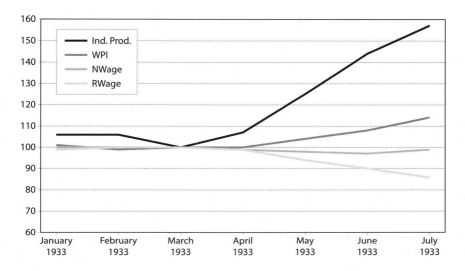

Figure 5.1. Industrial Production, the WPI, Real and Nominal Wages

rapidly. It is certainly easier to generate high rates of growth in a severely depressed economy, but even so, the 57 percent increase in industrial production between March and July is astounding. Roughly one-half of the ground lost during the previous four years was made up in a period of just four months.[2] And even if we assume that output was artificially depressed in March by the bank closures, we are still left with a July output peak that was nearly 50 percent above the levels of late 1932 and early 1933. In Chapter 6, we will see that this sort of rapid growth can be explained using one of the most sophisticated econometric models of the 1920s and 1930s.

We will consider three types of evidence for Roosevelt's dollar depreciation program causing the large increases in commodity and equity prices, as well as industrial production, during the first half of 1933. The next two sections show how the financial markets reacted to news pertaining to the dollar devaluation program. We will see that changes in the foreign exchange (or gold) value of the dollar during 1933 were a good indicator of monetary

---

2. Note that this does not mean that one-half of the output gap was closed; full employment output would have risen somewhat over the preceding four years.

policy during 1933—and more specifically, that policy statements can impact the exchange rate by altering *the expected future path of the money supply*. Then we will see that changes in the value of the dollar were highly correlated with changes in stock prices, commodity prices, and interest rate spreads. And finally, we will see that these correlations support the gold market approach to aggregate demand.

The Desperate Interregnum of 1932–1933

As during the previous occasion in which control of the presidency switched from one party to the other (1920–1921), the four-month interregnum in early 1933 was a period of intense economic distress. In 1932, output was already severely depressed, but financial conditions weakened even further as soon as it became apparent that Hoover was likely to lose, and they continued to deteriorate right up to the day of Roosevelt's inauguration. The underlying problem seems to have been uncertainty about Roosevelt's plans for the dollar.

As 1933 began, congressional proposals for "currency tinkering" brought a renewed attack on the dollar. The *New York Times* noted that

A European raid upon the dollar, reminiscent of last Spring, hit the foreign exchange market yesterday as news of Senator Borah's plan to introduce legislation to devalue the American monetary unit reached Paris and other foreign markets. (1/5/33, p. 29)

The Dow rose 5.2 percent on the news. With a new (and more proinflation) administration only two months away, equity markets now began to respond more positively to inflation proposals, even those that threatened to force the United States off the gold standard. Although the dollar would not come under severe pressure until late February, Roosevelt's refusal to accede to Hoover's call for a strong endorsement of the gold standard resulted in persistent inflation rumors throughout early 1933.

The conservative financial press was critical of Roosevelt's noncommittal attitude toward the gold standard and unfavorably contrasted FDR's vague promises of a "sound currency" with President-elect Cleveland's forthright endorsement of the gold standard during the pre-inauguration periods of 1885 and 1893. They also argued that this uncertainty was hurting the economy:

Yet it will not have been forgotten that, on numerous older similar occasions, doubt and mistrust prevailed with exceedingly bad effect on financial sentiment, until the President-elect took matters into his own hands and publicly avowed his purposes. . . . It is probable enough that the present spirit of hesitancy, not only on financial markets but in general trade, is more or less influenced by the lack of such reassurance. (*NYT*, 1/23/33, p. 19)

The next day, the *New York Times* reported that increasing calls for "inflation" had led to renewed pressure against the dollar.

On January 18, the *New York Times* (p. 27) noted that, "sentiment in Wall Street seems to be turning toward inflation in some form as a means of breaking the backbone of depression. The sponsors of this policy hope that inflation, rather than the allotment plan for agriculture, will be resorted to." Note that the term "inflation" refers not to higher prices, which could also be generated by crop limitations, but rather to monetary stimulus. The phrase "in some form" refers to policies such as open market purchases (OMPs), "printing money," and dollar devaluation. The conflict between proponents of output restrictions and monetary stimulus would become a central theme, perhaps *the* central theme, of Roosevelt's first term in office.

The attitude of the conservative financial press toward inflation during the interwar years might seem confusing to a modern day macroeconomist. At times they seemed to combine skepticism regarding the ability of inflation proposals to achieve any price increases, with a fear that the proposals would lead to hyperinflation. During the period prior to World War II, prices followed something close to a white noise process with zero trend. There was no concept of a steadily rising price level of the sort that we have experienced since the 1940s. For instance, referring to proposals to have the Fed issue more currency, the *New York Times* noted

[A]s against their assurance that currency thus issued will raise prices, the record shows that the currency supply has increased $965,000,000 since the end of 1929, yet that average prices have in the same period fallen 33 percent.

No one doubts that the outright issue of illimitable and irredeemable government fiat money would do more even than to restore the prices of 1929. Germany's experiment in that direction brought the average price level in the Autumn of 1923 . . . three million times as high as that of 1914. (1/30/33, p. 19)

And it wasn't just the *New York Times* that seemed oblivious to the possibility of an intermediate policy of modest inflation. In Chapter 11 we will see that the same blind spot appears in Keynes' writings from the mid-1930s.

The best way to make sense of prewar views of monetary policy is by ceasing to view different monetary proposals as representing mere quantitative differences in policy. Open market purchases within a gold standard regime, one-time devaluations, and expansionary fiat regimes were viewed as three *qualitatively* different proposals with vastly different implications for the price level. As the *New York Times* suggested, almost no one doubted the efficacy of fiat money regimes to promote inflation, the debate was over the desirability of such regimes. But, serious doubts arose as to the expansionary potential of monetary policies implemented in an environment where some linkage to gold was maintained.

During the winter of 1932–1933, conditions in the farm belt deteriorated rapidly and during mid-February, there was a sudden shift in the tenor of news reports on the economy. A February 13 *New York Times* headline (p. 1) cited "DANGER OF REVOLT" and "INFLATION DEMANDS GROW":

A few months ago there was in the minds of the people who wrote these letters [to Congressmen] only a sad bewilderment at the financial swamp in which they were sinking, appeals for help and angry protests. But now the predominant emotion in them is fear—fear of greater economic and business chaos, fear of revolution.

In the same article the *New York Times* noted that a recent survey of letters to various congressmen showed a dramatic shift in sentiment, not just among farmers, but also among normally conservative "small town bankers, lawyers, real estate men, insurance agents, heads of mortgage and loan companies, and merchants." And they also observed that

The most insistent demand found in these letters is for currency inflation. The writers do not care much what kind of inflation, whether a reduction in the gold content of the dollar, free silver, bimetallism, or straight inflation of the currency. They don't particularly care what happens to industry and the wage earner as the result of inflation.

When Roosevelt did finally devalue the dollar the policy was seen as favoring the rural sector, and labor was not particularly supportive.[3] The perception that inflation would hurt workers (which I think was mistaken) may have later pushed FDR into a high wage policy that proved very costly.

On February 14, the imminent failure of several large Detroit banks led the Governor of Michigan to declare a statewide banking holiday, and stock and commodity prices declined in response. The Michigan bank failures triggered a wave of bank panics and by the end of February most states had declared bank holidays. These restrictions on depositors led to an unprecedented[4] surge in currency hoarding, which added to fears of devaluation. The February 15 *New York Times* also reported that "HEAVY EARMARKING OF GOLD CONTINUES" and suggested (p. 29) that to "a large extent the movement is believed to be tied with Europe's reaction to the renewed outbreak of banking trouble here and to the recent discussions of inflationary proposals in Washington." The causality probably ran both ways, with banking troubles leading to fears of devaluation, and fears of devaluation leading to currency hoarding, and thereby triggering more banking holidays.

The following day an assassination attempt on Roosevelt reinforced the perception of a society fraying at the seams. On February 17, the dollar dropped below the gold point, falling to its lowest level since June 1932. A big drop in Treasury bond (T-bond) prices on February 20 provided additional evidence of a loss of confidence in the dollar. On February 27, a *New York Times* headline warned that "Financial Europe Sees Urgent Need for Sound Money Declaration by Roosevelt" and the *Times* also noted that

The unsettlement of last week's stock market, the recurrent weakness in the bond market, and the indication that hoarding of currency had

---

3. Even socialists like Norman Thomas opposed FDR's dollar devaluation program (*Commercial and Financial Chronicle* (*CFC*), 4/29/1933, p. 2838).

4. The public's holdings of cash rose 11.5 percent during February 1933. This compares to a 5.6 percent increase during October 1931 and a 3.6 percent increase during December 1930, months marked by two previous panics. It is likely that devaluation fears contributed to the February 1933 banking panic. See Wigmore (1987).

increased resulted partly from the not very skillfully handled Michigan episode, but they equally reflected the mental influence of the
mischievous talk of experimenting with the currency. (p. 23)

The real surprise, however, is that the financial markets didn't respond
even more dramatically to the 1933 financial crisis. It is true that, after several
months of relative stability, the Dow did fall by 15.6 percent between February 11 and February 27. But stocks never even approached their July 1932
lows, despite the fact that early 1933 saw the most severe U.S. financial crisis
of the entire Depression. And stocks actually rose steadily after February 27,
even though the foreign exchange crisis intensified dramatically during early
March. Commodity prices declined only modestly in late February.

The strength of the financial markets during the 1933 financial crisis may
have been related to expectations of an imminent change in policy; the inauguration of a new president was only a few days away. It is also important
to recall that during this period, the federal government was perceived by
investors as having a much greater ability to influence real asset prices than is
the case today. This second point may seem counterintuitive given that in 1933
government spending represented a much smaller share of the economy. But
equity markets had often moved dramatically on Hoover's policy initiatives,
and investors had every reason to believe that FDR would try something at
least as dramatic.[5] Paradoxically, this perception intensified the 1933 dollar
crisis, leading to large gold outflows, but also limited its impact on asset prices.

During the last half of February, stocks moved up and down with the
T-bond market. In early March, T-bond prices fell sharply as the crisis intensified and devaluation fears increased. And yet these same devaluation fears
now led to higher stock and commodity prices as the market looked forward
to possible currency tinkering by the incoming administration. The more

---

5. The *NYT* (2/15/33, p. 29) quoted Senator Thomas as follows:
Let me remind you that, during the past year, every legislative proposal even suggesting possible expansion of the currency . . caused an immediate and positive
upturn in commodity and stock securities prices and consequent renewal of hope
and confidence in the minds and the hearts of the people.
And then, just as soon as wise observers saw that such intimations were false
alarms, prices began to sag and hope and confidence began to wane.

severe the crisis became, the greater became the expectation of dramatic policy changes in the near future:

> The market and those who follow it appear to be building their hopes on the possibility of a sweeping psychological change after the Presidential inauguration. (*NYT*, 3/3/33, p. 25)

By the close of the Hoover administration, virtually the entire banking system was shut down and the U.S. government was losing gold at an unprecedented rate.[6] Yet, the only discernable macroeconomic consequence of this crisis would be a modest dip in industrial production during March 1933.

Despite all of these shocks, the forward markets showed little evidence that investors thought an immediate, and large, devaluation was imminent. On March 3, 1933, the three-month forward dollar sold at only a 1.2-percent discount against the pound. Yet by June 3, the spot pound had appreciated by nearly 14 percent. Instead, the large gold outflows during early March may have reflected concern that Roosevelt would move to further restrict gold outflows. In the short run this view was correct. Roosevelt made no immediate moves to devalue the dollar but did take steps to restrict both gold outflows and domestic hoarding.

In retrospect, fear over the soundness of the dollar appears to have been the primary factor that aborted the recovery in the fall of 1932 and led to a "double dip" in the economy in March 1933. And it was uncertainty over Roosevelt's plans for the dollar that was most responsible for this change in sentiment. Some uncertainty may have been unavoidable, but one can also make a good argument that FDR's conservative critics were right in blaming him for the crisis.

It is not surprising that many historians have given FDR something of a pass on his non-cooperative attitude toward Hoover during the interregnum. For three straight years, the rigid and inept Hoover had failed to develop any kind of effective remedies for the Depression. In contrast, Roosevelt was an enthusiastic reformer who relished knocking the high and mighty down a peg

---

6. The resulting hoarding of gold led to a 6.5 percent decline in the U.S. monetary gold stock during February 1933, and a 1.6 percent decline in *world* stocks.

or two. It is not difficult to guess which President attracts the natural sympathies of liberal-minded historians. And there *were* some cases where FDR's mischievous approach to conservative orthodoxy paid real dividends—as when he undercut the negotiations at the World Monetary Conference (WMC) in July 1933.[7] After he took office, dollar devaluation was the right policy. But the interregnum was different; FDR was not yet president.

Even in the 1930s, it was widely understood that financial markets were not capable of withstanding great uncertainty over the soundness of a currency. That is why it was (and still is) standard operating procedure for policymakers to deny any intention of devaluation right up to the last minute. It might be argued that one cannot ask public officials to lie about their policy intentions. But this issue is different—indeed, it is the very reason why Roosevelt campaigned on a platform of adherence to the gold standard. Given his later decision to devalue, it was inevitable that FDR would eventually have to break that promise. But the admission should have occurred in March; immediately after the election, he should have issued a Grover Cleveland–like statement of fidelity to the gold standard. It is easy to see the dispute between Hoover and Roosevelt in personal terms, but the cost of FDR's irresponsibility was the suffering of millions when the recovery fizzled out in late 1932 and output slumped again in early 1933.

Roosevelt's Dollar Depreciation Program

The Roosevelt Administration included supporters of at least four distinct approaches to macroeconomic policy. The conservatives advocated orthodox economic remedies such as a balanced budget and/or maintenance of the gold standard. A second group favored Keynesian remedies such as public works projects and were willing to accept deficit spending. Roosevelt was particularly supportive of proposals to raise the price level, especially commodity prices and wages. These goals were to be achieved through two sharply conflicting policies. One faction advocated a policy of depreciating the dollar in order to

---

7. Schuker (2003) applies the same sort of criticism to FDR's attitude toward the WMC. I don't agree with this specific criticism but do credit Schuker with changing my mind about FDR's behavior during the interregnum.

increase commodity prices.[8] Another faction favored cartelizing the economy in order to artificially restrict hours worked and output. This cartelization was to be achieved through programs such as the Agricultural Adjustment Act (AAA) and the National Industrial Recovery Act (NIRA).

During Roosevelt's first one hundred days there was a flurry of new legislation to deal with the economic crisis. From the perspective of investors, however, it was Roosevelt's gold policy that mattered most. To meet the ongoing crisis, FDR immediately instituted a national banking holiday and a temporary embargo on gold exports. With the banks closed from March 4 to March 14, 1933, business activity declined even further and the New York Stock Exchange also closed down.

Despite the fact that the forward discount on the dollar was even greater in March than in February, world monetary gold stocks rebounded 1.7 percent during March, an indication that Roosevelt's anti-hoarding policies were having some effect. Investors were now confident that Roosevelt's policies would prevent gold (and currency) hoarding from having an adverse impact on the money supply, and therefore they took a more tolerant view of exchange rate uncertainty.

Roosevelt's actions produced an immediate boost to the nation's morale, and when the stock market reopened on March 15, the Dow jumped 14.3 percent to 62.10. Yet despite the market's vote of confidence, over the next five weeks investors showed very little real enthusiasm for the new administration's program. Stocks traded in the 55 to 63 range of the Dow, essentially the same levels as prevailed during the preceding winter of discontent. Why did the stock market show so little enthusiasm for the first forty-five days of the New Deal, and why did an explosive stock market rally begin on April 19, 1933?

When the banks reopened, gold and currency hoarding dropped sharply as deposits exceeded withdrawals, and the dollar rose strongly on the foreign exchange market. But the very success of these early initiatives may have created some disappointment, as well. Even before the markets reopened, the *New York Times* noted that European sentiment was quite favorable toward the new administration, and that despite the gold embargo, "DOLLAR RATE

---

8. Wigmore (1987) provides a good analysis of how the gold standard contributed to the banking panic of 1933 and also how this led Roosevelt to initiate several important changes in U.S. gold policy.

MAY HOLD . . . Belief Is General in Preservation of the Gold Standard by the United States."[9] During the last days of the Hoover administration the markets had clearly factored in the possibility of inflation initiatives such as dollar devaluation. When Roosevelt's early initiatives appeared to quickly restore confidence, the possibility of inflation seemed to recede.

Of course FDR's early initiatives did provide a modest boost to the financial markets; at the very least, the gold embargo insured that monetary expansion could be undertaken without fear of external complications. The performance of the financial markets during the first forty-five days is probably best viewed as reflecting an outcome somewhere between the pessimistic fears of continued paralysis and the optimistic hopes for a vigorous policy of inflation. Referring to the strong dollar and the decline in stock prices during late March, the *New York Times* noted that

> As in the case of the foreign exchanges, the reason commonly assigned for yesterday's further decline was that speculation based upon a belief that common stock equities would be more valuable in an inflationary season had been halted by realization of the fact that the underlying significance of the Federal Administration's recent steps to end the banking crisis may have been misinterpreted. (3/22/33, p. 25)

On April 10, the Bank of International Settlements (BIS) resumed dollar trading, an indication that "all doubt whether the United States is still on the gold standard ended officially today as far as the world's chief central banks are concerned."[10] This attitude may seem surprising in light of the subsequent devaluation, but previous currency devaluations had generally occurred after a currency had already depreciated sharply, or during a period where speculation had put the gold reserve at risk. Neither of these conditions applied to the United States during April 1933, and thus any devaluation of the dollar would have been (correctly) seen as an unprecedented attempt to manipulate an otherwise sound gold-backed currency solely for purposes of economic stimulation.[11]

---

9. *NYT*, 3/13/33, p. 23.
10. *NYT*, 4/11/33, p. 27.
11. The *NYT* (2/27/33, p. 23) called this unprecedented policy a "voluntary devaluation."

In mid-April, political pressure for devaluation of the dollar began to increase, and on April 13, a strong speculative movement against the dollar led to sharp rallies in the stock and commodity markets. The market reaction may have been triggered by a meeting at which FDR seemed sympathetic to a proposal by Canadian Premier Richard Bennett that the dollar be devalued, as well as to the perception that recently announced programs such as the NIRA would require a more inflationary policy.

Throughout March and early April 1933 there was some recovery in output and wholesale prices. Yet, the Dow was at roughly the same level on April 17 (the day before the dollar was allowed to float), as it had been when the markets reopened on March 15, or for that matter, when FDR was elected in November 1932. FDR's decision on April 19, 1933, to temporarily abandon the gold standard ushered in one of the most remarkable years in the history of U.S. financial markets. It would be difficult to find any other period where movements in all of the markets were so dominated by the whims of a single individual.[12] Stocks, commodities, and speculative bonds all soared after the decision on April 19, and then again, early on April 20 in response to overnight news of a proposed bill to give FDR broad inflationary powers. Between April 18 and April 20 the Dow rose by 15.4 percent, the beginning of one of the great bull markets in U.S. history.

Although dollar devaluation signaled a shift toward a more expansionary monetary policy, T-bonds fell on both days, a sign that inflation expectations had increased. The April 20 *New York Times* (p. 2) noted that "among some of the conservative elements who have steadfastly held that inflation is anathema, the emphatic response of the financial markets to the imposition of the gold embargo caused bewilderment." Yet, this pattern would be repeated frequently throughout the remainder of 1933, as the administration pushed the value of the dollar lower and lower. By July 18, the Dow was up over 73 percent from its level three months earlier. And even more than by its size, this bull market was distinguished by the close relationship between stock prices and the international value of the dollar.

---

12. I will focus on how FDR's decisions influenced the markets, but the causation ran in both directions. For instance, Eichengreen (1992, p. 333) describes FDR using stock and commodity prices as a fairly sophisticated policy guide. At times he would respond to bearish market sentiment by pushing down the foreign exchange value of the dollar.

The Thomas amendment to the Agricultural Adjustment Act not only allowed the president to reduce the value of the dollar by as much as 50 percent, but also authorized the Treasury to print up to $3 billion in "greenbacks." When combined with the extra powers to appoint several more Federal Reserve Board members, the changes made the Fed little more than the "blind hand-maiden of the Government."[13] Even so, in the early days of the program there was still little awareness of the inflation that lay ahead. An April 21 *New York Times* article (p. 1) discussing Britain's experience after leaving the gold standard noted that "Brookings Study Shows Rapid Price Rises Did Not Follow Their Desertion of Gold." Of course, the pound's depreciation took place against a backdrop of severe (worldwide) deflation in commodity prices measured in terms of gold.

Why did FDR decide to suddenly shift course forty-five days after taking office? The *New York Times* cited administration advisors as indicating concern over continued deflation. In addition the *Times* indicated that

> The measures suggested by the administration to overcome deflation, such as loans to States for self-liquidating projects and a public works program of enormous proportions, apparently have failed to stimulate industry sufficiently and revive confidence that the country was on the road to recovery. (4/20/33, p. 1)

To a modern economist, the preceding quotation may seem odd. Surely it was too soon to draw any firm conclusions about the course of the economy. And industrial production during mid-April was already advancing briskly from the depressed conditions in March. The real problem lay in the sluggish performances of the stock and commodity markets; these markets were highly correlated with output during the interwar years, and their recent performances had provided little indication of hope for the future. The interrelationship between these markets and administration monetary policy was a hallmark of FDR's first year in office.

Between April 1933 and February 1934, the dollar declined dramatically against both gold and gold-backed currencies such as the French franc. The

---

13. *CFC*, 5/27/33, p. 3579. Wicker (1971) stated that during this period "the President assumed direct responsibility for the conduct of monetary policy."

Table 5.2. Exchange Rates, Stock Prices, and News, April–July 1933

Date	Change in the Dow	Related Monetary Policy News
4/19	+9.0%	U.S. dollar is floated
4/20	+5.8%	Inflation bill introduced
4/29	+6.2%	Inflation bill passed
5/23	+3.9%	Open market purchases
5/26	+3.2%	Discount rate cut
5/27	+3.7%	United States formally leaves the gold standard
6/12	+2.5%	FDR desires lower dollar at opening of WMC
6/19	+6.4%	FDR rejects currency stabilization at WMC
7/1	+2.8%	FDR rejects "current form" of stabilization proposal
7/3	+2.8%	FDR torpedoes the World Monetary Conference

decline was erratic and currency futures data indicate that the decline was also largely unanticipated. Most importantly, the more dramatic movements in the dollar were almost invariably linked with statements made, or actions taken, by the Roosevelt Administration. Table 5.2 shows the response of the U.S. stock market to important news relating to monetary policy during the first three months after the dollar was floated. The Dow increased by more than 65 percent between April 18 and July 3, 1933, and almost 90 percent of that increase occurred on the 10 news days shown in Table 5.2.

The market's strong approval of FDR's switch to a more inflationary policy does not mean that investors welcomed deficit spending. The April 29 *New York Times* noted (p. 19) that "as soon as the news was out that the proposal to use the 'greenback' currency authorized in the Thomas bill to pay the soldiers' bonus had been killed prices began to move up smartly." The next day the dollar fell on news that the Thomas amendment (suspending the gold standard) had been passed "in substantially the same form that was originally proposed" and stocks and commodities advanced sharply.

Although the defeat of the soldier's bonus and the falling dollar were cited as the primary market influences, another development that would prove to have momentous implications was also noted:

Part of yesterday's enthusiasm had its inspiration, no doubt, in the news from Washington that a "national industry recovery act," which seems to be one of the most ambitious legislative projects yet undertaken on behalf of the administration, was being speedily prepared. If the purposes have been correctly summarized in the Washington dispatches, a broad emergency control of industry is contemplated, with price-fixing, abrogation of the anti-trust laws and what-not. Apparently the plan has some sort of administration sponsorship, but details are lacking. At least the share market seems to be impressed by the possibilities. (*NYT*, 4/30, p. N7)

Bittlingmeyer (1996) showed that antitrust enforcement had a strongly negative impact on stock prices during the interwar era, and thus it is not surprising that the markets might have been favorably impressed by these early reports on the National Industrial Recovery Act (NIRA). In Chapter 6, we will see that the markets initially misjudged the essence of the NIRA, and that it would prove to have a strongly negative impact on both equity prices and real output.

After remaining fairly stable during the first twenty days of May, the value of the dollar began falling again in response to expansionary moves by the Fed. Significant open market purchases were announced on May 23, the discount rate was reduced on May 25, and the United States formally left the gold standard on May 27. It is interesting to contrast the stock market's enthusiastic response to the Fed's decision (on the evening of May 25) to reduce the discount rate with the previous nonreactions to the discount rate increases of October 10 and 17, 1931. With the Fed now able to adopt expansionary policies without fear of a run on the U.S. gold stocks, markets reverted to their traditional pattern of welcoming lower discount rates. Although stocks opened higher on May 26, not all of the day's increase can be attributed to discount rate cut. Stocks rose sharply in the last fifteen minutes of trading, and again on the morning of May 27, on news that a bill had been introduced to eliminate the gold clause in both public and private contracts, a move widely seen as foreshadowing the end of the gold standard.

The impact of floating the dollar went far beyond simply providing more flexibility to the Fed. When the war debts issue resurfaced in mid-June, the *New York Times* observed that

Wall Street notes a remarkable contrast between the attitude toward the war debt question last December and that at the present time. Last year, financial circles began to become apprehensive about the war debt question long before Dec. 15. . . . At the present time, although the war debt payments are due by next Thursday, there has been almost no discussion of the subject in financial circles, and the possibilities of wholesale default have left the markets unperturbed. (6/11/33, p. N5)

This is important because it shows that it was not the fiscal, but rather the *monetary* aspects of the war debts problem that was of greatest concern to the markets. Now that the dollar was being devalued, the markets no longer had to worry about the possible deflationary impact of a war debts dispute.[14]

On June 15, both stocks and foreign exchange plunged sharply on rumors of an imminent agreement to stabilize the dollar/pound exchange rate, and then rebounded on June 19 as it became clear that Roosevelt was still undecided on the issue. On June 22, the Dow fell 3.1 percent on rumors that France would leave the gold standard. Those rumors would continue to affect the stock market throughout the mid-1930s. Interestingly, however, when France finally did devalue in late 1936, the U.S. stock market responded positively. In Chapter 8, we will see why the market's reaction to French devaluation rumors depended on the broader monetary environment.

Although Roosevelt occasionally[15] indicated that he intended to raise prices back to their 1925 levels, financial markets initially seemed reluctant to accept the statements as administration policy. However, this perception began to change in late June and early July as Roosevelt continued to resist currency stabilization proposals. On July 3, FDR stunned the delegates at the World Monetary and Economic Conference (WMC) by stating his adamant opposition to any currency stabilization agreement. Furthermore, Roosevelt suggested that he was serious about a "commodity dollar":

So, too, old fetishes of so-called international bankers are being replaced by efforts to plan national currencies with the objective of giving

---

14. This time Britain took advantage of the Thomas amendment and made a token payment in silver, in contrast to December's full payment in gold.

15. See the *CFC* (7/15/33, p. 430).

those currencies a continuing purchasing power which does not greatly vary in terms of the commodities and need of modern civilization.

Let me be frank in saying that the United States seeks the kind of dollar which a generation hence will have the same purchasing power and debt-paying power as the dollar value *we hope to obtain in the near future.* (7/4/33, p. 1, emphasis added)

This was a clear indication that FDR's policy of devaluation represented more than just a negotiating tool to gain concessions at the WMC.[16] In retrospect, this statement can be seen as an intimation of the dollar-buying program adopted in the fall of 1933. Once again, stocks and foreign currencies rose strongly on the report.

Roosevelt's hand was undoubtedly strengthened by the fact that output was expanding at the most rapid rate in U.S. history. And this vigorous recovery was not being generated by a "beggar-thy-neighbor" exchange rate policy. The October 8, 1933, *New York Times* (p. xxi) reported that exports had increased a mere 3 percent above the previous year's levels in the first five months after the dollar began depreciating, whereas imports had soared by 20 percent, suggesting that it was rising domestic aggregate demand that was generating a recovery, not improved terms of trade. Regarding the question of dollar stabilization, (Chancellor of the Exchequer) Neville Chamberlain noted that

At the beginning of the [World Monetary Conference, officials from the United States Treasury came over, duly authorized to discuss this very question. . . . [T]here came a time in the United States when public sentiment closely connected the depreciation of the dollar with the rise in commodity prices. It was then impossible for the President to agree even to temporary stabilization without running the risk of checking the policy to which he had set his hand. (*Commercial and Financial Chronicle*, 7/15/33, p. 366)

---

16. Roosevelt's policy was very similar to Irving Fisher's famous "Compensated Dollar Plan." Prof. George Warren was regarded as the most forceful advocate of this plan within the "Brain Trust."

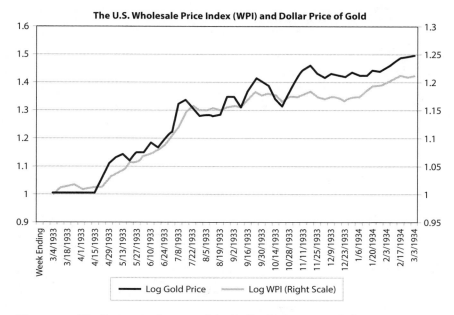

Figure 5.2. The Economic Impact of the Dollar Depreciation Policy

Of course, Roosevelt had no desire to have his policy checked. Figure 5.2 shows that the policy was achieving FDR's objectives, the wholesale price index (then measured weekly) was rising in tandem with the dollar price of gold:

The Economic Impact of the Dollar Depreciation Policy

Table 5.3 shows that the devaluation of the dollar had a major impact on commodity prices. A regression of (the first difference of the log of) the Moody's Commodity Price Index against the (first difference of the log of the) dollar price of French francs suggests that dollar depreciation raised U.S. commodity prices. Because available foreign exchange data reflect midday prices, one lag of the commodity index was also regressed on the price of French francs and again the coefficient was both positive and significant.

Between March and July 1933, the rise in prices was accompanied by a 57 percent increase in industrial production, *by far* the largest four-month increase in output in U.S. history. Although it is tempting to assume the re-

Table 5.3. The Daily Relationship between Commodity Prices and the Dollar Price of French Francs, April 17, 1933, to February 1, 1934

Independent Variable	French Franc				
Dependent Variables	**Coefficient**	**T-Statistic**	**D-W**	**R_2**	**n**
Commodity Price Index	.362	(7.12)	1.74	.179	229
Lagged Commodity PI	.218	(4.02)	1.67	.063	228

covery in output was triggered by the ongoing program of dollar depreciation, this hypothesis needs careful consideration. Whereas almost any macro model predicts a connection between dollar depreciation and inflation, a finding that dollar depreciation triggered a sharp recovery in output would have quite significant implications for Keynesian theories of monetary policy ineffectiveness during depressions as well as modern "real business cycle" models.[17]

Stock prices can provide important clues about causality. If the stock market is efficient, then only unanticipated changes in the exchange rate should affect stock prices. Although we now know that the dollar was sharply depreciated from mid-April 1933 through the end of January 1934, the three-month forward discount on the dollar remained in the ½ percent to 2 percent range throughout this period. Thus, the actual depreciation of the dollar was almost entirely unanticipated, *even after April 1933.*

Table 5.4 shows the results of a regression of the first difference of the log of the Dow (DOW) on the (first difference of the log of the) price of French francs. The coefficient is both positive and significant. As with commodity prices, I also regressed one lag of the Dow on the French franc, and again the coefficient was both positive and significant. The sum of the coefficients is

---

17. Both traditional Keynesian "liquidity trap" models and real business cycle models predict that monetary stimulus would fail to boost real output at near-zero interest rates. The Keynesians would claim that monetary stimulus would fail to boost aggregate demand, whereas RBC models predict that more demand would fail to boost real output.

Table 5.4. The Daily Relationship between the Dow Jones Industrial Average, Real Stock Prices, and the Dollar Price of French Francs, April 17, 1933, to February 1, 1934

Independent Variable	French Franc				
Dependent Variables	**Coefficient**	**T-Statistic**	**D-W**	**R$_2$**	**n**
DOW	.563	(5.21)	2.10	.103	229
LaggedDOW	.534	(4.92)	2.07	.093	228
RealDOW	.208	(2.39)	2.14	.020	227
LaggedRealDOW	.325	(3.81)	2.12	.057	226
DOW (4/17/33—7/18/33)	.510	(3.09)	2.20	.101	77
DOW (7/18/33—2/1/34)	.562	(3.88)	2.04	.085	152

slightly greater than one, which suggests that dollar depreciation may have resulted in a greater than proportionate increase in stock prices. Nevertheless, the coefficient is close enough to one to call into question whether the depreciation of the dollar was increasing *real* stock prices.

Temin and Wigmore (1990, p. 491) also noted that the stock market reacted favorably to dollar depreciation, and suggested that, "we cannot distinguish between expectations about the price level and about the expansion of industry." Table 5.4 also provides a couple of regressions using the Dow deflated by Moody's commodity price index (RealDOW) on the price of French francs. The positive and significant coefficient suggests that dollar depreciation raised real stock prices, a result that conflicts with equilibrium macro models where nominal shocks don't have real effects. Although the Moody's commodity index may not be the optimal way of deflating daily stock prices, the stock market rose by much more than any reasonably comprehensive price index during the period of dollar depreciation.

One way of distinguishing between real and nominal effects is to look at the effect of the dollar depreciation on bond spreads. In an equilibrium

Table 5.5. The Daily Relationship between Bond Yields and the Dollar Price of French Francs, April 17, 1933, to February 1, 1934

Dependent Variable: Aaayield

Independent Variable	Coefficient	T-statistic	D-W	Adj. R_2	n
French francs	.089	(5.21)	1.34	.103	229

Dependent Variable: Baayield

Independent Variable	Coefficient	T-statistic	D-W	Adj. R_2	n
French francs	.020	(−0.53)	1.04	.000	229

Dependent Variable: Spread

Independent Variables	Coefficient	T-statistic
DLFF	−.107	(−3.43)
SPREAD-1	.294	(4.68)

Adj. R_2 = .127, n = 229

Note: The first two regression equations show some indication of serial correlation. Diagnostic tests show no indication of serial correlation in the final equation. Spread-1 is the first lag of Spread.

business cycle model, inflation will not increase bond prices or reduce bond yields. Table 5.5 shows that dollar depreciation does seem to have increased Aaa bond yields, presumably through the Fisher effect. In contrast, there is no evidence that dollar depreciation affected Baa bond yields. Most importantly, the interest rate spread (Baa yield minus Aaa yield) is both negatively, and significantly, related to changes in the (first difference of the log of the) price of French francs.

The spread between the Baa yield and the Aaa yield is a good proxy for default risk. Expectations of more rapid growth would reduce default risk and reduce the Baa/Aaa spread.[18] Apparently, the depreciation of the dollar had just that effect. It is difficult to think of an explanation for this relationship that is consistent with either real business cycle models featuring

---

18. Temin and Wigmore (1990) make a similar observation, but without a formal test.

money neutrality or with Keynes's view that monetary policy had become ineffective by 1933.

What Does the Depression Tell Us about Price Indices?

In the preceding narrative we have seen numerous examples of the interwar WPI behaving very differently from modern price indices. Prices fell very sharply when monetary policy tightened in late 1929 and rose rapidly when the dollar was depreciated in 1933. It might be argued that this greater sensitivity to demand shocks reflects problems with early price indices, and that we are now fortunate to have much better data. I would argue just the opposite. It was relatively easy to measure changes in the prices of the sort of goods that dominated the interwar economy—such as coal, iron, and wheat—while it is much harder to accurately measure changes in the prices of software or consulting services.

Admittedly, the interwar WPI contains a somewhat limited sample of prices, often from the more procyclical industries, but even that might represent a hidden advantage. Stigler and Kindahl (1970) showed that changes in the sort of list prices measured by the BLS (U.S. Bureau of Labor Statistics) often lag well behind changes in transaction prices. And Friedman and Schwartz argued that

> While the wholesale price index generally shows a wider amplitude than the cost-of-living index or the implicit index, the differences [after the dollar was devalued] were much wider than usual. They reflect in part the differential impact of devaluation on goods entering international trade; those goods are more important in the wholesale price index than they are in the other indexes. But it may also be that the differences reflect in part an understatement of the price rise by the cost-of-living and implicit indexes; the *recorded* prices of many items included in those indexes, but not in the wholesale price index, are much more stable than the *actual* prices of those items. (p. 497, emphasis added)

In Chapter 13, I discuss research by Christopher Hanes that shows a lower proportion of sticky prices in the prewar WPI. The key question is not which index is best in some abstract sense such as for measuring the elusive "cost of living," but rather, which is of greater value for purposes of business cycle analysis. For instance, one could argue that when deciding whether to construct a new building what matters is the expected price at which one can sell or rent the project, not the current rents paid by tenants under long-term contracts.[19] If so, then the (flexible price) WPI may provide a sort of shadow equilibrium price level, which is especially sensitive to the impact of aggregate demand shocks on business conditions. Using interwar data to look at wage cyclicality, real interest rates, and purchasing power parity can illuminate important features of the economy that get overlooked when using modern indices full of dubious (sticky) price data.[20]

An article by Alchian and Klein (1975) addressed this issue from a slightly different direction, but reached similar conclusions. They started with the observation (p. 174) that the "appropriateness of a price index depends on the question to which an answer is sought" and then suggested that for many types of macroeconomic analysis the price index should include asset prices. They argued (p. 179) that "a decrease in the supply of nominal money . . . causes asset prices to fall relative to service flow prices and relative to the cost of producing new assets. . . . In turn, the reduced profitability of producing new assets decreases their production." They also noted that Friedman and Schwartz and Keynes, held similar views about the importance of a fall in the relative price of assets.[21]

---

19. Between 1933 and 1934 the consumer price index (CPI) measured by the BLS rose by 3.4 percent. The four components were as follows: food up 11.6 percent, furniture up 9.9 percent, apparel up 9.5 percent, and rent *down* 6.3 percent.

20. A recent example occurred when Bureau of Economic Analysis (BEA) consumer price data showed housing prices rising between mid-2006 and mid-2009 and declining thereafter. More market-sensitive housing indices showed exactly the opposite pattern. Chowdhry, Roll and Xia make an analogous argument using equity prices:

> Recognizing that relative PPP may not hold for the official inflation data constructed from commodity price indices because of relative price changes and other frictions that cause prices to be "sticky," we provide a novel method for extracting a proxy for *realized* pure price inflation from stock returns. We find strong support for relative PPP in the short run using the extracted inflation measures. (2005, p. 255).

21. They cite Friedman and Schwartz (1963b, pp. 229–31) and Leijonhufvud's (1968, pp. 335–38) study of Keynes.

Alchian and Klein (p. 180) lamented a "shocking" lack of availability of asset-oriented price indices, but suggested that some useful inferences could be drawn by "examining recent movements in common stock price indices relative to flow price indices." They also noted (p. 179) that the impact of monetary policy "will be underestimated by a current service flow price index compared to an index that also includes asset prices." In the preceding narrative we have seen numerous examples where commodity and stock indices seemed highly sensitive to monetary shocks, indeed much more so than modern price indices.[22] In Chapter 12, we will see that Alchian and Klein's conjecture also has important implications for recent research in monetary economics.

Why Was the Dollar Depreciation Program So Effective?

The events of early 1933 demonstrate the importance of policy actions that change the expected future time path of the money supply. In the final two years of the Hoover administration, Fed policy seemed to have little impact on the financial markets, or the economy as a whole. Instead, markets reacted strongly to news that hinted at regime change—that is, changes that might relax the constraints imposed by the international gold standard (such as the 1932 Glass-Steagall bill). In April 1933 the financial markets were finally given just such a regime change. Although conservative opinion on Wall Street was strongly opposed to dollar devaluation, money speaks louder than words, and equity traders greeted FDR's heterodox policy with great enthusiasm. Flexible stock and commodity prices rose in anticipation of a more expansionary monetary policy, and businesses responded by boosting real output at the fastest rate in U.S. history.

Traditional monetary studies that rely on money supply or interest rate transmission mechanisms are not able to account for the extraordinary rate of increase in asset prices and output during the spring of 1933. Both interest rates and the money supply[23] showed little change during 1933 (before rising

---

22. Actually, it is hard to know how responsive modern price indices are to monetary shocks, because it is now much harder to identify exogenous monetary shocks.

23. There is some ambiguity about the money stock data after many banks were temporarily closed. The assumption of little change represents Friedman and Schwartz's (p. 428–32) best guess on the issue.

sharply in 1934 and 1935). Friedman and Schwartz (p. 433) acknowledged that the "economic recovery in the half-year after the panic owed nothing to monetary expansion." But instead of citing the depreciation of the dollar, they went on to argue that, "the emergency revival of the banking system contributed to recovery by restoring confidence in the monetary and economic system." The behavior of the stock market would suggest otherwise. Stocks languished for weeks after the banking system was closed and stabilized in March, and soared on news of dollar depreciation.

Both McCloskey and Zecher (1976) and Temin and Wigmore (1990) emphasized one possible transmission mechanism: dollar depreciation could have raised the prices of traded goods, which may have reversed the deflationary trends of the previous four years. Another possibility is that the monetary regime change led to a dramatic change in expectations about the future path of monetary policy.[24] This second mechanism would immediately boost aggregate demand even if the presence of trade barriers and nontraded goods prevented purchasing power parity from being effective in the short run.

Although the gold market approach can help us to better understand the rapid recovery in the spring of 1933, it raises almost as many questions as it answers. If actual dollar devaluation was so bullish for stocks and commodities, then why did devaluation fears (which encouraged hoarding) have such a bearish impact on markets throughout much of the 1930s? And why were market reactions to the severe dollar crisis of early 1933 so ambiguous? To what extent did the various market responses depend on the size of the anticipated devaluation, and/or whether it was viewed as being imminent? Although we do not have definitive answers to these questions yet, the period from 1934–1938 provides clues that will be developed in later chapters.

The U.S. price level continued to increase in the second half of 1933, albeit more slowly. Unfortunately, the explosive recovery in industrial production fizzled out after July 1933. In the next chapter we will see how a mere two

---

24. See Temin (1989) and Eggertsson (2008). In his explanation of why expectations changed so dramatically during 1933, Eggertsson placed almost equal weight on expansionary fiscal and monetary policies. I found almost no evidence, however, that markets responded favorably to news about expansionary fiscal policy—in fact, the response often seemed quite negative.

weeks after FDR torpedoed the World Monetary Conference, the National Recovery Administration (NRA) began to force wages much higher, which negated most of the benefits flowing from the policy of dollar depreciation. Wigmore (1985, p. 451) reported that "Roger Babson, who had foreseen so many of the financial troubles between 1929 and 1933, suggested at the end of May [1933] that conditions might be back to normal within 12 months." Instead, the Great Depression would drag on for another eight and a half years.

6

The NIRA and the Hidden Depression

"When you say 'hill'" the Queen interrupted, "I could show
you hills, in comparison with which you'd call that a valley."
—Lewis Carroll, 1872

IN CHAPTER 5 we looked at the first great policy experiment of the Roosevelt administration, the attempt to reflate prices by depreciating the dollar. This policy proved to be a spectacular success for a few months. The dollar fell sharply against most major currencies, industrial production soared, and prices (particularly at the wholesale level) increased rapidly despite slack in the economy. However, something went wrong after July 1933; industrial production began declining and didn't regain its July 1933 peak for another two years. In this chapter, we digress from the gold market analysis to see how the recovery was aborted by the National Industrial Recovery Act (NIRA), FDR's second great policy experiment of 1933.

Other economists have argued that the NIRA slowed recovery from the Depression. I hope to show that the impact of the NIRA was much greater than almost anyone else has suspected—preventing what otherwise would have been a near full recovery by late 1934 or early 1935. Some have argued that U.S. output growth between 1933 and 1941 was rapid, but to paraphrase the Red Queen, by comparison with the initial growth surge after the dollar began to depreciate, the rest of the recovery was more like a contraction.[1]

---

1. I stole this quotation from Hawtrey (1947, p. 185), who used it in a slightly different context.

My conclusions differ from others for at least four reasons. Unlike most other researchers, I focus almost exclusively on the wage and hours aspects of the NIRA, taking no position on other elements of the program. Second, I assume that the price of gold is the proper indicator of monetary policy in 1933, not the money supply or interest rates. Third, I assume that the interwar American economy had a strong self-correcting mechanism. And finally, I use monthly rather than quarterly or annual output data. These four assumptions underlie my claim that a quick recovery would have been possible in the absence of the NIRA.

The Breakdown of Natural Rate Models after 1933

In retrospect, the aborted recovery of 1933 represented, not just a turning point in the Great Depression, but also a pivotal event in the development of macroeconomic theory. For despite the unprecedented severity of the Depression, the more sophisticated business cycle models of the 1920s were able to at least partially account for both the prolonged contraction of 1929–1933 and the explosive recovery over the following four months. Indeed, prior to July 1933, the contraction and initial recovery could be viewed as simply a more severe version of the 1920–1922 recession. As the 1930s dragged on, however, the American economy seemed to be mired in a state of permanent depression. As we will see, the breakdown of interwar macro models provides important clues as to why the recovery faltered.

During the 1920s, the prevailing view of mainstream economists was that the business cycle was primarily a "dance of the dollar." According to this view, the more stable the purchasing power of the dollar (i.e., the price level), the more stable the level of real output. This view reached its greatest refinement in the work of Irving Fisher (1925), who first estimated what is now referred to as the "Phillips curve." Fisher argued that the changes in the price level impacted real output with a lag. Figure 6.1 reprints a graph from Fisher's famous 1925 paper, which shows a strong correlation between fluctuations in monthly output (T) and a distributed lag of past inflation rates (P'), for the period from 1915 through 1922.

It is interesting to update Fisher's model to the 1923–1935 period. The correlation between predicted output and actual output falls from .941 during

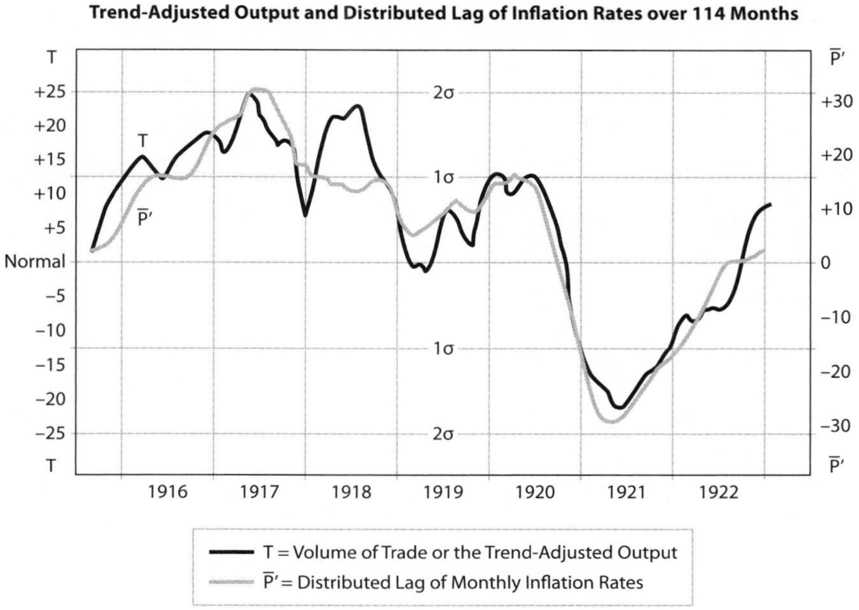
Trend-Adjusted Output and Distributed Lag of Inflation Rates over 114 Months
T
+25
+20
+15
+10
+5
Normal
-5
−10
−15
−20
−25
T
P̄′
+30
+20
+10
0
−10
−20
−30
P̄′
2σ
1σ
1σ
2σ
T
P̄′
1916
1917
1918
1919
1920
1921
1922
T = Volume of Trade or the Trend-Adjusted Output
P̄′ = Distributed Lag of Monthly Inflation Rates

Figure 6.1. Fisher's "Phillips Curve" Model from 1925

1915–1922, to .256 during 1923–1935. The actual decline in output between 1929 and 1932 is greater than predicted by Fisher's model. (This is consistent with the Bordo, Erceg, and Evans (2000) simulations discussed in Appendices 13c and 13d.) As can be seen in Figure 6.2, however, the decisive breakdown of Fisher's model does not occur until after July 1933. Between 1923 and July 1933, the correlation is still .851, quite respectable for an out-of-sample test. Thus, both the Great Contraction and initial recovery can be roughly explained[2] by Fisher's "Phillips curve" model. Then, after July 1933, Fisher's model fails completely, with actual output falling sharply even as predicted output rapidly converges on full employment levels. And this dramatic failure is not simply an artifact of specific flaws in Fisher's model; modern Phillips curve models also break down when applied to the early years of the recovery.

2. That Fisher's model "predicts" the Great Contraction (contingent on price data unavailable in 1929) is especially ironic in light of Fisher's well-known failure to predict the 1929 stock market crash and subsequent economic downturn. But surely the ability to make good *conditional* forecasts is the proper way to judge an economist, not the ability to make unconditional forecasts (which would be like judging a statistician by his ability at roulette).

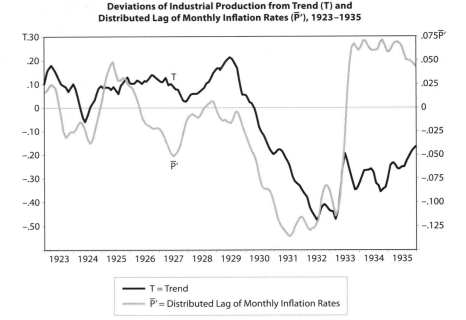

Deviations of Industrial Production from Trend (T) and Distributed Lag of Monthly Inflation Rates ($\bar{P}'$), 1923–1935

Figure 6.2. Out-of-Sample Forecast Properties of Fisher's Phillips Curve Model

The most important counterfactual question to be considered here is whether, in the absence of the NIRA, the economy would have achieved something close to full recovery by late 1934. To be sure, the extreme severity and duration of the Great Depression clearly led to unusually large amounts of internal migration and losses of human and physical capital, and this presumably made it nearly impossible to achieve *complete* recovery by 1934.[3] Higher marginal tax rates, Smoot-Hawley, and the RFC (Reconstruction Finance Corporation), may have also damaged the supply-side of the economy. Nevertheless, a good case can be made for the proposition that a nearly complete recovery was possible by late 1934, albeit to a level perhaps slightly below trend.

By July 1933, industrial production was roughly as far below potential as at the beginning of 1922. Yet, by December 1922, the recovery from the 1920–1921 depression was nearly complete.[4] And even though wholesale prices had already risen sharply by July, the additional increase in wholesale prices between

---

3. This is sometimes referred to as the "hysteresis" phenomenon.
4. Weinstein (1981) makes a similar point.

July 1933 and late 1934 was comparable to that of the entire 1921–1922 recovery. This is significant because (until July 1933) industrial production was highly correlated with the wholesale price index (WPI) during the interwar period. In other words, demand shocks seemed to drive the interwar business cycle.

We will consider six different pieces of evidence to support the hypothesis that the NIRA had a decisive impact on the economy during the mid-1930s. Much of this will consist of simple time series analysis. But because the wage shock administered by the NIRA in mid-1933 was far larger and more comprehensive than ordinary adjustments in the minimum wage and because it occurred in the midst of other dramatic changes in the economy, it seems unlikely that ordinary time series analysis can provide a definitive account of its impact. Thus, in addition to looking at co-movements of wages, prices, and output during the 1930s, we will also consider how the announcement of these wage policies impacted the financial markets. But first let's briefly examine some of the most important features of the NIRA.

The National Industrial Recovery Act

The primary purpose of the NIRA was to establish industrial codes that would serve to prevent "ruinous" competition by setting minimum levels for wages and prices. These above-market-clearing wages and prices were to be maintained by government-sanctioned industry cartels. Although the program was not completely mandatory, there were a number of enforcement mechanisms that made for a surprisingly high level of compliance, at least during the initial stages of the program.[5]

The NIRA was a complex program that has proven difficult to model. It is easier to consider the NIRA as two very distinct policies. After the President's Re-employment Agreement (better known as the "Blue Eagle" program) was enacted in July 1933, the average nominal wage rate rose by an astounding 22.3 percent in just two months.[6] However, the NIRA is probably best known as an attempt to cartelize industry in order to raise the price level.

---

5. See Roos (1937).

6. Because of oversampling of larger firms as well as governmental pressure on firms to conform to NIRA industry codes, it seems likely that the actual wage rate rose by somewhat less than the reported percentage. Nevertheless, contemporary accounts indicate that a large wage shock did occur at this time.

Although the NIRA almost certainly raised hourly wage rates, its impact on the price level is unclear. Both the NIRA, and its sister program, the Agricultural Assistance Act (AAA), may have tended to reduce output and raise prices during the last half of 1933. But prices had already been rising rapidly in the months before the NIRA was passed, and those changes were closely correlated with changes in the price of gold. And since changes in the dollar price of gold were highly correlated with exogenous policy shocks emanating from the Roosevelt administration and Congress, the causation presumably ran from dollar depreciation to inflation. As least with respect to traded goods, the sharp devaluation of the dollar was both a necessary and sufficient condition for the sort of rapid inflation experienced during 1933.

Because it is easy to demonstrate the impact of the Blue Eagle program on wages and because this wage shock was by itself capable of sharply depressing industrial production, I will focus on the wage rather than price aspects of the NIRA. This doesn't mean that the price-fixing arrangements might not also have an adverse impact on aggregate supply.[7] But it is difficult to see how the NIRA provisions that artificially raised prices could have played a decisive role in causing the economic recovery to stall in late July 1933. The subsequent contraction in output was actually accompanied by a significant *slowdown* in price inflation, even as wages were soaring by 22 percent in two months.

March 1933 is often viewed as the moment when the Great Contraction ended and the recovery began. By July, the policy of dollar depreciation had gone a long way toward ending the demand-side Depression. In the remainder of this chapter, I will argue that a second supply-side depression began in late July 1933, triggered by the NIRA. In the next section, we will briefly examine the co-movements of wages, prices, and output during 1933. Then, we will look at the response of the financial markets to news about the NIRA. In "Interpreting July 1933," I consider the key counterfactual raised by this analysis: What was the most likely path for output had the NIRA never been enacted?

The year 1933 presents especially severe problems of interpretation. Because the various New Deal policies were implemented in close proximity to one another, it is difficult to disentangle their effects. In "Previous Interpretations

---

7. The NIRA even resorted to restricting business purchases of new equipment as a way of raising prices. (*CFC*, 10/21/33, p. 2918).

of the NIRA and the Failed Recovery," I show why economic historians have greatly underestimated both the expansionary impact of dollar depreciation, and the contractionary impact of the NIRA.

Wages and Output during 1933

In Chapter 1 (Figure 1.2), we saw that one of the most distinctive features of the interwar economy was the highly countercyclical pattern exhibited by real wage rates. Stephen Silver and I (1995) showed that in a regression involving nominal wages, prices, and industrial production, a decisive breakpoint occurred in 1933. Prior to that date, the countercyclicality of real wages could be fully accounted for by the strong procyclicality of wholesale prices. After that date, however, even nominal wages became highly countercyclical. We argued that the difference could be explained by the interventionist labor market policies of the Roosevelt administration.

Table 6.1 shows monthly data for many of the key macroeconomic indicators during 1933. There are a number of striking correlations among the data in Table 6.1. As one would expect, the more commodity-intensive wholesale price index responded especially rapidly to the exchange rate changes. Yet during the period up until July 1933, nominal wages showed virtually no change. This might have been due to the extraordinarily high levels of unemployment, or it may simply reflect the short-run stickiness of nominal wages. In either case, the program of dollar depreciation initially depressed real wages in the United States.

The time path of nominal wages is perhaps the most interesting aspect of Table 6.1. After showing no increase at all between March and July of 1933 (despite a rapid increase in prices) nominal hourly wages jumped 22.3 percent (an annual rate of 230 percent!) in a period of just two months. Such a rapid increase in wages would be unusual during any period and is astounding for a period when nearly 25 percent of the workforce was unemployed. This increase occurred immediately after President Roosevelt issued an executive order creating the Blue Eagle program, which mandated that participating firms reduce hours by 20 percent with no change in total weekly wages. The wage increase was associated with a sharp decline in industrial production despite a continued modest increase in the price level. This is the first time during

Table 6.1. Selected Monthly Indicators, 1933

Month	Industrial Produc- tion	WPI	COL	Exchange Rate	Nominal Wages	Real Wages	Dow
1/33	106	101	103	100	100	99	99
2/33	106	99	101	100	100	100	91
3/33	100	100	100	100	100	100	100
4/33	107	100	100	100	99	99	101
5/33	125	104	101	115	98	94	128
6/33	144	108	102	118	97	90	143
7/33	157	114	105	140	99	86	171
8/33	151	115	108	131	113	98	156
9/33	143	118	109	144	120	102	165
10/33	135	118	109	140	122	103	146
11/33	128	118	108	164	122	104	152
12/33	129	118	108	154	124	106	161

*WPI (Wholesale Price Index), COL (Cost of Living Index), Dow (Dow Jones Industrial Average)

Note: The exchange rate is the dollar price of French francs. Both the exchange rate and Dow are mid-month figures. The real wage is deflated by the WPI.

the Great Depression when the path of prices and output began to sharply diverge. Figure 6.3 shows the relationship between real wages and industrial productions during 1933.

Because the real wage series is inverted, the two trends diverge over time as both industrial production and real wages were rising during this period. But the important correlations are the changes in slope; note how closely the key turning points are synchronized.

On four more occasions during the 1930s, federal policy appears to have had an impact on the aggregate nominal wage rate. These wage shocks include the tightening of NIRA codes during mid-1934, the labor organizational drives of 1936–1937 (facilitated by the passage of the Wagner Act of 1935), and minimum wage increases in late 1938 and 1939. As we will see in later chapters,

Figure 6.3. Industrial Production and Inverted Real Wages

these subsequent wage shocks were also associated with a stall in the recovery. Taken together, the five New Deal wage shocks caused a second supply-side depression during 1934–1940.

The NIRA and the Stock Market

In retrospect, it is surprising that the stock market did not show even greater strength during the spring and early summer of 1933. The economy seemed to be repeating the cyclical pattern of 1920–1922; output began recovering rapidly as soon as prices stopped declining. One factor that may have been restraining stock prices during this period was concern over the possible effects of New Deal legislation, particularly the NIRA.

During the spring of 1933, early reports on the proposed NIRA painted a picture of a pro-industry bill that would eliminate cutthroat competition. The April 30 *New York Times* (p. N7) saw the proposed bill as representing an "abrogation of the antitrust laws" and suggested that it might even have a positive impact on stock prices. At the same time, there were clear indications that industry was overestimating the efficacy of the NIRA at raising prices and underestimating its potential impact on wages. The business community was itself split, with the Chamber of Commerce in favor of the NIRA, and the National Association of Manufacturers (NAM) opposed to several key provisions. James Emery of the NAM noted that business was "slow to perceive the significance and effect of these [NIRA] proposals"[8] and correctly predicted that the NIRA would "nip in the bud the business recovery."

In Chapter 5, we saw that the ongoing rise in wholesale prices was primarily caused by dollar depreciation, and with the exception of certain agricultural commodities impacted by the AAA, that was also the view of contemporaneous observers.[9] Because the business press focused on the more controversial policy of dollar depreciation and because the NIRA's provisions were highly complex and constantly evolving, it is not surprising that many commentators initially underestimated the significance of Roosevelt's policy.

After FDR torpedoed the World Monetary Conference in early July, the press turned its attention to the NIRA. Business was benefiting from the higher price levels generated by dollar depreciation and the administration felt that the recovery would collapse unless some of this increased purchasing power was soon passed on to workers. Roosevelt named General Hugh S. Johnson as the NRA's Recovery Administrator, and Johnson immediately began to press for a rapid acceleration in the development of industry codes. A reporter who was sympathetic to the NIRA discussed industry concerns that the administration would not allow higher costs to be passed on in the form of higher prices, but also suggested that

> On the other hand, in preparing their codes, executives appear to be misunderstanding the intent of the Recovery Act. They seem trying to relinquish as little as possible to labor . . . . Considering this, it is not

---

8. *CFC*, 6/3/33, p. 3830. In addition, Emery argued that a policy of artificially raising prices was bound to fail owing to the lack of control over import prices.

9. Although some have argued that the spring 1933 increase in wholesale prices was caused by anticipations of the NIRA, McCloskey and Zecher (1984) showed that the WPI was highly correlated with the prices of foreign exchange during this period.

to be wondered that threats of rigid governmental control are hurled freely. (*NYT*, 7/9/33, p. N15)

There were also indications that the NIRA was beginning to adversely impact stock prices. Despite continued increases in the dollar price of gold, stock prices began to level off. The same issue of the *New York Times* (p. N5) noted that, "the intimation by the National Industrial Administrator that he was concerned over the gap between the recently accelerated production and consumer demand had a sobering effect upon the markets." There were indications that this concern over the "gap" between production and consumption might lead the administration to try to restrict output:

Another important point is that executives, who now bewail reduced working hours, are creating a situation whereby even shorter hours will be enforced if the present production pace continues. . . . The administration, already aware of the huge increase in output, may demand shorter hours to bring production into balance with consumption. (*NYT*, 7/16/33, p. N13)

The *New York Times* also noted that the threat of higher wages was restraining stock prices:

No doubt, the stock market was under some restraint because of the government's obvious impatience with the progress being made in its industrial recovery program. The possibility of a mandatory order which would fix minimum wages and limit the hours of labor pending acceptance of individual industrial "codes" was naturally disquieting. (7/16/33, p. N5)

At the same time, the *Times* suggested that because of recent progress in developing codes in the steel and oil industries the President might not have to intervene.

During May 1933, Roosevelt had asked business to increase wages with prices. The data indicate, however, little or no increase in the aggregate nominal wage rate during this period of rapid inflation, a situation that led Roosevelt to worry that the rise in output wouldn't bring real prosperity unless there were "buyers at high prices."[10] Like many others during this period, Roosevelt failed to see the distinction between the impact of an expansionary monetary policy that raised prices by boosting aggregate demand and the impact of a policy of *artificially* raising wages and prices above their equilibrium levels.[11]

During July 1933, business was engaged in the laborious process of setting up industry codes. On July 17, stocks rallied, perhaps in response to a report that "President and Johnson Agree General Wage Ruling Cannot Be Made Compulsory."[12] The next day, stocks reached their 1933 peak, and then immediately plunged in one of the greatest stock market crashes in U.S. history. On July 19, 1933, an impatient Roosevelt administration decided to force immediate adoption of the NIRA through the Blue Eagle program. The most important aspect of this program was a provision that sharply raised hourly wages and reduced hours worked for millions of workers. One indication that the full dimensions of the wage fixing scheme was at least partially unanticipated is the fact that the Dow fell 4.7 percent on July 19 and an additional 14.4 percent over the following two days, the third greatest crash[13] in modern stock market history:

> The New York Stock Market suffered one of the most noteworthy relapses in Stock Exchange history, and with such huge declines in prices on Wednesday, Thursday, and Friday that the only parallel to them for magnitude is to be found in the complete breakdown of stock prices in the autumn of 1929. (*Commercial and Financial Chronicle*, 7/22/33, p. 540)

The same issue of the *Commercial and Financial Chronicle* (p. 539) attributed the additional declines on July 20 and 21 to the aggressively anti-business statements made by General Johnson. Although the NIRA passed in June, the program that unfolded after July 19 appears to have shocked the business community:

---

10. *CFC*, 5/13/33, p. 3209.

11. During the 1932 campaign, Hoover had advocated policies that sounded much like the NIRA.

12. *NYT*, 7/17/33, p. 1.

13. The only comparable declines over any three-day period occurred during October 1929 and October 1987.

Rumors have been current for a long time that some . . . were urging that the Government should undertake regulatory control over business of every character and description, but it was not known whether President Roosevelt could be induced to give unqualified assent to a scheme of such all-embracing character and so far-reaching in its application. On Wednesday, however, all doubt in that regard was removed. (*Commercial and Financial Chronicle*, 7/22/33, p. 537)

Whereas the 1929 stock market crash seems to have been triggered by expectations of declining aggregate demand, the second half of the Depression was signaled by a stock market crash that reflected expectations of a drop in aggregate supply.

Temin and Wigmore (1990) attributed the July 19–21 stock market crash to the rise in the dollar between July 19 and July 21. Commodity prices declined along with the prices of foreign currencies. But a 4.2 percent dollar appreciation seems much too small to account for an 18.4 percent stock market crash.

The July 21 *New York Times* (p. 1) attributed the crash both to the decline in commodity prices and to "bearish rumors and reports from Washington that a crisis would occur in the nation's recovery program within sixty days unless wages were advanced further in order to increase the purchasing power of the public." Yet the *Times* continued to support the NIRA, arguing that it might help offset weakness in the economy resulting from the stock market crash! The July 30 *New York Times* (p. 37) noted that the recent production upswing had been "the most sensational trade advance in the economic history of the country" and suggested that a lull, not a severe reaction was to be expected. Instead, the economy plunged into renewed depression and industrial production declined over 18 percent by year end.

Another possible explanation for the stock market crash of July 19–21 is that the market perceived the Blue Eagle program as redistribution of income from capital to labor. Thus, the market decline does not necessarily refute the justification for the program—that is, that artificially boosting wages would increase aggregate demand and thus expand the economy. But the crash was also accompanied by a substantial increase in the risk premium on Baa bonds. It is difficult to see how a program could be expected to result in both more corporate bankruptcies, and more economic activity.

President Roosevelt was highly popular during the spring of 1933 as dollar depreciation seemed to be rapidly boosting output. As the following quotation illustrates, however, many conservatives feared an inflationary bubble that would soon burst. These attitudes would hamper Roosevelt later in the year:

> As the effects of the first jab in the arm wear off, the country is plainly more than a little worried over the cure-all drug called inflation. The first dose was just a promise—and what beautiful dreams it produced! Exchange was about to be stabilized, stocks and commodities were to go kiting, everyone was to be prosperous—long live the 50-cent dollar!
>
> Now the headache of the morning after is already unmistakable in many quarters. Such is the familiar inevitable history of the inflation treatment, and it is interesting to see even the first preliminary stage following the classic formula. Nothing is more certain to produce a temporary thrill, a delusion of wellbeing; nothing is more certain that, as the effects wear off, the patient feels worse than ever. That is the chief viciousness of inflation. It is in literal truth a habit-forming drug requiring ever larger and larger doses to keep the patient satisfied. (*New York Herald*, 4/27/33)

Although this appears to be a colorful parable of the "accelerationist hypothesis," April 27 was obviously much too soon for any cyclical relapse to have resulted from the dollar depreciation program. Even the collapse of industrial production after July 1933 occurred too soon to be plausibly regarded as the *long-run* effect of the expansionary monetary policy that didn't begin until April 1933. Nevertheless, this was exactly the argument that conservatives would make during the last quarter of 1933.

The adverse impact of this program on industrial output was both dramatic and immediate. Weekly indicators show output rising rapidly throughout the first half of July, and then breaking so sharply that the *level* of industrial production in August was 4.1 percent below July's level. When it became apparent in mid-August that the recovery had aborted, rumors of additional monetary inflation led to a rebound in stocks and further depreciation of the dollar:

> When everything else fails suggestions that the Administration intends to take active measures in the carrying out of the policy of infla-

tion to which it stands committed acts instantly as a stimulus to any flagging tendency in [stock and commodity] prices. (*Commercial and Financial Chronicle*, 8/19/33, p. 1284)

Between August 7 and August 9, FDR had a series of meetings with proponents of the "commodity dollar," including George Warren and Irving Fisher, and inflation rumors pushed the Dow 3.6 percent higher on August 8, and another 3.4 percent on August 9. The August 10 *New York Times* (p. 1) indicated that FDR's goal was first, a return to the average of the 1924–1926 commodity price level, and then, the adoption of a commodity dollar (i.e., a dollar with a stable purchasing power vis-à-vis a basket of commodities).[14]

By mid-August a perception began to develop that the Blue Eagle program would be more effective at raising wages than prices:

Iron and steel consumers . . . are unwilling to make further purchases of materials until they find a way out of some of the perplexities that have arisen from signing up under the Blue Eagle. Many of them, having raised wages and shortened hours, now fear that they cannot obtain compensatory increases in their prices, realizing only too well that the final arbiter on prices is the ultimate consumer. (*Commercial and Financial Chronicle*, 8/19/33, p. 1327)

Without further dollar depreciation, there were significant limits as to the extent to which the Blue Eagle program could raise industrial prices.

After mid-August the forward discount on the dollar did begin to gradually increase (see Table 8.2). These market expectations of further dollar depreciation may have short-circuited opposition to the Blue Eagle program:

The [steel] industry believes that if general business does not expand spontaneously it will be induced by an inflationary program at Washington. (*Steel*, 9/4/33, reprinted in *Commercial and Financial Chronicle*, 9/9/33, p. 1842)

And the August 15 *New York Times* (p. 25) also forecast that "if by chance these [NIRA policies] should not produce the desired effect, it is understood

---

14. Today this policy would be called price-level targeting, or a price rule.

that the administration would not hesitate to manipulate credit and money in such a manner as to bring about higher markets."

On August 22, General Johnson talked to the Fed about the need to expand credit to "speed up the NRA program,"[15] and on August 25, both the stock and foreign exchange markets rallied strongly on news that the Fed had renewed an aggressive policy of open market purchases.[16] The *New York Times* interpretation is particularly interesting:

> The renewal of the buying of "governments" on a scale unprecedented in the present Administration's credit-inflation program had been vaguely forecast this week, but the official announcement yesterday came as a surprise nevertheless. To the more reckless advocates of currency inflation it must have been a rude shock, indicating, as it undoubtedly did, that the administration was still avoiding the expediency of outright currency inflation. (8/25/33, p. 23)

To a twenty-first-century economist, the assertion that inflation proponents would receive news of open market purchases being instituted on an "unprecedented" scale as a "rude shock" must seem bewildering. But as we saw earlier, there was substantial doubt as to the effectiveness of policies such as the 1932 open market purchases. On the other hand, almost no one doubted the efficacy of "outright currency inflation," only its desirability. Of course, this time the United States was off the gold standard, and open market purchases had somewhat more potential to expand aggregate demand than had been the case in 1932. And the next day, stocks and foreign currencies did rally strongly. A few weeks later, however, commodity prices were again falling, and the administration again began to search for ways of depreciating the dollar. In Chapter 7 we will look at how FSR accomplished that goal.

---

15. *CFC*, 8/26/33, p. 1501–02.

16. The Dow rose 3.6 percent on August 25 and the French franc rose 1.9 percent on August 25 and 2.0 percent on August 26. The news came out the previous day "after business was ended on the various Exchanges" (*NYT*, 8/25/33, p. 23).

Interpreting July 1933

Consider the following hypothesis: rather than being a single event, "the" Great Depression was actually two distinction depressions. The first, demand-side depression, ended in late 1934, by which time output had returned to its "natural rate." A second, supply-side depression, began in late July 1933, sharply depressed the natural rate of output, and lasted for eight more years. As with the gold market shocks, we will examine this hypothesis from three perspectives: the predictions of economic theory, the relationship between various macroeconomic time series, and financial market responses to policy news. We will see that all three types of evidence support the "two depressions" hypothesis.

In order to better understand why the recovery faltered after July 1933, we need to go back and take a closer look at why Fisher's business cycle model broke down at precisely that date. Although Fisher did not explicitly use the term "aggregate demand," he implicitly assumed that price level fluctuations were generated by demand shocks. In retrospect, he probably should have made some attempt to account for the supply side of the economy. And he also should have tried to distinguish between anticipated and unanticipated inflation. But before we are too quick to condemn him for oversimplification, recall how even as recently as the 1970s, macroeconomists were caught off guard as oil shocks and changes in inflation expectations played havoc with their 1960s-era Phillips curve models. And Fisher (1934, p. 362) did recognize that "the introduction of codes under the NRA, as well as the processing of taxes under the AAA seemed to have a deterrent effect upon the activities of industry."

It is interesting that Fisher's model predicts a complete recovery from the Depression before the end of 1933. Because the model does a fairly good job of (conditionally) forecasting both the Great Contraction and the explosive recovery between March and July of 1933, it is tempting to look at the predicted path of output in Figure 6.2 as a policy counterfactual, that is, the likely path of output had Roosevelt refrained from his policy of mandating higher wages. I don't think that we can take this conditional forecast too seriously, but I do believe that this out-of-sample forecasting exercise has something useful to say about policy counterfactuals. Because this is such an important issue, we need to take a closer look at what this exercise is telling us.

Fisher's model is clearly inferior to recent "natural rate models" that postulate a relationship between output fluctuations and *unanticipated* changes in the price level. But remember that during the gold standard era there was very little evidence of any long-run trend toward higher prices. Indeed, Barsky (1987) showed that changes in the price level were almost completely unforecastable during the classical gold standard era. Thus, it is not clear that Fisher's failure to incorporate inflation expectations into his model would have been much of a problem for studies using interwar data. Of course, there are other more serious problems, such as Fisher's failure to include a variable for lagged output levels, which might have led to the unrealistic implication that a policy of rapid reflation would have been expected to generate an almost instantaneous recovery in output. And if we take a close look at Fisher's 1925 paper, we see an empirical business cycle study that is dominated by a single cycle, the depression of 1920–1922. Thus, its ability to forecast out-of-sample is going to depend on whether that early post-war depression was in some sense "typical." In addition, we need to think about the "Lucas critique." That is, would output respond in the same way to inflation created by dollar devaluation, as to earlier episodes of rising prices that occurred while the United States was still firmly attached to the gold standard?

Between early 1920 and mid-1921, a 40 percent fall in the wholesale price level was associated with a 32 decline in industrial production. After July 1921, wholesale prices leveled off for about nine months and then began rising. The end of the price deflation brought a rapid recovery in output, as industrial production soared by 55 percent between July 1921 and December 1922, reaching a level 6 percent above its 1920 peak. Although the Great Contraction was substantially deeper than the first postwar depression, there are a number of qualitative similarities.[17] The initial stages of the recovery, however, differed in two significant respects. The price level increased more rapidly in 1933 (despite an even more depressed economy) and the volatility of output was much greater.

One obvious question is whether it is reasonable to assume that the extra dose of inflation created by dollar devaluation would have been expected to lead to an even faster recovery during 1933 than occurred during 1921–1922,

---

17. Vedder and Gallaway (1993) attribute the greater severity of the Great Depression to the fact that wages were less flexible than in 1921. That might explain some of the differences, but it should also be noted that in both cases recovery did not begin until prices stopped falling.

when the dollar was still firmly attached to gold. We already saw that the policy of dollar depreciation was a mostly unanticipated monetary shock, and thus, most business cycle models would predict that it should have resulted in output rising at an even faster rate than during 1922 (when policymakers were essentially relying on the economy's self-correcting mechanism, i.e., wage cuts). And there is other evidence that the price rise was mostly unanticipated: there were no significant movements in either nominal interest rates or nominal wages. If the price level increase had been anticipated, both wages and interest rates should have risen to reflect higher inflation expectations. This suggests that the Lucas critique may not invalidate use of the Fisher model here; the dollar devaluation and resulting inflation were mostly unexpected.

Unfortunately, we only have four months worth of data to work with before the recovery was derailed by the NIRA. Thus, much of the "two depressions" hypothesis hinges on how seriously we take the 57 percent increase in industrial production during the spring and summer of 1933. It's nice that Fisher's model (conditionally) predicted just such an explosive recovery, but was it merely beginner's luck?

It turns out that modern natural rate models also suggest that dollar depreciation should lead to rapid recovery and also have difficulty explaining why unemployment rates remained so high during the later half of the 1930s.[18] For example, Temin and Wigmore (1990) observed that when the model of devaluation developed by Eichengreen and Sachs (1985) is applied to U.S. data, the actual level of output in 1935 is only *two-thirds* of its predicted value. Thus, at least in a qualitative sense, the "two depressions" hypothesis is also consistent with modern business cycle theory. But even if the latter half of the Depression was caused by an adverse supply shock, what evidence do we have linking the shock to federal labor market policies?

According to most neoclassical models of the labor market, an exogenous, government-mandated, wage hike would be expected to reduce employment. Although there has recently been some debate over the impact of modest increases in the minimum wage where firms have monopsony power, theory suggests that a mandated[19] 22 percent increase in the *average* hourly wage rate

18. Prescott (1999) and Cole and Ohanian (1999) both emphasize this point.

19. It is not entirely clear whether the wage codes should be regarded as "mandatory" or "voluntary." But for the purposes of this analysis, all that really matters is that the sharp wage increases of July through September would not have occurred without the NIRA.

during a period where prices increased only slightly would severely depress employment and output. But what can we say about the empirical evidence for this proposition?

In Chapter 13, we'll see that although real wages were highly counter-cyclical throughout the entire interwar period, nominal wages were essentially acyclical between 1920 and 1933 (when labor markets were relatively unregulated) and then became highly countercyclical for the remainder of the 1930s. In other words, higher wages don't reduce output when they reflect market forces (such as productivity gains) but do depress output when they reflect nonmarket factors. Although hardly definitive, this pattern is exactly what one would expect if New Deal policies began generating autonomous wage shocks in 1933. Thus, the wage cyclicality data is broadly consistent with the predictions of neoclassical theory—that is, that a government-mandated increase in real wage rates will depress output.

The response of the stock market to news of the President's Blue Eagle program provides an additional piece of evidence in favor of the "two depressions" hypothesis. In July 1933, dollar depreciation was creating expectations of higher prices, and industrial production had been rising rapidly for four months. Even if the public had not anticipated any further dollar depreciation, investors knew that in 1922, the economy continued to recover even without dollar depreciation. It would have been exceedingly odd if after 57 percent industrial output growth in four months, investors suddenly expected output to decline over the next two years. But if investors did not see this occurring before the Blue Eagle program was announced, then it would hardly be surprising to see the stock market react quite adversely to policy news that seemed likely to derail the recovery.

As we saw in 1987, stock market crashes do not always presage economic downturns. Nevertheless, it is hard to ignore the fact that immediately following the other two[20] of the three greatest (three-day) stock market crashes in American history, the economy performed very poorly relative to the output path that might have plausibly been expected a month or two earlier.

We don't know if the entire 18.4 percent decline in the Dow was due to news of the Blue Eagle program. As noted earlier, a small portion of the decline

---

20. October 25–29, 1929, and July 19–21, 1933.

was probably caused by the dollar's strength. But it is also possible that this drop understates the impact of the wage shock. As we saw in "The NIRA and the Stock Market," by mid-July investors were already somewhat concerned about the future direction of the NIRA program. The "new information" received from July 19 to 21 was not precisely a 22.3 percent wage shock but rather an increase in the perceived likelihood of such a shock. This means that the three-day stock price collapse may significantly *understate* the overall impact of the Blue Eagle program on equity values.

Also recall that if output had continued rising at the March through July pace, then by the end of 1933, industrial production would have greatly exceeded its 1929 peak. In contrast, even at their July peak, stock prices remained more than 71 percent below the levels of early September 1929. Despite soaring production, investors apparently did not foresee an uninterrupted boom in the economy. Concern over the New Deal in general, and the NIRA in particular, undoubtedly played a role in restraining the market during the run up to announcement of the Blue Eagle program.

Although some type of NIRA program was clearly expected, the scale of the July 19–21 stock market crash also suggests that the actual wage fixing policy was far more restrictive than had been previously anticipated. And it is also possible that a growing realization that FDR was serious in his high wage policy continued to depress stock prices even after the July announcement. It's worth noting that by September 1933, the business press was claiming that dollar depreciation was no longer boosting stock prices.[21] Yet, as Table 5.4 clearly shows, the correlation between the dollar and the Dow was nearly as strong during the period from July 19, 1933, to February 1, 1934, as during the preceding three months. One way of reconciling the business press's perceptions with the data is by assuming that the boost to stock prices provided by dollar depreciation from July 1933 to February 1934 was roughly offset by the restraining influence of higher wages, leaving the Dow on February 1, 1934, at almost precisely its mid-July level.

There is one piece of evidence that points against the two depressions' hypothesis. Recall that this hypothesis is based on the assumption that, in the absence of the Blue Eagle program, dollar devaluation would have led to a

21. *CFC*, 9/23/33, p. 2143.

rapid recovery in output. And one of the pieces of evidence for this view is that output did rise rapidly between March and July 1933. But some of that increase may be attributable to production increases in anticipation of the higher costs that would be imposed by the Blue Eagle program. Roos (1937, p. 431) suggested that "anticipation of increased costs and prices under the NRA must surely have led to some of the speculative buying which boosted production greatly in May, June, July, and August, 1933, and also in April and May, 1934, when the NRA again threatened shorter hours."[22] Roos' hypothesis is difficult to test because most real wage changes were probably unforecastable. Thus, the fact that interwar monthly output is not correlated with leads of real wages does not mean that speculation played no role in the spring 1933 boomlet.

On the other hand, even during June 1933 (when the economy was expanding vigorously), there were signs that uncertainty over the NIRA might also be *restraining* output:

> [S]elling orders [for steel] have halted to some extent owing to uncertainty as to the precise way in which the provisions of the Industrial Recovery Act, which are intended to insure a higher level of values, are likely to operate and likely to be enforced. (*Iron Age*, reprinted in *Commercial and Financial Chronicle*, 6/17/33, p. 4136)

It is also important to recognize that Roos's argument cuts both ways; we already saw that the greater the extent to which the higher costs were anticipated, the more likely that the 18.4 percent stock market crash understates the impact of the wage shock on market expectations of the economy's underlying health.

The view that the NIRA reduced aggregate supply and inhibited the recovery is increasingly widely accepted. But the same cannot be said for my hypothesis that sometime around the end of 1934, the first depression had ended and output had returned to its natural rate. That view is obviously based

---

22. Lyon, et al. (1972) made a similar observation. Roos (1937) indicated that the President's Re-Employment Agreement was rushed into effect in July precisely because of a fear that the economy was unstable due to speculation. But *Iron Age* noted that steel consumption increases "closely paralleled" production increases. (*CFC*, 7/1/33, p. 4). Roos also noted that NRA members like himself who anticipated a decline in production after implementation of the codes were labeled "reactionaries" (1937, p. 88).

on the assumption that the wage shock had dramatically raised the natural rate of unemployment. Of course, the precise timing of the counterfactual recovery path is unknowable; my guesstimate is based on the following assumptions. First, it is likely that some of the production increase during the spring was in anticipation of the Blue Eagle program, and thus, the 57 percent growth in industrial output which occurred during the first four months of Roosevelt's presidency probably overstates the economy's response to currency devaluation. Otherwise, that rate of growth would have led to complete recovery by November 1933!

Alternatively, we could use the 1921 depression as a benchmark. In the recovery of 1921–1922, it took seventeen months for industrial production to rise by 55 percent. Starting in March 1933, that rate of growth would have meant full recovery by roughly the end of 1935.[23] But that cannot be an appropriate benchmark—in 1933 output rose by over 57 percent in just the first four months of recovery! There are two reasons why the recovery from the 1921 depression almost certainly *understates* the economy's growth potential in 1933. Output in 1933 was even more depressed than in 1921 (recall that growth becomes more difficult as one approaches full employment), and the depreciation of the dollar provided a powerful monetary stimulus that was not available in 1921–1922. In contrast to 1933, prices were flat during the early stages of the 1921–1922 recovery.

To summarize, there are at least six reasons to believe that without the NIRA, dollar depreciation would have led to a relatively rapid recovery from the Great Depression:

1. Interwar Phillips curve models suggest that output should recover quickly once prices stop falling.

2. Unlike during 1921–1922, FDR did not wait for the economy's self-correcting mechanism to operate. Instead, he (successfully) pursued a highly inflationary monetary policy.

3. Output did rise by 57 percent between March and July 1933.

---

23. Here, I am using the industrial production level for December 1928 as a benchmark for the natural rate of output. In addition, I have allowed for a 2.7 percent per annum increase in the natural rate.

4. Output fell sharply after policymakers artificially raised wages by 22.3 percent during mid-1933, just as neoclassical theory would predict.

5. The stock market reaction to the announcement of the Blue Eagle program suggests that investors suddenly became much more bearish about the economy.

6. In later chapters, we will see that output rose strongly after the NIRA was repealed in mid-1935, and that wage shocks in mid-1934, early 1937, late 1938, and late 1939 were also associated with sharp slowdowns in output growth.

Friedman and Schwartz suggested that the NIRA (and related policies) might have also slowed the recovery by indirectly depressing aggregate demand. They argue that without the artificially high price level after 1933 there would have been:

> [A] still larger favorable balance of trade and hence a still larger gold outflow. The changed political and economic climate might well have invoked a greater demand for investment, a smaller decline in interest rates or perhaps even a rise instead of a decline, and a less rapid fall in the ratio of deposits to reserves desired by commercial banks. The rise in the stock of money would therefore probably have been greater on two scores: high-powered money would have risen more, and the ratio of the money stock to high-powered money would have declined less. (p. 499)

Their first argument hinges on whether gold inflows to the United States reduced or increased the world gold reserve ratio; only in the former case would the inflows be expansionary. But they are on firmer ground with the second argument—a stronger economy would very likely have resulted in a higher money multiplier, or in terms of our model, a lower demand for base money.

Previous Interpretations of the NIRA and the Failed Recovery

To a modern economist, the confusion exhibited during the early days of the New Deal can seem quite frustrating. As the following quotation indicates, the connection between dollar depreciation and economic recovery was well understood at the time:

> The Federal Reserve System after months of inaction renewed its drive towards easing credit by purchasing $25,000,000 in government securities, the New York bank reduced its rediscount rate from 3 to 2½ percent and President Roosevelt called for a law taking the country off the gold standard by statute.
>
> The immediate effect of these inflationary moves was to arrest at once any softening in commodity prices and, in some lines of industry, to cause a redoubling of efforts to place advance orders. The latter movement will undoubtedly spread and further stimulate the expansion now underway. (*NYT,* 5/28/33, p. N15)

Yet, later in the very same article, the *Times* also suggested that a policy of raising wages and reducing hours would help to provide the purchasing power required for the expanding economy.

Many interwar observers seemed to think that any policy boosting wages and prices would also boost purchasing power, regardless of whether the higher wages and prices were generated by more aggregate demand, or less aggregate supply. Today an economy-wide set of wage, price, and output controls would be viewed as being far more radical than a policy of dollar depreciation aimed at preventing deflation; in the 1930s, however, conservative opinion was much more receptive to the (now discredited) NIRA, than to any policy that even hinted at a move toward fiat money.

Temin and Wigmore (1990) and Eggertsson (2008) also saw the devaluation of the dollar as a regime change that sparked the economic recovery. In contrast, Eichengreen (1992, p. 344) argued that the dollar depreciation program failed to produce a sustained recovery because it was not accompanied by "rapid monetary expansion." He argued that, "recovery had to await stabilization of the dollar in 1934." But sustained recovery occurred only after mid-1935, when the NIRA was thrown out.

Although I agree with Temin and Wigmore's view of the importance of monetary regime change, they have a very different interpretation of the NIRA:

Weinstein . . . suggested that the [NIRA] . . . could have choked off the recovery by the threat of higher real wages. This seems unlikely. . . . We suggest instead that an apparent weakening of Roosevelt's commitment to devaluation halted the expansion. When Roosevelt ordered the Federal Reserve to support the dollar in July, the . . . [Dow] dropped from 108 to 88 in 4 days. Commodity prices fell, and both the New York Stock Exchange and the Chicago Board of Trade temporarily restricted trading volume. The value of the dollar had become a key index of the Roosevelt administration's commitment to its new regime. When he hesitated, expectations fell and production faltered. Fortunately, the dollar resumed its fall and the recovery was not aborted. (1990, p. 499–500)

There are two problems with this interpretation. Earlier, I argued that the rise in the dollar (4.2 percent) was much too small to explain the huge decline in the Dow between July 18 and 21. More importantly, the recovery *was* aborted and did not resume until the NIRA was repealed in mid-1935.

A few have gone even further than Temin and Wigmore, arguing that the NIRA and AAA may have actually contributed to the recovery from the Depression.[24]

Even during the 1930s, economists such as Keynes, Fisher and Hawtrey understood that the NIRA had probably slowed recovery from the Depression. More recently, studies by Weinstein (1981), Vedder and Gallaway (1993), Bordo, Erceg, and Evans (2000), and Cole and Ohanian (2004), reached similar conclusions. But I think it is fair to say that none went quite so far in arguing that, without the NIRA's high wage policy, the Depression would have essentially ended by late 1934.[25] There are at least four reasons I have reached somewhat more dramatic conclusions than most previous researchers.

---

24. Bittlingmeyer (1996) argued that cartels can boost output when there are significant fixed costs. DeLong and Summers (1986) suggest that less price flexibility may be stabilizing. And Eggertsson (2006) suggested that the NIRA may have raised inflation expectations. None of these papers specifically asserted that higher wages would promote recovery.

25. With no NIRA, Cole and Ohanian's model predicts a recovery by 1936. They also note that output growth was very rapid after many of the New Deal high wage policies were relaxed in the early 1940s. Vedder and Gallaway also thought that, if not for the NIRA, recovery by 1936 might have been possible.

Most of these researchers placed less emphasis than I have on the "wage shock" aspect of the NIRA.[26] The impact of higher prices and weaker antitrust laws is ambiguous. The price cartels may have depressed output, but we also know that a lot of cheating took place. Large firms had to meet competition from smaller firms not covered by the NIRA, as well as foreign competition. While wages jumped by more than 22 percent in the two months after July 1933, wholesale price inflation actually slowed, as did the rate of dollar depreciation. This is exactly what one would have expected if dollar depreciation were the key factor driving prices higher in 1933.

A second difference is that most studies have relied on quarterly or annual data, not monthly data. Even using quarterly data, the production spike in July 1933 seems far less dramatic, and with annual data, this mini-business cycle is completely obscured. Industrial production increased 9.5 percent between 1933 and 1934, and then by another 15.3 percent between 1934 and 1935.[27] These certainly look like healthy rates of growth, and thus don't seem to indicate that the economy had stalled after implementation of the NIRA. As we have seen, however, the monthly industrial production figures tell a very different story, with production leveling off for two years after July 1933. The rapid growth in the annual production data is due the fact that growth in industrial output was extremely rapid during the first half of 1933 and then again during the second half of 1935 (after the NIRA was declared unconstitutional).

An even more important reason for the differences in interpretation is that most other researchers have tended to look at probable causes in isolation. Some economic historians have studied gold and/or monetary questions; others have focused on structural issues related to the New Deal. But it is very misleading to analyze either set of issues in isolation. Consider the plateau in industrial production between mid-1933 and mid-1935. I have argued that both dollar devaluation and the NIRA had extraordinarily powerful effects on output, but that the two policies roughly cancelled each other out.[28] This

26. Of the researchers cited above, Vedder and Gallaway (1993) and Cole and Ohanian (2004) probably put the greatest emphasis on the wage problem and are, in that respect, closest to my interpretation.

27. Real GDP rose by 10.8 percent between 1933 and 1934 and by 8.9 percent between 1934 and 1935.

28. In this respect, the narratives by Hawtrey (1947) and Glasner (1989) are probably closest to the one presented in the book. They focused on how the U.S. economy was impacted by both gold market disturbances and New Deal labor policies.

means that a researcher focusing on monetary policy might see only modest evidence of the expansionary potential of the dollar depreciation program. Similarly, someone focusing only on the NIRA would tend to underestimate its contractionary impact.

And even if researchers did look at both monetary and wage policy, they may have used the wrong indicator of monetary policy. For instance, Weinstein (1981) did observe that in the absence of the NIRA, monetary expansion should have led to even more rapid economic growth during the mid-1930s. But Weinstein relied on money supply figures as a policy indicator, rather than the price of gold, and thus greatly underestimated the extent of monetary stimulus in 1933.

And finally, many other researchers seem to have underestimated the U.S. economy's ability to self-correct. Great Contractions are so rare that we don't really know much about the economy's properties at 25 percent unemployment. Although economists sympathetic to Roosevelt often point out that recovery from the Depression was rapid, I cannot help agreeing with Cole and Ohanian's (2004) view that the recovery was surprisingly anemic. The initial surge in output during the spring of 1933 showed that there were no technical impediments to extremely rapid growth. Yet between July 1933 and July 1935 industrial production actually declined. And as late as July 1940, more than *seven years* after the recovery began; the nonfarm unemployment rate is estimated to have been between 14 and 21 percent![29]

Concluding Remarks

We began this chapter by looking at a state-of-the-art interwar business cycle model, Fisher's famous "Phillips curve" paper. Although not all economists shared Fisher's views, the business cycle models of his most distinguished contemporaries[30] all shared the assumption that there would normally be a strongly positive price level/output correlation at cyclical frequencies. We also

29. The Lebergott-BLS estimate for 1940 is 21.3 percent. Darby (1976) excludes those in government relief jobs and comes up with an estimate of 13.9 percent. Because output was flat in early 1940 and grew rapidly in late 1940, the mid-year figures were almost certainly even higher than the annual averages.

30. Indeed Cassel (1922), Robertson (1922), Hawtrey (1923), Keynes (1923), and Pigou (1927) all saw price level instability as an important cause of the business cycle.

saw that the WPI was highly procyclical until July 1933. In subsequent chapters, I will argue that by looking at the breakdown of Fisher's model after July 1933, we can better understand—not just the unusual duration of the Great Depression—but also why monetary policy was deemphasized after 1933 and why Keynes' *General Theory* found such a warm welcome in America.

By the fall of 1933, it had become clear that the Blue Eagle program had failed to boost output, and this led Roosevelt to resume his dollar depreciation program. The second phase of the program was in some ways even more interesting than the first. No longer merely an indicator of the impact of various policy signals emanating from Washington, in October 1933, the buying price of gold became an actual *instrument* of monetary policy. In the next chapter, we will examine one of the most intriguing episodes in American monetary history, a policy perfectly suited to analysis using the gold market approach.

Table 6.2. Selected Weekly Indicators, April 1933 to February 1934

Week Ending	WPI	Gold Index	Exch. Rate	Dow	For. Disc.	Aaa Yield	Baa Yield
4/15/33	603	815	40305	6288	1.2%	4.74%	9.13%
4/22/33	604	819	42486	7224	1.4%	4.85%	8.97%
4/29/33	615	772	44776	7766	1.1%	4.78%	8.53%
5/6/33	619	750	45815	7761	1.0%	4.77%	8.02%
5/13/33	623	762	46230	8085	0.9%	4.59%	7.67%
5/20/33	630	779	45006	8021	0.7%	4.54%	7.54%
5/27/33	633	785	46564	8961	0.8%	4.51%	7.33%
6/3/33	638	773	46693	9002	0.9%	4.51%	7.25%
6/10/33	640	775	48091	9442	0.7%	4.49%	7.12%
6/17/33	645	772	47293	9023	0.5%	4.45%	7.12%
6/24/33	651	762	48906	9567	0.7%	4.41%	6.94%
7/1/33	663	774	50131	10092	0.7%	4.40%	6.80%
7/8/33	672	758	55455	10515	0.6%	4.38%	6.61%
7/15/33	689	742	56069	10610	0.5%	4.35%	6.47%
7/22/33	697	734	54375	8842	0.5%	4.35%	6.74%
7/29/33	692	733	53159	9454	0.8%	4.33%	6.60%

(Table 6.2 continued on the next page)

Table 6.2. Selected Weekly Indicators, April 1933 to February 1934, *continued*

Week Ending	WPI	Gold Index	Exch. Rate	Dow	For. Disc.	Aaa Yield	Baa Yield
8/5/33	692	770	53250	9262	0.8%	4.30%	6.65%
8/12/33	694	759	53025	9747	0.6%	4.29%	6.73%
8/19/33	693	764	53331	9832	0.7%	4.29%	6.75%
8/26/33	696	752	56711	10507	0.9%	4.30%	6.86%
9/2/33	697	713	56850	10366	0.9%	4.33%	6.94%
9/9/33	697	712	54748	9942	1.0%	4.31%	7.08%
9/16/33	705	725	58201	10532	1.2%	4.31%	7.09%
9/23/22	715	688	60639	9978	1.2%	4.41%	7.48%
9/30/33	711	693	60095	9482	0.9%	4.38%	7.60%
10/7/33	713	680	59078	9820	1.0%	4.35%	7.53%
10/14/33	711	695	56164	9559	1.0%	4.31%	7.37%
10/21/33	704	701	55013	8364	1.0%	4.31%	7.48%
10/28/33	709	692	58039	9201	1.3%	4.35%	7.48%
11/4/33	709	684	60660	9309	0.9%	4.40%	7.62%
11/11/33	712	663	62733	9610	1.0%	4.50%	7.78%
11/18/33	717	637	63550	9867	1.3%	4.60%	8.21%
11/25/33	710	618	61737	9928	1.5%	4.62%	8.15%
12/2/33	707	644	61028	9907	1.9%	4.57%	8.01%
12/9/33	709	646	61691	10292	1.4%	4.50%	7.67%
12/16/33	708	661	61390	9806	1.2%	4.48%	7.65%
12/23/33	704	639	61176	9804	1.5%	4.48%	7.80%
12/30/33	708	641	61991	9990	1.5%	4.44%	7.56%
1/6/34	710	646	61440	9694	1.5%	4.43%	7.57%
1/13/34	717	659	61471	9866	1.0%	4.36%	7.14%
1/20/34	723	643	62401	10552	0.7%	4.30%	6.70%
1/27/34	724	650	62228	10603	0.8%	4.29%	6.58%
2/3/34	728	653	63098	10941	0.7%	4.23%	6.27%

Note: The gold index is the Annualist Index of Commodity Prices measured in gold terms. The forward discount is the three-month forward discount on the dollar in terms of British pounds. The exchange rate is the dollar price of French francs.

7

The Rubber Dollar

EVEN IN A year of heterodox policy initiatives, President Franklin D. Roosevelt's gold-buying program stands out as a particularly odd policy. Between October 1933 and January 1934, Roosevelt (FDR) gradually raised the price at which the U.S. government purchased gold, with the avowed intention of depreciating the dollar and raising the price level. The idea of adjusting the official price of gold inversely to movements in the price level had been proposed in Britain more than a century earlier, during the post–Napoleonic War deflation.[1] Irving Fisher (1920) rediscovered and popularized the idea, dubbing it a "compensated dollar plan." By the late 1920s the plan enjoyed considerable support among economists, but remained completely untested.

Roosevelt's gold-buying program was highly controversial, both at home and abroad. The policy's transmission mechanism was something of a mystery to the financial press during 1933 and even today remains poorly understood. For instance, although referred to as a "gold-buying program," it is unlikely that the actual purchases of gold were large enough to significantly affect the market price of gold. Throughout the final two months of 1933, however, the official price of gold almost invariably diverged from the London (free market) price, often by a relatively large margin. This is important because the whole point of Roosevelt's policy was clearly to affect the *market* price of gold.

These facts have led some modern historians to view the program as being largely ineffective and to treat the policy as a minor footnote to Roosevelt's broader strategy of devaluing the dollar. In late 1933, however, the gold-buying

---

1. The policy was first proposed by Rooke (1824) and Williams (1892).

program was *the* big news story, far overshadowing any of FDR's other policy
initiatives. And both the press and financial markets did pay close attention
to the daily announcements of the government's official gold purchase price.
During the period when Roosevelt was most aggressively increasing the buying price of gold, his policies were seen as sharply depressing both the value
of the dollar and long-term Treasury bond prices. The scheme was so controversial that several of Roosevelt's top economic advisors resigned in protest
over the policy.

In this chapter we'll see how the gold market approach can provide insights
into this program that are inaccessible through conventional monetary theory.
The section "The Policy of Dollar Depreciation" reviews the broader policy
goals of the Roosevelt administration and explains why during late 1933 Roosevelt turned to what Eichengreen (1992, p. 338) called "peculiar quarters" for
advice on macroeconomic policy. The following four sections show the impact
of the gold-buying program on the value of the dollar, as well as its effect on
commodity, stock, and bond prices. In the section "Previous Evaluations of
the Gold-Buying Program" I argue that the program has been widely misunderstood, and in "The Gold-Buying Program and Macroeconomic Policy"
I show why it made sense for Roosevelt to choose such a roundabout strategy
for devaluing the dollar. We will see that the program has important implications for contemporary monetary theory.

Roosevelt's gold-buying program has been unfairly maligned by both contemporaneous critics and modern historians. Its relatively sophisticated use
of market expectations gave the program both tactical and strategic advantages over alternative policies, particularly in light of institutional constraints
on Roosevelt's ability to control monetary policy. We will see that what was
essentially a policy feedback rule (linked to flexible market prices) represented
a remarkably modern approach to the problem of promoting rapid reflation
through the use of expansionary monetary policy. Indeed, Svensson (2003a)
recently advocated a similar policy as a cure for Japan's "liquidity trap."

The Policy of Dollar Depreciation

After the dollar was allowed to float on April 17, 1933, its value initially fell
by only about 10 percent. In sharp contrast to many other countries leaving

the gold standard during the early 1930s, the United States was not "forced" off the gold standard; in fact, its holdings of gold were the largest in the world. Rather, the decision to talk down the value of the dollar was made pursuant to the broader macroeconomic objectives of the Roosevelt administration (i.e., reflation). Even within the administration, however, there were widely differing views as to the merits of depreciating the dollar.

Between April and July 1933, the market price of gold increased from $20.67 to over $29 per ounce and the dollar depreciated sharply against both gold-backed currencies, such as the French franc, and floating currencies such as the pound sterling. In some respects, the October gold-buying program merely formalized or made explicit the policy of dollar depreciation that Roosevelt had already been pursuing for six months. But there was one key difference; after October 21 the buying price of gold would become an actual *instrument* of monetary policy.

In Chapter 5, we saw evidence that dollar depreciation triggered sharp increases in stock and commodity prices, as well as industrial production. Between July and October 1933, however, the value of the dollar leveled off and stock prices, commodity prices, and industrial production all suffered sharp setbacks. As the Blue Eagle program began to depress output there was growing frustration over the pace of recovery. By late August, administration pressure led the Federal Reserve to step up its open market purchases to a rate of $35 million per week, and the dollar resumed its decline in September.

On August 30, the *New York Times* announced (p. 27) that "the share market turned sharply upward shortly before the close of business on the Stock Exchange yesterday following publication of the news that President Roosevelt had modified the gold embargo." By allowing newly mined gold to be exported at world prices, Roosevelt took the first step toward establishing a gold market, which he could then manipulate to devalue the dollar. On September 8, the Treasury set the price of newly mined gold at $29.62/ounce. Subsequently, the price was adjusted daily according to conditions in the world gold market (i.e., roughly according to the dollar/gold bloc exchange rates).

As the open market purchase (OMP) program accelerated in mid-September, the dollar began to fall sharply, but stocks seemed less responsive than during previous months. Signs that output was now declining rapidly led to renewed demands for inflation. The *New York Times* attributed modest stock price

increases on September 11, 13, 14, and 16 to rumors that a more inflationary policy would be adopted but also noted that falling output was hurting
stocks. And bond prices, which had rallied during the spring and summer,
now declined on "sudden fears of currency inflation and severe weakness in
the dollar."[2] As increasing amounts of gold were hoarded, wholesale prices
measured in gold terms[3] declined sharply and foreign stock markets showed
an increasing tendency to react adversely to the falling dollar. For the first
time since taking office, President Roosevelt faced strong opposition to his
program. Surprisingly, however, the opposition was directed not at the NIRA
but rather at the dollar depreciation:

> When the policy of the Administration . . . was first disclosed, and busi-
> ness recovery quickly followed . . . the disposition everywhere was to let
> the authorities at Washington unfold their plans . . . and to accord the
> program a sort of quasi-approval. . . . Latterly, however, the temper has
> changed as device after device has been put into effect looking toward
> credit inflation, all supporting the conclusion that apparently there is
> no limit as to how far credit expansion is to be carried. Accordingly
> . . . anxiety is being manifested and criticism is no longer withheld.
> (*Commercial and Financial Chronicle*, 9/23/33, p. 2143)

On September 21, a *New York Times* headline reported that "ROOSE-
VELT CHECKS INFLATION DEMAND."[4] Stocks fell by a total of 7.7
percent on September 20 and 21, and the following day's *New York Times*
(p. 27) attributed the decline to "the disappointment of those traders who
had counted too heavily of the prospect of currency inflation." Another sharp
decline on September 27 was also attributed to signs that FDR would oppose
inflation. But just a few days later the *Times* hinted that further steps would
be necessary because "The NRA, it is held, has brought about unsettling influences in several industries and curtailment of operations in some."[5]

---

2. *CFC*, 9/23/33, p. 2162.

3. See Table 6.2

4. The same issue (p. 29) even noted that some were advocating a plan "to let new money
drop from airplanes."

5. *NYT*, 10/1/33, p. N7.

By mid-October it was apparent that the Fed's open market purchases would not be sufficient to offset the strong worldwide deflationary pressures resulting from gold hoarding. Stock, commodity, and foreign exchange prices continued to decline on news that the Treasury planned a bond refinancing program:

> The refinancing proposal was construed immediately as an answer by the administration to "left-wing" inflationists who have been demanding payment of maturing government obligations with "printing-press" money. (*NYT*, 10/12/33, p. 1)

> All the financial and commodity markets adjusted themselves yesterday to the altered conditions arising from the announcement, over the Columbus Day holiday, of the government's bond conversion plan. The dollar advanced sharply, as did the bond market, but stocks and commodities broke widely. (*NYT*, 10/14/33. p. 21)

The October 15 issue of the *New York Times* (p. N7) assured readers that "the financial community . . . seems to be reasonably well satisfied that the inflation movement has been defeated." This complacency would not last long. Over the next week the dollar continued to rise on European war scares and rumors of a French devaluation. By October 21, stocks had reached their lowest point since May, and the administration finally decided to act.

The Gold-Buying Program

Roosevelt was under increasing pressure from farm groups to raise commodity prices, and growing doubts about the effectiveness of the Agricultural Adjustment Act (AAA) led Roosevelt to again turn to dollar depreciation as the method of implementing that goal. On October 20, Roosevelt met with Henry Morgenthau Jr. and George Warren to develop a strategy for depreciating the dollar. Prior to 1933 Warren was a relatively unknown agricultural economist at Cornell University and a friend of then Governor Roosevelt. Warren had been a long-time advocate of stabilizing the price level through adjustments in the dollar price of gold.

In a "Fireside chat" on the evening of October 22, 1933, Roosevelt announced a dramatic switch in administration policy:

> [A]lthough the prices of many products of the farm have gone up . . . I am not satisfied. . . . If we cannot do this [reflation] one way we will do it another. Do it, we will. . . . Therefore the United States must firmly take in its own hands the control of the gold value of the dollar . . . I am authorizing the Reconstruction Finance Corporation [RFC] to buy gold newly mined in the United States at prices to be determined from time to time after consultation with the Secretary of the Treasury and the President. (*NYT*, 10/23/33, p. 3)

The headlines in the following day's *New York Times* indicated the confusion generated by the speech: "President's Gold Plan Is Held Unprecedented and Bewildering," "Some Circles See in the Speech a Move Toward the 'Commodity Dollar.'" The *New York Times* (p. 1) also argued that the plan was "completely at variance with tested monetary precepts." Another article (p. 3) reported that Warren viewed the plan as leading to a dollar of "fixed value and a rubber weight," the same metaphor employed by Fisher to describe his "Compensated Dollar Plan" (CDP). Fisher's plan for adjusting the gold weight of the dollar in proportion to changes in the wholesale price index (WPI) had garnered considerable support during the 1920s and in 1932 had been incorporated into the Goldsborough Bill.[6]

Between October 21 and October 25, 1933, the price of gold in London rose from $29.06 to $30.93 per ounce, and the dollar depreciated on the European exchanges by a roughly proportionate magnitude. The Dow soared by 11.8 percent. The October 25 *New York Times* (p. 2) noted that the actual purchases were merely a "drop in the bucket" and that it was believed that the "announcement" of higher prices would presumably lead to the same sort of inflation as would be generated by an actual devaluation in the dollar. In the same issue (p. 29), the *New York Times* suggested that "there was some dispute among theorists whether it were possible to quote a gold price higher than

---

6. A poll of economists taken in 1927 showed that 252 out of 281 supported a policy of price level stabilization, and 70 even supported Fisher's CDP. During the 1920s and 1930s, Congressman Goldsborough introduced several bills to implement a policy of price level stabilization, and in 1932 his bill garnered considerable support.

the world level" since the world price would presumably adjust immediately to the quoted price.

The October 26 *New York Times* headlines noted that "Gold Buying Opens at $31.36, Only 27¢ over World Price" and "DOLLAR HAS AN ODD RISE." This reaction was attributed to the fact that the RFC price:

> was disappointing to some, as it was only slightly higher than that prevailing in London, the consensus was that the advance in foreign exchange rates recently and the decline in the value of the dollar were largely in anticipation of a price above the world parity. The feeling is that the method will be effective in depreciating the dollar . . . and many believe that there is little doubt that the price of gold will be increased gradually until commodities are selling at around the 1925–26 level, which is the goal of the administration. (10/26/33, p. 29)

On the following day, the quoted price increased another 18 cents and the London price again failed to keep pace. The *New York Times* headline reported that "Capital Denies Setback" and the paper also noted that although the increase in the RFC price was:

> less than had been expected . . . If the government should continue depreciating the currency by increasing the price of gold until commodity prices are at the 1925–26 level, the belief is that stock prices should advance. However, if for any reason the policy should be abandoned . . . many speculators do not see why stock prices should advance. (10/27/33, p. 29)

Although the preceding quotation suggests that "Wall Street" was in favor of the gold-buying program, the truth was somewhat more complex. We have already seen that both real and nominal stock prices were closely correlated with changes in the value of the dollar throughout the entire April 1933 through January 1934 period of dollar depreciation. Yet Roosevelt's program was strongly opposed by many of the more conservative financial leaders on Wall Street, in the financial press, and even within the Treasury.[7]

---

7. Interwar conservatives were much less likely than their modern "supply-side" counterparts to regard the stock market as a barometer of policy effectiveness.

Over the next several days, the administration was frustrated by a continuing decline in the market price of gold, and the October 28 *New York Times* (p. 21) noted that Wall Street was both confused and disappointed by the gold program. On October 29, the administration decided that additional steps were necessary, and the following day's headlines indicated that "ROOSEVELT DECIDES TO BUY GOLD IN WORLD'S MARKETS" ... "FIRST STEP IS NOT ENOUGH." ... "Three-Hour Meeting Discusses Ineffectiveness of Domestic Purchase Policy." Other headlines indicated a fear that Roosevelt's action might trigger a series of competitive devaluations: "Washington Hopes to Avoid Monetary War" and "BANKERS FORECAST GOLD RETALIATION."

The preceding quotations raise two interesting questions. Why was the gold-buying program already being viewed as "ineffective" a mere four days after being implemented? And why did the administration believe that foreign gold purchases would be any more effective than domestic purchases? Obviously, the perceived ineffectiveness related not to the performance of the macroeconomy, but rather the failure of London gold prices to move upward in tandem with the RFC price. It is apparent from these quotations, however, that even the interwar press understood the concept of market efficiency; markets move on expectations of future policy initiatives and thus the primary impact of the Roosevelt policy would have been expected to occur after the October 21 announcement, not the October 25 implementation. The Roosevelt administration appears to have implicitly adopted a criterion for success that would have required the policy to be more expansionary than anticipated!

It is *theoretically* possible for even fully anticipated increases in the RFC price to have generated proportionate increases in the free market price of gold. The efficient market hypothesis only precludes anticipated gold price increases that exceed the nominal return on other assets of comparable risk. But in this case the expected price rises must have been small. We do lack direct evidence as to the expected dollar return on gold assets held in London. But if one combines the extremely low short-term nominal interest rates in the United States with the fact that arbitrageurs could freely purchase gold-backed currencies, it seems unlikely that the anticipated *daily* change in the market price of gold ever reached levels of much more than $1/100$ percent. If so, then we can view actual changes in the London gold price during this period as being almost entirely unanticipated.[8]

The preceding discussion raises several other puzzling issues. In retrospect, we know that the RFC buying price was increased almost daily between October 25 and December 1, 1933, when it reached $34.01/ounce. And, although the exact timing and magnitude of the increases was a carefully guarded secret (and was decided on a day-by-day basis), the markets certainly knew that any changes would be in an upward direction. If markets moved in anticipation of future changes in the price of gold, then why would the administration not simply have opted to immediately increase the RFC buying price by the full $2.65 on October 25? To answer this question, we first need to consider an even more fundamental issue: Why should changes in the RFC buying price have had any impact on the market price of gold in London?

If the RFC had been willing and able to buy or sell unlimited quantities of gold at the quoted price, then this price would have certainly become the effective market price. But at no time during the gold-buying program was the RFC quote equal to the market price of gold. Since the RFC purchases were clearly too small to set the market price, it is not clear why the RFC quote would have had *any* impact on the price in London.

In many respects, the RFC gold purchases are just as perplexing as the daily changes in the RFC purchase price. Economic theory suggests that the only mechanism by which RFC gold purchases could affect London gold prices would be through their impact on the world demand for gold. During 1933, the gold bloc currencies were still rigidly fixed to gold, and even the sterling bloc maintained a relatively stable exchange rate vis-à-vis the gold bloc currencies, and hence gold itself. Therefore, during 1933, increases in the real value of gold would have tended to depress the price level of most industrial countries, particularly in Europe. And, since the U.S. money supply was not directly impacted by RFC actions, the resulting fall in the foreign exchange value of the dollar would represent a higher real value of foreign currencies rather than (the administration's goal of) a lower purchasing power for the dollar.

---

8. During this period, the mean (of the absolute value of the) daily variation in the London gold price was 1.28 percent.

The preceding discussion suggests that the administration appeared to have confused nominal and real gold prices. The October 31 *New York Times* (p. 29) reported that one reason markets were skeptical about Roosevelt's program was that inflation required more money to be placed in circulation. Printing money would raise commodity prices, including the nominal price of gold, and also depreciate the domestic currency. In contrast, buying gold raises the *real* price of gold and causes gold bloc currencies to appreciate. If Roosevelt wished to raise commodity price indices to their 1926 levels, it would seem that a more sensible method would have been to *sell* gold, rather than to buy it. In either case, the size of the U.S. monetary gold stock would ultimately be determined by Fed policy, and Roosevelt's influence was limited to the dollar price of gold, that is, the exchange rate. For any given exchange rate, the lower the U.S. demand for gold, the higher the world price level would be.

Even if one accepts the premise that RFC gold purchases could be an effective tool in increasing the price level, the October 29 decision to begin purchases in foreign markets is difficult to comprehend. The ostensible reason for this decision was that international markets were where the market price of gold was actually established. Once again, however, the theoretical basis for this policy shift remains unclear. Although the United States did not have a free gold market at that time, newly mined gold could already be exported at the RFC's price.[9] Thus, when the RFC switched from buying domestic newly mined gold to purchasing gold in foreign markets, it had the effect of increasing the export of newly mined gold by an amount equal to the RFC's foreign purchases. It is unclear why this change would have had any impact on the world gold market. Nevertheless, the policy shift was treated as a major news event and the price of gold in London rose by nearly 3 percent on Monday, October 30.

The preceding discussion provides abundant reasons why both contemporary observers and modern historians found Roosevelt's gold-buying program to be so perplexing. In the next section, I discuss why Roosevelt chose such an unusual program and provide evidence that the program may have been more effective than almost anyone has recognized.

---

9. Existing gold hoards had to be turned over to the Treasury at the pre-1933 par value of $20.67/oz.

Explaining the Gold-Buying Program

A full understanding of the gold-buying program requires an answer to the following question: Why didn't Roosevelt simply devalue the dollar in October 1933? Only three months later, Roosevelt did devalue the dollar when he raised the legal (or par) value of gold from $20.67 to $35 an ounce. And, after the devaluation the market price of gold quickly increased to approximate parity with the new par value. Even in October 1933, Roosevelt had full legal authority to raise the legal price of gold as high as $41.34/ounce. Why, then, would Roosevelt rely on such a convoluted strategy?

In his October 22 Fireside chat, Roosevelt directly addressed this issue:

> Some people are putting the cart before the horse. They want a permanent revaluation of the dollar first. It is the Government's policy to restore the price level first.[10]

This explains why Roosevelt did not opt for a permanent devaluation in October, but it does not explain why he refrained from a series of incremental changes in the par value of the dollar as a method for determining which exchange rate would best achieve his price level objectives. Instead, the par value remained at $20.67 as the RFC price was gradually raised.

As noted earlier, the popular "Compensated Dollar Plan" (CDP) would have involved frequent[11] changes in the par value, that is, the legal price of gold, in order to offset incipient movements in the price level. Although there may have been some technical problems with implementing some of the specific CDP proposals, these were certainly not insurmountable.[12] Rather, it seems more likely that there were political obstacles to pursuing a series of incremental devaluations.

It is useful to recall that during the ninety-two years from 1879 to 1971, the par value of the dollar was adjusted only once. To a much greater extent than today, the (inverse of the) price of gold was viewed as *the* value of the

---

10. *CFC*, 10/28/33, p. 3013.

11. The plans generally involved monthly or even bimonthly changes. See Fisher (1920).

12. See Patinkin (1993) for a discussion of some of these problems. Sumner (1990b) showed that Fisher's CDP was technically feasible. And Bordo, Dittmar, and Gavin (2003) show that the policy would have significantly reduced price level and inflation uncertainty.

dollar. Any decision to devalue would have been extraordinarily controversial. Even as noted a critic of the gold standard as Keynes viewed devaluation as a temporary, and unfortunate, expedient.[13] To Keynes, devaluation was a tool to be used sparingly, when required, to accommodate necessary fiscal and monetary policies. He did not favor manipulating the exchange rate as a method of reflating the economy. Keynes supported Roosevelt's policy of depreciating the dollar through July 1933 but then favored stabilizing the dollar at a value corresponding to a gold price of $28/ounce.[14] He opposed Roosevelt's policy of trying to sharply depreciate the dollar.

This dilemma was also understood by contemporary observers. The *New York Times* observed that "devaluation, once effected, cannot be repeated and the country which acts last can choose the level which suits it best."[15] And Paul Einzig added that

> The most common argument which was used in attempting to persuade the United States to agree to the currency truce was that it would not be binding upon her future monetary policy. In light of practical experience this argument sounds most unconvincing. It has been found that, whenever an inconvertible currency is kept stable for a while at a given level, it becomes increasing difficult to change that level without provoking strong opposition. (1933, pp. 122–23)

Perhaps the most dramatic example of the political obstacles to using devaluation as a routine policy tool occurred in 1938, when Roosevelt *failed* to devalue the dollar. Friedman and Schwartz noted that there were rumors the dollar would be devalued during the recession of 1937–1938. These rumors coincided with widespread private hoarding of gold, a frequent symptom of currency crises. And speculators had good reason to expect the dollar to be devalued. Prices and output declined very rapidly during late 1937 and early 1938. Because the 1933 devaluation had been accompanied by sharply higher stock and commodity prices, as well as large gains in output, it was natural to

---

13. For instance, note that Keynes was *not* recommending a devaluation of the pound during 1931. Also note that Keynes was instrumental in developing the Bretton Woods system, which involved pegging the dollar to gold at $35/oz.

14. See the *Collected Writings of J.M. Keynes*, Vol. 21, p. 272.

15. *NYT*, 5/29/33, p. 17.

expect Roosevelt to again attempt a monetary "shot in the arm."[16] His failure to do so provides an indication of how, even during a major depression, any reduction in the par value of the dollar would be viewed as a radical policy move.

If Roosevelt did operate under the assumption that any legal devaluation was likely to be permanent, then he would naturally have been reluctant to firmly commit to a new par value until it was clear that this value would be consistent with his price level objectives. When viewed from this perspective, Roosevelt's policy options were quite limited. The traditional tools of monetary policy included discount loans and open market operations, but these were under the control of the Federal Reserve. The Roosevelt administration had essentially two choices: print greenbacks or devalue the dollar. In May 1933, Congress had granted the president the authority to issue up to $3 billion in greenbacks, but this would have been even more controversial than devaluing the dollar.[17]

Throughout the period of depreciation most of Roosevelt's top advisors were opposed to his efforts to establish what they derisively referred to as a "commodity dollar." But the president himself was apparently entranced by Professor Warren's charts, which showed a close correlation between the price of gold and the price of a basket of commodities. Because Roosevelt wished to hold off from a formal devaluation until his price level objectives were met, he either intentionally or unintentionally adopted a policy of manipulating the free market price of gold through both public statements and RFC price increases.

Even a presidential statement will not impact the gold market unless it alters expectations of the future course of monetary policy. Roosevelt's statements to the effect that a higher price level was desirable might have altered expectations in two ways. If the dollar was devalued, the nominal value of the existing monetary gold stock would increase, and the Fed could respond with an increase in the money supply. If they did not, gold would flow into the

---

16. See the *CFC* (1937, p. 1783 and p. 2590).

17. The monetary base in mid-1933 was roughly $8 billion. Given that nominal income in 1933 was still barely one-half of its 1929 level, even the greenback proposal does not look all that radical from a modern perspective. The fact that this was widely viewed as a wildly inflationary proposal that Roosevelt was wise to reject provides another indication of the striking "conservatism" of interwar attitudes toward monetary policy.

United States, putting even more pressure on the Fed to inflate. In his fireside chat of October 22, Roosevelt alluded to an additional option: "If we cannot do this one way we will do it another. Do it, we will." This was probably a veiled reference to his authority to issue greenbacks and an implicit warning to his opponents in the Treasury and the Federal Reserve.

Throughout the spring and summer months, Roosevelt was able to keep the financial markets off balance with a series of statements that pushed gold, commodity, and stock prices sharply higher. By October, however, gold prices had fallen somewhat from their July peak, and Roosevelt was under growing pressure from farm groups to boost commodity prices. On October 18, Roosevelt called Warren to the White House to help prepare a new policy designed to raise the price of gold.

The gold-buying program involved the purchase of gold at "official prices," but the quantity of gold purchased was small relative to the size of the world gold market.[18] For this reason the purchases proved ineffective at making the official price coincide with the market price. The gold-buying program had the form but not the substance of a gold standard. Yet, at least initially, the market did seem to respond to the new policy. Traders apparently understood that Roosevelt was signaling an intention to take future steps that would have a meaningful impact on prices, probably a formal devaluation of the dollar.[19]

If one views the gold-buying program as an attempt to manipulate the gold market, without issuing greenbacks and without a formal devaluation, then some of the more perplexing aspects of the program begin to make more sense. Given the real or imagined constraints that Roosevelt operated under, nothing short of massive gold purchases would have insured that the RFC's official buying price coincided with the market price of gold. And massive RFC

---

18. According to the *CFC* (12/23/33, p. 4409), between October 25 and December 21, 1933, the RFC purchased about $62 million worth of gold. Although this may have represented close to 10 percent of world gold output, the relevant comparison is with the *stock* of gold. The world monetary gold stock exceeded $15 billion in late 1933, and billions more were held privately. By comparison, after Britain left the gold standard in September 1931, the Bank of France purchased nearly $900 million worth of gold. And the nominal gold stock in (pre-devaluation prices) was far lower in 1931.

19. Brown (1940) provides a similar interpretation.

purchases would have been very costly, possibly illegal,[20] and more likely to promote deflation overseas than inflation in the United States.

If the gold purchases were not essential to the program, why purchase any gold at all? In principle, Roosevelt might simply have announced a new gold price each day. In fact, the gold price announcements were generally the headline news story, whereas the gold purchases were mostly ignored by the press.[21] But a "gold-buying program" without any purchases of gold would have represented an even more transparent attempt to manipulate the gold market. If it were apparent that markets were moving solely on changing perceptions of Roosevelt's ultimate intentions, rather than on a *real* factor such as gold purchases, then there would have been even more pressure on Roosevelt to show his hand and make a permanent alteration in the value of the dollar. Even with the gold purchases, perceptive observers like Keynes saw the game Roosevelt was playing with the markets:

> This game of blind man's bluff with exchange speculators serves no useful purpose . . . is extremely undignified . . . and is responsible both for the irritation and for a certain lack of respect which exist abroad. (*NYT,* 12/31/33)

Roosevelt was very sensitive to the perception that he treated the value of the dollar too cavalierly. In his October 22 speech, Roosevelt emphasized that the gold-buying program was "a policy and not an expedient." If Roosevelt's policy utterances were to have any effect on markets, then it was essential that they have credibility. The gold-buying program certainly looked like a *policy*, and thus arguably had more credibility than would a set of statements (or prices) which merely conveyed Roosevelt's long-term policy goals.

Market Reactions to the Gold-Buying Program

This section provides evidence that (despite the rocky start) markets did react to the gold-buying program as a set of signals about future policy intentions.

---

20. Even some members of the Roosevelt administration questioned the legality of the gold purchases. This explains the odd procedure of having the RFC exchange debentures for gold.

21. The quantity purchased each day was a secret, but occasional press reports indicated that the amounts were believed to be trivial.

Table 7.1. Selected Economic Indicators: October 21, 1933 to January 15, 1934

Date	RFC Gold Price	London Gold Price	T-Bond Price	Dow	Moody's Index
10/21/33	—	29.06	98.72	83.64	1,209
10/23/33	—	29.85	98.62	88.13	1,228
10/24/33	—	30.63	98.53	91.35	1,229
10/25/33	31.36	30.93	98.41	93.54	1,254
10/26/33	31.54	30.97	98.31	92.02	1,248
10/27/33	31.76	30.93	98.19	93.22	1,262
10/28/33	31.82	30.53	98.09	92.01	1,252
10/30/33	31.96	31.42	97.62	88.43	1,254
10/31/33	32.12	31.11	97.50	88.16	1,239
11/1/33	32.26	31.57	97.50	89.62	1,231
11/2/33	32.36	32.17	97.25	90.54	1,237
11/3/33	32.57	32.25	96.97	93.60	1,242
11/4/33	32.67	32.18	96.88	93.09	1,245
11/6/33	32.84	32.20	96.62	92.50	1,236
11/7/33	32.84	31.84	*	*	*
11/8/33	33.05	32.63	96.75	95.54	1,263
11/9/33	33.15	33.09	96.00	96.40	1,283
11/10/33	33.20	33.34	95.00	95.06	1,280
11/11/33	33.32	33.12	95.88	96.10	1,278
11/13/33	33.45	33.19	96.19	95.98	1,288

Table 7.1 shows the official RFC gold price, the closing price of gold in London (set after the RFC price announcement), the price of long-term U.S. Treasury bonds,[22] the Dow, and the Moody's commodity price index during the gold-buying program. All but two of the RFC price changes occurred between October 25 and December 1, 1933. Therefore, this sample period was used to test the relationship between the RFC gold price and the price in London.

---

22. Treasury bonds with a coupon rate of 3 percent and a maturity date of 1951–55.

Date	RFC Gold Price	London Gold Price	T-Bond Price	Dow	Moody's Index
11/14/33	33.56	33.81	96.00	95.50	1,296
11/15/33	33.56	34.84	95.47	94.36	1,290
11/16/33	33.56	35.42	94.94	99.01	1,301
11/17/33	33.56	33.90	95.25	98.09	1,289
11/18/33	33.56	33.62	95.25	98.67	1,278
11/20/33	33.66	33.92	94.97	101.28	1,284
11/21/33	33.76	34.11	94.47	100.29	1,280
11/22/33	33.76	34.24	93.69	100.07	1,266
11/23/33	33.76	33.48	94.31	98.59	1,250
11/24/33	33.76	32.76	95.44	99.52	1,256
11/25/33	33.76	32.84	95.88	99.28	1,248
11/27/33	33.76	31.92	96.62	95.77	1,232
11/28/33	33.85	32.50	96.00	96.23	1,240
11/29/33	33.93	32.75	95.88	98.14	1,251
12/1/33	34.01	32.43	95.97	98.89	1,244
12/16/33	34.01	32.34	94.66	98.06	1,236
12/18/33	34.06	32.61	94.41	97.20	1,234
1/13/34	34.06	32.55	94.75	98.66	1,297
1/15/34	34.45	32.99	95.62	103.19	1,327

Sources: Gold and bond prices are from the *New York Times*, various issues. The Dow is from the Dow Jones Co. (1991). Commodity prices are from the various issues of the *Commercial and Financial Chronicle*.

Equation 1 shows an OLS regression of the first difference of the log of the London price (P_L) on the first difference of the log of the RFC price (P_{RFC}):

$$P_L = 2.68*P_{RFC} \quad N = 31, \text{ t-statistic} = 2.05, \text{ Adj } R^2 = .096 \tag{1}$$
prob. value = .05, Durbin-Watson = 2.05

With such a small sample period it is difficult to draw any firm conclusions. It is clear, however, that although the coefficient on P_{RFC} is positive, there is no evidence of a *close* relationship between the RFC price and the free market price of gold. This is, however, exactly what one would expect. As noted earlier, a perfect correlation would imply either market inefficiency or a completely random process for generating the RFC price.

It will be more useful to analyze market responses to the *information* that the Roosevelt administration and its critics were conveying to the markets. For instance, between the October 22 speech, and the initiation of the daily RFC price quotes on October 25, the free market price of gold soared by 6.2 percent.[23] This provides a good indicator of the market's initial perception of the credibility of Roosevelt's initiative. And the concurrent 3.7 percent increase in the Moody's commodity price index suggests that markets anticipated the program would raise not just gold prices but the broader price level as well.

As noted earlier, Roosevelt's October 29 decision to allow RFC gold purchases in foreign markets did not involve any substantive change in policy. It did, however, send a clear signal that Roosevelt would do whatever was necessary to drive up the price of gold. And his signal had enough credibility to send gold prices up an additional 2.9 percent on the following day. After an early rise, however, both stock and commodity prices fell on doubts about the program and fear of foreign retaliation, and the next day the London price of gold also fell by one percent. (Because of the time difference, the closing gold price in London was determined well before the U.S. stock and commodity markets closed.)

During early November the press continued to pay close attention to the daily RFC price announcements. Numerous stories discussed a "sound money revolt" and on November 4 it was reported that the New York Chamber of Commerce was demanding a return to the gold standard. Within the administration a vigorous battle was being fought over whether to abandon the policy. On November 7, for the first time since the program began, the RFC gold price quote was not increased. The price of gold in London fell 1.1 percent.

On November 7, the London gold price was still well below the RFC quote, an indication of the market's uncertainty regarding Roosevelt's ability to carry

---

23. Only about one-half of the increase occurred immediately after the announcement. Over the next several days, however, the Roosevelt administration issued a series of statements intended to strengthen the credibility of the proposed policy. As we saw with the Blue Eagle program, it is not unusual for the market reaction to a complex policy announcement to be spread over several days as investors respond to clarifying comments from policymakers.

forward his policy of reflation. The next day saw the largest daily increase during the entire month of November, 21 cents, and the London price rebounded 2.5 percent. The November 9 issue of the *New York Times* reported a "note of exultation" in the pro-devaluation camp. On November 10 the London gold price closed *above* the RFC quote for the first time since the program was initiated. The November 10 issue of the *New York Times* described the market as "panicky" and noted (p. 2) that the dollar was being driven down by fears of inflation, not gold buying. Another story (p. 33) reported rumors that France would soon be forced to devalue. These inflation fears also produced a sharp sell-off in government bonds. Given the fact that 1933 was perhaps the only year in U.S. history when the Treasury bond market had to face an administration with an *avowed* policy of inflation, the real surprise was the remarkable stability in the bond market during the initial period of dollar depreciation (from April to July, 1933).

Over the next several days the *New York Times* made numerous references to the fact that commentators were "puzzled" by the fact that stock and commodity prices were now lagging behind the rise in gold prices (in sharp contrast to the pattern observed during the first few months after the dollar began to float in April). The following three equations show the results of regressing the first difference of the logs of commodity prices (MOODY'S), bond prices (TBOND), and stock prices (DOW), on the first difference of the log of the free market price of gold in London (P_L), during the period from October 25 to December 1, 1933:

$$\text{MOODY'S} = .266^*P_L \quad \text{T-statistic} = 3.04, \text{Adj } R^2 = .222 \tag{2}$$

$$N = 30, \text{Prob. value} = .005, \text{D-W} = 1.98$$

$$\text{TBOND} = -.204^*P_L \quad \text{T-statistic} = -4.53, \text{Adj } R^2 = .402 \tag{3}$$

$$N = 30, \text{Prob. value} = .000, \text{D-W} = 1.69$$

$$\text{DOW} = .252^*P_L \quad \text{T-statistic} = 1.19, \text{Adj } R^2 = .014 \tag{4}$$

$$N = 30, \text{Prob. value} = .244, \text{D-W} = 2.09$$

These regressions show that during November 1933 both the stock and bond markets appear to have responded less favorably to the policy of dollar depreciation than had been the case during the spring and summer of 1933.

One explanation for their disappointing performance is that, in contrast to the spring and summer, administration policy was now having a significant impact on inflation expectations. By mid-November the London gold price exceeded the RFC price, the forward discount on the dollar was increasing, and long-term Treasury bond prices were declining. During this period the relationship between the rate of inflation and the rate of change in stock prices exhibited the negative correlation typically observed in the postwar period, rather than the positive correlation found during most of the interwar period.[24]

On November 15 the *New York Times* tried to reassure its readers with the observation that the position of Secretary of the Treasury remained in the hands of sound money advocate William Woodin. Ironically, Woodin resigned on the very same day, and the price of gold in London rose on November 15 to its highest level of the year.[25] The following day, Under Secretary Dean Acheson also resigned. Dollar depreciation advocate Henry Morganthau was appointed acting secretary.

November 15 also marked the first of four consecutive days when the RFC price of gold was not increased. The fact that London gold prices did rise sharply on the fifteenth, even without a change in the RFC price, could be used as an indication that Roosevelt's program was ineffective. More perceptive observers, however, understood that the RFC price was just one of many forms of information received by the markets:

> The behavior of the foreign exchange market yesterday offered another illustration of the fact that the decline in the dollar is due not so much directly to the daily advances in the RFC's gold price as to the government's avowed intention of cheapening the dollar which these rises in the gold quotation indicate. Yesterday the RFC's gold price was left unchanged from the previous day, but the market ignored the implication that the RFC was content for a moment not to push further the cheapening of the dollar. Instead it fastened its attention on the news of the changes in the Treasury Department's administration, which

---

24. Glasner (2011) showed that the correlation reverted back to positive after 2008, which matches the perception that this period was a sort of "little depression."

25. Between November 13 and 15, the London price of gold rose 5.0 percent to close at $34.84/oz.

it interpreted as still further reducing the influence of those opposed to drastic dollar depreciation. (*NYT*, 11/16/33, p. 37)

The preceding quotation shows how the problem of interpreting the impact of RFC price changes is complicated by the partial endogeneity of the RFC price. The temporary hiatus in RFC price increases after November 14 was probably attributable to administration concern that the Woodin and Acheson resignations not disrupt an already fragile Treasury bond market. The anticipation of a sharp rise in the free market price (due to the resignation) may have actually *caused* the RFC not to announce a price increase. Thus a simple regression equation is unable to capture the full impact of Roosevelt's policy.

The November 17 *New York Times* (p. 2) reported rumors that President Roosevelt was trying to force France off the gold standard. Even if this story was fictitious, there is little doubt that the policy of dollar depreciation was putting the franc under great stress, and this was during a period when budgetary problems in France had already caused an outflow of foreign capital. The sharp increase in the forward discount on the franc was an indication of the growing fears that France would abandon the gold standard.[26]

The gold-buying policy was putting the franc under pressure for several reasons. In addition to the direct (negative) impact of the dollar's depreciation on the competitive position of French firms in the tradable goods sectors, the depreciation also exerted downward pressure on prices in the gold bloc. The same issue of the *New York Times* (p. 2) cited the *Times* of London:

So far as his campaign has gone at present, it has had less effect in raising prices in America than in depressing prices and checking recovery in the rest of the world. It must moreover, continue to exert a deflationary influence until there is some plain indication of the level to which President Roosevelt intends to drive the dollar.

---

26. The three-month forward discount on the French franc against the British pound increased from ¼ percent to nearly 1 percent during November 1933. Although this discount was not computed in terms of gold, the fact that the forward Swiss franc (a more stable gold currency) remained at par with the pound provides an indication that the French franc was almost certainly also at a forward discount against gold.

During this period commodity price indices in the United States rose by less than the price of gold, and Fisher's weekly price index measured in gold terms declined by 11.8 percent between October 21 and November 25, 1933 (see Table 6.2).

There are several possible links between the gold-buying program and deflation. As noted earlier, the purchase of gold tends to increase its value, and hence depress prices in gold terms. The direct impact of RFC purchases, however, was probably less important than the indirect impact on private gold hoarding. We have already seen that during the interwar period, currency crises and/or expectations of exchange rate depreciation were associated with increases in private gold hoarding that resulted in sharp decreases in the growth rate of the world monetary gold stock.

During the entire period from December 1929 to December 1934, the monetary gold stock increased by an average of $43 million per month (measured at $20.67/ounce). Between April 30 and October 31, 1933, the world monetary gold stock increased by only about $16.4 million per month, an indication that the uncertainty associated with dollar depreciation was increasing private gold hoarding.[27] And during the final two months of 1933 the world monetary gold stock declined by over $126 million (more than $200 million below trend, even at the old price of $20.67/ounce). This suggests that the private hoarding induced by the gold-buying program may have had a greater impact than the RFC purchases, which totaled only $131 million at market prices during the entire gold buying program. Gold hoarding put deflationary pressure on European economies in late 1933, and this tended to lessen the (inflationary) impact of the dollar depreciation on U.S. prices.[28] It was like ascending a ladder resting on a sinking platform.

---

27. The gold stock data are from the Federal Reserve Bulletin, September 1940, p. 1000.

28. The *NYT* (11/18/33, p. 10) estimated that "FLIGHT OF DOLLAR SET AT ONE BILLION" and also noted that "the movement of American capital in this present phase of its flight is through sterling into gold. Gold is being bought for private American accounts in the open market from stocks of newly mined metal received in London."

The End of the Gold-Buying Program

During the second half of November, Roosevelt's gold policy became more controversial and sparked an intense policy debate.[29] After four days without an increase in the RFC price, the price of gold in London had declined 3.2 percent below its peak. Then on November 20 and 21, the RFC price rose by a total of 20 cents per ounce and the London price of gold rose 49 cents. On November 22 the *New York Times* headline reported "SPRAGUE QUITS TREASURY TO ATTACK GOLD POLICY" and on page 2, "Administration, Realizing This, Vainly Tried to Persuade Him to Silence on Gold Policy." As with the Woodin resignation, Sprague's resignation led to a temporary hiatus in the RFC gold price increases, this time lasting five days.

Over the next several days the controversy continued to increase in intensity. The November 23 *New York Times* reported "RESERVE'S ADVISORS URGE WE RETURN TO GOLD BASIS; PRESIDENT HITS AT FOES" other stories reported opposition by J.P. Warburg, and a debate between Warburg and Irving Fisher (a supporter of the plan).[30] Another story was headlined "WARREN CALLED DICTATOR." The November 24 *New York Times* headline suggested that "END OF DOLLAR UNCERTAINTY EXPECTED SOON IN CAPITAL; RFC GOLD PRICE UNCHANGED." Nevertheless, over the next few days the *New York Times*'s headlines showed the battle raging back and forth:

ROOSEVELT WON'T CHANGE GOVERNMENT'S GOLD POLICY, IGNORING ATTACK BY [former New York Governor Al] SMITH (11/25/33)

SMITH SCORES POLICY . . . Says He Is in Favor of Sound Money and Not 'Baloney' Dollar . . . ASKS RETURN TO GOLD . . .

29. Davis (1986, p. 294) noted that Roosevelt's October 22 speech touched off "such lengthy, fervent, and highly educative national public debate of monetary policy as there had not been since Bryan's Cross of Gold campaign in 1896."

30. Fisher regarded Roosevelt's policy as being essentially equivalent to his Compensated Dollar Plan. Although there were important differences, the rhetoric used by Roosevelt to justify the policy was remarkably close to the rationale behind Fisher's plan.

Critical of Professors Who 'Turn People Into Guinea Pigs' in Experiments (11/25/33)

GOLD POLICY UPHELD AND ASSAILED HERE AT RIVAL RALLIES . . . 6,000 Cheer [Father] Coughlin as He Demands Roosevelt Be "Stopped From Being Stopped" (11/28/33)

In retrospect, Father Coughlin's rally in support of FDR was too late. There were three more small increases in the RFC price at the end of the month, but these probably reflected little more than Roosevelt's pique at critics who were predicting an end to the program. For a variety of reasons, Roosevelt then decided to refrain from any further significant moves until January,[31] when he again raised the price of gold and then permanently devalued the dollar. But why did Roosevelt abandon the program long before he had reached his goal of returning prices to their 1926 level?

President Roosevelt's decision to refrain from further attempts at dollar depreciation appears to have been motivated by both political and economic factors. The political opposition was intense, and not just from conservatives in the financial community. Labor groups such as the American Federation of Labor strongly opposed it as well. Interestingly, manufacturers were actually split on this issue. Recall that immediately after the dollar began depreciating in April, prices rose sharply while nominal wages were almost unchanged, and this led to much higher industrial production. Only after the NIRA wage codes were instituted during the late summer of 1933 did real wages regain the ground lost in the early stages of the depreciation. Thus, in the short run dollar depreciation boosted profits and depressed real wages.

The November 24 *New York Times* reported that many top economists had also gone on record opposing the plan. In some cases the criticism involved open ridicule of the role played by George Warren. Keynes likened the policy to a "gold standard on the booze."[32] Although the Republican Party was very weak in 1933, there was also strong opposition from important factions of the Democratic Party, both in the east and in some of the silver producing

---

31. The only increase during this period occurred on December 18, when the RFC price was raised by 5 cents and the London gold price rose 27 cents.

32. *NYT,* 12/31/33.

western states. The steady stream of resignations, including Woodin, Sprague, Acheson, and Warburg, clearly put pressure on the administration. And opposition from Europe was almost unanimous.[33]

Even with the intense opposition, it is not clear that Roosevelt would have changed course solely on the basis of political pressure. Although his popularity had declined somewhat from the heights reached during the summer of 1933, he would still have been able to push through the maximum 50 percent devaluation authorized by the Thomas amendment. Instead, there is some evidence that disappointment with the immediate effects of the program contributed to his decision.

As noted earlier, during November the effects of dollar depreciation differed from the spring and summer pattern in two important respects. The Treasury bond market declined substantially, and the financial press attributed this decline to the policy of inflation. In addition, the stock and commodity markets appeared to respond less enthusiastically than during the earlier period:

> It is indeed difficult to find out exactly what are Wall Street's views with regard to the monetary question. When former Governor Smith made public his letter and stocks were going up, there seemed to be little doubt that Wall Street wanted sound money. But yesterday, faced with the sharpest break of the month, opinion veered toward inflation again. As one broker expressed it, it begins to appear as if Wall Street would like to see enough inflation to double the price of stocks and commodities, but little enough so that Liberty bonds can sell at a premium. (*NYT*, 11/28/33, p. 33)

One explanation for this ambiguity is that investors distinguished between once and for all changes in the price level and changes in the rate of inflation.

---

33. Fear of a round of competitive currency devaluations might conceivably have played some role in Roosevelt's decision. Both Roosevelt and Warren, however, seemed to genuinely view their policy in domestic terms, that is, as a way of increasing prices rather than as a "beggar thy neighbor" decrease in the real exchange rate. And a complete breakdown of the gold standard, a real possibility in late 1933, might have given Roosevelt even more leeway to pursue an independent course with his gold policy.

During the early stages of the dollar depreciation, long-term interest rates held fairly steady, and the three-month forward discount on the dollar (against the pound) remained below 1.5 percent. The market apparently viewed the depreciation as a one-time monetary stimulus, which would not lead to persistent inflation. Investor confidence was shaken during November, however, when persistent administration attempts to force the dollar down were associated with falling bond prices and an increase in the forward discount on the dollar. Consistent with this interpretation, the Dow rose 4.6 percent in mid-January 1934, following the Administration's announcement that a decision was imminent to raise, *and then fix,* the price of gold. The *New York Times* noted that

> The satisfaction found by stock and commodity markets in the inflationary implications of the program was nearly matched by the bond market's enthusiasm for the fact that the government had announced limitations to dollar devaluation. (1/16/34, p. 1).

This episode highlights the difficulty in finding a stable relationship between stock and bond prices, and inflation. During the gold standard period, the price level was approximately a white noise process with zero trend and stocks seemed to react positively to price level.[34] As long as the dollar was firmly tied to gold, price level increases did not necessarily raise expectations of future inflation and/or nominal interest rates. Under these circumstances, price level increases would raise nominal stock prices by pushing up the nominal value of corporate assets and could raise real stock prices if the higher commodity prices led to expectations of economic recovery. Conversely, in the postwar period higher inflation has generally led to higher inflation expectations, and (perhaps since inflation tends to increase the real tax on capital[35]) a reduction in real equity prices.

President Roosevelt appeared to sincerely believe in Warren's ideas, but he was also a pragmatist. The early New Deal years are best characterized as a period of relentless experimentation. Roosevelt listened to a variety of advisors and occasionally supported mutually incompatible policies. When the

---

34. In contrast, by the 1970s the price level was closer to a difference stationary process, and stocks appeared to react negatively to inflation.

35. In the U.S., taxes are imposed on the *nominal* returns on capital, including that portion that merely compensates for inflation.

response of financial markets to his gold-buying policy was less enthusiastic than expected, he was quite willing to place the policy on hold and shift his focus to other issues.

Previous Evaluations of the Gold-Buying Program

There has been widespread misunderstanding about the nature and effects of the gold-buying program. Friedman and Schwartz (p. 465) comment that, "for a time, the large scale of RFC purchases abroad made the announced price for newly-mined domestic gold the effective market price. From the end of November, however, until the end of January 1934, the announced price exceeded the market price abroad." In addition to being factually incorrect,[36] this statement misses the way in which Roosevelt's policy attempted to manipulate expectations. Thus, when Friedman and Schwartz argue (p. 466) that "essentially the same effects on the dollar prices of internationally traded goods would have followed from the same dollar volume of government purchase of wheat or perfume or foreign-owned art masterpieces," they miss the that fact that a program featuring these other commodities would not have been interpreted by the financial markets as a signal of a future dollar devaluation.

Eichengreen is somewhat more perceptive but still fails to see the essential nature of the program:

> Warren's link between gold prices and commodity prices suffered from two significant sources of slippage: that between the dollar price of gold and the exchange rate, and that between the exchange rate and commodity prices. The link between the dollar price of gold and the exchange rate was loosened by the U.S. gold embargo, which disrupted arbitrage between the U.S. and European gold markets. Without the embargo, arbitrage in the gold market would have raised the dollar price of French francs and the dollar price of gold by the same proportion. But with arbitrage disrupted, the exchange rate could move independently, to an extent. (1992, p. 340)

---

36. The RFC purchases were not particularly large in aggregate, and at no time were they large enough to equate the RFC price with the free market price in London.

To the extent that there was slippage between the dollar price of gold (i.e., RFC quote) and the exchange rate (London gold price), the problem was that the RFC price usually *exceeded* the world price. It is hard to see how ending the embargo would close this discrepancy since U.S. gold exporters would presumably rather sell to the RFC than into the free market. The problem, of course, was that the RFC bought far too little gold to make its price effective.

Eichengreen belongs to a revisionist group of economic historians who view the gold standard as being an important causal factor in the Depression and who argue that, almost without exception, devaluation was the key to recovery for both individual nations and for the world as a whole.[37] Yet, Eichengreen calls Warren's views "peculiar," and then discusses evidence that the correlation between gold and commodity prices was not *exact*. Although Eichengreen is correct in noting that there was "slippage" between RFC gold prices, exchange rates, and commodity prices, one is inclined to ask, so what? The correlation between policy tools and targets is almost never perfect. Since Eichengreen clearly believes that the decision to devalue the dollar was wise, and his research also supports the view that there was a close correlation between devaluation and reflation, it is odd that he would uncritically accept the view that Warren was "peculiar." Warren's contemporaries also saw him as something of a crackpot, but primarily because he *advocated* dollar depreciation.[38]

Barber (1996, p. 80) called the effects of the gold-buying program "decidedly disappointing" because the WPI only increased by 3.4 percent between October 1933 and February 1934. (Note that an annual inflation rate of more than 10 percent is actually a fairly impressive achievement for monetary policy in a severely depressed economy.) And Kenneth Davis (1980) also expressed skepticism about the program's effectiveness:

> Roosevelt realized that his gold purchase program was not having the effect Warren had predicted it would have. The lowering of the gold value of the dollar was *not* reflected in rising commodity prices; as a

---

37. This group also includes Bernanke (1995) and Temin (1989). Note that they do not regard the 1930s devaluations as traditional "beggar thy neighbor" policies which only worked by lowering real exchange rates but rather argued that even a uniform global devaluation would promote recovery by spurring aggregate demand.

38. Skidelsky (2003, p. 131) suggested that the program "was regarded as bizarre by many at the time . . and a longer perspective has not altered this verdict."

matter of fact, these prices declined slightly in November, with farm prices going down the most. (1986, p. 302)

Since raising commodity prices was the raison d'être of the entire program, it is worth examining this assertion in more detail.

Equation 2 showed a positive correlation between changes in the market price of gold and changes in commodity prices, and Pearson, Myers, and Gans (1957, p. 5647) also show that during late 1933 there was a fairly close correlation between the level of the market price of gold and an index of 17 commodity prices. But the comparison that interested Roosevelt's critics was the relationship between commodity prices and the RFC price. In particular, commodity prices declined in late November 1933, even as the RFC price increased slightly.

Equation 5 shows the results of an OLS regression of the first difference of the log of Moody's commodity price index on the first difference of the log of the RFC gold price:

$$\text{MOODY'S} = 1.696 * P_{RFC} \quad N = 30, \text{T-statistic} = 2.49, \text{Adj } R^2 = .15 \quad (5)$$

Prob. value = .019, Durbin-Watson = 1.95

These findings certainly don't support the view that Roosevelt's policy was ineffective. And these results appear even more impressive if one recalls that (according to the efficient markets hypothesis) even if Roosevelt's policy had been completely effective, commodity prices should have only reacted to unanticipated changes in the RFC price. Thus the estimated correlation in Equation 5 probably understates the actual impact of the RFC price changes.

The late November decline in commodity prices undoubtedly contributed to the perception that the program was ineffective. Both Roosevelt and his critics, however, failed to understand the role of expectations. For instance, during the month of November, there were ten occasions when the RFC refrained from increasing its purchase price.

Presumably the markets knew that a price decrease was highly unlikely, and thus we can assume that on each of those ten days the RFC price was below market expectations. During the ten days in question the market price of gold declined by an average of over 27 cents (or 0.8 percent) per day and the Moody's commodity price index also declined (by an average of roughly ½ percent per day). Also note that nine of the ten days when the RFC price was not increased occurred during the latter half of November. It was during this period that the policy was perceived as being ineffective. Thus, the RFC price appeared to lose its ability to raise the market prices of gold and commodities, just at the time when the market began to (correctly) perceive that Roosevelt was about to yield to intense pressure and refrain from further attempts at dollar depreciation.

The preceding discussion helps explain the relationship between the RFC gold price and commodity prices but fails to account for the weakness in wholesale prices. Although day-to-day movements in commodity and gold prices were correlated, the broader price indices, such as the WPI, failed to increase during November and December. This is especially problematic because, even though the market price of gold declined in the latter part of the month, it remained well above its pre-October 22 price throughout all of November.[39] In one sense, the resolution of this problem is simple; gold prices outperformed commodity prices because the prices of commodities on a gold basis (i.e., the prices of commodities in Europe) were falling during late 1933. This leads to perhaps the most powerful criticism against the gold-buying program, that is, the European view that the program led to gold hoarding and thus was more successful in depressing prices overseas than in raising prices in America.

There is no easy resolution to the question of what caused the gold hoarding. It would be extremely difficult to discriminate between the gold hoarding caused by fear of dollar depreciation and hoarding due to factors such as fear of French devaluation. Certainly a decision to quickly and permanently devalue the dollar in October 1933 would have reduced gold hoarding generated by fears of dollar depreciation during late 1933. It is also true, however, that the more successful the U.S. policy was perceived to be, the greater were the pressures on the remainder of the gold bloc, and hence the greater was the likelihood of European gold hoarding.

Given all of these uncertainties, one could hardly blame Roosevelt for concentrating on raising U.S. prices back to their 1926 levels and letting Europeans make their own monetary decisions. From a modern perspective, a good argument can be made that Roosevelt's greatest failing was in not aggressively

---

39. The market price of gold was $29.06 on October 21. During the latter half of November, the market price never fell below $31.90.

pursuing RFC price increases until commodity price reflation was complete, or at least until the dollar had been devalued by the full 50 percent authorized by the Thomas amendment. (If this forced France from the gold standard, then its economy might have been much stronger during the mid-1930s.) The key was to move fast; once the dollar was re-pegged the gold hoarding would stop, and the value of gold would stop increasing.[40]

The widely divergent reactions to the gold-buying program of economists such as Fisher and Keynes provide an interesting insight into their views on the role of monetary policy. During the 1930s, Keynes began to question the view that a suitably expansionary monetary policy could generate economic recovery. Leijonhufvud (1968) argued that Keynes's statements regarding the ineffectiveness of monetary policy must be viewed in context of interwar policy constraints (such as the gold standard), which limited the choices available to central bankers. There is undoubtedly some truth to this assertion, yet it remains curious that Keynes refused to support existing proposals for radical monetary actions such as extreme devaluation or "greenbackism." For instance, when the United States returned to the gold standard in January 1934, Keynes suggested that Roosevelt

> has adopted a middle course between old-fashioned orthodoxy and the extreme inflationists. I see nothing in his policy that need be disturbing to business confidence. (*Collected Writings*, Vol. 21, p. 312)

This suggests either that Keynes was more apprehensive about inflation than has been generally acknowledged (as Meltzer [1988] has argued), or that Keynes simply failed to understand that a suitably expansionary monetary policy could rapidly return nominal spending to pre-Depression levels.

As noted earlier, the gold-buying program was widely viewed as the adoption of a "commodity dollar" policy, of which Fisher's Compensated Dollar Plan was the most famous example. Not surprisingly, Fisher strongly endorsed

---

40. Bernanke and Woodford (1997) discuss a "circularity problem" with this sort of targeting scheme. If investors anticipated that the gold buying price would increase until the commodity price target was reached, then commodity prices should have immediately moved to the target, thus denying policymakers a useful signal. As a practical matter, this problem would have probably only slightly reduced the precision of FDR's price level targeting scheme (which lacked some credibility).

Roosevelt's policy and vigorously debated Roosevelt's critics. During this period, Fisher's policy views were seen as being much more radical than those of Keynes. These differences reflected fundamentally different approaches to monetary theory.

Unlike Keynes, Fisher believed that under a fiat money system the central bank could essentially peg the price level within a narrow band, and thus monetary policy was capable of effectively stabilizing the economy. Despite the peculiar role of gold prices, in its essentials the CDP is strikingly modern. As with recent proposals for monetary feedback rules, Fisher's plan recognizes, and even requires, a monetary system where the central bank has unlimited ability to influence nominal aggregates. The residual role of gold in Fisher's plan was simply a token to reassure the public that the dollar would still have a stable value (albeit in terms of commodities, not gold). As noted above, a similar redundancy was inherent in Roosevelt's policy.

President Roosevelt's gold-buying program can be seen as a very crude precursor to modern monetary policy feedback rules designed to target nominal aggregates. Unfortunately for Roosevelt, he attempted to implement the program in a policy environment that was both intellectually and politically hostile to the idea that central bankers should control the price level. In this environment, he achieved the limited success of pushing the price of gold up to $35/ounce, much higher than most observers (or the markets) thought likely. And an increasing body of literature suggests that during the 1930s both the timing and the magnitude of economic recovery were closely linked to currency depreciation.

The Gold-Buying Program and Macroeconomic Policy

Beyond the narrow question of whether the gold-buying program raised commodity prices, there is the broader question of whether this program was sensible as a matter of macroeconomic policy. As noted earlier, Keynes was strongly opposed to this phase of the dollar depreciation programs, and many others have accepted his critique.[41] Most other accounts of the Depression

---

41. For instance, see Davis (1986).

take an ambivalent view at best.[42] Only rarely, as in Pearson, Myers, and Gans (1957), is it argued that the gold-buying program was an effective tool that should have been used much more aggressively. In this section I will argue that the policy deserves more respect, particularly from Keynesians.

Today, most economists would accept the view that an expansionary monetary[43] policy would have been desirable in 1933, and many would even be comfortable with Roosevelt's expressed goal of reflating prices to their pre-Depression levels. Modern economists might be uncomfortable, however, with Roosevelt and Warren placing greater emphasis on commodity prices than on the overall price level. This emphasis was based on their view that the Depression was caused by disequilibrium among the various prices in the economy. We've seen that during the major interwar deflations, price indices with a heavy commodity weighting (such as the WPI) tended to fall much more rapidly than the broader price indices, such as the cost of living or the GDP deflator. And, these prices also rose much more sharply in the immediate aftermath of the April 1933 depreciation of the dollar. If one accepts the view that monetary shocks can have real effects in the short run, then the observed procyclicality of real commodity prices during the interwar years *does* suggest that monetary shocks may have been able to raise real commodity prices in the short run. Thus, the Roosevelt–Warren rhetoric should not be interpreted as indicating that they naively believed monetary policy could permanently impact real farm prices.[44]

---

42. For instance, see Kindleberger (1973); Eichengreen (1992); and Friedman and Schwartz (1963a).

43. If one accepts the notion that the gold purchases were relatively small and unimportant, then the policy can be evaluated primarily as a nominal or monetary shock. Some might be uncomfortable with the designation of the policy as "monetary," since changes in the price of gold had no *direct* impact on the money supply. During the interwar period, however, the term "monetary" was applied not just to changes in the quantity of money, but also changes in its *value*. In addition, there is an important mechanism by which a devaluation of the dollar could indirectly impact the money supply. Devaluation would lead to an inflow of gold, which would allow for an increase in the monetary base. This is exactly what occurred during 1934. If one accepts the preceding interpretation of Roosevelt's policy (i.e., that it was sending signals about a future devaluation), then the market responses can also be viewed as an anticipation of an imminent increase in the quantity of money.

44. Warren probably understood this distinction more clearly than did Roosevelt.

The distinction between flexible (commodity) prices and a sticky overall price level is crucial to any understanding of Roosevelt's policy. For instance, when Roosevelt decided to formally devalue the dollar in January 1934, many prominent economists, such as E.W. Kemmerer, predicted runaway inflation. Prices did rise modestly but remained well below pre-Depression levels throughout the 1930s. Pearson, Myers, and Gans quote Warren's notes to the effect that when the summer of 1934 arrived without substantial increases in commodity prices:

> The President (a) wanted more inflation and (b) assumed or had been led to believe that there was a long lag in the effect of depreciation. He did not understand—as many others did not then and do not now— the principle that commodity prices respond immediately to changes in the price of gold. (1957, p. 5664)

Warren understood that commodity markets in late January 1934 had already priced in the anticipated impact of the devaluation, and that commodity price indices were signaling that a gold price of $35/ounce was not nearly sufficient to produce the desired reflation. Most modern macroeconomists continue to make this mistake, taking a wait and see attitude toward initiatives such as "quantitative easing," whereas the inflation expectations embedded in the Treasury Inflation-Protected Securities (TIPS) markets provided immediate evidence that the policy was nowhere near sufficient.

The disadvantage of targeting commodity prices is that these prices may be an unrepresentative sample of all prices and may provide a misleading indicator of the stance of monetary policy. The advantage is that they respond immediately to monetary policy innovations. One can think of the gold-buying program as a monetary feedback rule designed to circumvent the problem of policy lags. Because many prices are slow to adjust, it is difficult to know precisely how much monetary expansion was required to raise the overall price level to its 1926 level. Commodity prices provide an admittedly imperfect indicator, but one that at least has the virtue of responding immediately to monetary policy.

For instance, suppose that Roosevelt had raised the RFC gold price high enough to push commodity indices back to their 1926 levels. One could then interpret the concurrent market price of gold as providing an indicator of the magnitude of dollar devaluation that would be expected to force the Fed to

adopt an expansionary enough monetary policy to provide for complete reflation. Both the actual expansion of the money supply and the actual increase
in the overall price level would come later. The market expectations that are
embedded in commodity prices would be a particularly useful indicator for
policy, however, because once a formal devaluation has occurred, policy is
essentially set in stone. At that point, any attempt to pursue a policy of dollar
devaluation further would have met intense political resistance.

Even if we assume that there were no institutional constraints on Roosevelt's choice of monetary policy, it is not clear that any of the other popular
targets, such as the money supply or interest rates, would have been more
effective than dollar depreciation in achieving his goal of reflation. And if we
consider the fact that Roosevelt's influence over the Fed was limited, then the
case for using dollar depreciation is even stronger. Perhaps Roosevelt should
have exercised his authority to issue $3 billion in greenbacks. From the per-
spective of the twenty-first century, however, it is difficult to understand how
deeply ingrained the fear of inflation was during 1933 and how extraordinarily
controversial such a decision would have been. Even his gold-buying program
represented an "extremist" position in the context of interwar ideology.

The gold-buying program was much too brief to draw any firm conclusions
regarding its impact on broader economic aggregates such as real GDP. After
rising 57 percent between March and July 1933, industrial production declined
by 18.8 percent in the four months following implementation of the NIRA
wage codes. Production reached a trough in November, when the gold-buying
program was in full swing, and then increased by 13.8 percent over the next
four months. Thus monthly data for industrial production do not support the
view that the program was ineffective. At worst, gold hoarding and problems
in France caused a brief delay in its expansionary impact.[45]

Historians have generally treated the gold-buying program as just a minor
footnote to the New Deal. Whereas the program was viewed as highly disrup-
tive by most contemporaneous observers, modern historians are more likely to
view the program as being essentially ineffective. The previous analysis sug-

---

45. At first glance the gold hoarding problem may seem similar to the policy constraints
under the gold standard, which inhibited the 1932 OMPs. This is an inappropriate analogy
however, as the gold-buying program was a fiat money regime. Either dollar depreciation
would continue indefinitely (and dominate any increase in the real value of gold), or it would
end, and gold would then be dishoarded (as actually occurred in 1934).

gests that the program was marginally effective at raising commodity prices, and, if one accepts the proposition that reflation would ultimately promote economic recovery, then it could be argued that the policy's greatest drawback was the timidity with which it was pursued.

Concluding Remarks: Interpreting 1933

Because governments are reluctant to do controlled policy experiments, it is difficult to identify exogenous policy shocks. Yet 1933 contained not one, but *two* of the most dramatic policy experiments ever conducted by the U.S. government. And given the size and unforeseen nature of these experiments, it could be argued that more information can be gleaned from a close examination of their impact, than from a VAR-type analysis of postwar data. In fact, during the brief 1933–1934 devaluation episode, one can identify more independent monetary policy shocks than Romer and Romer (1989) found in their entire analysis of postwar Fed policy.

Although the gold-buying program lasted for only a brief period, the various financial market reactions show us how expectations of future money supply growth impacts the current level of variables such as prices and interest rates. It also highlights the difficulties encountered in VAR analyses of a particular indicator of monetary policy. For example, the dollar's exchange rate may provide a useful indicator of monetary policy during periods where it is being targeting (i.e., 1933), but an unreliable indicator of policy during periods when the nominal exchange rate for the dollar essentially parallels real exchange rates (i.e., during recent decades) and is not being targeted by the monetary authority.

Another important lesson from 1933 is that the only avowedly inflationary policy ever pursued by the United States was accompanied by rapid inflation in all of the price indices, despite high unemployment. The fact that this aggregate demand shock was accompanied by unprecedented output growth would seem to confirm the standard textbook model of the upward-sloping short-run aggregate supply curve. And the fact that the recovery aborted immediately following a government-mandated 22 percent wage increase (a classic adverse supply shock) provides additional confirmation of the basic aggregate supply/aggregate demand (AS/AD) model.

If we take a closer look, however, it is not at all clear that the preceding interpretation of the events of 1933 is supportive of modern business cycle theory. Mankiw and Reis identify "three key facts" of modern business cycle theory:

1. "*The Acceleration Phenomenon* . . . inflation tends to rise when the economy is booming and falls when economic activity is depressed."

2. "*The Smoothness of Real Wages* . . . real wages do not fluctuate as much as labor productivity."

3. "*Gradual Response of Real Variables* . . . The full impact of shocks is usually felt only after several quarters." (2006, p. 164)

In the preceding three chapters we have seen evidence of rapid inflation in an extremely depressed economy, rapid change in real wages (even before implementation of the NIRA), and industrial production responding almost immediately to monetary shocks.

Obviously, I have not formally tested any of the preceding three stylized facts, but at least the first of these "facts" would be exceedingly difficult to reconcile with the observed changes in the U.S. price level after the dollar was devalued. Rather, the stylized facts of 1933 actually seem more consistent with the more "old-fashioned" interpretation of the Phillips curve—the Irving Fisher/Milton Friedman view that the causation ran from (unanticipated) changes in inflation to changes in output. Again, this is just one episode, but given how difficult it is to identify truly exogenous monetary shocks, it is disturbing that the most powerful and clearly identifiable monetary shock seemed to produce effects that don't conform very closely to those predicted by the standard new Keynesian model.

At least the new Keynesian model allows for monetary shocks to have real effects. There are numerous alternative approaches, ranging from old (or post-) Keynesian to new classical, which have raised doubts about the efficacy of monetary policy during a severe depression. Some have suggested that money-output correlations may be highly misleading because of the possible endogeneity of monetary policy. One of the reasons I provided such a detailed account of the political factors associated with dollar depreciation is to show that many of the major changes in the value of the dollar were associated with actions or statements made by the Roosevelt administration. In many respects, a better case can be made for monetary policy exogeneity during April 1933 through February 1934, than during the postwar data so favored by modern macroeconomists.[46] Monetary policy doesn't get much more exogenous than this:

> One morning (it was Friday, November 3), when Morgenthau came to the bedside tense with worry over some pressing problem and suggested that the [gold] price change that day be considerably greater than the 10 to 15 cents of immediately preceding days, Roosevelt promptly announced that the increase would be 21 cents. Why *that* figure? Because "three times seven" is a lucky number, said Roosevelt, his face straight but his blue eyes twinkling at Morgenthau's recoil from such frivolous dealing with a serious matter (quoted in Davis, 1986, p. 294)

The policy experiments of 1933 also had an important impact on policy developments during the mid to late 1930s. One reason the gold bloc currencies were under so much pressure during the fall of 1933 was the perception that a successful U.S. devaluation would force other nations to follow. As the recovery faltered in late 1933, pressures on the gold bloc currencies eased.

Temin (1989, p. 124) noted that the after the popular front took office in 1936, its policies were "almost the same as the labor measures introduced in America under the NRA. But they were introduced in a very different context, before rather than after devaluation." Temin argued that during a depression, a high wage policy can increase productivity if accompanied by a credible policy to raise prices, such as devaluation. Yet the French experience of 1936–1938 seems remarkably similar to that of the United States under the NIRA—sharply rising real wages followed by two years of stagnating output. Ironically, had the NIRA not been adopted then the dollar depreciation program might well have been so effective that France would have been forced to devalue in late 1933, but without the U.S. devaluation of 1933 (which softened the impact of the NIRA) France might never have tried its own wage fixing policy.[47]

---

46. Bernanke (1993) notes that one of the implications of Eichengreen's (1992) extensive account of the interwar gold standard is that the findings present a direct challenge to the RBC (real business cycle) approach. Eichengreen provides international evidence for a close link between (exogenous) devaluations and economic recovery.

47. Temin (1989) also suggested the Nazi's low wage policy might have helped boost employment in Germany after 1933. (Although he also argues that it slowed technological progress in Germany.)

After the dollar was again fixed to gold in January 1934, the price of gold remained stable for the remainder of the decade. Although the United States was no longer "on the gold standard," gold flows continued to influence U.S. monetary policy, perhaps even more so than prior to 1933. Indeed, in the next three chapters we will see how the interaction of international gold market shocks and changes in U.S. labor market regulations can also explain much of the volatility of U.S. industrial production throughout the last half of the Depression.

PART IV

Back on the Gold Standard

8

The Demise of the Gold Bloc

IN PREVIOUS CHAPTERS I argued that economic historians overlooked the significance of certain gold market shocks during the first five years of the Depression. But at least there is an awareness that the gold standard played a role in the Great Contraction and that dollar devaluation contributed to recovery. In contrast, almost no attention has been paid to the role of the world gold market in the commodity price bubble of 1936–1937, or the severe contraction that accompanied the fall in commodity prices during 1937–1938. In the next three chapters, we will see that gold market shocks played a key role in the late 1930s, indeed, probably an even more important role than the fiscal and monetary policy shocks on which most other economic historians have focused. And just as during 1933, the interaction of gold and wage shocks explains much of the volatility of industrial production in the late 1930s.

Although 1933 is often viewed as the year when the United States permanently left the gold standard, in one key respect U.S. monetary policy became even more firmly tied to gold after February 1934 than it had been prior to 1933. After the price of gold was pegged in early 1934, the (free market) dollar price of gold stayed fairly stable for another thirty-four years. There are three generally accepted characteristics of a gold standard: maintenance of a fixed price of gold, free convertibility of the currency into gold, and adherence to the rules of the game—that is, a relatively stable gold reserve ratio. While prior to 1933, the United States did conform to the first two criteria, it did not even come close to adhering to the rules of the game. After 1934, the dollar was no longer freely convertible into gold, but its market price was still fixed, and changes in the monetary base were closely correlated with changes in the monetary gold stock.[1]

While the par value of gold was raised by more than 69 percent during 1933–1934, wholesale prices rose only about 20 percent during the period of dollar depreciation, and another 5 percent between February 1934 and August 1940, when World War II inflation began in earnest. This meant that the dollar was seriously undervalued during the mid-1930s, and the now overvalued gold bloc currencies faced a series of speculative attacks. The high dollar price of gold also triggered increases in the output of gold mines, which accelerated growth in monetary gold stocks during the mid- to late 1930s.

Why was inflation not more rapid between 1934 and 1940? It is tempting to point to factors such as high unemployment and the depressed economy. But that isn't a satisfactory answer; inflation had been very rapid during 1933 when unemployment was nearly 25 percent. Other factors such as low nominal interest rates undoubtedly played a role; by increasing the real demand for currency and bank reserves, low nominal rates would increase the demand for monetary gold and hold down the rate of inflation. Low nominal interest rates also tended to increase private gold demand.[2] And although the U.S. monetary base closely tracked the gold inflows into the United States after 1934, the Federal Reserve (Fed) did not monetize the sudden one-time increase in nominal gold stocks that resulted from the change in the dollar's par value, and thus the gold reserve ratio jumped sharply between 1933 and 1934.

Although prices rose only modestly between 1934 and 1940, there were some important fluctuations along the way. Wholesale prices rose gradually during 1934, but all of the increase was in the agricultural commodities, presumably reflecting the impact of the "dust bowl." During the six-and-a-half year period from March 1934 through Sept 1940 there were only two dramatic

---

1. See Friedman and Schwartz (p. 507). Actually, their views are a bit conflicted on this issue. On page 474 they deny the United States was on a true gold standard after 1934, arguing that the volume of gold did not "determine directly or even at several removes the volume of money." But elsewhere (as on pages 544–45), they repeatedly argued that the money supply expansion of the mid- to late 1930s was an exogenous event and cite the fact that the increases were closely associated with the gold inflows from Europe.

2. See Sumner (1993a) for evidence that under the classical gold standard (1845–1913), low nominal interest rates depressed prices by reducing both the monetary and non-monetary demand for gold.

movements in the wholesale price index (WPI): a price level "bubble" lasting from September 1936 to June 1938, when wholesale prices first rose and then fell by roughly 10 percent, and then a 5 percent increase in the WPI between August and October 1939, clearly associated with the outbreak of hostilities in Europe. In Chapters 9 and 10 we will see that a substantial portion of the price level bubble of 1937 can be attributed to a surge in private gold dishoarding, followed by renewed hoarding in late 1937.

Many economists have argued that 1934 to 1940 was a period of rapid recovery from the Depression. The growth rates were high when compared with the long-term trend in U.S. output, but on closer inspection the recovery looks much less impressive. Unemployment rates remained extremely high as late as mid-1940, more than seven years after the recovery had begun. And high frequency fluctuations in output continued to be quite pronounced throughout the recovery. During periods when growth was not being held back by the hoarding of gold, or perverse labor market policies, industrial production grew at a blistering pace, suggesting that there were no structural barriers preventing a much more rapid recovery from the Depression.

The Second Wage Shock

During the fall and winter of 1933–1934 the dollar gradually fell toward its new par value (set at $35/ounce of gold). This should have helped the economy, and for a time output and prices did rise briskly. But growth slowed sharply during the spring of 1934 when nominal wages once again began to rise. Although this second round of National Industrial Recovery Act (NIRA) wage increases boosted the aggregate nominal wage by only 4.4 percent between March and July 1934, with nonfood prices no longer increasing, the wage shock was enough to temporarily derail the recovery. The weekly *New York Times* index shows output peaking in late April and then falling sharply during the summer of 1934. The FRB (Federal Reserve Board) industrial production index peaked in May and then declined 15 percent by September.

There is some evidence that the stock market may have anticipated that the second wage shock would again abort the recovery. After rising about 8 percent during the early part of 1934, the Dow began a modest decline on February 23, 1934. The next day the *New York Times* (p. 19) referred to rumors of tightening of NIRA codes. On March 8, the *New York Times* (p. 29) reported that a key factor depressing stock prices was an "intimation that General Johnson, the Recovery Administrator, was preparing to enforce a blanket reduction in industrial working hours and a corresponding increase in wages." When steel output fell in mid-March, the *New York Times* (3/19/34, p. 25) pointed to an "overclouding of hopes for further expansion by the intrusion of labor controversies" and also referred to a "not unfriendly British economist of high repute [presumably Keynes] who remarked, last Autumn, that our government seemed to him to be endeavoring to ride two horses at once, going in opposite directions." The next day the *New York Times* (p. 31) suggested that Wall Street's attitude to labor disputes was of "grave concern," that "labor unrest may be spreading" and "The recent comments concerning a 'showdown' and a 'decisive struggle' obviously have had their effect upon sentiment in financial circles."

According to Roos (1937), the high level of output during April and May 1934 was due to firms trying to beat the wage increases. As with the wage shock of 1933, it is difficult to prove or disprove this assertion (on either empirical or theoretical grounds). Industrial production had already increased 13.8 percent between November 1933 and March 1934, most likely in response to President Roosevelt's (FDR's) gold-buying program. The rumors of further wage increases during March 1934 may have briefly boosted output even further, but output grew by only another 1.9 percent between March and May 1934. We can explain the price level, wage rate and industrial production co-movements during 1934 without recourse to Roos' expected wage change mechanism.

For most of the 1930s, stock prices tracked business activity fairly closely. Thus the *New York Times* (3/28/34, p. 33) noted how unusual it was that rapidly rising output should be associated with falling stock prices. One possibility is that Wall Street was already beginning to discount a summer downturn. When the slowdown finally arrived, share prices fell, but not as sharply as in 1933. Having already seen one boomlet fizzle out during the latter half of 1933, investors had become much more aware of the potential impact of NIRA wage policies. Thus, much of the impact of the higher wages was priced into stocks even before the economic slowdown had begun.

Once the economy began to slow in early May 1934, the press cited concern over both labor difficulties and a lack of inflationary proposals, particularly the

Table 8.1. Selected Monthly Indicators, 1933–1934

Month	Industrial Production	WPI	Core WPI	Nominal Wages	Real Wages	Dow
11/33	100	100	100	100	100	100
12/33	101	100	100	101	101	99
1/34	104	102	101	103	102	104
2/34	109	104	102	103	101	109
3/34	114	104	102	103	101	104
4/34	114	103	102	105	103	105
5/34	116	104	102	106	104	94
6/34	114	105	101	107	105	101
7/34	106	105	102	107	106	98
8/34	105	107	101	107	106	93
9/34	99	109	101	108	106	88
10/34	103	108	101	107	106	96

Note: The Dow is measured at mid-month. The core WPI excludes food prices. The real wage is deflated by the core WPI.

fact that "no further cheapening of the dollar need be expected."[3] In contrast to 1933, when wage increases were accompanied by further depreciation of the dollar, there were no significant monetary initiatives to soften the impact of the 1934 wage increases. The WPI did rise substantially in 1934, but mostly due to the impact of crop failures on farm prices. Table 8.1 shows that, excluding food, the WPI was almost flat during 1934. Thus, when nominal wages began rising after March 1934, output leveled off and then declined in the second half of the year. For the second time in a year, a promising recovery triggered by dollar depreciation was derailed by a NIRA wage shock.

Silver Monetization and the Gold Clause Case

The slide in stock prices was interrupted on May 17 as the Dow jumped 3.5 percent on the announcement of plans for a silver monetization program.

3. *NYT,* 5/8/34, p. 33.

A few days later some of the details of the silver plan came out and stocks fell modestly as investors (correctly) saw that the program was mostly symbolic.[4] Nevertheless, during the summer months, the press was full of reports of "Inflationist Talk and Markets"[5] and gold flows into the United States slowed dramatically. There was no outflow of gold, however, as there was a growing perception that many of the continental European countries might also be forced to devalue their currencies:

> In informal discussions among executives, the opinion was frequently voiced that the government, watching closely the depressed state to which many lines have fallen, will give business "another shot in the arm" to assist the expected Fall momentum.
>
> Possibility that European countries, such as Germany and France may go off the gold standard and that England may depress the pound further was considered as a prelude to further reduction of the gold content of the dollar by President Roosevelt.
>
> (*NYT*, 6/24/34, p. N15)

On August 9, 1934, the long-awaited silver program was finally unveiled: "ROOSEVELT NATIONALIZES ALL SILVER AT A PRICE OF 50.01 CENTS AN OUNCE; PROMISES NATION BROADER NEW DEAL."[6] The dollar fell 0.63 cents, the Dow rose 2.7 percent, and bond prices broke sharply on the announcement. But FDR refused to move to a true bimetallic system, as was advocated by proponents of easy money. Instead, the silver purchase program became little more than a commodity price support program, which FDR used to placate western mining interests. On August 10, stocks lost most of the gains from the previous day, and bonds recovered.

Although the silver program may not ultimately have been very effective,[7] there was some concern that it might be a prelude to more inflationary poli-

---

4. Wall Street actually paid more attention to the ineffectual silver program than to the other elements of this historic reform package, such as proposals for a national labor relations board, a workers' compensation program, and a social security system.

5. *NYT*, 7/12/34, p. 27.

6. *NYT*, 8/10/34, pp. 1 and 27.

7. Burdekin and Weidenmier (2005) present evidence that the program was effective. If silver purchases did not merely displace open market bond purchases, but added to the monetary base, then the program might have modestly reduced the U.S. gold reserve ratio. It

cies. By late August, silver purchases were being blamed for a gold outflow from the United States. Increased gold market activity in London suggests that private hoarding was increasing, and beginning in September the growth in the world monetary gold stock did slow down. The *New York Times* noted

> The subsidence of aggressive pressure against Federal obligations and the dollar coincided with the publication of cautious reassurance by the Secretary of the Treasury with respect to the government's monetary policy. Mr. Morgenthau indicated that no change in this policy was contemplated at this time, but this did not remove altogether the apprehensions arising out of recent developments which, correctly or not, have been interpreted as a forecast of further inflation of the currency . . . when Mr. Morgenthau's statement was broadcast yesterday the stock market immediately displayed a sagging tendency. (8/24/34, p. 23)

Between late August and mid-September, stocks declined and Treasury bond (T-bond) prices rose as reduced concerns about inflationary policies restored confidence in the dollar.[8] Stocks reached their 1934 low on September 17. In the primary elections on the following day there was a strong showing by left-wing candidates and stocks began to rise on rumors that these election results would lead to more inflationary policies if the economy failed to recover. Democrats did do well in the election held on November 6, and on the eighth the *New York Times* (p. 35) noted that a rise in stock and commodity prices "was interpreted to mean that speculative interests were viewing the emphatic approval of New Deal policies in the light of the possible effect on price levels." The same article suggested that, "the renewal of the agitation for currency inflation is regarded by many in the financial district as an inevitable sequel to the impressive gains made by the majority party." There was a certain irony in that "this explanation is not entirely gratifying to the financial community, a large part of which, it may be surmised, voted for losing candidates."[9]

---

would be difficult to estimate its impact without knowing the extent to which the Fed tried to offset its impact.

8. *NYT*, 9/8/34, p. 33.

9. *NYT*, 11/10/34, p. 21.

As the economy began growing again during the fall, expectations of de-valuation were replaced by expectations of dollar *revaluation*. This crisis was precipitated by a case before the Supreme Court that tested the constitutional-ity of FDR's decision to abrogate the gold clause in all private contracts. On January 12, 1935, the *New York Times* (p. 23) reported that great uncertainty in the financial markets was generated by "pointed questions which members of the court have directed to attorneys for the government." And the same issue described a

> MARKET WRENCHED BY THE GOLD CASES . . . Gold Clause
> Federal Bonds Soar, Stocks and Commodities Drop, Dollar Rises
> . . . The criss-cross movement in the bond market was without pre-vious parallel. While Liberty bonds and other Treasury obligations issued prior to the abrogation of the gold clause soared 4–32ds to 23–32ds point, other Treasury securities of equal standing, save for the gold clause, fell 2–32ds to 8–32ds point. (p. 1)

On January 16, the Dow dropped 2.2 percent and the next day the *New York Times* (p. 27) reported that stock and commodity prices were declining on "fresh anxiety" that if the government lost the case it would be forced to revalue the dollar back to the pre-1933 gold price.

Of course, there was no possibility of the court actually ordering such a revaluation. Rather, the administration might have been forced to revalue the dollar because (assuming an adverse court decision) debtors would find it almost impossible to meet their obligations in contracts featuring a gold clause at the existing exchange rate. Enforcement of the gold clauses of debt contracts would have effectively increased those debts by nearly 70 percent in dollar terms. By mid-February there were even signs that the gold clause case was slowing the economy:

> The uncertainty over the decision . . . has brought about a decline in business . . . It is stated that export trade has suffered probably more than domestic because export and import trade are based on foreign exchange and commitments in foreign exchange offer dangerous pit-falls if the yardstick of values suffers a fundamental alteration. Until the decision is handed down, it is believed that general business activity

will continue to decline, and for that reason many persons hope that there will be little further delay in clearing up the situation. (*NYT*, 2/12/35, p. 31)

It may seem odd that the uncertainty over dollar revaluation had the same sort of deflationary impact as did uncertainty over devaluation during 1931 and 1932. But in this case a decision was expected in the near future, and thus, the effect of near-term changes in the value of the dollar outweighed any effects on the world demand for gold. This was essentially the mirror image of the situation during the first few days of March 1933, when the possibility of a near-term dollar devaluation had boosted stock prices.

The February 17 *New York Times* (p. 13) reported that stocks had recently risen because of an expectation that in the event of an unfavorable decision, "remedial legislation" would be passed to "meet any emergency." Two days later the decision was greeted with a (perhaps unwarranted) burst of optimism: "COURT BACKS GOVERNMENT ON GOLD; 5–4 FOR BOND PAYMENT IN NEW DOLLAR; BUSINESS SURGES FORWARD, STOCKS RISE." Trading was the heaviest in seven months and both stocks and commodities rose sharply at the opening.[10] A few days later, however, stocks had given up all of their gains and business certainly did not "surge forward" during the first half of 1935. Although there is no evidence that this case had a significant impact on the overall economy, it foreshadowed the much larger gold panic of 1936–1937, when a revaluation scare *did* have an important impact on prices and production.

The Belgian Crisis

On March 6, 1935, the *New York Times* (p. 29) reported a sharp fall in the pound and asserted that, "the pound's fall is disastrous for Belgium." They also noted that "an unaccountable wave of pessimism swept over the security markets yesterday and prices were reduced quite sharply," although no linkage between the two events was discussed. It wasn't until five days later that the *New York Times* finally reported (p. 25) that the pound had been "disturbing" Wall Street and that "gold hoarding once more is being indulged in on

---

10. Stocks opened nearly 5 percent higher, but the Dow finished the day up 2.5 percent.

a large scale." By March 16, the *New York Times* (p. 21) indicated that, "prospects of devaluation of the gold-bloc currencies are discussed in Wall Street these days—not much else is being talked of." A March 19 headline (p. 38) emphasized the deflationary impact of this crisis "GRAIN PRICES CUT BY HEAVY SELLING . . . FOREIGN CRISIS A FACTOR."

In retrospect, these events marked the beginning of an eighteen-month crisis that would culminate in the demise of the gold bloc. Whereas the gold clause case ended before much damage could be done, the gold bloc crisis would prove long-lasting and clearly did have a major impact on the international gold market. World monetary gold stocks declined significantly during the spring of 1935, and again during the spring of 1936. Yet, despite turmoil in the financial markets, this crisis does not appear to have significantly impacted American prices or production.

An article entitled "Inflation or Deflation" in the March 20 *New York Times* discussed the difficulty of modeling the fallout from a collapse of the gold bloc:

> There is considerable difference of opinion in financial circles whether a breakdown of the gold bloc would be seriously deflationary in its effects upon this country. It is conceded that the dollar likely would rise sharply and that, if prices and business here have received any stimulation from the fall of the dollar in foreign exchange, a rise might, presumably, reverse that condition. On the other hand there are those who believe that the abandonment of gold by the gold bloc would lead to all-around inflation, since it would involve a world-wide appreciation in the money value of gold stocks and there are still others who hold that it might lead to general stabilization of currencies—a move which is almost universally considered conducive to recovery. (p. 31)

There are at least five plausible scenarios for how a gold-bloc crisis might impact the United States:

1. The crisis could lead to gold hoarding (as in the early 1930s), which would be deflationary.

2. Actual devaluation could lead to gold dishoarding, which would be inflationary.

3. The devaluation of gold bloc currencies could impact the terms of trade, which could lead to deflation in the United States.

4. There might be an international currency war (competitive devaluations) leading to inflation in the United States.

5. There might be a general currency stabilization agreement, leading to gradual economic recovery in the United States.

We now know that only the second, and to a lesser extent the fifth, scenarios were borne out in practice. But none of this was obvious during 1935.

There are several possible reasons for the surprising stability of prices during the extended gold bloc crisis. Perhaps the most important factor was the asymmetrical responses of central banks to gold flows triggered by devaluation fears. During 1935–36 the gold bloc central banks did not allow the gold outflows to proportionately reduce their currency stocks, yet the United States *did* allow its equally large gold inflows to dramatically expand its monetary base. Thus, the world gold reserve ratio declined during the crisis. This helped to offset the deflationary effects of private gold hoarding.

There is another important difference between the currency crises of the mid-1930s and those of 1931. The deflationary impact of the German and British crises did not end with their decisions to devalue and/or restrict gold outflows. Rather, resolution of their crises simply triggered a loss of confidence in other currencies, particularly the dollar. By 1935, the situation was much different. The French franc was the last major currency that had not been adjusted to reflect the deflationary environment of the 1930s. It was widely believed that a decision to devalue the franc would quickly be copied by the smaller gold bloc members, especially the Dutch and the Swiss. The Belgian devaluation of March 1935 was important to financial markets because it triggered expectations of further devaluations and led to large gold outflows from the gold bloc. But if investors correctly foresaw the benign consequences of the final collapse of the gold bloc, then it is easy to see why the final crisis of the international gold standard had much less impact on the world price level than did the earlier German, British, and U.S. crises.

Stocks began to rise modestly in early April. The April 15 *New York Times* (p. 27) attributed the April rally to a "distinct subsiding of European 'war talk' and in the resolute attitude maintained by the 'gold bloc' countries after

Belgium's surrender." Despite the heavy gold hoarding during April and May, markets were already looking ahead to the restoration of currency stability:

> Recent estimates have placed the total of gold being hoarded in the world at about $2,000,000,000 and half of that is thought to be lying in the vaults of banks in London for the account of hoarders all over the world. When the hard struggle back to world-wide currency stability is achieved, the release of this store of hoarded gold will be an important contribution to the monetary stocks of central banks and governments. (*NYT*, 5/4/35, p. 19)

Ten days later, the head of the World Bank went so far as to (accurately) forecast that "a general return to gold would serve to raise instead of lower prices."[11]

The Repeal of the NIRA

In retrospect, the Supreme Court's rejection of the NIRA appears to have been the most significant economic event of 1935. Yet, after news of the decision hit Wall Street on the afternoon of May 27, stocks rose only slightly in the final twenty minutes of the trading session. The May 28 *New York Times* noted both the concern over the potential for "cutthroat competition" and the hope engendered by "the feeling that a yoke has been lifted." Then, on the following day stocks dropped back on deflationary fears attributed to both the demise of the NIRA and the renewed crisis in the French franc:[12]

> Out of the welter of conjectures as to the immediate future of trade and industry as a result of the wind-up of NRA enforcement, the markets arrived yesterday through the trial-and-error method at the conclusion that some deflation will have to be faced. The confusion that existed in financial circles seemed to match exactly the state of mind of Washington officialdom as indicated by the dispatches; to add to the fog that all but obscured the markets was the disturbing French financial situation. (*NYT*, 5/29/35, p. 31)

---

11. *NYT*, 5/14/35, p. 1.

12. The Bank of France raised its discount rate from 2.5 percent to 6 percent between May 23 and May 28.

The administration was split on how to react, and the June 1 *New York Times* (p. 1) noted that "stocks and commodities declined sharply yesterday following the publication by news tickers of President Roosevelt's reaction to the Supreme Court's NIRA decision." Roosevelt indicated that without the NIRA, deflation was likely to occur. It is interesting to note, however, that is was Roosevelt's labor advisors who were most concerned about the defeat of the NIRA. By June 7 the *New York Times* was reporting (p. 1) that "LABOR DEMANDS NEW NRA" . . . "PAY OF 1,000,000 HELD CUT," and that many saw Roosevelt's passive attitude as a "surrender to the opponents of national recovery."

Over the ensuing months it became more and more apparent that ending the cartelization of U.S. industry would not result in deflation and that the more enduring impact would be wage cuts. As stocks entered into an almost uninterrupted two-year bull market, attitudes toward the NIRA and the AAA began to change:

> Having witnessed a dynamic rise in business activity and the stock market since last May, when the court declared the NRA unconstitutional, the financial district, it is said, is prepared for a decision invalidating the AAA and believes that such a ruling ultimately would have stimulating effects on business. (*NYT*, 10/6/35, p. F1)
>
> Six months ago, Wall Street probably would have received an adverse decision on the constitutionality of the AAA with trepidation, on the ground that commodity prices would decline and business recovery might receive a blow. The situation is somewhat different today and many brokers believe that a ruling *upholding* the AAA might cause a bad break in stock prices. (*NYT*, 9/20/35, p. 31, emphasis added)

During the twenty-two months from July 1933 to May 1935 the economy moved forward in a slow and erratic fashion, with industrial production actually declining slightly. Then, over the following twenty-two months, industrial production soared by nearly 44 percent. The December 30, 1935, *New York Times* (p. 25) noted that "trade revival started almost immediately after the 'New Deal's' vital machinery had been shattered on May 27 in the courts."

The trends in wages and prices do suggest that repeal of the NIRA helped to trigger the recovery. Nonfood wholesale prices fell slightly in the former period before rising slightly in the latter period. It is with wages, however, that we see a really dramatic change. Nominal wages rose 7.4 percent between March 1934 and June 1935, and then actually fell by slightly over 1 percent during the subsequent fifteen months. Ironically, labor had previously complained that the NIRA was too pro-business. Since the economy was actually much stronger during the latter period, repeal of the NIRA presumably contributed to the lower wages. That was also the view of contemporaneous observers.

The impact of the repeal of the NIRA went far beyond the changes in wage and price trends. By reducing the cartelization of the economy, the repeal boosted economic efficiency. Not only were wholesale prices slightly higher after repeal of the NIRA, but they were also much more likely to represent market-clearing prices. Under the NIRA, there was strong pressure on firms to report prices in line with industry codes, which often exceeded the actual market prices.

Renewed currency stability in Europe may have also contributed to the economic recovery in the United States. On June 2, a referendum that would have forced Switzerland off the gold standard was easily defeated, and this seemed to temporary stabilize the gold bloc:

> The gold bloc crisis came to a spectacular end yesterday when the currencies of France, Switzerland and the Netherlands rallied strongly, routing speculators who had counted on their early collapse. The rally cut off the flow of gold from Europe to the United States. (*NYT*, 6/4/35, p. 33)

The Dow rose by 1.6 percent on June 3 and another 1.9 percent on June 4.

War Scares and Inflation Scares

In the years leading up to World War II, the stock market was hit by frequent European "war scares." The first major scare occurred in July 1934, when fighting in Austria led to a sharp break in U.S. stock prices on extremely heavy volume. In September 1935, the Ethiopian crisis again shook U.S. stock markets and led to a big gold inflow. Romer (1992) has argued that the gold inflows triggered by fears of war in Europe boosted the money supply and contributed to economic recovery in the United States. There are several ways that war scares could have impacted the U.S. economy, and not all would have been expansionary.

During October 1935, the Dow frequently rallied on news stories suggesting that peace might be preserved. The markets were less concerned with the Italian–Ethiopian conflict itself than with the possibility that it could trigger a wider European conflict. But markets faced a world situation that was fraught with uncertainty. The British and French had adopted a policy of appeasement that preserved peace in the short run while laying the groundwork for future crises as the fascist states saw that their expansionist aims would not meet serious opposition.

On September 19 and 20, the stock market fell sharply and the next day the *New York Times* (p. 1) reported that, "WAR FEARS SHAKE STOCK MARKETS." Then at 2:00 p.m. on October 2, stocks broke lower on news of an outbreak of hostilities between Italy and Ethiopia. Just a few days later, however, the war news seemed transmuted into a bullish factor:

> An acceleration of the rise that had been resumed on Thursday [Oct. 3] and extended on Friday was evident yesterday in the financial markets. Almost overnight, the war scare was converted into ammunition suitable for speculators committed to the rise. Stocks, wheat, copper and other commodities, with the exception of cotton, joined in an assault on some of the high records for the year.
>
> Misgivings over the possibility that the war might *extend its frontiers* were forgotten. (*NYT*, 10/6/35, p. F1, emphasis added)

These contradictory market reactions may have reflected perceptions that a massive rearmament program would be bullish so long as it did not result in an all-out European war. This shows how difficult it is to draw inferences from market reactions to war scares.

On January 6, 1936, the Supreme Court struck down the Agricultural Adjustment Act (AAA), and although the stock market closed slightly lower for the day, the next day's *New York Times* (p. 31) also noted that "markets seethed with excitement as the financial news tickers gave the gist of the decision;

securities and commodities were bid up rapidly." Over the next several weeks both the AAA decision and the congressional enactment of the "bonus bill" for veterans led to rumors of new inflation initiatives:

> The markets last week were very definitely under the spell of inflation psychology. What with Congress in a spending mood and the Treasury's large holdings of gold and silver offering temptation for currency manipulation, stocks rose, commodities edged higher, government bonds declined, and the dollar dropped sharply. (*NYT*, 1/26/36, p. F1)

On January 31, the dollar fell below the gold export point for the first time since September 1934, and a sizable gold outflow developed during February. The *New York Times* called this flow "one of the most arresting developments of the day, and at the same time the least understood" and then nicely captured the uncertainty:

> Psychologically, the fact that such exports are in progress should be reassuring, in that it implies that the Treasury is prepared to defend the position of the dollar by giving up gold—gold that can easily be spared. However, if the gold drain were to continue for a considerable time—there are no guesses as to how long the new movement may continue—it is quite likely that a nervous situation would result, since it would imply that Europe was repatriating funds. (2/4/36, p. 31)

A sharp drop in stock prices on March 9 was attributed to Germany's surprise move to reoccupy the Rhineland.[13] Stocks fell again on March 12 and 13 on renewed tensions among the European powers but then recovered swiftly when the crisis eased in mid-March. By June, there were reports of heavy purchases of steel in anticipation of "labor difficulties." This was the first sign of a major wage shock that would begin pushing up nominal wages in October. The most likely cause of the 1936 wage shock was the passage of the Wagner Act in 1935, which made it easier to form labor unions. During late 1936 and 1937, the membership of both the American Federation of Labor

---

13. Surprisingly, however, the sharpest declines did not occur until late in the day.

(AFL) and especially the more aggressive Congress of Industrial Organizations (CIO) grew rapidly.

Over the course of 1936, the federal government became increasingly concerned that an overheating economy would lead to an upsurge in inflation. Throughout the first half of 1936, there had been persistent rumors that the Fed might act to slow the economy, probably by increasing reserve requirements. The July 15 *New York Times* headlines announced "RESERVE REQUIREMENTS INCREASE 50 PER CENT TO BAR CREDIT INFLATION . . . GOLD INFLOW THE REASON . . . 'EASY MONEY' POLICY KEPT." The negative Treasury bond market reaction on the next day was widely regarded as a response to this action (suggesting that the move was at least partially unanticipated). Stocks rose to new highs in early trading, while T-bond prices broke early and closed down in the heaviest volume in over a year. The increase in stock prices is odd given the consensus view of modern economic historians is that the reserve requirement increases of 1936–1937 were a mistake, and may have helped trigger the 1937–1938 depression. It could be argued that the announced change was smaller (i.e., less contractionary) than had been anticipated, but that view fails to account for the accompanying rise in the yields on Treasury securities.[14]

Despite the higher reserve requirements, as well as subsequent moves such as gold sterilization, the United States was entering into a major inflation that would push wholesale prices up by 11 percent between June 1936 and April 1937. Thus, the Fed's inflation worries were not entirely unfounded. And the markets presumably agreed that these steps were necessary to maintain steady, but controlled, expansion in an economy experiencing large gold inflows. As we will see in Chapters 9 and 10, this does not necessarily mean that the Fed's action played no role in the 1937–1938 depression, but it does indicate that the action was not as obviously foolish as is suggested in some modern accounts. And, by now, it should be abundantly clear that the stock market's apparent approval of Fed restraint was not due to it having a "conservative" point of view on monetary policy issues.

---

14. The Fisher effect does not seem to have been a factor in market responses during the period when the United States was on the gold standard.

The Tripartite Agreement

The United States did not escape entirely unscathed from the renewed gold bloc crisis that began in April 1936. The Dow, which had been rising almost continuously ever since the court rejected the NIRA eleven months earlier, fell nearly 10 percent over the last few weeks of April. On April 22 the *New York Times* (p. 35) suggested that the currency crisis in France might be depressing markets in the United States. The following weekend saw Poland abandon the gold standard as well as increased election uncertainty in France. On April 28, the *New York Times* (p. 1) reported "Stocks Drop 1 to 9 Points in Selling Rush; French Vote, Roosevelt Talk Held Factors." On May 3 the Socialists did well in the second round of the French elections, and two days later, the *New York Times* (p. 31) again suggested that French politics were depressing U.S. stock prices.

During both April and May, gold hoarding increased dramatically as gold bloc currencies sold at large discounts in forward markets. Unfortunately, the quality of world monetary gold stock data declines in the late 1930s. Increasing amounts of gold were held secretly in "Exchange Equalization Accounts." In Appendix 8.a, I discuss how these estimates of the size of these accounts might alter the findings of this study.

The outbreak of the Spanish Civil War in August 1936 did not appear to have a major impact on Wall Street, although a sharp break in stock prices on August 21 was attributed to fears that other European powers might be drawn into the conflict. On several occasions during late September, the *New York Times* suggested that the French crisis was modestly depressing equity markets in the United States. But the *Times* also noted that the devaluation of the franc had already been heavily discounted and was not expected to have a major impact on stock prices, particularly if it led to a currency stabilization agreement. On September 27 the *Times* reported (p. F1) that a "Tripartite Agreement" for currency cooperation between the United States, Britain, and France had helped boost the U.S. stock market.[15]

---

15. This was an informal agreement to avoid competitive devaluations. France agreed to devalue by no more than 25 percent.

In the short run, the Tripartite Agreement was successful in restoring some measure of stability, but unsettled conditions in Europe prevented any major return flow of funds from the United States:

> Fear that heavy repatriation of foreign funds lodged in this country would immediately follow devaluation of the erstwhile gold-bloc currencies was dispelled last week, and the stock market closed the week with a vigorous advance. (*NYT*, 10/4/36, p. F1)

Three days later the *New York Times* (p. 41) suggested that "speculative interest in the stock market has risen to the highest level witnessed since last February" and "Wall Street continues to believe that the spark that touched off the recent rise in stocks was the devaluation in foreign currencies." In addition, commodity prices, which had been gradually rising for several years, began increasing rapidly in October.

The massive dishoarding of gold touched off by the Tripartite Agreement raised the world's monetary gold stock by almost 3 percent in just the month of December. Although some dishoarding was anticipated, the press suggested that the rate of dishoarding was greater than expected, and that the willingness of European powers to absorb those hoards was less than anticipated:

> It was widely believed that if the gold bloc nations devalued, the flow of gold here would cease and even turn about in the other direction. . . . When the gold bloc did capitulate last September, however, nothing of the sort occurred. Gold continued to come here as before. It no longer came directly from the Bank of France and other central banks but it came from all the gold mines of the world and from private hoards. (*NYT*, 6/13/37, p. E3)

Even though the "international gold standard" was now reduced to the United States and Belgium, the international gold *market* was playing an increasingly important role in the world economy. Although nominally operating under a floating rate regime, the important sterling bloc maintained a relatively stable exchange rate with the dollar, and thus with gold. Thus, the inflation of 1936–37 was a worldwide phenomenon. Figure 8.1 shows how the rapid rise in the world monetary gold stocks between mid-1936 and mid-1937 was associated

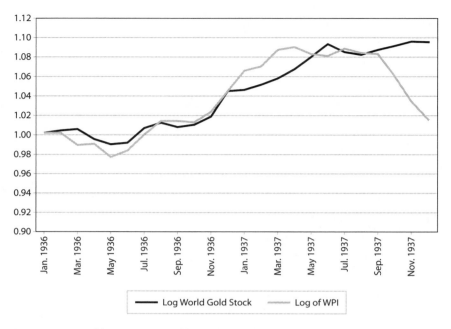

Figure 8.1. World Monetary Gold Stock and U.S. WPI

with rapid increases in the U.S. price level, especially during December 1936. Note that commodity prices are forward-looking, and thus rose even more rapidly than gold stocks during early 1937.

The final crisis of the gold bloc provides an interesting contrast to the British devaluation of 1931. Whereas the British devaluation helped create an international monetary crisis, the gold bloc crisis helped to restore stability to the international monetary system, at least for a brief period. And the fact that these two devaluations had very different effects on the U.S. price level suggests that the impact of foreign devaluations on the U.S. terms of trade *was much less important* than their impact on the international gold market. Both the British and the French devaluations turned the terms of trade against the United States. But the British devaluation of 1931 also led to a huge increase in gold hoarding, which reduced stock and commodity prices in the United States. In contrast, the gold bloc devaluations led to massive gold *dishoarding*, which raised stock and commodity prices in the United States.

Summary

In this account of the Great Depression, the two-and-a-half year period from February 1934 to September 1936 represents the eye of the hurricane. The purchasing power of gold was fairly stable, and (because the dollar was pegged to gold) a stable gold market meant a relatively stable price level. As gold flowed back from the gold bloc to the United States, the world gold reserve ratio declined. Thus, the deflationary impact of private gold hoarding (as well as currency hoarding) was roughly offset by the inflationary impact of gold flows. Most of the events described in this chapter and the next—the devaluation scares, revaluations scares, wage shocks, and war scares—were short-lived and now seem faint echoes of the traumatic events that came before and after. Not surprisingly, the stock market became much more stable in the period after the dollar's link to gold was reestablished in early 1934, and this stability continued until the fall of 1937, when the dollar again came under attack.

A gold price of $35/ounce was capable of supporting a much higher price level (and did so during the Bretton Woods era). The low but gently rising prices of the mid-1930s reflected two offsetting factors: a sharp increase in the price of gold during 1933, and a simultaneous sharp increase in the U.S. gold reserve ratio. The 1933–1934 devaluation gave the Fed all the flexibility it needed; it simply chose not to monetize the increase in the nominal value of its existing gold stock. Indeed, given its stable price level policy preferences, it would have made no sense to adopt a more expansionary policy.

Modern economic historians often criticize the Fed for having an almost pathological fear of inflation during the mid-1930s. But the unprecedented labor market interventions make this period difficult to evaluate. Absent the large NIRA wage shocks, the expansionary monetary policy (and rising WPI) of the 1933–1936 period would have been more than adequate to generate full recovery. The Fed might reasonably have argued that they did all they could, or at least all that was prudent. But because of the wage shocks, this monetary stimulus was only sufficient to generate a partial recovery. From this perspective, those arguing that the Fed should have been more expansionary during 1934–1936 are actually arguing that the Fed should have taken it upon itself to repeal FDR's high wage policy. That is a defensible argument, but also one that raises a number of complex issues, both theoretical and political. The Fed may have been too conservative during 1934–1936, but their policy was nowhere near as indefensible as during the 1929–1933 contraction.

In the next two chapters we will see that this period of steady growth was disrupted by two new problems, or rather by the recurrence of two problems that had previously occurred in the early 1930s: fast-rising wages and then widespread gold hoarding by the public.

Appendix 8a
Exchange Equalization Accounts

The Federal Reserve data that this study relies upon do not include gold held in non-central bank accounts, most notably, the Exchange Equalization Accounts (EEAs) that governments used to control exchange rates. The most important of these funds was the British EEA, which began accumulating gold at the end of 1932. Initially the amounts were rather small, and adding them to the official reserves would not materially affect the conclusions from the earlier part of the Depression. After 1935, however, the gold purchases of the British EEA were substantial.

Paish (1939) estimates that the British EEA gold holdings rose from about $300 million in April 1935, to nearly $1.5 billion in April 1938. After that date, the gold holdings fell sharply, as Britain used these reserves to pay for its rearmament program. Total central bank gold stocks (excluding Russia) rose by about $2.6 billion, or 11.2 percent, during that three-year period. If one were to add the British EEA gold accumulations to that total, the increase would have been about 17.8 percent, certainly a significant difference. Paish also reports that EEA gold holdings rose by over $460 million in just the spring and summer of 1937, before falling slightly in the final quarter. Then gold stocks rose modestly in the first quarter of 1938, and fell rapidly during the rest of 1938.

Although this data is rather sketchy, it suggests that the major stylized facts that I will present in the next two chapters actually *understate* the changes that were occurring in the world monetary gold stock. If we added Paish's estimate of British EEA gold to the Fed's central bank estimates, then world gold stocks would have almost certainly risen right up to September 1937, instead of peaking in June, as shown in Figure 8.1 (on page 292). But the EEA data would not alter the claim that world monetary gold stocks were relatively flat in the nine months after September 1937. Thus, the slowdown in the growth rate of the world monetary gold stock is probably even more dramatic than suggested by the Fed estimates. Later, I will argue that this sudden shift in the world gold market popped the commodity price bubble and moved the United States from an inflationary to a deflationary environment after September 1937.

Fortunately, the narrative in these chapters does not hinge on having precise gold stock data, but merely that there was a large inflow of gold to central banks during late 1936 and early 1937 and a renewed period of hoarding after September 1937. As we will see, there were numerous reports in the financial press of exactly these sorts of gold inflows and outflows. Thus, although we cannot be certain of the exact size of government gold stocks, the direction of change is almost certainly consistent with the Federal Reserve's central bank data, and indeed that data may understate the turnaround in the world gold market during late 1937.

9

The Gold Panic of 1937

THE PRECEDING NARRATIVE has focused on two broad themes: the impact of wage shocks and the impact of changes in the demand for gold. In the eighteen months following the Tripartite Agreement, each of these factors took on increased importance. Just as in 1933, however, gold and labor market shocks tended to partially offset each other, and only through a careful examination of the historical record can we see their actual importance. The economic impact of the 1937 gold scare, in particular, has not received the attention that it deserves. This eighteen-month period is one of the best examples of how the gold market approach to aggregate demand can provide insights not available from the traditional monetary or expenditure approaches. Thus, we will devote two full chapters to the 1936–1938 business cycle.

The Election of 1936

During October 1936, investors began to pay increased attention to the forthcoming national elections, although politics was nowhere near as important a market influence as had been the case in 1932. Notwithstanding the famous *Literary Digest* poll (which predicted a Landon victory), most knowledgeable observers expected President Roosevelt (FDR) to be reelected. The November 1 *New York Times* (p. 1) forecast a result similar to 1932, with Roosevelt favored in states with 406 electoral votes, Landon in states with 93 votes, and 32 unknown.[1] It was also suggested that a Landon victory would boost

---

1. The same issue suggested that the Supreme Court, not FDR, had brought recovery.

utility stocks, because the New Deal regulation had been so hostile to those firms. This forecast will help us to interpret the election results.

With the reelection of Roosevelt widely anticipated, the *New York Times* noted that

> [T]he main hope of the financial community had been that anti-New Deal representation in Congress would be increased. But business judgment is not swayed by sentiment; the strength of the security and commodity markets yesterday was impressive. (11/5/36, p. 41)

At both the presidential and the congressional levels, the actual election results were much more favorable to the Democrats than almost anyone had forecast, and stocks, bonds, and commodities all soared on expectations of continued monetary ease. The notable exception was the Dow utility index, which fell by 3.3 percent.

Even though the reelection of Roosevelt had been widely anticipated, the strength of his victory was so overwhelming as to produce a sea change in the U.S. political and economic environment. The election was viewed as an enthusiastic endorsement of the New Deal, and previously hostile business and financial interests immediately adopted a more conciliatory attitude. Prior to the election, labor had been having difficulty getting business to accept the provisions of the Wagner Act, which many felt would eventually be ruled unconstitutional.[2] Now labor made rapid gains in both membership and wages.

In retrospect, the financial markets misjudged the impact of the New Deal landslide. Roosevelt would begin his second term advocating policies to increase wages and restrain price inflation. In fact, Roosevelt felt so strongly about this issue that he even opposed a plan to index steel industry wages to the CPI on the grounds that it would *prevent* real wages from increasing.[3] By 1937, he had combined an anti-inflationary program with a policy of high wages, a poisonous combination for the equity markets. Figure 9.1 shows the wholesale price index (WPI) as well as nominal and real wages during 1936–1938. Note that the WPI increased first, and this was associated with rapid gains in output during 1936 and early 1937. After the election nominal wages began increasing

---

2. See Hall and Ferguson (1998, p. 143).

3. *NYT*, 11/14/36, p. 1.

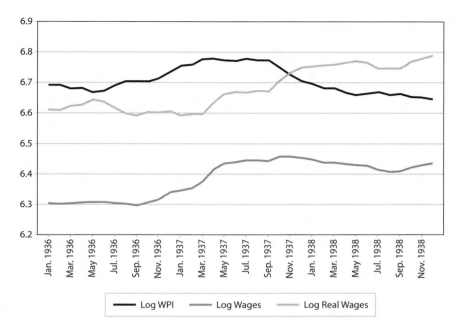

Figure 9.1. Wholesale Prices and Nominal and Real Wages

more rapidly, so that by the spring of 1937 real wages were rising rapidly. At this point industrial production leveled off. When the WPI began falling sharply in the fall of 1937, real wages increased still further, and severe recession occurred.

Labor was viewed as having played an important role in generating the huge turnout that produced the electoral landslide, and not surprisingly they now began a much more aggressive push to achieve what they regarded as their just reward. One item on the agenda was a "New NRA," which would eventually become the Wage-Hours Act of 1938. Just days after the election, wage increases were announced in the steel, auto, and oil industries, and even many nonunion firms began to raise wages sharply as a way of averting future labor troubles.[4]

The political situation in the United States was now much more stable than in most of Europe. Although the U.S. economy had been robust for many months, the November 14 *New York Times* (p. 25) suggested that "the

4. See the *NYT*, 11/7/36, p. 1; and 11/11/36, p. 1.

election result had to be made known before Europe as a whole would be convinced that the New Deal policies were to be continued. Then the money poured across the Atlantic." Four days later the Dow reached its 1936 peak (and, in real terms, its peak for the entire 1931–1951 period) as stocks were boosted by rumors that curbs on foreign investment would not be imposed.[5]

By mid-December it was clear that the stock market was not keeping up with the worldwide commodities boom and the *New York Times* noted that "the reassuring business reports might be expected to exert greater force were it not for the disconcerting spread of labor disputes."[6] Of course, prior to the New Deal, nominal wages generally followed market-sensitive prices with a significant lag. For instance, nominal wages actually declined during the March through July 1933 period, when the WPI increased by 14 percent. Thus, the wage shock of 1936–1937 was probably not caused by the concurrent commodity price boom (the CPI showed a much smaller increase), but rather by political factors such as the Wagner Act and the 1936 election. The union share of the nonfarm workforce leaped from 13.2 percent in 1936 to 21.8 percent in 1937, and then 26.6 percent in 1938.[7] And, in addition to wage increases associated with the unionization drives, at the beginning of 1937 business faced a new payroll tax that boosted employer labor costs by another 2 percent.

As early as October 30, the *New York Times* (p. 35) had discussed how "the continued rise of excess reserves due to the influx of gold . . . has stirred up some talk of the possibility of another increase in reserve requirements," and also predicted that "a second increase in reserve requirements would scarcely be received as easily as was the first." By mid-December it was clear that the August increase in reserve requirements had failed to restrain the speculation in commodity markets that had been triggered by worldwide gold dishoarding. The second step in the Fed's anti-inflation program was announced after the markets closed on December 21, 1936. This plan called for the sterilization of all gold imports into the United States, and as with the higher reserve requirements, it was received relatively[8] calmly by the financial markets.

---

5. See the *NYT*, 11/18/36, p. 37.

6. *NYT*, 12/20/36, p. F1. And it was not just commodity prices that were soaring. In the five weeks from November 7 to December 12 the *NYT* business index jumped from 101.3 to 108.6.

7. This data is taken from Freeman (1998, p. 292).

8. The Dow rose by 0.8 percent on December 22.

At first, these policies lacked credibility, and commodity prices continued to accelerate. Even Roosevelt's message to Congress (which promised a balanced budget) was viewed as bullish because "the inference is that if the Federal budget is to be balanced on schedule, trade and industry must continue at a high rate of activity and there must be no drastic deflation of commodity prices."[9]

On January 30, the Federal Reserve (Fed) announced that the third and final step of its anti-inflation program would involve two additional increases in bank reserve requirements. These increases were set to occur on March 1, 1937, and May 1, 1937, and would bring the required reserve ratio up to its legal maximum. As with the first increase, this announcement was followed by a slight *increase* in stock prices. By early 1937 inflation was an even greater concern than had been the case in July 1936. And the December 28 *New York Times* (p. 23) was echoing the conventional wisdom when it suggested (five years prematurely) that, "1936 has proved unmistakably the definite ending of the cycle of depression."

The overwhelming electoral victory led Roosevelt to overreach at the beginning of his second term. On February 5, Roosevelt announced his intention to pack the Supreme Court with six additional justices and the next day the *New York Times* (p. 1) reported that Congress was "expected to approve" the measure. They also noted that "STOCKS DROP FAST ON COURT MESSAGE," not surprisingly since the Supreme Court was now the only bulwark against what the financial community perceived to be radical New Deal legislation.[10] Although the market reaction to the previous November's election could be interpreted as approval of the New Deal, with the gold clause case already decided, the Supreme Court would have no further say on those elements of the New Deal which were approved by stock investors (i.e., expansionary aggregate demand policies), but would have a say on the regulatory aspects of the New Deal which so exercised Wall Street. In addition, Roosevelt's proposal may have been (correctly) viewed by Wall Street as a sign that he would adopt a more aggressively anti-business stance during his second term.

---

9. *NYT* (1/10/37, p. F1).

10. Although stocks declined by only 1.3 percent on February 5, the *NYT* noted that stock prices had been increasing until midday when "summaries of the message were flashed on the financial news tickers, the market hesitated momentarily and then sold off rapidly" (2/6/37, p. 25).

The court packing scheme was the first of a series of steps that greatly strained relations between the Roosevelt administration and the much more conservative financial community during 1937–1938. Wall Street pundits would later argue that Roosevelt's antibusiness stance was the cause of the 1937–1938 depression. Certainly, Roosevelt's commitment to a high wage/high tax/low price policy at the very least made it much more difficult to formulate effective countercyclical policies.

Organized labor became increasing assertive at the beginning of 1937, and by early March labor unrest had become the most talked about economic issue in the United States. On March 4, the *New York Times* reported that a steel settlement had pushed stocks up and suggested that the pact should not hurt earnings as long as consumers didn't resist price rises. They also argued (p. 33) that, "any control over the cost of living has long ago passed from Wall Street to Washington." In fact, "Washington" was already attempting to slow the economy, and only a month later wholesale prices reached their cyclical peak. After another few months the steel industry would be forced to sharply contract output.

The Gold Panic

In addition to labor unrest, there was increasing concern over the rapid increase in the supply of gold during the spring of 1937. On March 8, France removed controls on gold in order to reduce hoarding, and on March 14 the *New York Times* (p. F1) suggested that the policy seemed to be working. Stocks reached their depression highs (in nominal terms) on March 10, and the next day the *New York Times* (p. 33) reported that "inflationary sentiment in the commodity markets continues to run riot." At about the same time the Russians began dumping large quantities of gold onto the London market.

On March 19, the *New York Times* (p. 35) reported that Treasury bond (T-bond) prices increased and stocks fell sharply after Administration officials expressed concern about inflation. The markets were beginning to fear that FDR would overreact to the high commodity prices. Roosevelt was becoming increasing concerned that wages were lagging behind prices and that attempts by workers to catch up were producing violent labor conflicts. The March 18 *New York Times* headlines capture the climate of this period: "STRIKERS

DEFY COURT ORDER AT DETROIT PLANTS" . . . "CHAOS IS FORE-
SEEN" . . . "MOB RULE FEARED" . . . "FASCISM HELD POSSIBLE"
. . . "Wild Riot Rages in Chicago Loop As Taxi Drivers Battle Police." On
March 23, stocks rose on rumors that the administration might act against
sit-down strikes. A week later it was announced that FDR would push for a
federal minimum wage law, although it would not be enacted for another year.

The fear that we were headed for "another 1929"[11]—that is, a speculative
bubble—led the administration to impose curbs on federal purchases of commodities and durable goods as a way of restraining inflation. The April 3 *New
York Times* (p. 6) noted that recent statements by both the administration
and Fed officials had "indicated a change in the trend of the government's
recovery measures away from the emphasis which has been placed upon the
stimulation of industrial activity and recovery of prices." They also noted
that after the President announced this new policy, stocks fell "at once." This
policy shift triggered a very unusual crisis in the gold market—a worldwide
fear of currency *revaluation*.

Throughout recorded history there are relatively few examples of formal
revaluations of currencies in terms of gold. Yet just such a rumor developed
vis-à-vis the dollar during the spring of 1937. On April 8, both stocks and commodities fell sharply and the next day the *New York Times* cited rumors of a cut
in the gold price as a market influence. The *New York Times* also suggested that

> Unneeded gold continues to flow to this country and, at best, the re-
> cent procedure of "sterilizing" . . . has been a makeshift to get around
> a situation fraught with grave financial and economic consequences.
> (4/9/37, p. 33)

Two days later the rumor had become headline news "ROOSEVELT
DENIES PLAN TO CUT GOLD, BUT FRANC PLUNGES," and the *New
York Times* (p. 1) noted that such a move would "be deflationary, checking
prices and tending to lessen the influx of foreign money to this country, a
tendency over which the President has expressed concern." The *New York
Times* (p. 23) also reported that the U.S. "stock market got off to a bad start

11. *NYT*, 4/3/37, p. 6, quoting both Henry Wallace and Fed chairman Marriner Eccles.

but rallied on the President's statement." And the rumor had an impact on markets worldwide:

> Dispatches reaching London tonight from all the financial centers of the British Empire indicate how complete was the unsettlement of the exchange, commodity and security markets as a result of rumors that the United States Government intended substantially to reduce its buying price of gold. . . . Frenzied scenes were enacted in Throgmorton Street tonight, when operators, taking courage from the President's denial, rushed in to buy gold and copper shares and United States securities. For an hour the street was impassable to traffic. (4/10/37, pp. 1, 7).

Despite high rates of inflation, investors understood that the Roosevelt administration did not wish to reduce the price of gold, but it was believed that the huge gold inflows would ultimately force such an action:

> The rapidly growing production of gold in Russia which the U.S. has to absorb, it is held here, is especially pushing Washington toward revaluation.
>
> The effect of these considerations upon speculators and the large European corporations which have their reserves now in gold bars is, bankers here explain, to encourage them to put their gold on the market. It is reported that there still are large quantities of this hoarded gold left. Dehoarding of this gold, in addition to the new gold that is coming from the mines . . . only adds to the pressure on Washington to cease buying at so high a price, thus increasing the danger of a sudden upset in the general price structure. One odd result is that the bankers who a year ago were denouncing the hoarders of gold for not bringing it out are now praying that they won't dehoard. (*NYT*, 4/13/37, p. 37)

Two additional factors that reduced the credibility of government denials were the recent abandonment of the silver purchase program and the desire to balance the budget:

> Before the United States abandoned its policy of buying foreign silver, it was besieged with tenders of the metal from all points of the compass; so long as this country is the only nation to buy gold continuously

and freely at $35 an ounce, it will not want for offerings, through London, from South Africa and India, and now from Soviet Russia. In the meanwhile, the Treasury must finance the Federal deficits and carry the added burden of paying for this unneeded gold. (*NYT,* 4/18/37, p. F1)

In a sense, the gold panic of 1937 was the mirror image of the sort of "expectations trap" discussed by Paul Krugman (1998). Krugman suggested that monetary injections might fail to arrest deflation if the policy was expected to be reversed in the future. With the gold panic, there were attempts by the government to slow the growth in the money supply with reserve requirement increases and gold sterilization. But gold sterilization is costly, forcing the Treasury to increase its borrowing. The markets thought that the United States would eventually be forced to monetize at least a part of the huge gold inflows triggered by the $35/ounce price, the war fears in Europe, and the lack of other buyers.

During April, May, and June, the already rapid growth in the world monetary gold stock accelerated further as de-hoarding was spurred by fears of an imminent decrease in the price of gold. A sharp drop in stocks and commodities on April 26 was attributed to "persistent rumors regarding a lowering in the price of gold."[12] In a letter to Congress made public late on April 27, Roosevelt issued another statement about inflation, and on April 29 the *New York Times* (p. 1) reported that the previous day's market "was weak from the start on the overnight news of President Roosevelt's warning against the 'present hazard of undue advances in prices, with a resulting rise in the cost of living.'" The same issue noted that excess reserves had been increasing much more rapidly that expected, casting further doubt on the effectiveness of the Fed's anti-inflation measures.

Several articles noted that the relatively high buying price of gold created an excess supply of gold for the same reason that price support programs for wheat led to grain surpluses. There was speculation that the gold sterilization policy would eventually collapse under the pressure of market forces, and that a revaluation of the dollar was almost inevitable. There are two important differences, however, between gold and wheat markets. First, the medium-term

---

12. See the *NYT,* 4/27/37, p. 31.

(i.e., one to five years) elasticity of supply of gold is almost certainly far lower than for wheat. More importantly, unlike wheat, gold was the medium of account in the United States, and thus FDR could not change the dollar price of gold without having a profound impact on the entire price structure.

Because the 1937 gold panic was in some respects the mirror image of the devaluation scares of 1931–1932, it might have been expected to increase the U.S. price level. For a time during late 1936 and early 1937, the flood of dishoarded gold did push wholesale prices sharply higher. But, just as the dollar crisis of 1933 became a bullish factor once investors began to fear an *imminent* devaluation of the dollar, the last stages of the gold panic led to rumors of an imminent revaluation of the dollar, and that put downward pressure on commodity and equity prices. The strongest evidence for this comes from the commodity markets and gold mining stocks; both plummeted sharply on news relating to the gold panic. The U.S. wholesale price index fell only slightly between April and June, but the rapid inflation of 1936–1937 had come to an end.

Ironically, the panicky reaction to revaluation rumors may have prevented the very problem that so worried stock and commodity speculators. Stocks rose modestly in early May, and on May 6, the *New York Times* (p. 37) argued that the rumors had "served to remind the world that it has a vital interest at stake in the maintenance of the existing value of gold" and that as a result the British and Dutch governments were now buying gold to assist the United States in that endeavor. The revaluation rumor would not die easily, however, and after stocks dropped 3.4 percent during the week of May 10–15, the *New York Times* reported that

> The plans announced last week by the Swedish Government for monetary measures to check a possible inflation, including, if necessary, an upward revaluation of the currency, attracted interest in Wall Street banking circles as a portent of the changing trend in world monetary affairs. (5/16/37, p. F1)

Although that rumor eventually turned out to be false, the *New York Times* also reported that in London:

> The suggestion that the Swedish krona should be revalued in terms of sterling caused a flutter . . . similar to that occasioned by the United States gold scare, although less severe. (5/24/37, p. 29)

Stocks broke again on June 1, and the next day's *New York Times* (p. 33) suggested that a Bank of International Settlements (BIS) report recommending gold revaluation was worrying London financiers, and that despite the fact that "GOLD CUT DENIED AGAIN BY TREASURY" . . . "Europe in Rush to Sell Dehoarded Gold." On June 3 the one-day volume of gold transactions on the London gold market hit a new record ($16 million), a clear sign that dishoarding was accelerating. On the following day another record was set ($20 million), and on June 5 the *New York Times* (p. 23) reported that even more gold had to be turned away "for the simple reason that there were insufficient trucks to contain it."

On June 4, stocks rallied on Roosevelt's reassuring statement that there was no change in government policy, but the next day the *New York Times* noted that these denials did not solve the problem of credibility:

> But the persistence of this fear about gold, in the face of denials by the highest authorities, reflects the public's loss of faith, all over the world, in the word of governments where money is concerned. Devaluation and its concomitant, abrogation of gold clauses, was a breach of faith on the part of the devaluing governments, however much it may have been demanded by the circumstances. Moreover, devaluation was preceded everywhere by solemn assertions that it would not occur. People became inured to disregarding official pledges on the currency because they saw that the force of economic events was nullifying such pledges. Similarly now it appears to many as though the current gold situation, involving governments in the costly purchase of huge unwanted stocks of the metal, is too difficult to continue unchanged for very long, regardless of what governments say. (6/5/37, p. 23)

The same issue indicated that the British were highly skeptical of the ability of the United States to maintain the gold price, particularly in light of rapidly growing Soviet production, which was reported at 73.5 million ounces ($2.57 billion) in 1936. This report is relevant for two reasons. First, it may help us to understand why the anti-inflationary steps taken by the Fed in 1936 and early 1937 had so little impact on commodity prices. But the report is also important because it was apparently incorrect. Soviet production was probably nowhere near as high as reported, and as this became better known to market participants commodity prices began to soften.

Understanding the Gold Panic

Although modern economic historians[13] have paid little attention to this episode, contemporaneous observers understood the importance of the gold panic. Paul Einzig provided an entertaining critique of the views Gustav Cassel expressed during the middle of the gold panic:

On June 9, 1937, this veteran monetary expert published a blood-curdling article in the *Daily Mail* painting in the darkest colours the situation caused by the superabundance of gold and suggesting a cut in the price of gold to half-way between its present price and its old price as the only possible remedy. He took President Roosevelt sharply to task for having failed to foresee in January 1934 that the devaluation of the dollar by 41 percent would lead to such a superabundance of gold. If, however, we look at Professor Cassel's earlier writings, we find that he himself failed to foresee such developments, even at much later dates. We read in the July 1936 issue of the *Quarterly Review of the Skandinaviska Kreditaktiebolaget* the following remarks by Professor Cassel: "There seems to be a general idea that the recent rise in the output of gold has been on such a scale that we are now on the way towards a period of immense abundance of gold. *This view can scarcely be correct.*" . . . Thus the learned Professor expected a mere politician to foresee something in January 1934 which he himself was incapable of foreseeing two and a half years later. In fact, it is doubtful whether he would have been capable of foreseeing it at all but for the advent of the gold scare, which, rightly or wrongly, made him see things he had not seen before. It was not the discovery of any new facts, nor even the weight of new scientific argument that converted him and his fellow-economists. It was the subconscious influence of the panic among gold hoarders, speculators, and other sub-men that suddenly opened the eyes of these supermen. This fact must have contributed

---

13. Eichengreen fails to mention the gold panic in his 400-page treatise on the interwar gold standard. Friedman and Schwartz also ignore this episode.

in no slight degree towards lowering the prestige of economists and of economic science in the eyes of the lay public. (1937b, pp. 26–27)

This is a fascinating statement, but I think that both Cassel and Einzig have it wrong. Cassel was mistaken in his 1937 views, but he was not wrong to be influenced by the market "sub-men," just as academic "supermen" were not wrong to revise their views in late 1997 when panic selling among Asian financial market traders provided them with new information about East Asian economic growth prospects and structural inadequacies. Markets are often wrong (and were wrong in 1937), yet remain the most informed opinion we have. Rather, Cassel's mistake is in his retrospective criticism of policymakers. It wasn't just Cassel who didn't foresee the superabundance of gold in 1934, or even early 1936, the markets also failed to anticipate this problem. Cassel is making the same error as those who retrospectively criticized the Fed's tight money policy of 1928–1929, the discount rate increases of 1931, or the reserve requirement increases of 1936 and 1937—pretending to be smarter than the markets. And, of course, an entire book could be written on this phenomenon during the post-2007 global economic crisis.

Einzig's comments also illustrate the sea change in market views between 1936 and 1937, and raise the question of what caused this change. It makes no sense to view the high wholesale prices of mid-1937 as the inevitable effect of the devaluation of 1934, even if, *ex post*, it is possible to trace a chain of causation between those two events. These high prices did not exist at any other time between 1931 and 1939, and financial markets did not anticipate them in the summer of 1936.

If markets are efficient then traders should have received new information during the period when commodity prices were rising. And the most rapid increases occurred during the winter of 1936–1937. Einzig suggested that:

Even though the "alarming" figures for 1936 [gold stocks] became available in January 1937, it was not until three months later that their sinister significance was discovered. From April onwards it became fashionable to present gold statistics in the gloomiest possible light. The one-sided presentation of the facts and figures of past production would in itself have caused but little harm, but when they were used as the basis for forecasting future gold supplies, the prophets indulged in extreme exaggeration. (1937b, p. 28)

Once again, Einzig seems only partly correct. The "sinister significance" of rapidly growing gold stocks was probably influencing commodity prices in early 1937; rapid inflation is exactly what one would expect from the growing perception that gold supplies would increase rapidly over time. The intelligentsia generally picks up on a problem some time after market participants become aware of the problem. Then, in April 1937, the markets began reacting to signs of how the *political establishment* would respond to the ongoing market trends. More specifically, the markets began to fear that governments would respond by revaluing their currencies. This pattern of financial market movement—government policy reaction–market response was more important in the experimental policy environment of the 1930s than at any other time in American history.

The June 13 *New York Times* discussed the gold problem in depth ("UNCLE SAM, UNHAPPY MIDAS," p. E3) and concluded that there were five possible solutions. The current policy, sterilization, was viewed as too costly to maintain in the long run. The legalization of private gold ownership in the United States was seen as being ineffective; few would want to hold gold if its price were about to be reduced. Desterilization was seen as a potentially inflationary policy, whereas revaluation was viewed as deflationary. Instead, the *New York Times* suggested that a "world agreement to curtail gold production" was the "only really promising solution." Ironically, a few weeks after this article was written, the problem vanished for good. First, the gold inflows ceased for one year. Then, when the gold flows resumed, they were fully absorbed by huge increases in excess reserves beginning in 1938. In essence, commercial banks relieved the U.S. Treasury of the burden of buying the world's surplus gold.

During mid-June the French franc came under increasing pressure, and this eventually brought the panic to an end. The July 1 *New York Times* (p. 41) noted that "devaluation of the franc hardly implies deflation of world prices" and on July 19 (p. 23) they suggested that French currency problems had ended speculation of a cut in the price of gold and led to a resumption of hoarding. Although the world monetary gold stock declined in July, the prices of commodities rose modestly as fears of a revaluation of the dollar subsided.

A Switch in Time Saves Nine

While the gold panic was the focus of Wall Street during the spring of 1937, labor disturbances were also an important market influence. Given the hypothesis outlined in the previous chapter, it is surprising that the midday April 12 announcement of the Supreme Court decision upholding the Wagner Act had only a small (negative) impact on Wall Street.[14] One possibility is that the Wagner Act played a smaller role in the unionization drives than I had assumed. Another, is that this decision made it less likely that the court-packing scheme would succeed. The April 14 *New York Times* (p. 37) noted that even in the mildly negative reaction to the Court's decision, Wall Street was out of step with much of public opinion. They indicated that the Wagner Act had received an "enthusiastic response" from "conservative as well as liberal" opinion. Given that the country was being racked by violent labor disputes, it is not surprising that the dispute resolutions incorporated in the Wagner Act should have received such a positive response. The *Times* also wondered, however:

> If the validating of the Wagner act may be said to re-establish certain aims contained in the outlawed NRA, the next question is whether other provisions of this act will be taken up piecemeal. Taken alone, the Wagner act should make for industrial labor stability, but in Wall Street the "inflation" topic will not [die] down, and the question of how some industries will fare in trying to pass along increased costs is still pertinent. (4/14/37, p. 37)

Wall Street was clearly more supportive of that part of the National Industrial Recovery Act (NIRA) aimed at promoting higher prices, but the administration was actively working to slow the ongoing inflation.

By mid-June 1937, labor disturbances were once again dominating the news, and the June 14 *New York Times* (p. 27) indicated that although the market had become used to workers striking when "industrial activity is high," the markets were especially disturbed by the fact that "not a word is said by the national government regarding the more lawless of them." And on the following day they indicated (p. 33) that "followers of the stock market are greatly concerned over the widespread industrial labor trouble, not alone on

---

14. See the *NYT*, 4/13/37, p. 1.

the score of companies directly concerned, but as it may be thought to imperil the whole recovery movement." Without the boost to commodity prices provided by the resolution of the gold panic in early July, the depression of 1937–1938 might well have begun at this time.

In addition to the resolution of the gold crisis, stocks were helped in July by the failure in Congress of the bill aimed at packing the Supreme Court. As early as May 19, the *New York Times* (p. 35) had reported that an adverse committee vote on the bill had "coincided with a sharp advance in share prices," and again on July 20, they reported (p. 31) that stocks were advancing on the apparent failure of the bill. This failure was viewed as meaning that "the legislative power of the New Deal has been weakened" and that as a result Wall Street was "less apprehensive over the early passage of some other measures affecting industry." Over the next twelve months it would be the international gold market, rather than Washington policymakers, that would severely depress U.S. equity prices.

Summary

There are several alternative explanations for the 1936–1937 inflation. At the time, many commentators argued that an international armaments race was driving up prices. Others have pointed to the delayed effects of monetary and fiscal expansion in the United States. But, only the gold market approach can explain precisely why prices began rising rapidly after the Tripartite Agreement, why prices suddenly stopped rising with spring 1937 rumors of revaluation, and why they fell sharply during the fall of 1937.

This episode of American monetary history also provides support for those who argue that monetary policy should not be viewed in terms of the current setting of a particular monetary instrument, but rather that "monetary shocks" are events that change the entire expected future path of those instruments. The massive dishoarding of gold led to inflation fears, and the offsetting actions taken by the Fed were not perceived as *credible*. Thus the large increase in the U.S. (and foreign) wholesale price indices during 1936–1937 was triggered by expectations of *future* monetary expansion.

Of course, we now know that the markets were wrong. But there is no reason to presume that the forecasts were irrational, based on the information available to investors at the time. By late July, even Irving Fisher had come to the reluctant conclusion that the price of gold would have to be cut, and recall that Fisher had been an enthusiastic support of reflation during FDR's first term.[15] Investors knew that gold sterilization was costly and had good reason to believe that the massive gold inflows to the United States would eventually be monetized. What they did not foresee is that by the time those inflows were monetized in the late 1930s, commercial bank demand for excess reserves would have risen to an extraordinarily level and that this would absorb much of the dishoarded gold. In addition, both Soviet production and private dishoarding turned out to be smaller than what was projected during the height of the panic.

15. See Barber (1996, p. 103n).

10

The Midas Curse and the
Roosevelt Depression

THE 1937–1938 CONTRACTION was roughly comparable in depth and duration to the 1920–1921 contraction, which makes it one of the most severe downturns of the twentieth century. In the brief period from August 1937 to May 1938, industrial production plunged by 31.5 percent.[1] And wholesale prices lost all of their gains from the previous 14 months. By mid-1938, critics were referring to the "Roosevelt Depression."

Both fiscal and monetary policymakers have been blamed for the depression of 1937–1938, but neither hypothesis is entirely persuasive. Although a 2 percent increase in payroll taxes undoubtedly slowed the economy somewhat during early 1937, it hardly seems a plausible explanation for the sudden sharp plunge in stock and commodity prices, or industrial production, during late 1937. Nor is there much evidence that a modest tightening of fiscal policy can explain a slump of this magnitude.[2] In 2013 payroll taxes were raised by the same 2 percent, income taxes were also raised, and a budget "sequester" slashed spending. And yet economic growth *accelerated*.

---

1. From peak to trough, industrial production fell 32.4 percent in 12 months. By comparison, industrial production fell 32.5 percent over thirteen months during 1920–1921, and 30.5 percent over seventeen months during 1929–1930.

2. Consider several recent examples from the 1990s: A massive Keynesian stimulus failed to put much of a dent in the high unemployment rates in East Germany. Massive budget deficits failed to generate significant growth in Japan. And a tight fiscal policy was accompanied by rapid growth in the United States during the late 1990s. Romer (1992) reported that the budget deficit fell from 4.4 percent of GNP in 1936 to 2.2 percent in 1937. She also performed simulations that show fiscal policy having almost no impact on the path of GNP between 1933 and 1941.

In some respects, the monetary hypothesis seems to offer a more plausible explanation for the depression. Reserve requirement increases and gold sterilization would be expected to slow growth in the monetary aggregates, which could help explain the deflation that accompanied the sharp fall in output. But the timing seems all wrong; the tightening occurred during late 1936 and early 1937 when wholesale prices were still rising at double-digit rates. Monetary restraint should have had an immediate impact on the prices of goods traded in auction-style markets, yet the sharp drop in commodity (and equity) prices didn't occur until late 1937.

Figure 10.1 shows the monetary base and the level of U.S. monetary gold stocks during 1936–1938. Throughout most of the new Deal period monetary policy was very passive, with the monetary base rising in lockstep to gold flows into the United States. The one exception occurred during 1936–1938, when the gold sterilization program caused the base to level off nearly a year before the gold stock reached a plateau. Note that the slowdown in base growth was associated with rapidly rising commodity prices, whereas the gold stock de-

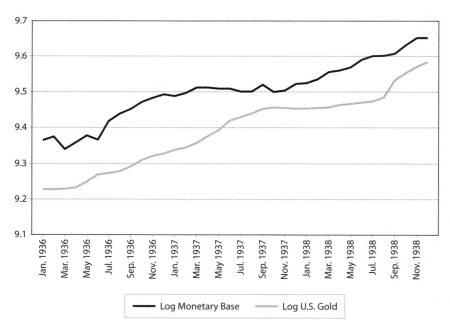

Figure 10.1. U.S. Monetary Gold and the Monetary Base

celeration occurs at about the time when stock and commodity prices crashed in late 1937.

In the next few sections, we will see that although the traditional monetary and fiscal mechanisms may have played some role in the downturn, a surge in private gold hoarding is the most plausible explanation for the sharp break in the economy that occurred during the fall of 1937.

From the Gold Panic to the Dollar Panic

During the period between March and August 1937, the U.S. economy was treading uneasily along a precipice. Industrial production had increased rapidly for nearly two years after the National Industrial Recovery Act (NIRA) was ruled unconstitutional, but by early 1937, wages were again rising rapidly and output leveled off during the spring and summer months. Although the sharp wage increases triggered by the Wagner Act and the 1936 elections had slowed the economy, there was no danger of a severe recession as long as prices remained at the lofty heights reached during the gold panic. In other words, during mid-1937 the reduction in aggregate supply caused by higher wages was roughly offset by the impetus to aggregate demand resulting from the massive dishoarding of gold, *and expectations of more dishoarding to come.*

Figure 10.2 and Table 10.1 both show that stocks continued to trade at relatively high prices as late as mid-August 1937, and thus we know that investors did not yet foresee a severe recession, even though all of the putative causes which others have advanced were already in plain view. So what happened in late 1937?

Between August 1937 and March 1938, the stock market lost roughly 40 percent of its value, ceding all of the gains from the long 1935–1937 bull market. It will be useful to segment this bear market into three parts. Between mid-August and mid-September, the Dow fell by 14 percent, while commodity prices were essentially unchanged. Then, between mid-September and late November, stocks, commodities, and industrial production all declined precipitously. During the winter of 1937–1938, each series continued to fall, but at a much slower pace.

On August 14, the Dow reached its summer peak on reports that Congress would adjourn without voting on the Black-Connery bill (to institute a

Figure 10.2. Stock Prices, Wholesale Prices, and Industrial Production

minimum wage in the United States), and news of renewed gold flows from Russia to the West. The financial press initially attributed the stock declines of late August to the outbreak of the Sino-Japanese War. Even so, the August 19 *New York Times* (p. 19) continued to argue that, "prospects are bright for business expansion." By September, it was clear that the London stock market was being less severely impacted than Wall Street, despite being far more heavily exposed to Asian investments. At this point, concern over fall business prospects began to be cited as a bearish factor.

We know that nominal wages rose rapidly during the first 10 months of 1937, and that this increase provides a plausible explanation for industrial production leveling off after March 1937, and then declining modestly in September. But these wage increases were already factored into the market by August, and can hardly explain the sharp collapse in the financial markets after mid-September. As late as August 21, the *New York Times* (p. 19) was still reporting that the "prospects are bright for business expansion." Some reports

Table 10.1. Selected Indicators, 1936–1938, Monthly

Month	Industrial Production	WPI	Nominal Wages	Real Wages	Dow
6/36	100	100	100	100	100
7/36	102	102	100	98	106
8/36	103	103	99	96	107
9/36	105	103	99	96	107
10/36	107	103	100	97	114
11/36	110	104	101	97	118
12/36	113	106	103	97	117
1/37	113	108	104	96	120
2/37	114	109	105	96	121
3/37	117	111	107	96	122
4/37	117	111	111	100	117
5/37	117	110	113	103	109
6/37	116	110	114	104	108
7/37	116	111	115	103	116
8/37	116	110	115	104	122
9/37	112	110	115	104	105
10/37	103	108	116	108	88
11/37	94	105	116	110	83
12/37	85	103	116	112	81
1/38	83	102	115	112	87
2/38	83	101	114	113	81
3/38	83	101	114	113	79
4/38	81	99	113	114	75
5/38	79	99	113	115	74

Note: The Dow is measured at mid-month. The real wage is deflated by the WPI.
All figures indexed to 100 in June 1936.

also suggested, however, that the optimism was predicated on business's ability to pass higher costs onto the consumer:

> Continued indecision of the stock market reflects above all else the mixed views with respect to the extent of the seasonal Autumn pick-up in industry and trade. In the main, the outlook is viewed with a fair show of optimism. But the point at issue has to do with the effects of *higher price levels made necessary by higher wages* and attendant higher costs of raw materials. (*NYT*, 9/1/37, p. 23, emphasis added)

Less than two weeks later the *New York Times* noted that the previous week's crash on Wall Street had also depressed prices in London, and that

> after a long interval, sentiment in the City has come, once again, under the influence of Wall Street trends. . . . [N]ow British investors are examining United States trade trends and prospects more closely and are conning figures on production and developments in the field of wages and working hours. From these studies it is becoming increasingly evident that rising operating costs are rearing difficulties for American industry and railroads, and former bullish British views [of the United States] are currently being modified. (9/13/37, p. 31)

Figure 10.3 shows the two real wage shocks of 1937 (note the real wage series is inverted to make it easier to see the correlation with output). The first wage shock occurred in the spring, as nominal wages rose rapidly following union organization drives. Just as during 1933 and 1934, higher wages brought a promising recovery to a standstill. But, this time the results would be far worse, as another dollar panic was about to produce the sort of severe deflation that the United States had not experienced since Hoover was president. This led to a second real wage shock in the fall, higher real wages caused by falling prices.

The Dollar Panic of 1937

Even without the 1937–1938 deflation, the ongoing wage shock would have slowed business considerably during late 1937. It was prices, however, that provided the big surprise of late 1937. Rather than continuing to rise, the price

Figure 10.3. Industrial Production and Inverted Real Wages

level in early September was about to begin a sharp plunge that would return wholesale prices to the level of early 1936. Add in the additional burden of higher nominal wages and the result was a near free fall in output during the fall of 1937. In order to explain the sharp contraction in real output that began in September, we need to first explain the concurrent decline in wholesale prices during late 1937 and early 1938.

The decline in commodity prices after mid-September seems to have been caused by a reversal of the factors that had previously pushed prices higher during late 1936 and early 1937. Whereas the previous inflation was aggravated by gold dishoarding following the Tripartite Agreement, the renewed period of deflation is at least partially attributable to gold hoarding triggered by currency instability in France and, more importantly, by devaluation fears in the United States. The world monetary gold stock had soared by 11.5 percent between mid-1936 and mid-1937, but monetary gold stocks actually declined slightly over the following twelve months, as the public again began hoarding gold in large quantities. This helped turn worries about "runaway inflation" associated with a "superabundance" of gold into renewed fears of deflation.

The steady rise in wages may have already been depressing output and stock prices during the late summer of 1937, even as commodity prices remained relatively stable. Yet although the cyclical peak[3] occurred in May 1937, the key inflection point didn't occur until mid-September. The *New York Times* (weekly) production index shows output declining gradually from mid-August to early September, and then falling precipitously from the week ending September 11 until the end of November. Then, output declined at a slower rate up through the spring of 1938. Thus, the period of sharply falling output coincides almost precisely with the period of plunging stock and commodity prices. (See Figure 10.2.)

September 1937 is also important because it was at this point that the stock and commodity markets in the United States and UK became synchronized. Recall that commodities are traded in a world market and thus deflation in the United States meant deflation in all countries with relatively stable currencies (such as the sterling bloc). The U.S. wage shock was a problem for the U.S. economy; the fall in U.S. commodity prices was problem for the world economy.

The correlation between declining stock and commodity prices and falling output doesn't necessarily favor any particular theory of the business cycle. If the gold market approach developed in the preceding nine chapters is to have any value here, we need to find some sort of gold market shock that could plausibly explain the declines in all three variables, and that is not itself a necessary consequence of economic recession—that is, it would help if we could identify a gold market shock that did not occur, for example, during the first year of either the 1920–1921 or 1929–1930 contractions.

As with the 1929 stock market crash, the financial press could find no obvious explanations for most of the sharp price breaks during late 1937. The September 11 *New York Times* (p. 21) reported that Wall Street was in a "bewildered state of mind" regarding the previous day's crash, and suggested the "possibility that the market was 'discounting' a recession in business of unexpected proportions." The same issue noted that the French franc was now under pressure. This observation is important to keep in mind, as a later issue of the

3. The NBER (National Bureau of Economic Research) peak in May 1937 is a bit closer to the point where wage increases slowed the economy. The Miron-Romer peak is in August 1937, and is closer to the point where gold hoarding began to sharply contract the economy.

New York Times reported that a renewal of gold hoarding had been triggered by this weakness in the French franc.

On September 13, the Treasury announced it would desterilize $300 million in gold. Normally, such a move would be expected to boost stock and commodity prices, but the next day's *New York Times* reported that, in this case, it had had a "reverse effect" on the stock and commodity markets. The drop in stock prices was modest, but the tremendous volume on the exchange, the highest since March, suggested a high level of uncertainty regarding the administration's intentions.

The September 14 *New York Times* noted that a late August cut in the discount rate (to a record low of 1 percent) had been justified as meeting the "expected Autumn credit demands" and that since then all signs had pointed to a diminished demand for credit. Thus, "in spite of official disclaimers . . . the financial community was convinced that there was a very direct link between the break in stocks and the new credit-expansion measure." They went on to suggest that the action was "criticized strongly in Wall Street yesterday as a gesture designed to restore bullish sentiment *which was unequal to the purpose*" and that as an attempt to restore "boom psychology" it represented a reversal of previous policies.[4] The following day's *New York Times* (p. 33) noted that strong Soviet gold sales had resulted in a resumption of significant U.S. gold imports for the first time in weeks, although no link was made with the 3.1 percent gain in the Dow.

The U.S. monetary authorities would not take any further expansionary moves until spring, by which time the contraction would be almost over. Interestingly, a few weeks later the *New York Times* suggested that the Fed's action had scared markets because the steps taken seemed "excessive and indicated, possibly, some hidden menace to business."[5]

The tight money/high wage policy adopted by the administration in late 1936 left President Roosevelt (FDR) unprepared to meet the oncoming dollar crisis. Business interests asked for tax relief, particularly with respect to the undistributed profits tax, but FDR's antagonism toward the "economic royalists" made him deaf to those pleas. The recent battles over the reorganization

4. *NYT*, 9/14/37, p. 33, emphasis added.
5. *NYT*, 10/3/37, p. F4.

bill and especially the court packing fight had increased the bitter feelings between FDR and conservatives. Occasionally the *New York Times* suggested that political factors were worrying Wall Street:

> Labor unsettlement continues, and the visit of the C.I.O. leader to the White House caused some misgiving. No signs as yet point clearly however to renewal, after last Summer's defeat, of the mass attack on great manufacturing plants. As Saturday's stock market indicated, the recurrent uneasiness over Washington policies was not abated by the President's speech on Constitution Day, when something very different [i.e., more conciliatory] had been expected. (9/20/37, p. 33)

When the government did act, it was in a perverse fashion. On September 23, the administration floated a proposal to tax "hot money," that is, foreign short-term investments in U.S. financial markets, and stocks dropped sharply in the final hour and then again on the following day. It is not clear what caused these declines, but the September 25 *New York Times* (p. 23) noted that after receiving this news from Washington "not only was there liquidation in the London market, but wires to the United States hummed with selling orders from British investors in Wall Street." A day earlier the *New York Times* (p. 31) had called the plan a "Check on Gold Flow."

By October 1, the *New York Times* was reporting a complete turnabout in the world gold market:

> The recent acute weakness of the franc with its accompanying unsettlement of confidence in other currencies has completely altered the popular sentiment toward gold. Fears for the price of that metal, which existed last Spring and which caused extensive dishoarding in Europe, have been driven out by the renewed fears for the future of currencies, and gold is once more in active demand in London for purposes of private hoarding. (p. 31)

Although this report of increased gold hoarding occurred roughly three weeks after commodity prices had began declining, it is evident that the *New York Times* was referring to a process that was already well under way by October 1. The following day the *New York Times* (p. 25) suggested that "apprehension over another French 'financial crisis' probably contributed to the mild sell-off in share prices in the morning" and led to even more gold hoarding in London.

There were also numerous reports that business had misjudged the situation. With regard to FDR's April 2 speech advocating that wages be brought into line with prices, the *New York Times* noted "it now appears, the full deductions to be drawn from the statement were lost from sight" and because of this miscalculation by industry "the problems of taxation and labor . . . will be aggravated by the business recession, instead of vanishing in another upward surge of production and sales."[6] In other words, there was insufficient nominal spending to support production at current wage and payroll tax levels.

The October 5 *New York Times* (p. 35) noted that a disappointing FDR speech proposing a special session, which was viewed as a threat to raise taxes and impose a minimum wage, had helped depress stock prices on the previous day. Roosevelt indicated that rather than try to restore the complete NIRA, he would only attempt to restore its minimum wage features. On the following day the Dow plunged another 5.3 percent. The October 6 *New York Times* (p. 35) attributed this decline to falling commodity prices and to disappointment over another speech in which FDR failed to meet "hopes that the President might issue a statement . . . reassuring to business." The next day, the *New York Times* noted (p. 41) that the speech also led to expectations of a major rearmament program, but that those expectations had failed to boost stock prices.

During October, there were more and more reports that gold hoarding was continuing to increase in London. It would be several more weeks before the *New York Times* would mention concerns over the possibility of dollar devaluation. The conservative press was reluctant to even print these rumors, but there were already some hints in early October.[7] The October 4 *New York Times* mentioned worries over a "desire to experiment" in U.S. monetary policy. An October 8 *New York Times* article (p. 35) entitled "The About-Face on Gold" discussed the formation of the "Committee for the Nation," which advocated raising the price of gold from "$35 an ounce to $41.34 in order to combat the 'steady fall of commodity and security prices.'"

---

6. *NYT*, 10/3/37, p. F1.

7. Eichengreen (1992, p. 377) reported that spreading rumors of currency devaluation was illegal in France during the 1930s.

During October 1937, stocks, commodities, and industrial production all plunged sharply. Unfortunately, on days of some of the sharpest price breaks there was little news other than reports of sharp declines in steel output. After a 7.8 percent drop on October 18, the stock market became front-page news. Two days later the *New York Times* (p. 1) reported that stocks fell almost 10 percent before rebounding to unchanged, amid "rumors and demands for official action" on the largest volume of trading since July 21, 1933 (following announcement of the Blue Eagle program). Then, on October 20 stocks, commodities, and bonds all rallied strongly on news of a Roosevelt speech discussing the need for the Federal Reserve (Fed) to coordinate policy.

Clearly, there was great uncertainty about monetary policy, but it wasn't until October 30 that the *New York Times* (p. 25) finally conceded that revaluation fears had been replaced by devaluation rumors, and that these rumors had been floating around Wall Street for weeks. It was also reported that the French franc was now rising on rumors that gold would soon flow back to France.

During late October the financial press became very hostile to what they perceived as administration incompetence. The October 24 *New York Times* (p. F1) indicated that on Wall Street the two prevailing views were that either monetary management had failed, or that it had been thwarted by anti-business policies in other areas. They cited (p. 5) an August 18 speech where FDR had accused his critics of being opposed to democracy. And there were also numerous stories suggesting that the administration didn't understand the severity of the business decline, with particular concern expressed (p. E2) over a possible special session of Congress that might implement a minimum wage rate, government reorganization, and/or crop control—hardly what business interests were looking for.

Although Roosevelt was in an anti-business frame of mind, the huge Democratic majorities in Congress faced mid-term elections in 1938, and the plunging markets began to bring forth demands for remedial policies to assist business. On October 29, the *New York Times* (p. 1) reported proposals for business tax revision and less strict labor regulation. Business taxes were at most a minor factor in the sharp stock collapse of late 1937, but this issue was viewed as being very important by the financial press. Stocks rebounded 8.7 percent during the last full week of October. The political mood was changing rapidly and the special session that Wall Street had previously feared was now viewed as a potential savior of business.[8]

From October 29 to November 8, there were almost continuous declines in stock and commodity prices as well as an increasing run on the dollar. The November 2 *New York Times* (p. 39) reported "Rumors of Gold Price Rise Depress Dollar," and not surprisingly there were expectations of a gold outflow. They also discussed a key problem raised by the hypothesis that dollar crises were deflationary:

> The movement of foreign funds away from New York continues to be hastened by the willingness of European money centers to entertain the rumors that "further devaluation of the dollar is inevitable." The current action of the stock market, however, scarcely lends any comfort to this topic. (*NYT*, 11/5/37, p. 33)

As we saw with the market reaction to the 1931 and 1932 dollar panics, the bearish influence provided by the gold outflow would often more than offset the bullish influence provided by expectations of devaluation, particularly if no imminent currency adjustment was expected. The *New York Times* also indicated that the problem of gold hoarding was not confined to private individuals:

> According to bankers here in touch with European markets, the scare abroad over a second devaluation of the dollar is not confined to irresponsible or ignorant elements but is shared by a good many important banks, particularly on the Continent, which have been buying gold to protect themselves. (*NYT*, 11/5/37, p. 33)

On November 6, the *New York Times* (p. 21) reported that the gold outflow did not mean confidence in European currencies, but rather fear of a U.S. devaluation, and then suggested that "European rumor-mongers" believed that the "gold price must be raised again if a serious deflation of prices is to be avoided." The next day the *New York Times* (p. F1) was full of stories that "NEW RUSH FOR GOLD HURTS THE DOLLAR . . . for First Time Since 1933 the Metal Is More Prized Abroad Than Our Currency . . . DEFLATION

---

8. See the *NYT*, 11/5/37, p. 33.

328 | *Back on the Gold Standard*

FEARED HERE" and they also (p. F8) observed that "curiously enough, the current dollar scare seems to be confined almost entirely to Europe. In contrast to the fears there that the dollar will be further 'inflated,' the markets here give rein to the deepest fears of deflation."

Of course, if the French franc had also been linked to gold, then deflationary fears would have existed there as well. Although the *New York Times* was now attributing the ongoing decline in U.S. stock prices to the gold outflow, they still failed to see how devaluation rumors could cause deflation of commodity prices: "There was little change in the general run of the news to account for the continued decline in wheat prices, which has been underway for eight straight days." (11/7/37, p. F8)

A front-page story in the November 8 *New York Times* ("FLOW OF GOLD NOW AWAY FROM U.S.A.; CREDIT BASE FIRM") can help us to understand why so many in the United States were confused by the crisis. They reported that Treasury officials "find comfort in the fact that the United States can lose up to about $1,270,000,000, the amount of its 'sterilized' gold, without experiencing the type of reaction *which sometimes has followed such flight of capital*" (emphasis added). But just as the sterilization in early 1937 had not prevented the ongoing inflation of commodity prices, so the sale of sterilized gold would not prevent a deflation of prices. In early 1937 there had been a fear that a much higher world gold stock would eventually force a more inflationary monetary policy; now market expectations of the future world monetary gold stock were falling dramatically, and so were expectations of future price levels.

At least the *New York Times* (11/8/37, p. 1) acknowledged the fact that a "serious slump . . . on some occasions in the past, has followed a sudden outward movement of foreign capital." They also reported that the gold outflow began in mid-October, but that private withdrawals began in mid-September, at first obscured by the fact that until early October the major central banks were continuing to augment their dollar reserves.

By November, many Europeans had become very pessimistic about U.S. economic prospects. The French saw FDR following the failed high wage policies of the Blum government.[9] As capital fled to London, the price of

---

9. See the *NYT*, 11/8/37, p. 27.

gilts soared by 1.5 to 3.5 points. The following day, it was reported (p. 33) that "DOLLAR DESERTION GAINS MOMENTUM" and that the French government had chosen to import gold rather than let the franc appreciate.

After the markets closed on November 8, Secretary Morgenthau announced the export of more than $10 million in gold to France and also indicated that the United States would "let gold go willingly."[10] On November 9, it was announced that gold would be released for shipment to Europe and the *New York Times* commented that

> Europe seems to have worked up enough excitement over the rumors of a further dollar devaluation to have raised some doubts about our attitude toward gold exports. The fact that the Treasury did not merely release the gold *but advertised the fact that it had done so* must have helped to discredit the rumors. (11/10/37, p. 39, emphasis added)

On November 9 and 10, the stock market, the commodity markets, and the dollar all rallied strongly, with positive tax news out of Washington also cited as a market influence. Despite the Treasury's moves to release gold, the dollar remained under pressure and the *New York Times* indicated that gold flows were actually much larger than central bank statistics would indicate due to the heavy flows in and out of inactive funds.[11]

The *New York Times* contrasted the recent passivity of the administration to the energetic activity that had characterized FDR's first hundred days in office. They attributed the drop in stock prices during the week of November 14–20 to a disappointing speech by Roosevelt on November 15, and indicated that in London the prevailing view was that

> The President's views are considered here as too indefinite for any hope that recovery can be built on governmental action. . . . Frankly, London is disappointed over what is considered a fine opportunity to gain credit for lifting the United States out of yet another depression being missed by the President. (11/22/37, p. 27)

---

10. *NYT*, 11/9/37, p. 33.

11. *NYT*, 11/21/37, p. F1. During the late 1930s, some central banks kept a portion of their gold reserves "off the books," in what were called "exchange stabilization accounts," which is why the press reports of massive gold hoarding may be more meaningful than official gold reserve statistics.

Stocks plunged to their yearly low on November 22, and the next day the *New York Times* reported that FDR had moved to limit Congress to consideration of his program, and that there was now little or no prospect of business tax relief during the 1937 session of Congress.

In late November, a modest rebound in the stock market was attributed to congressional moves to reform taxes, a more conciliatory administration attitude toward business, and signs that labor turmoil was waning. In December, stock and commodity prices leveled off, and although the monthly industrial production figure for December showed another sharp decline, weekly figures from the *New York Times* show industrial production leveling off after the first week of December. On December 20, the *New York Times* (p. 35) suggested that if the recession ended soon, which then appeared likely, FDR would stay the course; otherwise more extreme measures could be expected.

The "Capital Strike" of 1938

In late December 1937, the administration resumed its confrontational stance toward big business, and forecasts that the contraction might be over proved to be premature. Stocks fell 3.1 percent on December 27 and another 3.7 percent on the next day, and the *New York Times* observed that, "obviously, the stock market was disturbed yesterday by Assistant Attorney General Robert H. Jackson's radio address on Sunday night. The popular interpretation was that this speech by a government spokesman might be the prelude to an active antitrust campaign."[12] The drop on December 28 was also attributed to a hostile administration attitude toward business, and two days later the *New York Times* noted that because of recent instability in France, gold hoarding in London was increasing again.

The December 31 *New York Times* (p. 1), reported that Harold Ickes said the public needed to call the "bluff" of "big business" in its "sit-down strike." The "capital strike" rhetoric emanated from the more radical wing of the administration and represented a way of simultaneously deflecting attention from some of the more controversial tactics employed by labor and of blaming business

---

12. *NYT*, 12/28/37, p. 31.

for the new depression. Whatever the political objective, the administration's confrontational tone worsened business confidence. With the economy severely depressed and the administration adopting an anti-business policy stance, there was little investment and the natural rate of interest (in real terms) fell to very low levels. As prices were also falling rapidly, short-term nominal interest rates approached zero, where they would remain throughout the remainder of the 1930s. This sharply increased the demand for excess bank reserves and reduced the Fed's ability to boost the economy through conventional measures. And, FDR rejected the one "foolproof" method of escape from a liquidity trap, currency depreciation.

During the first half of January 1938, stocks rose on inflation rumors and conciliatory statements by the administration. By January 5, the *New York Times* (p. 29) was suggesting that rising commodity prices were "giving some encouragement to the security markets" and two days later they asserted (p. 27) that "the inflation topic as suggested by the outlook for continued government spending on a large scale, seemed to be the basis for the brisk rise in the stock market." The next day the *New York Times* reported that a bill calling for the federal government to reverse its deflationary monetary policy with a goal to restoring the 1926 price level had been introduced in Congress.

The markets were not helped by a January 25 speech where "ROOSEVELT FIGHTS PAY CUTS; HOLDS INDUSTRY MUST LEAD THE WAY TO REDUCE PRICES."[13] Stocks fell late on that day and opened much lower on the next day, closing down another 4.0 percent. The following day's *New York Times* (1/27/38, p. 29) suggested that "President Roosevelt's opposition to linking wage cuts to reductions in prices seemed, more than anything else, to prompt the dumping of stocks at the opening of the market." With wage cuts opposed by the administration, price increases would seem the only way of restoring profitability to U.S. businesses. Not surprisingly, another run on the dollar began in late January. The January 28 *New York Times* (p. 29) reported that "DOLLAR AND FRANC DROP . . . Revived Fears of Devaluation." On February 1, the *New York Times* (p. 25) recalled that in November, the first run on the dollar had been contained by the Treasury's readiness to export gold

---

13. *NYT*, 1/26/38, p. 1.

and that the most recent run on the dollar was triggered by FDR's statement on the need to boost "purchasing power." This was apparently a reference to a warning contained in FDR's January 25 speech:

> If industry reduced wages this Winter and Spring it would be deliberately encouraging the withholding of buying and fostering a downward spiral, he said; and if that happened, industry would have made it necessary for its government "*to consider other means of creating purchasing power.*" (1/26/38, p. 1, emphasis added.)

This was presumably a reference to the possibility of further dollar depreciation, a move that would have been strongly opposed by the financial elite.

During February, ominous developments in central Europe also began to impact the international gold market. On February 6, the *New York Times* (p. F1) reported that "frightened capital from Continental Europe, continues to pour into London." Surprisingly, the U.S. stock market was not significantly impacted by German threats against Austria on February 14. Then on February 18, stock and commodity markets broke on an FDR statement of opposition to both wage cuts and inflation: "the remark that the Administration's program does not mean inflation, touched off considerable selling of commodities as well as securities." The inflation comment was assumed to represent a denial of any devaluation plans and the dollar rebounded on the news. Ironically, all FDR had to offer was a revival of RFC (Reconstruction Finance Corporation) loans, an ineffectual policy adopted by Hoover back in 1932. As with Hoover, FDR's commitment to the gold standard prevented him from offering any effective policies for boosting the price level.

The German annexation of Austria on March 11, 1938, sparked several weeks of instability in the world's financial markets. Austrian bonds immediately lost nearly half of their value, an indication that despite the February threats the annexation was almost entirely unexpected. On March 13, the *New York Times* (p. 1) referred to "near panic" in the world's foreign exchange markets as capital fled from the smaller European countries. Heavy demand for gold in London pushed up the pound price of gold, but surprisingly, the dollar price of gold fell. There was talk that "hot money" would now flow back to the United States, as no European country was viewed as being entirely safe. On March 15, the hot money flows pushed U.S. stock and commodity prices sharply higher, and the United States resumed its imports of gold. But the very next day, a European war scare sent U.S. stock prices back down, while the dollar continued to strengthen.

The final ten days of March present a major puzzle, stocks fell sharply in the United States, but the March 28 *New York Times* (p. 21) noted that it was hard to blame the unsettled conditions on Europe since European markets were rebounding during this period. And commodity prices failed to accompany stocks on some of their sharpest declines. A *New York Times* reporter who was relatively sympathetic to the administration noted that stocks were continuing to fall despite the repeal of the undistributed profits tax, the "No. 1 demand of business."[14]

There is some evidence that the administration's attitude toward business was having negative impact on Wall Street. Certainly the rhetoric was white-hot during this period; in an aggressively anti-business speech on March 23 FDR asserted that, "SELFISH FEW BLOCK NATION . . . He Assails Feudalism as Like Fascism, and Hits Communism Also."[15] His reference to fascism and communism may have been a way of deflecting criticism that his administration was itself moving in that direction. While in hindsight these fears seem excessive, recall that he now had a massive majority in Congress and had just attempted to pack the Supreme Court. With the economy again sliding into depression, and with fascism appearing ascendant in Europe and Asia, there was some concern that the United States might be moving toward a dictatorship.

The March 31 *New York Times* (p. 27) argued that "short of unwanted inflationary measures, what the stock market needs more than anything else just now is a clear-cut statement from some high officer in the government, preferably from President Roosevelt, calculated to reassure the business and financial community" and then suggested that the main problem was "the strained relationship between government and business." But short of "unwanted inflationary measures" it is unclear just what Roosevelt could do. Nominal wages had begun to decline, which made it even less likely that he would back off on his demand for a minimum wage bill.

14. *NYT*, 3/27/38, p. F8.
15. *NYT*, 3/24/38, p. 1.

Friction between business and the administration had been building since the "capital strike" rhetoric began to be employed in late December. The *New York Times* sarcastically observed that administration rhetoric seemed to increasingly view the business as the enemy:

> To some minds it has suggested that the idea of severe reaction, deliberately caused by finance and industry as a lesson to the New Dealers, still has possession of some minds at the capital. This somewhat crude conception may have been based on the legendary Hindoos who committed suicide on the doorstep of a disliked individual, in order to show what they thought of him. But it hardly belongs to sober American thinking. (3/7/38, p. 25)

And the March 28 *New York Times* (p. 21) suggested that Roosevelt's speech on March 23 may have been "a veiled attempt to charge Big Business with having deliberately contrived the setback" and that "the spirit of hopefulness which might otherwise have been encouraged by disposition in Congress to 'help business' has been dampened by the Administration's continuing attitude of hostility."

During late March 1938, the Government Reorganization Bill (which would have strengthened the Administration) became the focal point of business fears of the Administration. The bill's progress in Congress was cited as a factor in the steep break in stocks prices on March 29:

> If a single item were to be singled out from the day's news grist, it would necessarily have to be the Government Reorganization Bill. Surely the bill in itself . . . could not be responsible for the outpouring of securities yesterday. But the point is that many traders had been led to believe that business would receive some long awaited consideration from executive and legislative circles. After long delay it became apparent that the tax burden was to be eased to a certain extent, but this knowledge seems to have come too late to benefit the markets. In other words, many traders contend that improvement in political, if not yet in business, trends may be too slow to repair the damage that has been done. (*NYT*, 3/30/38, p. 29)

One way to evaluate the importance of this particular piece of legislation is to evaluate the market reaction as it progressed through Congress.

On March 31, stocks fell to their lowest point of the 1937–1938 depression, and commodities prices fell as well. The next day the *New York Times* (p. 1) reported that "REORGANIZATION WINS TEST IN TURBULENT HOUSE SESSION; PASSAGE TOMORROW SOUGHT." But the bill ran into trouble, and stock prices rallied strongly on the news:

> No doubt some of the improvement in sentiment in the stock market was due to the refusal of the House of Representatives to rush through the Government Reorganization Bill, which, from a slow start, has now developed into a highly controversial issue. As Wall Street views it, the furor over the bill has more to do with the mere idea of increasing Presidential power than with the actual provisions of the bill itself. (*NYT,* 4/3/38, p. F1)

This quotation demonstrates an extraordinary lack of confidence in the ability of an American president to effectively govern during an economic crisis. Even though the financial press was very conservative, the current attitude of financial *markets* was quite different from that exhibited during the administration's first hundred days, when a radical policy of dollar devaluation was boosting stock and commodity prices.[16] After the markets closed on April 8, the House narrowly rejected the Reorganization Bill (by a vote of 204–196) in a surprise vote that was widely viewed as being a repudiation of the president. On April 10 a *New York Times* headline (wrongly) predicted that "DEFEAT OF REORGANIZATION MAKES WAGE-HOUR PASSAGE UNLIKELY" and noted that "STOCKS RISE 2 TO 6 ON DEFEAT OF BILL." The Dow soared by 5.2 percent on April 9.

FDR Reverses Course

The lack of any signs of economic recovery, combined with the severe break in stock prices during March, led the administration to finally propose

---

16. Also recall just how adversely the markets responded to many actions taken by the conservative Hoover administration.

a series of expansionary policies during April. The Dow rose by 3.9 percent on April 8, and the next day's *New York Times* (p. 21) noted "there is little question that the markets were governed yesterday by a single topic, and the title was 'inflation.'" They also reported that, "FEDERAL BONDS HIT BY INFLATION TALK."

During the following week, stocks continued to rise on rumors of additional inflationary steps and on April 14 FDR announced a policy of gold desterilization as well as a reversal of the reserve requirement increase from the previous May. The next day the *New York Times* noted (p. 1) that the "sweeping character" of the proposals took the financial community by surprise, that "the President was "firing the heaviest guns remaining in the monetary arsenal," but that they "doubt the efficacy" of the proposals. Commodity prices soared, the dollar fell, and stocks and Treasury bonds (T-bonds) also increased modestly. After being closed on April 15, the stock and T-bond markets soared on April 16 while the dollar fell sharply.[17]

These steps initiated the third phase of the administration's macroeconomic policy. An expansionary policy was in place for most of FDR's first term, gradual moves toward a contractionary policy began in mid-1936, and now the administration had switched back to an expansionary policy:

> By its action in "desterilizing" about $1,400,000,000 of gold and reducing member bank reserve requirements about $750,000,000, the government has made a sweeping retreat from its "anti-inflationary" credit policy begun two years ago. Monetary management, after having been directed for some time toward guarding against a possible inflationary boom, has turned, under the pressure of the business depression, toward the other extreme—an attempt to stimulate credit expansion. The current effort represents the biggest credit-expansion gesture ever made. (*NYT*, 4/17/38, p. F1)

Whether or not one views these steps as the U.S. government's largest attempt at credit expansion, it is clear that their impact was modest. There was no sustained follow-up to the brief spurt in commodity prices that followed

---

17. T-bill yields fell from 0.146 to 0.061 during week while the Dow rose by 4.9 percent.

the announcement, and by mid-1940 the wholesale price index (WPI) was even lower than in April 1938.

We have already seen examples from the early 1930s where attempts at monetary expansion triggered gold outflows, and that this prevented the policies from boosting aggregate demand. On April 19, the *New York Times* (p. 31) acknowledged the possibility that FDR's recent expansionary steps could lead to a similar outcome but then argued that recent political instability in Europe had reduced the possibility of any large gold flows in that direction. The enormous size of the U.S. gold stocks made it unlikely that even a highly expansionary policy would force the United States off the gold standard. Any devaluation would be made pursuant to FDR's broader macroeconomic goals, but the recent expansionary steps made such an action that much less likely. Devaluation rumors did recur occasionally throughout the spring of 1938, but no more frequently than during the previous six months, and, although private gold hoards continued to increase for several more months, there were no dramatic changes in gold flows.

It is certainly possible that the expansionary steps taken in April contributed to the economic recovery that began in late June. However, stocks remained weak until a vigorous upswing began on June 20, suggesting that investors had little faith in the efficacy of these policies. Instead, the occasional stock market rallies during the spring of 1938 coincided with devaluation rumors, or signs that the Wage-Hour bill was having difficulty in Congress. In the end, passage of the bill had little impact on Wall Street, perhaps owing to the fact that at the last minute the bill was watered down to appease Southern employers.

In late May 1938, the deteriorating Czechoslovakian situation was blamed for declines in stock and commodity prices, as well as for an increase in gold hoarding in London. The falling commodity prices led to a new round of devaluation rumors in early June, and modest stock price increases in early June were linked to rumors that the dollar would be devalued immediately after Congress adjourned on June 16.[18] A drop in stock prices on June 13 was

18. *NYT*, 6/4/38, p. 19, and 6/5/38, p. F1. The dollar held up well, perhaps due to rumors that other currencies would also be devalued at the same time. (*NYT*, 6/15/38, p. 33)

338 | *Back on the Gold Standard*

attributed to a denial of the rumor by Morgenthau, but administration denials were not regarded as sufficiently categorical, and uncertainty continued. For a brief period in mid-June, gold hoarding in London reached levels of three to four times the norm. Much of this hoarding was by "wealthy individuals in the United States [who] sought to take out devaluation insurance by buying gold in London and storing it there."[19]

During the week of June 19, several pieces of news led to a dramatic turnabout in the financial markets. First, on Sunday, June 19, Wall Street began to receive reports that suggested business was beginning to recover from the recession. In addition, the dollar crisis came to a definitive conclusion. There had been no devaluation after Congress had adjourned, and on June 20 Morgenthau issued a much more forceful denial of rumors that the dollar might be devalued.[20] The *New York Times* noted that the rumors had been "spiked with emphasis" and added that

> Investors and traders in the security and commodity markets looked hopefully yesterday toward the probable effect of the government's spending-and-lending program on the ailing business situation and prices were strong all around. More official denials that dollar devaluation is a near-term prospect failed to lessen enthusiasm in the markets. On the contrary, the denials *aided* market sentiment. (6/21/38, p. 29, emphasis added)

The final sentence of the *New York Times* quotation is particularly interesting. The implicit assumption is clearly that devaluation rumors would normally boost the stock market, but that this time the market was aided by the suppression of those rumors. What the stock market most wanted was clarity. A devaluation of the dollar would boost prices, but decisive steps to restore confidence in the dollar would lessen gold hoarding, and this would also tend to raise prices. The worst of all possible worlds was an open-ended period of uncertainty with neither currency devaluation nor a credible policy of adherence to the gold standard.

---

19. *NYT*, 7/10/38, p. F1.

20. Public works were also mentioned, but this information was already in the market by June 16.

There is a striking similarity between the 1938 summer rally in stocks and commodities and the comparable bull markets during the late summer of 1932. Both were triggered by the realization that the dollar was once again firmly tied to gold. The *New York Times* reported that "Dollar Continues Recovery on Assurances by Morgenthau Against Devaluation Move" and that stocks and commodities continued to show gains. They also noted that

> Foreign participation here coincided with the diminution of the hoarding demand for gold in London . . . . In other words, with the dollar devaluation topic laid on the shelf temporarily, at least, floating funds are drifting into equity investments. (6/22/38, p. 35)

And on the very next day the *New York Times* (p. 1) reported that a "CUT IN STEEL WAGE BROACHED TO LEWIS AS RECOVERY SPUR." With Congress adjourned, big business felt it was an opportune time to walk away from the "Ford Doctrine" of maintaining high wages during depressions. This plethora of "good news" contributed to an extraordinary weekly gain of 16.5 percent in the Dow. A recovery was finally underway.

There is some evidence that not only did renewed confidence in the dollar aid recovery, but that economic recovery also helped restore confidence in the dollar. It is interesting to contrast the June 21 report on the impact of Morganthau's remarks with the following quotation from several weeks later:

> One consequence of the rising market was the drying up of rumors of dollar devaluation, which had been persistent a week or two ago. In the face of a more optimistic appraisal of the economic outlook, due to the stock market, the idea that further tinkering with the currency would be needed to start a revival ceased to have much appeal. The demand for gold in London for hoarding dropped off. (*NYT,* 7/4/38, p. 21)

The U.S. monetary gold stock grew rapidly from mid-1938 through 1940, but then slowed sharply over the following twelve months. Because growth in the U.S. monetary base closely paralleled movements in the monetary gold stocks, one might have expected high inflation during the late 1930s, followed by a slowdown in 1941. Surprisingly, just the opposite occurred. Wholesale prices trended slightly downward between June 1938 and August 1940, except for a brief spike at the outbreak of World War II. Then prices rose by over 21 percent between August 1940 and December 1941.

For the period after mid-1938, price level movements in the United States are more easily explained with traditional macro models than by the gold market approach. Keynesians often point to the near-zero nominal interest rates of the late 1930s and argue that increases in the monetary base amounted to little more than "pushing on a string." Monetarists emphasize how the high levels of excess reserves reduced the money multiplier, and suggest that the Fed should have targeted the broader monetary aggregates.

The extraordinarily high demand for excess reserves tended to indirectly increase the demand for monetary gold, thus preventing the rapidly growing gold stocks from having the inflationary impact one might have normally expected. Prices only began to rise after the European war intensified in mid-1940, and the United States embarked on a massive rearmaments drive. This would have been expected to increase the equilibrium real interest rate, inflationary expectations, or both. Yet nominal rates remained quite low, and so the sudden increase in the money multiplier after mid-1940 remains unexplained.[21] In any case, the money multiplier began to rise in late 1940 and the growth in the broader aggregates accelerated despite a slowdown in the growth of the gold stock, and the monetary base. This is one period where both monetarist and gold market models performed poorly.

The Wage Shocks of 1938 and 1939

Although the gold market approach does not offer any special insights into the last two years of the Depression, the labor market analysis developed earlier can help explain the uneven path of recovery. Between May and November 1938, industrial production increased by 23 percent. Over the following six months, however, production rose by only 1.5 percent. Then output again soared by 22.4 percent between May and November 1939. And once again, the recovery faltered, with production falling by 2 percent over

---

21. Friedman and Schwartz make this point and suggest that perhaps the lower level of excess reserves was a delayed reaction to the increased soundness of the banking system.

the next six months. In wasn't until 1941 that the economy finally recovered from the Great Depression, with industrial production expanding by nearly 40 percent between May 1940 and December 1941. As we will see, both of the growth pauses can be explained by federal labor market legislation.

During the first nine months of 1938, nominal wages fell by 3.8 percent, presumably a lagged response to falling prices and high unemployment. Then in the last three months of 1938, they rose by 2.6 percent (an annual rate of over 10 percent) in a still severely depressed economy. Is there any explanation for the sudden turnaround in wages? The most likely culprit was the Wage-Hours bill enacted during June, which put a minimum wage rate of 25 cents/hour into effect on October 24, 1938.

Wages started falling again in July and August 1939, and the outbreak of war in Europe led to a sharp increase in the WPI during September and October, which further softened the impact of the minimum wage law. Industrial production rose rapidly during the July to October period. Then, on October 24, 1939, the minimum wage was raised to 30 cents/hour, and wages rose by 3.9 percent during the last three months of the year. Industrial production peaked in November and immediately began falling.

The final recovery from the Depression was associated with rapidly rising prices; the WPI rose by 21 percent between August 1940 and December 1941. Although nominal wages also rose by 19 percent, real wages actually declined during this period. Industrial production soared by over 33 percent during this sixteen-month period, reaching a level 49 percent above the 1929 peak. Thus, the Depression was over even before the United States entered the war. If there is any truth to the widely held assumption that "World War II got us out of the Depression," it was not the outbreak of the war in 1939 (the economy seemed to be going nowhere in mid-1940), nor was it the actual U.S. involvement in the war, which began in December 1941. Rather, in an economic sense, World War II began in mid-1940 when the swift German advance on Western Europe ended the so-called phony war and led to a massive armaments drive in the United States and elsewhere. Whether due to its direct (Keynesian) effects, or its indirect effect via a reduced demand for excess reserves (and thus, monetary gold), this event triggered a sudden and dramatic upsurge in both prices and production in the United States.

The War Scares and the Stock Market

After July 1938, the dollar devaluation story was essentially over and rumors of war would dominate the stock market over the next several years. Friedman and Schwartz (1963a) and Romer (1992) offer monetary explanations of how World War II might have ended the Depression, arguing that war (or fear of impending war) in Europe led to massive gold flows across the Atlantic, which in turn boosted the U.S. money supply and helped promote an economic recovery. Romer (1992) did some policy simulations that suggested, in the absence of these gold inflows (and dollar devaluation) the U.S. economy would not have recovered in the 1930s or early 1940s. She differs from Friedman and Schwartz in arguing that the U.S. economy lacked a self-correcting mechanism during the 1930s.

As we will see in Chapter 13, gold flows by themselves don't impact the world price level unless they also lead to a reduction in the world gold ratio. Although the gold statistics from the late 1930s are somewhat imprecise, it does seem likely that the gold flows to the United States tended to reduce the world's gold reserve ratio, and thus, may indeed have had the expansionary impact. Unfortunately, it is difficult to find confirmation for this war scare → gold flow → economic recovery hypothesis in the response of financial markets to political news.

With the exception of an upward blip during September 1939, the United States experienced mild deflation throughout most of the late 1930s and into the first half of 1940. In addition, stocks seemed to generally react adversely to "war scares." This suggests that any positive impact of war scares on the U.S. economy coming from gold flows was more than offset by the negative impact flowing from private hoarding of gold and/or dollars, or from fears for the stability of international trade and finance.

Beginning in August 1938, the Czech crisis led to a flow of central European capital into gold and dollars:

> The stock market last week suffered its first severe reaction of the Summer . . . and, while war clouds contributed somewhat to the unsteadiness of prices, the decline must be set down as purely a technical correction. . . . With the decline in share prices viewed as purely technical, the most disturbing movement of the week and one which

may prove to have been most important was the accelerated flight of capital out of the European moneys and into gold and the United States dollar. (*NYT*, 8/15/38, p. 23)

By August 18, the *New York Times* (p. 29) was reporting that "DEMAND FOR GOLD ABATES" due to a "Calmer View of International Politics" and three days later (p. F1) they attributed the recent rise in stock and commodity prices to a "lessening of political tension in Europe."

By the end of August, renewed political uncertainties were again driving stock and commodity prices lower.[22] And whereas "hot money" had recently been flowing to Britain, now it was leaving.[23] A few weeks later, stock prices plunged sharply just after a wire story of an ultimatum on the Sudeten situation. The reaction of commodity prices was more complex:

European developments yesterday caused wide fluctuations in most commodities. Those staples that are considered absolutely essential to the waging of a war generally advanced sharply [grains, copper], but those not vitally required for such an undertaking were lower. . . . Some traders said the action of the commodity markets was not dissimilar to that immediately preceding the breaking out of hostilities in Europe in 1914. (*NYT*, 9/14/38, p. 33)

This pattern certainly doesn't provide much support for the view that European war scares helped to boost the overall level of aggregate demand in the United States. And by September there were warnings that the European crisis could retard the recovery in the United States:

Under the influence of the warlike alarums from Europe it bounded widely about and fell to levels lower than it had touched since June 25. . . . The problem was: Is the decline a mere temporary response to the war scare, or does it mean that the continued strain of the European crisis has put a damper on our own recovery. (*NYT*, 9/18/38, p. F1)

The huge increase in the world's monetary gold stock suggests that private dishoarding was occurring, but the reality was more complex. All of Europe

22. *NYT*, 8/30/38, p. 25.
23. *NYT*, 9/4/38, p. F1.

was now viewed as being unsafe, and gold hoarding was still illegal in the United States. Under these conditions, many investors viewed the U.S. dollar as the most desirable substitute for gold:

> The United States is having a spell of its old complaint—the touch of Midas. Once again we have become a powerful magnet for gold and the yellow metal is pouring in here in record-breaking fashion. As Secretary of the Treasury Morgenthau explained it last week: "All over the world they want to buy dollars, and the only way they can get their dollars here is by shipping gold." (*NYT*, 9/18/38, p. F1)

Over the next several days the market reacted positively to reports that Britain and France would adopt a policy of appeasement:

> From a strictly market viewpoint the news of the decision of the Czech Government to capitulate to the demands that it cede the Sudeten area to Germany was favorable. Prices, quite naturally, improved as the threat of war seemed to recede. But this was "good news" with a difference; hardly the sort of good news to capture the imagination of individual traders and evoke a spirit of bullishness. Even in Wall Street, where the mental processes are supposed to be exceedingly realistic, there was a sufficiently powerful sense of the tragedy involved in Czechoslovakia's surrender and the unhappy role that Britain and France played in bringing it about to dampen the normal speculative impulses. (*NYT*, 9/22/38, p. 33)

Even beyond the few quotations provided above, one can find abundant evidence that the stock market reacted negatively to the frequent war scares of the late 1930s. But when we look at the reaction of Wall Street to the war itself, things get a bit more confusing. The Dow rose more than 10 percent during the first five days of September 1939 in reaction to the German invasion of Poland. The outbreak of hostilities was also associated with a sharp rise in commodity prices. But stocks then remained flat for about seven months before falling 21.7 percent during May 1940, when the Germans swept through France and the Low Countries with unexpected speed. And the Dow performance was lackluster, particularly in real terms, during the (high growth) period of U.S. involvement in the war.

Note that none of these events were obvious to investors in the late 1930s. One could easily imagine a number of scenarios, including a European war with or without U.S. involvement. And war could impact corporate profits in any number of ways. While high prices and production would certainly boost profits, disruption in trade and investment, as well as price and profit controls could reduce profits. Thus the reaction of the stock market to the war scares, while suggestive, is not capable of either proving or disproving Romer's hypothesis.

Certainly the gold flows to the United States, *ceteris paribus*, should have boosted the monetary base and aggregate demand. This effect may have been partially offset by increased private gold hoarding, and/or hoarding of dollars. And, even if the gold inflows did have a net positive effect, there isn't much evidence to suggest that war scares played a significant role in the U.S. recovery. Despite the huge gold inflows, U.S. wholesale prices actually declined by 12 percent between April 1937 and August 1940. One might argue that without the added gold reserves prices would have declined even more rapidly, but that sort of counterfactual requires an implausible level of passivity on the part of the Roosevelt administration. There were already significant rumors of devaluation in late 1937 and early 1938, and FDR almost certainly would have further reduced the gold content of the dollar rather than allowing even sharper rates of deflation to occur.

Despite the preceding reservations regarding Romer's policy counterfactuals, I agree with her overall view that fiscal policy was relatively unimportant and rising U.S. gold stocks contributed to the recovery. Less persuasive is Romer's assumption that the recoveries of 1933–1937 and 1938–1941 were very rapid, and that absent monetary expansion the interwar U.S. economy lacked a strong self-correcting mechanism. It is misleading to draw any conclusions about the economy's self-correcting capabilities from the very erratic growth rates of industrial production, which partially reflected the impact of wage shocks. And, although monetary policy was expansionary throughout 1933–1937 and 1938–1941, part of this merely offset the deflationary tendencies produced by increases in money demand at very low nominal rates.

Here it might be useful to partition the recovery into three components. If we exclude the period of July 1933 through May 1935, when the NIRA high wage policy prevented any growth in industrial production, then the economy's growth performance looks much more robust. But excluding only the NIRA period would probably overstate the economy's self-correcting capabilities, as it includes the periods of March 1933 through July 1933 and September 1940 through December 1941, when expansionary monetary policy pushed prices up sharply and industrial production grew at explosive rates. The best evidence of the economy's ability to self-correct comes from periods of fairly stable prices[24] such as May 1935 to October 1936, when industrial production rose 31.5 percent in seventeen months, and May 1938 to September 1940, when industrial production rose 60.9 percent in twenty-eight months. And, even this may *understate* the economy's natural self-correcting forces, as the latter period includes the two growth pauses associated with minimum wage increases.

Concluding Remarks

Although a number of explanations have been offered for the 1937–1938 depression, none are particularly satisfactory. Keynesians pointed to the tightening of fiscal policy between 1936 and 1937, which reduced the budget deficit from 4.4 percent to 2.2 percent of GNP. One has to ask, however, why a modest reduction in the budget deficit after a period of strong economic growth would lead to one of the worst depressions of the twentieth century.[25] And, why were the financial markets in 1937 so unconcerned with budget issues, with stock prices still near their cyclical highs as late as mid-August, when the fiscal tightening was nearly over?

The monetarist explanation for the 1937–1938 depression is that the reserve requirement increases of 1936 and early 1937 reduced the money multiplier, and thus the monetary aggregates. But this hypothesis also seems incompatible with the behavior of the financial markets. These increases had little or no impact on the stock market, which only began to decline sharply in late

---

24. The WPI rose by less than 2 percent in the former period and fell slightly in the latter period.

25. A large part of the decrease in the deficit reflected the fact that the large (one-time) bonus paid to veterans in the spring of 1936 was not repeated in 1937 or 1938. In addition, a 2 percent payroll tax was introduced in 1937. Neither factor seems a remotely promising explanation for one of the biggest depressions of the twentieth century.

August 1937. Nor did the stock market respond enthusiastically to the steps taken to reverse this tightening in August 1937, September 1937, and April 1938.

Friedman and Schwartz noted that rumors of devaluation led to an outflow of gold from the United States between October 1937 and February 1938, but don't attach much importance to this issue. They also avoided the issue of private gold hoarding, and its impact on the world monetary gold stock. Oddly, they did not view the United States as being on the gold standard during 1937–1938. But their argument that the post-1934 gold standard was analogous to an agricultural price support program misses one important characteristic; during 1934 through 1940 the monetary base was closely linked to the U.S. gold stock, not to agricultural stocks.[26]

The problem with the administration's tight money policy was that it lacked credibility so long as they remained committed to buy gold at \$35/ounce. Investors saw the massive dishoarding of gold triggered by the collapse of the gold standard in Europe as a tsunami that would overwhelm the government's attempt to restrain inflation. Wholesale prices only began falling in mid-September, 1937, when it became clear that forecasts of future gold stocks had been way too high.

We also need to recall that without the tight money policies of late 1936 and early 1937, the WPI would have reached even higher levels by August 1937. Perhaps we should be thankful that the price level didn't rise even higher during 1936–1937, after all, by late 1938 one of the reserve requirement increases and all of the gold sterilization had been reversed, and yet prices had still fallen back to roughly their pre-bubble levels. If the 1937 peak in the WPI had been even higher, then during the subsequent dollar panic the fall in wholesale prices might have been even greater. The Fed tightened *before* and *during* the post-Tripartite commodity price boom, and loosened before and during the 1937–1938 commodity price deflation. As a policy of "fine-tuning," the Fed's steps were probably no worse than acyclical and may well have been countercyclical, at least with respect to the market-sensitive commodity prices that respond immediately to policy. Given FDR's commitment to the \$35/ounce gold peg,

---

26. See Friedman and Schwartz (p. 472). And they do present evidence (pp. 281, 337, and 507) that gold stocks had at least as important an impact on monetary policy after 1934, as before 1933.

the 1936–1937 worry over an "inflationary bubble" is less foolish than it seems from a modern (fiat money) perspective. There were serious consequences to allowing an unsustainable decline in the value of gold.

It is interesting to reread Friedman and Schwartz's account of the reserve requirement increases in light of the now almost universal view that they were a blunder. They do admit (p. 526) that, "the desire to take restrictive action in early 1937 is understandable" but then add that "it is difficult to have much sympathy with the [Fed's] argument." By focusing their criticism on the Fed's reasoning process, they implicitly acknowledge that (with the WPI up almost 50 percent from the 1933 lows) there was some reason to be concerned about accelerating inflation. A policy aimed at price stability was certainly defensible under those circumstances. Friedman and Schwartz criticize Harrison severely for blaming the recession on nonmonetary factors, and contrast his poor performance in 1937 with his enlightened support for expansion during the early 1930s. Their criticism seems devastating:

> His situation was in many respects precisely that of his opponents in 1930. His experience is a striking illustration of how difficult it is for anyone—whether in practical affairs, politics, industry, science, the arts—however able and disinterested, as Harrison was in unusual measure, to reverse a strongly held intellectual position. (p. 529)

But is this fair? Even in the trough of the 1938 depression, prices were at the same levels as mid-1936, but wages were much higher. In contrast, by late 1930 prices had fallen sharply and there had been no increase in wages. The severe recession of 1937–1938 was due to a dramatic turnaround in the world gold market and the wage shock, neither of which were the Fed's fault.

Despite very real weaknesses in the monetarist interpretation of the 1937–1938 depression, it would be unwise to totally reject the possibility that reserve requirement increases and gold sterilization contributed to the downturn. Indeed, once the 1937–1938 contraction got underway there were numerous news reports suggesting that investors had misjudged the impact of the earlier moves by the Fed to tighten policy. Recall that even a policy that lacks credibility can still have a delayed impact, particularly if the policy environment changes unexpectedly. Once traders saw the economy slowing, they sharply raised their forecasts of the demand for gold and excess reserves and sharply lowered their forecasts of the future price level. The government's tight money initiatives only began to influence markets when investors no longer feared that a massive inflow of gold would force the Fed to reverse course and expand the money supply. This points to another important lesson: that it is easy to confuse a lag in the impact of monetary policy with delays caused by something very different, a delay in the public's *willingness to accept that the policy change will persist.*[27]

The Fed's role in the 1937–1938 depression should not be evaluated in isolation but rather needs to be examined in the context of the broader policy environment. The immediate impact of monetary policy (especially on sensitive market indicators) reflects the current expectation of how policy will impact the future expected path of the money supply. Investors initially had little reason to believe that the monetary tightening would significantly affect either the long-run value of gold or the long-run path of the money supply, and thus in late 1936 and early 1937 the government's policies seemed to have had little impact on market expectations or the broader macroeconomy. But as the economy slowed under the weight on higher wages, and as devaluation fears stopped growth in the monetary gold stocks, and as falling interest rates led to increased demand for excess reserves, these seemingly innocuous steps toward policy restraint began to sharply reduce aggregate demand.

In the preceding account, I have shown that devaluation fears led to gold hoarding in late 1937, which reduced expectations of future monetary growth and led to a collapse of equity prices, commodity prices, and industrial production. It is likely, however, that the inflection point for the economy slightly preceded the run on the dollar. While there was already some gold hoarding during the summer in response to instability in France, this did not significantly depress commodity prices. More likely, it was the steadily rising wages that finally tipped the economy into a mild recession in late August 1937. Approximately one month later, the economy's weakness became apparent and gold hoarding began to increase in response to devaluation fears. It was

---

27. A similar phenomenon may explain why the post–World War II economy seemed to react with such a long lag to expansionary moves by the Fed. Commodity traders would be reluctant to bid up prices until it was clear that the Fed was really serious about changing the trend rate of inflation, *something unheard of prior to World War II.* Once convinced, velocity would rise and prices would sharply accelerate to catch up to the previous monetary expansion.

this gold hoarding that caused the WPI to fall sharply, turning a mild recession into a major downturn.

Does this more nuanced interpretation make the gold hoarding merely an endogenous factor, with no causal role in the ensuing depression? I think not, for at least five different reasons:

1. Gold hoarding is not generally a characteristic of U.S. business cycles; it did not occur during the very similar 1920–1921 and 1929–1930 contractions. It does not occur when the dollar peg is unquestioned, nor under a fiat money regime.

2. When devaluation fears did lead to gold hoarding in 1931 and 1932, there were similar periods of falling stock and commodity prices and contracting output.

3. Price theory predicts that gold hoarding should increase the real value of gold, and, when gold serves as the medium of account, should also reduce the broader price level.

4. The gold hoarding hypothesis is also consistent with some aspects of monetarism. The U.S. monetary base closely tracked U.S. gold stocks between 1934 and 1941. The gold hoarding of 1937–1938 brought rapid growth in both the United States and world monetary gold stocks to a halt and reduced expectations of future monetary growth.

5. Financial markets treated the run on the dollar as an exogenous shock. Neither the Fed's tightening in 1936 and early 1937, nor its easing in late 1937 and April 1938, had any discernible impact on stock and commodity markets. In contrast, the stock and commodity markets plunged sharply during the dollar panic (which was often cited in the press as a bearish influence), and only began to rally after the dollar panic came to a decisive end in late June 1938. The stock market rally that occurred during the week of June 19 was one of the largest in history.

If gold hoarding was the primary factor behind the drop in aggregate demand during late 1937, and if that spending decline is largely responsible for the sharp drop in U.S. prices and output, then why was the recession of 1937–1938 much more severe in the United States than in the rest of the world? Eichengreen (1992, p. 387) argues that because the international gold standard collapsed in 1936, there was no longer a mechanism by which contractionary policies in America could be transmitted to the rest of the world (as had occurred in the early 1930s). This explanation overlooks the international dimensions of the increase in the real value of gold. Although the international gold standard had collapsed by 1937, most major economies still had currencies pegged to gold, and thus, should have also experienced a decline in aggregate demand. A more plausible explanation would focus on specific American factors such as the wage shock of 1937. The deflation of 1938 merely brought wholesale prices in gold terms back to their 1936 levels. But in America, nominal wages remained far above 1936 levels. Both gold hoarding and the 1937 wage shock, considered in isolation, were capable of producing a mild recession in the America; together they produced a severe recession.

As was the case in 1933, the events of 1937 are hard to disentangle because of the overlay of monetary instability and autonomous wage shocks. But if we view 1937 as part of a larger set of New Deal policies, then some interesting patterns keep reoccurring. Consider the five examples of autonomous wage shocks that we have examined. All were policy-driven, and all diverted nominal (and real) wages from the path that otherwise might have been expected. And four of the five had remarkably similar effects of the path of output (see Table 10.2).

The 1936–1937 wage shock that accompanied the post-Wagner Act unionization drives is hard to date because it occurred over a relatively long period of time. During the early stages of that wage shock output continued to rise, as gold dishoarding pushed up prices even faster than wages. Only when inflation slowed after March 1937 did real wages rise sharply. It was at that point that output growth came to a sudden halt, just as in the other four cases.

Table 10.2. Four-Month Growth Rates for Industrial Production

	Before	After
1933 wage shock	+57.4%	−18.8%
1934 wage shock	+11.9%	−15.0%
1938 wage shock	+15.8%	+2.5%
1939 wage shock	+16.0%	−6.5%

Note: The dates of the wages shocks are assumed to be 7/33, 5/34, 11/38 and 11/39. The growth rates are not annualized.

The five wage shocks of 1933–1939 effectively created a supply-side depression that lasted from mid-1933 through mid-1940, when a vigorous recovery finally got underway. This depression was partially hidden by the expansionary impact of dollar depreciation on aggregate demand. But it was very real to the workers who continued to face extraordinarily high unemployment rates as late as mid-1940, more than seven years after the recovery began.

Modern economists have often focused on the seemingly high growth rates of the recovery period. These would be high rates of growth during normal time periods, but were less than what would have been expected to occur in an economy recovering from a deep depression. During those periods free of wage shocks and deflationary policies, industrial production *invariably* grew at a blistering pace, testimony to the economy's powerful self-correcting mechanism. And when aided by effective steps at monetary expansion (as in March through July 1933) the growth rates were truly extraordinary.

Postscript

There are some great ironies in the widespread view that higher reserve requirements contributed to the 1937–1938 depression. The mechanism would presumably have been either a lower money multiplier, or a higher demand for base money (specifically bank reserves). I have argued here that this policy occurred too soon to cause the 1937–1938 depression and may have moderated the preceding inflation. But on October 6, 2008, the Federal Reserve instituted a very similar policy, and in this case, the timing could not have been more unfortunate.

The Fed's decision to begin paying interest on reserves in October 2008 almost certainly contributed to the extraordinary increase in the demand for excess reserves (although it wasn't the only factor). The Fed's rationale was that they wanted to keep control over the Fed funds rate as they injected large amounts of liquidity into the banking system. This essentially meant that they wanted to prevent nominal rates from immediately falling to zero. Thus, the effect was contractionary, and at almost the worst possible time.

Some have defended the Fed by pointing to the relatively low level of interest on reserves, which started at about 1 percent and eventually fell to 0.25 percent. But the 1937, doubling of reserve requirements had an almost identical effect on nominal rates, raising them by roughly 0.25 percent. If the 1937 decision was as harmful as many economists have assumed, then it is unclear why there was so little criticism of the Fed's 2008 decision. If we have learned anything from our study of the Depression, as well as the situation in Japan during the 1990s, it is that nominal rates are not a reliable indicator of the stance of monetary policy. Here is what Ben Bernanke wrote in 1999:

> The argument that current monetary policy in Japan is in fact quite accommodative rests largely on the observation that interest rates are at a very low level. *I do hope that readers who have gotten this far will be sufficiently familiar with monetary history not to take seriously any such claim based on the level of the nominal interest rate.* One need only recall that nominal interest rates remained close to zero in many countries throughout the Great Depression, a period of massive monetary contraction and deflationary pressure. In short, low nominal interest rates may just as well be a sign of expected deflation and monetary tightness as of monetary ease. (p. 11, emphasis added.)

Ironically, just nine years later, Bernanke was chairman of the Federal Reserve as it ran a deflationary monetary policy that was also wrongly thought to be expansionary. Most pundits were complacent about Fed policy in late 2008 due to the low nominal rates and the large increase in the monetary base. Unfortunately, the large increase in the base was sterilized by the interest on reserve policy, and low nominal rates are actually reflective of a deflationary policy environment, not easy money.

And here is an even greater irony. In 2003 Bernanke had recommended that the Japanese follow FDR's policy of aiming for reflation:

> What I have in mind is that the Bank of Japan would announce its intention to restore the price level (as measured by some standard index of prices, such as the consumer price index excluding fresh food) to the value it would have reached if, instead of the deflation of the past five years, a moderate inflation of, say, 1 percent per year had occurred. (I choose 1 percent to allow for the measurement bias issue noted above, and because a slightly positive average rate of inflation reduces the risk of future episodes of sustained deflation.) Note that the proposed

price-level target is a moving target, equal in the year 2003 to a value approximately 5 percent above the actual price level in 1998 and rising 1 percent per year thereafter. Because deflation implies falling prices while the target price-level rises, the failure to end deflation in a given year has the effect of increasing what I have called the price-level gap.

This sort of approach is generally called "level targeting," and has the effect of stabilizing expectations when the economy is hit by an adverse shock. But when prices started falling in late 2008 the Fed refused to adopt a higher inflation target in the United States. As a result, 2009 saw nominal GDP fall at the fastest pace since 1938. Let's hope this is the last time the Fed adopts a policy aimed at encouraging money hoarding in the midst of a recession.

PART V

Conclusion

11

The Impact of the Depression on Twentieth-Century Macroeconomics

Finally, what emerges clearly from this study of Keynes's views on monetary policy are the close links between theory and policy. For every change in the problem at hand came new proposals growing out of previous theory or, if previous doctrine could not accommodate the new situation, shifts in his theoretical position. This is clearly illustrated (from a Keynesian point of view) by the evolution of Keynes's views under the impact of British (and world) events between 1925 and, say, 1934. This interrelationship was the hallmark of Keynes, the economist.
—Donald E. Moggridge and Susan Howson (1974, p. 247)

As I see it, we have advanced beyond Hume in two respects only; first, we now have a more secure grasp of the quantitative magnitudes involved; second, we have gone one derivative beyond Hume.
—Milton Friedman (1975, p. 177)

WHILE WORKING ON this project I have gradually come to the conclusion that modern macroeconomics, macro history, and the history of thought are a seamless whole; it is impossible to really understand any one field without also having deep knowledge of the other two.

Why Do We Need Macroeconomic History and the History of Thought?

One implication of the preceding narrative is that knowledge of the history of economic thought can illuminate important problems of economic history. Consider the problem of identifying monetary shocks. We have already seen that what really matters isn't so much the current stance of policy but rather the impact of policy actions on the expected future time path of various monetary instruments. But which instruments? The history of monetary economics shows that at various times, economists have viewed monetary policy as the rental cost of money (short-term interest rates), the quantity of money, or the price of money (in terms of some other currency or commodity). Each instrument is associated with a radically different view of the essential nature of "monetary policy." Unless one is aware of all of these different perspectives, one can easily overlook the importance of a given monetary policy shock, which may dramatically impact one policy instrument while having little or no discernible impact on another.

One way of seeing the interrelationship between economic history and the history of thought is by observing how different institutional settings led to radically different ways of conceptualizing monetary economics. The earliest monetary theories were almost certainly a branch of price theory. In ancient times, "the economy" was little more than a small collection of commodity markets, with one commodity often designated as the medium of account. Monetary "policy," if it existed at all, consisted of little more than the debasement of coins. In this environment, monetary theorists naturally tended to evaluate policy through a Mundellian "price of money" perspective.

As financial systems became more sophisticated, paper money was developed and central banks began to influence short-term interest rates. Monetary theory then evolved in two new directions, with both the quantity of money and nominal interest rates becoming important policy indicators. But there were important differences between these two indicators. In a primitive economy without financial markets, changes in the money supply can only impact goods prices, not the prices of financial assets. And even if financial markets exist, if there is perfect wage and price flexibility then a change in the quantity of money will simply result in an instantaneous change in all nominal aggregates, with interest rates being unchanged. Thus, despite its name, an interest rate–oriented model such as Keynes' *General Theory* is a *special* theory that applies only to economies with sticky prices and well-developed financial markets.[1] Monetarism is actually the more "general" theory.

---

1. Brunner (1981) argued that "the evidence drawn from inflation (or deflation) experiences of countries with (at best) rudimentary 'money' or capital markets (Turkey, Israel, Belgium,

Today, most mainstream economists rely almost entirely on the interest rate approach to monetary analysis. This might be defended on the grounds that primitive economies are merely of academic interest and that even as far back as the Great Depression most developed economies featured substantial price stickiness and well-developed financial markets. But these institutional changes have not caused the more primitive transmission mechanisms to suddenly disappear. Consider a one-time, unanticipated, 50 percent currency devaluation in a small country that is part of an international gold standard. This policy should immediately increase the prices of traded commodities (and equities), and over a longer period of time should double the overall price level. But because of the interest parity condition, this sort of policy shock would have no impact at all on the time path of nominal interest rates.

During 1933–1934, the dollar did not depreciate all at once, and the United States did not have a small economy. Nevertheless, the depreciation was mostly unanticipated, and the economy responded pretty much as one would expect using a "price of money" approach. Prices rose sharply, and then more gradually, and the devaluation had little or no impact on the path of nominal interest rates. The policy shock that Mundell (1975, p. 143) called "one of the most important events of the century" is almost invisible when viewed through the lens of interest rate-oriented monetary models.

It might be argued that, although nominal interest rates were not a good indicator of policy actions during 1933, the decrease in the real interest rate provided the transmission mechanism for that policy. But once again, a study of monetary history shows that this cannot be the whole story. There must be other transmission mechanisms for primitive commodity-based economies that lack financial markets, and these other mechanisms certainly don't magically disappear as economies become more developed. Models that use an interest rate transmission mechanism assume that policy first impacts nominal and real interest rates, then investment and output, with inflation only beginning to rise as the economy approaches full employment. But in 1933 the prices of key commodities (and equities) responded immediately to the

the Netherlands, Korea, South America, and others) is hard to reconcile with a 'Hicksian' substitution pattern. It appears that the 'Hicksian' interpretation expresses a somewhat parochial 'City of London syndrome.'" Brunner's point is very important, although one might easily find even more "primitive" examples in extremely low-income countries or in earlier epochs of world history.

depreciation program of 1933–1934, despite 25 percent unemployment. Thus, an important part of the transmission mechanism ran from dollar depreciation to higher prices to rising output.

Modern graduate programs in economics have marginalized the history of economic thought. As a result, during the past two decades, we have been treated to an outpouring of analysis of Japan's "liquidity trap" (and more recently, that of the United States) by economists with only a vague recollection that Keynes had some interesting views on absolute liquidity preference but thought it was unlikely to occur in reality. In the next two sections I will argue that Keynes's views on liquidity preference have virtually no relevance to the recent so-called liquidity trap in Japan (and have led to great misunderstanding of that situation). Yet, Keynes's views on "absolute liquidity preference" were central to his worldview and had a much greater impact on the *General Theory* than he acknowledged.

Without adequate knowledge of the history of thought, economists have been forced to endlessly "reinvent the wheel," as various proposals for liquidity trap escape mechanisms are considered and then discarded. One prominent economist ended up suggesting that devaluation was a "foolproof" solution, and explicitly cited Franklin D. Roosevelt's (FDR's) dollar depreciation program.[2] It is ironic that this program represented FDR's attempt to implement the policy recommendations of George Warren, who (as we saw in Chapter 7) was at the time widely viewed as something of a monetary crank, and still is. And forty years before Warren, Williams (1892) was recommending currency depreciation as a cure for deflation. And decades before Williams, Rooke (1824) made a similar argument. Indeed, as far back as 1692, John Locke was debating advocates of the monetary ineffectiveness proposition, using a *reductio ad absurdum* argument to show that sufficient currency depreciation (specifically coinage debasement) was a foolproof way of generating inflation.

The policy analysis of early macroeconomists is often seen as being inferior to that of modern economists. Sometimes it is. But in many cases their unconventional views reflect a different view of policy instruments, the monetary

---

2. No sarcasm is intended here; I support Svensson's (2003a) proposal. (Note that most modern economists are probably unaware of just how much the National Industrial Recovery Act (NIRA) inhibited FDR's dollar depreciation program, and thus just how effective it actually was.)

transmission mechanism, or use of different price indices, or even the fact that the structure of the economy was quite different one hundred years ago. Some of these perspectives are still quite relevant to current monetary issues.

What Was the Keynesian Revolution Really All About?

I will examine the impact of the Great Depression on the development of macroeconomic thought in four stages. An obvious starting point is the Keynesian Revolution. In trying to identify the essence of Keynesian economics, the focus will be not so much on what Keynes "really meant" or what his followers thought he meant, but rather on how Keynesian economics differed from other pre-Depression models. Then, we will consider how the Depression impacted the development of Keynesian economics, and more specifically, how Keynesian economics can be seen as arising from a misreading of some of the policy initiatives discussed in earlier chapters. This view of the formation of "traditional" or early Keynesianism will help us to better understand some of the macroeconomic policy errors of the postwar period. And finally, we will see that as those policy errors exposed flaws in the traditional Keynesian model, a "new Keynesianism" emerged, which combined aspects of both traditional Keynesianism and monetarism. We will conclude by briefly examining a similar dialectic at work in another area of economic policymaking.

Many undergraduates are taught that the standard textbook aggregate supply/aggregate demand (AS/AD) model featuring a natural rate of output and sticky prices is "Keynesian" economics and that the model was developed in the 1930s because flexible price classical models were unable to explain why nominal shocks would have real effects. Those with even a passing knowledge of the history of economic thought know that this is a myth. Pre-Keynesian macroeconomists clearly understood how wage and price stickiness could lead to the short-run nonneutrality of money. And Keynes clearly rejected the concept of a natural rate of output. In some respects, modern macroeconomics[3] is closer in spirit to the work of Wicksell, or Fisher, than to the model developed by Keynes in the *General Theory*. One side effect of the growing awareness of

3. Woodford's *Interest and Prices* (2003) is perhaps the most important recent compendium of new Keynesian monetary theory. It is interesting that Woodford calls his model "neo-Wicksellian." Irving Fisher is now regarded as the inventor of the "Phillips Curve."

the sophistication of pre-Keynesian business cycle models is that it has become more difficult to identify what was truly innovative about the *General Theory*.

Elsewhere, I have argued (1999) that until the 1970s Keynesian economics was implicitly built upon two fundamental assumptions. First, that the nominal interest rate is the appropriate instrument and indicator of monetary policy. And second, that monetary policy is not a reliable tool for stabilizing the macroeconomy. Later, we will return to the difficult problem of whether that unreliability was caused by monetary policy being weak and ineffective, or by an implicit assumption that it would be constrained by exchange rate considerations. And, in the next section, I will add a third assumption—the concept of permanent underemployment equilibrium. But first we need to take a closer look at the problem of transmission mechanisms.

In an earlier paper (2004b), I showed that the development of Wicksellian (interest rate-oriented) monetary theory reflected two broad structural changes. The growing sophistication of financial markets led to interest rates becoming a more and more important part of the transmission mechanism, and the evolution from a commodities-based economy to a more sophisticated goods and services economy made prices much stickier. Both changes were necessary conditions for the development of monetary models using an interest rate transmission mechanism, but Keynes made several additional assumptions, most importantly that monetary policy was an ineffective tool for boosting aggregate demand during a depression.

When evaluating the *General Theory*, it is helpful to begin with the views of two of Keynes's shrewdest readers, John Hicks and Milton Friedman. When Hicks first formalized Keynes's insights into the IS-LM[4] apparatus, he noted two key differences from the preceding "classical" tradition, the multiplier equation and the liquidity preference doctrine. While Hicks saw the former as being "a mere simplification, and ultimately insignificant," he also suggested, "it is the liquidity preference doctrine which is vital." But even here, Hicks saw continuity with the Marshallian tradition, which also allowed for the possibility that money demand could be influenced by the rate of interest. Finally, Hicks concludes that the "most important thing in Mr. Keynes' book" is the

---

4. Originally termed IS-LL.

possibility of a flat LM curve—that is, the liquidity trap.[5] It is this special case that allowed Keynes to question the effectiveness of monetary policy and to call for increased public works spending.

One problem with Hicks's interpretation is that in the *General Theory* (p. 207) Keynes indicated that he knew of no previous examples of a complete liquidity trap. So perhaps Hicks's interpretation is wrong. But Friedman (1974, p. 169) also argued that "absolute liquidity preference" played an essential role in the *General Theory*.[6] Did Hicks and Friedman merely impose their own agenda rather than analyze Keynes in his own terms? To evaluate that question, we need to look at Keynes's work in its historical context. There is no doubt that, among other things, Keynes intended the *General Theory* as a critique of the macro theory of his contemporaries.

During the 1920s, the more progressive monetary economists had favored monetary policy rules aimed at stabilizing prices or nominal income.[7] Keynes made it quite clear that he was not convinced that monetary policy, unaided, was capable of stabilizing the macroeconomy. Because Keynes doubted the effectiveness of such policies, he focused on issues such as inadequate investment, the paradox of thrift, and using fiscal policy[8] to stabilize the economy—the sort of issues that have little or no relevance in an economy where the monetary authority is *willing and able to target nominal GDP growth*. If one approaches the *General Theory* as a critique of the state of interwar macroeconomics, it's

---

5. This is not to argue that Hicks's paper contains the only "correct" IS-LM model. Rather, Hicks's version seems to best represent the views of Keynes and his followers during the 1930s. De Vroey (2000) showed that Modigilani's (1944) later version, which emphasizes wage rigidity instead of the liquidity trap, is probably closer to spirit of modern Keynesianism. De Vroey argued that once the concept of an absolute liquidity trap began to seem implausible "the only bequest from the Keynesian revolution was a rudimentary pragmatic general equilibrium model, the IS-LM apparatus in general, devoid of any specific Keynesian trait." (p. 304)

6. Friedman suggested that "one consequence of my rereading large parts of the *General Theory* . . . has been to reinforce my view that absolute liquidity preference plays a key role. Time and again when Keynes must face up to precisely what it is that prevents a full-employment equilibrium, his final line of defense is absolute liquidity preference." (1974, p. 169)

7. See Fisher (1920), Cassel (1922), Robertson (1922), Hawtrey (1923), Keynes (1923), and Pigou (1927).

8. Here, I am referring not just to the *General Theory*, but also to Keynes's other writings during the 1930s.

hard to escape the conclusion that the concept of monetary policy ineffectiveness occupied a central position in the Keynesian revolution. Without this assumption, many of the *General Theory's* most distinctive ideas simply *make no sense.*

Policy Failures and the Keynesian Revolution

In several earlier studies, I argued that although Hicks and Friedman were probably correct about the centrality of monetary policy ineffectiveness to the *General Theory*, it is not at all clear that Keynes equated this concept with "absolute liquidity preference." We saw in Chapter 4 that Keynes misunderstood the reasons for the failure of the spring 1932 Federal Reserve (Fed) open market purchases. What had looked like a liquidity trap was actually an example of the constraints of the interwar gold standard. But it seems unlikely that this misunderstanding can fully account for Keynes's views on monetary policy effectiveness. Even in late 1933, when the dollar had been floating for eight months, Keynes continued to doubt the effectiveness of monetary policy in his comments on Roosevelt's gold-buying program:

> The other set of fallacies . . . arises out of a crude economic doctrine commonly known as the quantity theory of money. Rising output and rising incomes will suffer a setback sooner or later if the quantity of money is rigidly fixed. Some people seem to infer from this that output and income can be raised by increasing the quantity of money. But this is like trying to get fat by buying a larger belt. (*NYT*, 12/31/33)

This is a clear example of what is often referred to as the "pushing on a string" view of monetary policy ineffectiveness. But notice how Keynes subtly shifts his argument in the very next paragraph, as he turns from money's effect on real output, to its effect on prices:

> It is an even more foolish application of the same ideas to believe that there is a mathematical relation between the price of gold and the price of other things. It is true that the value of the dollar in terms of foreign currencies will affect the prices of those goods which enter into international trade. In so far as an overvaluation of the dollar was impeding the freedom of domestic price-raising policies or disturb-

ing the balance of payments with foreign countries, it was advisable
to depreciate it. But exchange depreciation should follow the success
of your domestic price raising policy as its natural consequence, and
should not be allowed to disturb the whole world by preceding its
justification at an entirely arbitrary pace. (*NYT,* 12/31/33)

Here, Keynes switches from a positive to a normative argument. And he
carefully avoids applying the monetary ineffectiveness proposition to prices,
merely noting that the relationship between the exchange rate and the price
level is not precise. Because the U.S. price level *did* rise rapidly during 1933, he
would have looked very foolish if he had claimed that currency depreciation
was incapable of boosting prices.

Keynes was a lifelong opponent of free-floating fiat money regimes (which
is what George Warren and Irving Fisher were promoting), once calling them
even worse than a rigid gold standard:

At all stages of the post-war developments the concrete proposals which
I have brought forward from time to time have been based on the use of
gold as an international standard, whilst discarding it as a rigid national
standard. The qualifications which I have added to this have been always the same, though the precise details have varied; namely (1) that
the parities between national standards and gold should not be rigid,
(2) that there should be a wider margin than in the past between the
gold points, and (3) that if possible some international control should be
formed with a view to regulating the commodity value of gold within
certain limits. (1933, *Collected Writings,* Vol. 21, p. 186)

Only a few weeks after criticizing Roosevelt's gold-buying program, he
praised the President for announcing an intention to reestablish a dollar gold
peg at $35/ounce, and even went so far as to congratulate Roosevelt for reject-
ing the policy advice of the "extreme inflationists." This is hardly the sort
of rhetoric one would expect from an economist who doubted whether an
expansionary monetary policy could raise prices.

Can all of Keynes's various statements on monetary policy effectiveness be
reconciled? Probably not, but some sense can be made of the varied assertions
if we assume that Keynes's thought process was highly compartmentalized.

Under "normal" conditions, monetary policy would be at least somewhat constrained, perhaps by a gold standard (although Keynes actually preferred a slightly more flexible arrangement such as the Bretton Woods regime). Under these sorts of policy constraints, monetary policy alone might have proved incapable of generating an adequate level of aggregate demand. In contrast, under "abnormal" conditions (such as the post–World War I hyperinflations), a central bank might print large quantities of fiat currency and allow an extreme depreciation in its currency. Keynes saw this sort of regime as being highly inflationary, but for some reason he never contemplated an intermediate case—that is, he never foresaw the possibility of an unanchored fiat money regime that targeted inflation at a low but positive level.[9]

Although Keynes never addressed the apparent inconsistencies in his views on monetary policy ineffectiveness, the preceding "compartmentalization" hypothesis is not entirely ad hoc. During the interwar period, one can find numerous similar examples of such inconsistency in the conservative business press, where commentators simultaneously doubted the effectiveness of monetary schemes to raise the price level and warned that radical monetary reforms might lead to hyperinflation. And in 2001 there was a similar inconsistency in statements made by officials at the Bank of Japan, who warned that quantitative easing would be ineffectual, but also that such a policy might lead to runaway inflation.[10] Keynes would not have been the only monetary policy analyst to exhibit this sort of compartmentalization in his thinking.

To summarize, a misreading of monetary policy during the Great Depression, and particularly the 1932 open market purchases in the United States, led Keynes to wrongly believe that, unaided, monetary policy might not be able to assure adequate growth in nominal spending. But what about the other core idea in the Keynesian revolution, the belief that an unregulated capitalist system has no self-correcting mechanism to return to full employment? Here again, it seems likely that Keynes's views were partially based on a misreading of U.S. policy initiatives.

---

9. Meltzer (1988) makes a similar observation. I am not arguing that were Keynes alive today he would oppose the sort of inflation targeting fiat money regimes which have proven relatively successful in many nations. Rather, I am arguing that he never seemed to have contemplated such a regime.

10. See the *Economist*, 6/2/2001, p. 74.

Even before the Great Depression, Keynes worried that capitalist economies would tend to suffer from a chronic problem of high unemployment as a result of a shortfall in aggregate demand. Indeed, Britain had experienced relatively high unemployment rates throughout much of the 1920s. But in the late 1920s the United States was by far the largest and most important capitalist economy in the world and the British problems were often seen as a special case, blamed by conservative American and French economists on the pernicious influence of "the dole."[11] As long as the United States showed an ability to rebound quickly from downturns, Keynes would have difficulty convincing others to question classical macroeconomic orthodoxy, which said that Say's Law would hold except during relatively brief transitional periods.

Even the high unemployment experienced by the United States during the early 1930s could be explained by interwar business cycle models, such as the one developed by Fisher (1925). Recall that Fisher's model predicted that an end to the deflation would lead to a quick recovery in output. And that is exactly what seemed to be happening during the spring and early summer of 1933, when industrial output rose by 57 percent in just four months. As we saw in Chapter 6, the 22 percent wage shock associated with the National Industrial Recovery Act (NIRA) aborted the recovery and led to seven more years of depression. Fisher's model failed spectacularly at this point, and the idea of a self-correcting economy went out of favor for the next forty years.

In retrospect, it seems clear that Keynes failed to grasp the significance of interwar labor market policies that reduced aggregate supply. Instead, he saw the persistence of high unemployment in market economies as evidence of both inadequate demand and also the absence of a self-correcting mechanism. Price flexibility alone would not be capable of restoring output to its "natural rate" in the long run. Today, the sort of chronic unemployment experienced by Britain in the 1920s (or the eurozone in recent decades) is generally attributed

---

11. American economists make similar arguments today about the high unemployment rates throughout much of the eurozone. Benjamin and Kochin (1979) present evidence that unemployment compensation programs raised the British natural rate of unemployment during the interwar years and also discuss interwar economists such as Jacques Rueff who held similar views. I find this hypothesis plausible, but would caution against the use of ambiguous and misleading distinctions between "voluntary" and "involuntary" unemployment.

to supply-side problems such as rigid labor markets and/or generous unemployment compensation.

The two policy initiatives that I have focused on, the 1932 open market purchases and the NIRA of 1933, occurred just as Keynes was developing the core ideas of the *General Theory*. This is not to suggest that these two policies were the only aspects of the Depression that contributed to Keynesian revolution. In some respects, the situation during the late 1930s was just as important. From 1938–1940, unemployment in the United States remained abnormally high despite nominal interest rates having fallen to near-zero levels. It is not surprising that by the late 1930s, many younger American economists were attracted to a model that argued the economy lacked a self-correcting mechanism and that monetary policy was often ineffective.

Nor is the Great Depression the only source of the Keynesian revolution. Elsewhere, I have argued that the *General Theory* is less a "depression model" than a "gold standard model," as it implicitly relies on assumptions that only make sense under a gold standard regime. One assumption is that monetary policy may not be an adequate stabilization tool, which we have just seen was based on confusion over the constraints of the gold standard. But there are other assumptions that are also implicitly linked to the gold standard world, as when Keynes explicitly denies the possibility of a Fisher effect in nominal interest rates (except in abnormal circumstances such as hyperinflation). Or when Keynes implicitly rules out the possibility that higher inflation expectations might lead to shifts in the Phillips curve that would automatically return output to its natural rate.[12] Recall that under a gold standard, the rational expectations' expected rate of inflation is near zero, and thus price level changes were mostly unforecastable during Keynes's lifetime. This means that there was little evidence of a Fisher effect during Keynes's lifetime, and the Phillips curve was much more stable than during the post-1960 period.

The publication of the *General Theory* came three years after the start of the New Deal. In retrospect, it seems doubtful that this book would have had the same impact if the U.S. economy had achieved something close to full recovery during 1934. Rather, the entire 1929–1934 episode might have been seen as a decisive vindication of the more activist mainstream economists

---

12. See Sumner (1999).

such as Fisher and Keynes (of the *Tract on Monetary Reform*) who advocated
a managed currency to maintain stable prices, and a decisive repudiation of
the more conservative mainstream economists who had argued that the gold
standard was the most effective way of maintaining price stability.

The Demise of Bretton Woods
and the Crisis in Keynesian Economics

The free market dollar price of gold was fixed at $35 an ounce from Febru-
ary 1934 to March 1968.[13] Obviously, this period did not meet all the criteria for
being a gold standard regime (although it's not clear that any other period fully
met those criteria either). But the dollar-gold peg was just binding enough to
keep both actual inflation and inflation expectations in the low single digits
for most of that period.[14] Of course, changes in the world economy led to a
dramatic fall in the real demand for monetary gold between the interwar gold
exchange standard and the postwar Bretton Woods regime, and this showed
up in a substantial one-time increase in the world price level in gold (or dollar)
terms between 1934 and 1968, much of which occurred during the war years.
Yet, as long as inflationary expectations were reasonably well anchored, there
was no reason to question the fundamental tenets of the Keynesian model.

No sooner had the United States shifted to a fiat money regime than it
began to experience increases in the expected rate of inflation, higher nominal
interest rates, and rightward shifts in the Phillips curve. At about the same
time, the "natural rate" of unemployment increased in many countries, as
the supply side of these economies steadily deteriorated under the burden
of increased taxes and other disincentives. In this environment, the traditional Keynesian policy guideposts proved unreliable. Stagflation was misdiagnosed as deficient aggregate demand, and rising nominal interest rates

13. Mundell (1968) noted that the dollar was made vulnerable by the 1967 devaluation of
the British pound. France was not very cooperative and the U.S. authorities preferred expansionary monetary policies to the constraints of the $35/ounce gold peg. Not much had changed
since the early 1930s.

14. Klein (1975, p. 472) argued that "even as late as 1964 firm expectations must have been
held that a long-term monetary policy necessary to maintain foreign convertibility of the dollar at $35/oz. would be followed," and that therefore expectations of inflation were quite low.

were misinterpreted as "tight money." These policy failures led to a revival of interest in monetarist ideas, and particularly the Friedman/Phelps natural rate model.

Beyond the problem of shifting inflation expectations, there is a more subtle reason why high inflation rates are so destructive to the simpler Keynesian models. In a high inflation environment it becomes difficult to account for nominal variables using expenditure models where money is pushed to the background. Not surprisingly, quantity theoretic monetary models have always tended to be most popular during periods of high inflation. During the post–World War I period of high inflation, even Wicksell and Keynes temporarily abandoned their interest rate approach and adopted a quantity theoretic mode of analysis. As Friedman observed:

> Double-digit inflation and double-digit interest rates, not the elegance of theoretical reasoning or the overwhelming persuasiveness of serried masses of statistics massaged through modern computers, explain the rediscovery of money. (1975, p. 176)

If Keynes was the most important macroeconomist of the gold standard world, then Friedman was the same for the fiat-money world.

One might ask why I have put such emphasis on the effectiveness of monetary policy at influencing nominal variables; after all, the Great Depression was a sharp decline in *real* GDP. But recall that Keynes assumed that depressions were caused by an insufficiency of nominal expenditure. If monetary policy is always capable of generating high inflation, then ipso facto, it is also capable of boosting nominal expenditure. Not all depressions are not due to insufficient nominal expenditure, but it was this sort of problem that Keynes addressed in the *General Theory*. The perception that, under a fiat money regime, central banks can almost effortlessly boost nominal spending with monetary injections makes fiscal policy seem like little more than a fifth wheel of stabilization policy. Indeed that view became new Keynesian dogma, at least until nominal rates again fell to zero in the recent recession.

Keynes's misreading of the Great Depression contributed to the policy confusion of the 1970s in two distinct ways. Throughout much of the postwar period there was an inflationary bias to policy as governments sought to avoid the chronically high unemployment of the interwar period. It was understood that policy errors could lead to occasional bouts of inflation, but there was little appreciation of the implications of persistent changes in inflation expectations. Nor was it widely understood that monetary restraint was the *sine qua non* of aggregate demand control. In 1968 the U.S. government attempted to slow inflation by increasing income taxes. Only when this policy failed did it switch to monetary restraint, but the traditional Keynesian (interest rate-oriented) policy framework was woefully inadequate for a world of fiat money regimes featuring high and unstable inflation expectations.

Throughout much of the 1970s, monetary policy was assumed to be tighter than it actually was. Interest rates were at historically high levels, and there was still insufficient appreciation for the distinction between real and nominal rates. In addition, throughout most of the 1970s and early 1980s unemployment rates were well above the 4 percent figure then assumed to represent full employment. In the simple Keynesian model the high nominal interest rates signaled that monetary policy was already "tight," and the high unemployment rates suggested that aggregate demand was inadequate.

Beyond its narrow impact on demand management, the Keynesian revolution had led to a general mistrust of free market ideologies, particularly the view that in a market economy wages and prices would adjust over time and that Say's Law would hold in the long run. When "tight money" failed to stop inflation, and unemployment remained high, it was not surprising that Keynesian policymakers would turn to "incomes policies"—that is, wage and price controls. We now know that these policies were merely treating the symptoms of inflation, which at the deepest level is a depreciation of the purchasing power of money—a process that cannot be halted by artificial controls on prices. But the policies were quite popular in the period after the price of gold was allowed to float.

In some respects the preceding account is a bit of a caricature of postwar Keynesianism. By the late 1960s the more sophisticated Keynesians had at least some awareness of these weaknesses in 1930s-style Keynesianism. But most Keynesians still failed to fully appreciate the potency of monetary policy, the importance of inflation expectations, and the size of policy-induced shifts in the natural rate of unemployment.[15] After the oil shocks that began in

15. Nelson blames the great inflation of the 1970s on "the monetary neglect hypothesis . . . Other explanations of the Great Inflation are ruled out, with one exception (the output gap

1973, many Keynesians came to (wrongly)[16] believe that the coexistence of persistently high inflation and unemployment could be explained by simply tacking aggregate supply shocks onto the traditional Keynesian model. But this explanation seemed less and less plausible as time went by, and it certainly did not provide many attractive options to policymakers. By the late 1970s, it was apparent that the problems with the Keynesian model were not so easily remedied, and policymakers began to look at alternative policy frameworks.

Monetarism is a model that is especially well suited to explaining large shifts in the trend rate of inflation. Thus it is not surprising that monetarism became increasingly popular during the period from the 1960s to the early 1980s, when much of the world experienced dramatic increases in actual and expected rates of inflation. In retrospect, monetarism can be seen as playing an important role in the transition from the Keynesianism of the 1960s to the new Keynesianism of the 1980s.

Monetarism Slays the Inflation Dragon, But Is Killed in the Process

Much of the narrative in Chapters 2 through 10 can be read as a critique of Friedman and Schwartz's account of the Depression. And Keynesians such as Temin and Eichengreen have also questioned Friedman and Schwartz's tendency to relegate the international gold standard to the periphery of their analysis. How then can we account for the enduring success of the *Monetary History,* even as monetarism has faded in importance?

---

mismeasurement hypothesis), which supplements the monetary policy neglect hypothesis" (2005, p. 1). Note that monetary neglect resulted from the traditional Keynesian view that monetary policy was not very effective, and the mismeasurement of the output gap reflected the traditional Keynesian assumption that any increase in unemployment must be due to a lack of aggregate demand. In other words, Nelson's two sources of policy errors are both linked to the misreading of U.S. policies during 1932–1933.

16. I'm not suggesting that the oil shocks had no impact on prices and employment, but it is interesting to note that once central banks switched to inflation targeting, the sort of sharp run-up in oil prices that occurred in 2004–05 seems to have had little impact on the price level. And the persistence of high unemployment into the 1980s and 1990s in the eurozone countries suggests that the 1970s employment problems related more to deep structural problems rather than the transitory effects of energy price shocks.

Of course, the *Monetary History* is an extraordinarily impressive work of scholarship. But I also believe that the success of *Monetary History* is partly related to the timing of its publication. In a sense, *Monetary History* can be viewed as an "as if" account of American monetary history—that is, a normative evaluation of American monetary history under the assumption that the Fed had control over a fiat money supply. And the book was also fortuitously timed, published just before the major central banks moved toward exactly this type of policy regime. Ironically, its *policy implications* are perhaps more relevant to the post-1968 era than to the 1867–1960 period which they examined.[17]

Even though the post–Bretton Woods policy environment was nothing like the 1930s, it was perfect for Friedman and Schwartz's central message: that fluctuations in nominal spending are caused by unstable monetary policy. Consider their hypothesis that a more expansionary monetary policy could have prevented a 50 percent fall in nominal GDP during the early 1930s. It is much easier to make that sort of argument in a world where most countries are experiencing very rapid money supply growth rates, and that growth seems to be generating rapid increases in nominal income. Indeed, by the end of the 1970s, if the term "monetary policy ineffectiveness" was used at all, it was invariably in reference to real GDP; almost no one questioned the ability of central bankers to influence nominal GDP growth.

We have already seen that the traditional Keynesian model was particularly ill-suited for fiat money regimes featuring dramatic changes in the expected rate of inflation. Friedman and Schwartz criticized the Keynesian model by showing that nominal interest rates were a highly misleading indicator of the stance of monetary policy during the Depression and that the fall in the money stock showed that policy was actually quite restrictive during the early 1930s. As we have seen, the dramatic increase in the gold reserve ratio during the early 1930s supports Friedman and Schwartz's conclusions. But their analysis actually understates the flaws in the Keynesian approach to monetary indicators, because under a fiat money regime there will be even larger shifts in inflation expectations than under a gold standard, and hence,

---

17. As noted earlier, I think many of their conclusions are defensible even under the constraints that faced gold standard–era policymakers; it's just that the some of their assertions about monetary policy would be even more persuasive had policymakers not faced those constraints.

the nominal interest rate will become an even less reliable indicator of the stance of monetary policy. Their critique of Keynes's monetary policy ineffectiveness proposition is even more relevant to the fiat monetary environment of the 1970s, than to the gold standard environment of 1932.

It is not surprising that the early critiques of Friedman and Schwartz focused on doubts about the effectiveness and/or exogeneity of monetary policy, issues at the center of the early Keynesian/monetarist debates. But after the high inflation 1970s and the Volcker disinflation seemed to confirm the potency of monetary policy, the critics shifted their focus to the issue of how the gold standard constrained policymakers. The following quotation from Peter Lindert discusses Friedman and Schwartz's suggestion that an extra $1 billion of reserves would have helped greatly during the early 1930s:

> If it is conceded that extra reserves would have propped up the money stock, a gainsayer would then have to argue that the extra money stock would have no effect whatsoever on aggregate demand. The extensive empirical literature on the money-income relationship precludes this extreme view. And once one concedes that extra reserves and money have some significant effect on aggregate demand, the debate is largely over: for any given desired effect on GNP, there must be *some* dosage of extra reserves, if not one billion exactly, that would have done the job. (1981, p. 130)

Elsewhere, I have used a similar argument against the possibility of a liquidity trap under a fiat money regime, yet today it seems odd to apply this argument to the *Monetary History*, which covers a period when reserves still needed gold backing.[18] His statement was made at a time when traditional Keynesian ideas were giving way to new Keynesianism and is both backward-looking (in its confusion between gold standard constraints and liquidity preference) and forward-looking (in its confidence in the efficacy of monetary policy). By 1981, the debate over the efficacy of monetary policy was largely over,[19] but another debate (over the constraints of the interwar gold standard) was just beginning.

---

18. See Sumner (2002) and (2003).

19. Perhaps I should say temporarily over, since the recent problems in Japan have revived the debate. Temin (1976) is an example of the early debate over the efficacy/exogeneity of monetary history, and Temin (1989) is an example of the more recent focus on the gold standard.

Earlier, I argued that we will probably never be able to resolve the dispute over the extent to which the gold standard constrained U.S. monetary policy during the Depression. But to younger economists who came of age after 1968, the dispute is of purely academic interest. Even if we assume the "worst case,"—that is, that Temin and Eichengreen were right in their critique of the *Monetary History*—it still doesn't mean that monetary policy wasn't to blame for the Great Depression. Rather, from a modern perspective, it simply means that monetary policymakers (broadly defined) should have abandoned the gold standard and printed enough fiat money to restore full employment. Friedman and Schwartz's error, if they made one, was simply to blame the wrong component of the monetary policy apparatus for the excessively tight money of the 1930s. Today we have a unified policy apparatus, and thus this dispute is merely a historical curiosity. Therefore, any weaknesses in the *Monetary History's* normative policy critiques in no way detract from its usefulness as a cautionary tale to modern policymakers.

This favorable appraisal of Friedman and Schwartz's *Monetary History* begs the question of why monetarism didn't triumph after the traditional Keynesian model fell apart in the 1970s. After all, the monetarists were the first to see that monetary policy was the primary determinant of growth in nominal spending and prices, and Friedman's natural rate model also helped restore faith in the economy's self-correcting mechanism. Monetarism even had successes on the policy front; soon after the Fed adopted money supply targets in 1979, inflation fell to relatively low levels, where it has remained ever since. Ironically, it was the very success of this anti-inflation policy that seems to have marginalized monetarism within the mainstream of contemporary macroeconomics.

Although Friedman and the other monetarists offered a compelling critique of traditional Keynesianism, they had trouble developing a persuasive and coherent model of their own. Part of the problem was beyond their control. The "interest rate approach" to monetary policy is much easier to understand than the quantity of money approach—in fact it's virtually the only approach used by the general public and the news media. But the monetarists also made some errors in their modeling strategy that ultimately led to their downfall.

Monetarists understood at a theoretical level that what mattered was not so much the current change in the money supply, but rather the expected change in the future path of the money supply. But monetarism was developed before the rational expectations revolution, and hence this insight was never fully incorporated into empirical monetarist analyses such as the *Monetary History*. For instance, although monetarists stressed the importance of asset markets in the monetary transmission process, they failed to adequately utilize asset prices as monetary policy indicators. Thus, they missed the full significance of an event like the 1933 devaluation of the dollar, which changed the future expected time path of the money supply, and which also showed up much more forcefully in forward-looking asset prices than in contemporaneous changes in the money stock.

This blind spot also led them to underestimate the potential volatility of money demand. When inflation expectations in the United States fell sharply in the early 1980s (indeed, more sharply than almost anyone had anticipated), the demand for money increased, velocity slowed, and the Fed decided to switch back to interest rate targeting. After 1982, inflation in the United States leveled off at about 4 percent, high enough to prevent a liquidity trap, but low and stable enough so that the nominal interest rate could once again become a useful instrument for monetary policy. And once inflation expectations became well anchored, policy lags proved to be a less worrisome problem than the monetarists had anticipated. Ironically, the very success of the monetarist anti-inflation program of 1979–1982 made the world safe for a revival of Keynesian operating procedures.

What's So Keynesian about "New Keynesianism"?

The return to interest rate targeting did not mean a revival of traditional Keynesianism. Rather, a "new Keynesianism" emerged which was a synthesis of traditional Keynesianism and monetarism. This model featured monetarist elements such as the natural rate model, an assumption that nominal spending growth can and should be determined by monetary policy rather than fiscal policy, and a greater sensitivity to the distinction between real and nominal interest rates. Younger economists might also emphasize the model's incorporation of the rational expectations hypothesis. Rational expectations is a useful modeling strategy, perhaps even essential, but after the demise of flexible price (new classical) models of the business cycle, rational expectations

Table 11.1. The New Keynesian Model

Classical Aspects	Keynesian Aspects
1. Self-correcting economy	1. Sticky wages and prices
2. Monetary policy determines aggregate demand	2. Interest rate transmission mechanism
3. Rational expectations	3. Interest rate targeting

played only a peripheral role in the dialectic that led to new Keynesianism. Even a monetarist critique founded on adaptive expectations was sufficient to undermine much of traditional Keynesianism.

The Keynesian model did retain certain aspects of traditional Keynesianism, most notably a focus on the interest rate transmission mechanism, and also the belief that the interest rate is useful as both an instrument and an indicator of monetary policy. But new Keynesianism has not retained all that much of what was really distinctive about the Keynesian revolution. New Keynesianism is distinguished by its more sophisticated understanding of the potency of monetary policy and also its awareness that long-run wage and price flexibility give the economy a self-correcting mechanism. Keynesians no longer see fiscal policy as the primary tool of demand management (at least outside the zero interest rate boundary) and no longer believe that demand management policies can cure the sort of persistently high unemployment rates recently experienced by the eurozone countries. Both of these insights can be seen as a belated recognition that Keynes misinterpreted both the apparent failure of the Fed's 1932 open market purchases, and also the chronically high interwar unemployment rates triggered by policies such as the NIRA.

Woodford's *Interest and Prices* is perhaps the best recent example of new Keynesian economic analysis. As such, it is interesting that Woodford skips past Keynes and calls his work "neo-Wicksellian." Wicksell (1907) was the first important proponent of the interest rate approach to monetary economics, and in reaching back to Wicksell, Woodford may be implicitly suggesting that Keynes contributed little of enduring value to this tradition.[20] It is true

---

20. Of course this is not to deny that Keynes made important contributions in many other areas of macroeconomics.

that there has recently been renewed interest in one of Keynes's innovations, the liquidity trap, but most new Keynesians have preferred to explain recent events in Japan using an expectations trap framework, which is equally compatible with monetarist analysis.[21]

The Evolution of Monetary Theory

Does the preceding account suggest that the entire Keynesian revolution was based on a set of mistakes by a single individual? Obviously, that would be too simplistic an explanation. In a previous work (2004b), I argued that the evolution of macroeconomic theory has been influenced more by outside events than by the internal dynamics of theoretical innovations in macroeconomics. The quantity, price, and interest rate approaches to monetary economics each have their strengths and weaknesses, and each is arguably best suited to a particular policy environment. For instance, were the major European powers to adopt separate, free-floating currencies, and dramatically different money supply growth rates, then one might expect renewed interest in the quantity theory of money[22] and its corollaries, the Fisher effect and purchasing power parity.

The Keynesian revolution represented the economics profession's best attempt to confront an exceedingly complex and confusing set of problems. One might argue that at its most basic level, it was a call for policymakers to take greater responsibility over the level of aggregate demand. And in that sense the revolution was a success. It is hardly surprising that Keynes misread some of the policy errors of that period. If they had been obvious, it seems unlikely that policy would have been so destructive. Steindl (2000) noted that during the early thirties, even Irving Fisher seemed to move away from a quantity theoretic approach, as he joined Keynes in questioning the effective-

---

21. An expectations trap occurs when monetary injections fail to boost aggregate demand because they are expected to be temporary. Sumner (1993b) provides a monetarist explanation for an expectations trap. Krugman (1998) applies this concept to the recent situation in Japan. Eggertsson (2006) looks at how FDR escaped the expectations trap in 1933.

22. As Friedman observed in 1975: "Double-digit inflation and double-digit interest rates, not the elegance of theoretical reasoning or the overwhelming persuasiveness of serried masses of statistics massaged through modern computers, explain the rediscovery of money" (p. 176).

ness of the Fed's 1932 open market purchases. But Dimand (2000) showed that Fisher soon moved back to the quantity theory, perhaps due to the (limited) success of Roosevelt's dollar depreciation program of 1933.

The preceding analysis links the rise and fall of traditional Keynesian economics with some misperceptions about U.S. policy during the Depression but also with the growing sophistication of the financial system, increasing price stickiness, the gold standard, and post–Bretton Woods fiat money regimes. As with most assertions about intellectual history, however, it is difficult to find testable implications for these hypotheses. Nevertheless, many developments in twentieth-century macroeconomics can be correlated with regime change and/or structural shifts in the economy:

1. **1900–1914**: Financial systems become increasing sophisticated. The classical gold standard keeps inflation expectations near zero. Wicksell (1907) develops an interest rate–oriented approach to monetary economics. Keynes (1911) also uses an interest rate approach.

2. **Early 1920s**: Postwar fiat money regimes. Some European countries experience high inflation or hyperinflation. Nominal interest rates are no longer a good indicator of monetary policy. Keynes (1923) adopts a quantity theoretic approach, and Jonung (1988) reports that at roughly the same time Wicksell also began to evaluate monetary policy in terms of growth in the money supply.

3. **1925–1931**: The international gold standard is restored and inflation expectations return to near-zero levels. Keynes (1930 [1953]) reverts back to an interest rate approach. Monetary policy is still seen as being fairly effective in most circumstances.

4. **1932**: The Fed policy of open market purchases seems to fail, creating an impression that the economy is stuck in a liquidity trap. Laidler (1999, p. 259n) calls this perceived failure "one of the key 'stylized facts' underlying the evolution of monetary economics in the 1930s and 1940s." Keynes loses faith in the efficacy of monetary policy. Even Fisher temporarily abandons the quantity theory. Only Currie (1934 [1935]) correctly sees the problem as a failure to expand the U.S. money supply (due to gold outflows), not a failure of monetary expansion to generate recovery.

5. **1933:** The NIRA aborts a promising recovery triggered by dollar depreciation, and the Depression drags on for another seven years. Keynes develops a model with monetary policy pushed to the margins and where the economy is assumed to have no self-correcting mechanism. The model is published three years later in the General Theory.

6. **Late 1930s:** United States experiences near-zero nominal interest rates. Hoarding increases. The Keynesian model becomes popular with younger American economists.

7. **Mid-1940s through mid-1960s:** The Bretton Woods regime anchors U.S. inflation rates at relatively low levels and constrains monetary policymakers in Europe. The Keynesian model becomes entrenched in academia and among central bankers. Low and stable inflation rates allow for interest rate targeting, but fiscal policy is also seen as a potent stabilization tool.

8. **Late 1960s–1980:** Major currencies begin to sharply depreciate against gold. Fiat money regimes allow for high and variable inflation rates. Interest rate targeting becomes less effective. Quantity theoretic approaches to monetary economics regain popularity. Fiscal restraint fails to slow inflation. Friedman (1968) and Phelps (1967) develop natural rate models where changes in inflation expectations shift the Phillips curve.

9. **Early 1980s:** Tight control of monetary aggregates reduces inflation and output in the United States. Monetary policy now viewed as more powerful that fiscal policy (which had been expansionary during this period). Velocity becomes unstable as inflation expectations fall sharply. When inflation stabilizes at a low but positive rate, interest rate targeting once again becomes highly effective. Policymakers now show greater awareness of the distinction between real and nominal rates (as in the Taylor rule).

10. **Mid-1980s through 2008:** After unemployment begins to fall back toward the natural rate during the mid-1980s, all the pieces are in place for the new Keynesian policy revolution. Because natural rate models imply that money doesn't impact output in the long run, central bankers now move toward inflation targeting. Fiscal policy is no longer

widely used as a stabilization tool. With commodities no longer comprising a large share of GDP, broad price indices become highly sticky and the monetary transmission mechanism is now assumed to run from monetary policy to output to inflation, rather than from policy to inflation to output, as Fisher (and Friedman) had assumed.

There is one anomaly in the preceding account. Liquidity traps shouldn't happen in an unconstrained fiat money regime. Yet just such a situation was widely perceived to have developed in Japan during the late 1990s and early 2000s, and more recently in the United States. One explanation is that despite their fiat money regime, the Bank of Japan was in fact constrained by the fear that sharp depreciation of the yen would trigger retaliation from the United States.[23]

I believe that there is a much simpler explanation: Japan did not experience a liquidity trap but was instead successful at maintaining an inflation target of roughly 0 to –1 percent per annum. The term "trap" implies a predicament that one tries but fails to escape. But did they really try? Twice during the past decade, the Bank of Japan tightened monetary policy as the (core) inflation rate was approaching zero, *from below.*[24] In each case, the tightening successfully prevented Japan from achieving positive inflation, and a moderate deflation resumed. Japanese central bankers seem to have successfully achieved low but stable rates of deflation. Despite their public protestations, their actions provide no evidence that they are dissatisfied with this result. Inflation only began rising in 2013, right after a new government enacted a 2 percent inflation target.

A more interesting question is, why have so many contemporary economists seemed willing to accept the Bank of Japan's (BOJ) statements at face value? Much of the criticism that did occur was directed at the BOJ's failure to prevent Japan from slipping into a liquidity trap in the first place, not its policy once nominal rates hit zero. There seems to have been surprisingly wide acceptance of the notion that a central bank operating under a fiat-money regime might actually have difficulty debasing its currency. A greater knowledge

---

23. McKinnon (2000) made a similar argument.

24. This occurred in 2000 and again in 2006. In 2006 the Japanese core rate was roughly zero, but if they had excluded the fast-rising energy prices (as in the United States), it would still have been in negative territory (at roughly –0.4 percent).

of monetary history, and particularly of how the "price of money" approach was successfully utilized by FDR in 1933, might have led to more skepticism about the BOJ claims of impotence. Perhaps it is time to reread John Locke.

A similar misconception occurred in the United States during late 2008. Interestingly, the perception that monetary policy had become ineffective was not shared by the Fed. Indeed, the Fed was so worried about the inflationary implications of their massive liquidity injections that they began paying interest on reserves for the first time in American history in early October 2008. The Fed conceded that the action was aimed at preventing interest rates from falling below their target. The policy continues to this day. In another paper (2009) I pointed out that if the Fed actually wanted a more expansionary monetary policy, they would have paid a negative interest rate on reserves (i.e., charge a penalty rate on excess reserves). Lars Svensson persuaded the Swedish Riksbank to adopt this sort of policy a few months later.

When Ben Bernanke was asked in 2009 why the Fed didn't aim for a higher inflation target, he didn't claim the Fed was unable to generate higher inflation but rather argued that it would be undesirable. Indeed, it would have been exceedingly odd for Mr. Bernanke to claim the Fed was powerless at the zero rate bound, as he had frequently ridiculed that idea when it was offered as an excuse for the Bank of Japan's passivity in the late 1990s. Oddly, there seems to have been a fairly widespread misunderstanding of this point, particularly among economists who have not kept up with the latest development in monetary economics. This is not to say that all was well with monetary policy in the current recession. I have been a relentless critic of Fed policy since 2008, arguing that the Fed moved far too slowly and timidly in September 2008, when it became clear the economy was deteriorating rapidly. Indeed, they failed to take any steps at the FOMC[25] meeting soon after Lehman failed (i.e., the Fed funds target remained at 2 percent), despite the fact that all sorts of financial market indicators were signaling that policy was far too tight.

Classical Liberalism, Modern Liberalism, and Neoliberalism

We have seen that new Keynesian macroeconomics is a synthesis of classical (or monetarist) ideas and older versions of Keynesianism and also how

---

25. Federal Open Market Committee.

the synthesis had roots in a reappraisal of U.S. policy during the early 1930s. Here I would like to suggest that a similar dialectic occurred in the broader field of economic policymaking.

Long before the onset of the Great Depression, the laissez-faire approach to economic policy had begun to go out of style. By the late nineteenth century, there was a growing perception that unfettered capitalism led to unjust concentrations of power and extreme income inequality. But the Great Depression undoubtedly accelerated the trend toward progressive policy reforms, as capitalism began to be seen as not just an unfair system, but also as a system that simply *didn't work very well*.

By the middle of the twentieth century, statist economic models were accepted in one form or another by virtually all governments, both right and left wing. The most characteristic features of statism are high levels of regulation (particularly limits on price competition and market entry) as well as extremely high marginal tax rates on the wealthy. Outside of the United States, there was also widespread government ownership of large-scale enterprises.

In addition to statism, the twentieth century also saw a pronounced movement toward egalitarianism in many countries, as evidenced by the large increase in the share of national income devoted to social programs. If classical liberalism is seen as laissez-faire, and modern liberalism (social democracy in Europe) incorporates both statism and egalitarianism, then perhaps the neoliberal revolution of the past thirty years can be seen as a synthesis of these two earlier forms of liberalism, embracing egalitarianism but largely rejecting statist economic models. Surprisingly, the Great Depression, and more specifically the two key policy failures of 1932–1933 discussed above, played essentially the same role in the neoliberal revolution in economic policymaking as it did in the new Keynesian revolution in monetary policymaking.

Recall that the constraints of the gold standard led many to erroneously conclude that conventional monetary tools were ineffective, and then, just as currency devaluation was about to generate a rapid recovery in the United States, its expansionary effect was counteracted by the NIRA's high wage policy. These two policy failures led to the mistaken impression that the market was not a very effective way of allocating resources. Governments of all political stripes leapt at the opportunity to take on much greater powers, and at least initially, many of these statist models seemed to perform fairly well. By the late 1970s, however, statist economies seemed to be underperforming, both in comparison to other, less statist policy regimes, and/or in comparison to their own past growth rates. Tentative moves toward market reforms began in such disparate locations as Britain, Chile, and China.

It is important to avoid focusing too much on the specific local factors behind the initial experiments in neoliberalism. By the late 1980s, those initial reforms seemed to be paying off and neoliberalism became a worldwide phenomenon, with privatization, deregulation, and sharp cuts in marginal income tax rates occurring in virtually all the major economies. As with the earlier adoption of statist models, neoliberalism was essentially a nonpartisan phenomenon, with local conditions affecting only the magnitude of the changes, not the direction. And as with new Keynesianism, the neoliberal revolution in policymaking is largely attributable to a broader reevaluation of the "lessons" of the Great Depression. Once it became apparent to most economists that the Great Depression was an anomaly of some sort, they reverted to the classical view that, for most purposes, the market is better at allocating resources than the state.

Liberals did not give up on the dream of egalitarianism, but now looked for a "third way" between laissez-faire and socialism. The relatively market-oriented Nordic countries, and to a lesser extent, the smaller Anglo-Saxon economies,[26] seemed to offer models that combined a vigorous private sector and an extensive social welfare state. Even the sharp cuts in marginal tax rates for the rich, which at first glance seemed anti-egalitarian, were actually directed at reducing the government's role in the allocation of resources. These cuts were combined with a reduction in tax preferences, which insured that the rich continued to pay a substantial portion of the cost of maintaining the still-extensive welfare states.[27] By the end of the twentieth century, the dominant economic model was probably something like the British neoliberal regime introduced by Thatcher and refined by Tony Blair.

Today, most economists believe that the Great Depression did not show the folly of relying on free markets (with the possible exception of banking) but

---

26. Britain, Ireland, Canada, Australia, and New Zealand.

27. The shift in the United States from "welfare" to the earned income tax credit is another example. The government hasn't cut spending on the poor, but now acts with more awareness of the importance of (labor) market incentives.

rather the need to avoid deflationary monetary policies. With the advantage of hindsight, it now seems clear that Friedman and Schwartz's reconsideration of the causes of the Great Depression contributed not just to the renewed respect for monetarism, but more generally to the increased prestige of free market economics. During the 1960s and 1970s researchers from the "Chicago school" emphasized the power of markets, and by the 1980s and 1990s this research led to numerous Nobel prizes. Nevertheless, it is important not to overstate the conservative nature of neoliberalism. Earlier, we saw that new Keynesianism combined ideas from both sides of the 1960s monetarist–Keynesian debate. Similarly, neoliberalism incorporates ideas from both sides of the age-old struggle between capitalism and socialism.

In 1989, Temin (p. 136) argued that capitalism thrives during periods of economic stability, and socialism advances during periods of instability. With the benefit of nearly two decades of neoliberal policy reforms, it now appears that the impact of economic turmoil also depends on the prevailing intellectual climate. When socialist models are popular, an economic crisis leads to calls for statist economic "reforms." But when neoliberalism is popular, economic problems in a single country often lead to calls for market "reforms."

In the previous several sections we saw how the NIRA slowed the recovery and contributed to the subsequent development of Keynesian, and then new Keynesian, monetary theory. Now we can see that it also contributed to vastly more consequential developments in modern liberalism and neoliberalism. To summarize, both traditional Keynesianism and modern liberalism were partially founded on a misreading of the Great Depression. The flaws in these ideologies led to policy errors during the postwar period, which in turn led to a reconsideration of some older, more right-wing ideologies during the 1970s. Finally, in the 1980s, a new synthesis emerged that incorporated the "best of each" approach. In macroeconomics, the synthesis is called "new Keynesianism." In the broader field of economic policymaking, it is often termed "neoliberalism."

It is probably too soon to know whether the current crisis will cause the sort of leftward shift in policymaking that we saw during the Depression. In my view, this crisis has been misdiagnosed in a very similar way to the Great Depression. As in the 1930s, the current recession was associated with a severe drop in nominal spending (relative to trend), caused by excessively tight money. Of course, the mainstream view is that the recession was caused by a financial crisis, and that monetary policy was actually relatively expansionary.

This certainly puts me in the minority, but I would point to two occasions where problems once viewed as nonmonetary eventually came to be recognized as monetary. The first was obviously the Great Depression itself, which at the time was thought to be caused by the failure of the domestic and international financial system, but is now widely attributed to the failure of monetary policy to keep nominal GDP from falling in half. Similarly, the onset of the great inflation of the 1960s and 1970s was originally attributed to deficit spending and powerful unions. In fact, the budget deficits in the United States were not particularly large and the great inflation is now generally viewed as being caused by a failure of monetary policy. That doesn't make my current view correct, but there is certainly precedence for the majority of pundits initially focusing on the symptoms of falling nominal GDP, such as banking distress, and ignoring the deeper monetary causes.

12

What Caused the Great Depression?

Yet it is also true that small events at times have large consequences,
that there are such things as chain reactions and cumulative forces.
. . . Because no great strength would be required to hold back
the rock that starts a landslide, it does not follow that the landslide
will not be of major proportions.
—Milton Friedman and A. Schwartz (1963a, p. 419)

IN THE FIRST ten chapters, I showed how gold and labor market shocks destabilized output during the 1930s. Then, we examined how this narrative could shed new light on the development of monetary thought both during and after the Great Depression. In this final chapter, we will consider two fundamental questions: Does all of this analysis shed any new light on the *root causes* of the Depression, and what does it tell us about previous economic histories of the Depression?

Economic Theory, Macro History, and Financial History

In the introductory chapter, I suggested that the persuasiveness of any economic analysis was at least partly related to its "coherence"—that is, its ability to make sense of a number of widely disparate phenomena under a single conceptual framework. It may be useful to begin with a brief summary of how much we can explain with the gold shock/wage shock analytical framework. Then, in "Policy Counterfactuals and the 'Root Causes' of the Depression," we can compare these findings with some previous explanations of the Great Depression.

The gold market approach to the price level can offer a coherent analytical framework on three different levels: theory, macro history, and financial history. At a theoretical level, a gold market approach to price level determination under a gold standard makes sense. Basic economic theory suggests that commodity values are determined by supply and demand, and in the United States the price level was simply the (inverse of the) value of gold throughout most of the 1920s and 1930s. And even during 1933, prices were varying with changing expectations of where gold would be pegged in 1934.

At the level of macro history, the preceding narrative offers a coherent explanation for all of the major price level movements of the 1930s. The initial decline in prices after 1929 was associated with a dramatic increase in the world gold reserve ratio. The banking panics that began in late 1930 led to an increase in the real demand for currency, which then triggered further increases in the demand for monetary gold. The gold market approach becomes even more useful during the period from mid-1931 to early 1933, when public and private gold hoarding associated with devaluation fears again put downward pressure on the world price level.

The gold market approach is especially well suited for explaining the extraordinary changes in the price level that began after the dollar was allowed to float in April 1933, and the dollar price of gold began to be used as an instrument of monetary policy. After the dollar–gold peg was restored in January 1934, wholesale price inflation slowed abruptly. When massive gold dishoarding began in late 1936, prices again began rising rapidly. This reversed after the gold panic ended in mid-1937. By late 1937, devaluation fears led to a renewal of private gold hoarding, and prices fell just as rapidly as they had risen over the previous twelve months.

This analytical framework can also account for many of the financial market responses to gold market disturbances during the Depression. In some cases, the linkages are only suggestive, such as when the stock market crashed at roughly the same time as the major central banks began increasing their gold reserve ratios. But, as time went by, the linkages became more and more obvious. During the exchange rate crises of the early 1930s, fears of devaluation and/or increases in private gold hoarding were associated with declining equity prices. Of course, this approach doesn't resolve all of the monetary puzzles from this period. More research needs to be done to explain why markets seemed to respond more bearishly to vague and uncertain fears of future devaluation than to expectations of imminent devaluation.

During the period of dollar depreciation, the linkages between the gold market, stock market, and commodity markets became especially close, and these linkages provide strong support for the hypothesis that gold market shocks were driving price level changes (and output changes as well). After the dollar–gold peg was restored in early 1934, the financial markets continued to be buffeted by gold hoarding, dishoarding, and/or changing expectations of the future exchange rate. On numerous occasions the gold market was the lead story in the financial press's coverage of equity and commodity markets. Like a canary in a coal mine, these highly sensitive markets often provided an early indication of how gold market disturbances would eventually impact nominal spending and the overall price level.

The sharp decrease in nominal spending during 1929–1933, and again during 1937–1938, can explain much of the Depression, but aggregate demand shocks cannot account for all output movements during the 1930s. After mid-1933, labor market disturbances also began to have an important impact on output. And once again, the labor market approach to output offers a coherent analytical framework at three levels—theory, macro history, and financial history.

Virtually any neoclassical labor market model would predict that the announcement of a mandated 22 percent wage increase would reduce output sharply. And output did fall significantly after July 1933, particularly when considered against the output path that would have been expected from the highly expansionary monetary policy during 1933. The stock market also fell sharply on the news. A similar, but much milder, wage shock hit the U.S. economy during the spring of 1934.

By 1937, nominal wages were again rising at a brisk rate and once again the increase seems tied to federal labor legislation (in this case the Wagner Act). As in 1933, output growth fell below the rate expected to occur during a period of rising prices and economic slack. And when prices stopped rising and turned downward in late 1937, real wages rose sharply and industrial production plummeted. Even in the final stages of the recovery (1938–41) there were two six-month periods when increases in the minimum wage rate led to a temporary pause in the growth of industrial production.

Many of the ideas in this book have been discussed in previous accounts of the Great Depression. Nevertheless, I would argue that much of this account is novel, in the sense that it is the first book to provide an explanation of all of the high-frequency output fluctuations in the United States during the 1930s. Here are just a few of the events that previous studies have not been able to adequately explain, but which are at least partially accounted for in the preceding narrative:

1. Why the onset of the Depression occurred in late 1929.
2. The role of monetary policy in the 1929 stock market crash.
3. How to partition blame among the central banks for the onset of the Depression.
4. Why output leveled off in early 1931.
5. The impact of private gold hoarding during 1931–1932.
6. Why industrial production rose 57 percent between March and July 1933 and then declined over the following two years.
7. How the 1933 gold buying program worked.
8. Why output declined in the summer of 1934.
9. Why inflation suddenly accelerated in late 1936, and why prices fell sharply in late 1937.
10. Why the recovery stalled in late 1938, and again in late 1939.
11. Why the discount rate increases of 1931, as well as the reserve requirement increases of 1936–1937, had little impact on financial markets.
12. Why movements in the Dow were strongly correlated with the price of German Young Plan bonds (YPBs) during 1931–1932, but not otherwise.

This study also has many other implications for macroeconomic theory, some of which will be explored later in this chapter. These include:

1. A critique of the monetarist view of policy lags.
2. A critique of new Keynesian monetary theory.
3. A new view of the transmission mechanism for gold market shocks.
4. A new interpretation of liquidity traps under a gold standard.

Policy Counterfactuals and the
"Root Causes" of the Depression

Even with all of the insights in the previous eleven chapters, it is not clear that we have identified a "root cause" of the Great Depression. One would like an explanation that is rooted so deeply in the interwar political and economic systems that in retrospect, the Depression seems almost inevitable. But we would also like an explanation that would not have been obvious to the financial markets in mid-1929. This is not easy to do. The Depression was probably an endogenous response to preexisting weaknesses in the world economy rather than simply the result of an exogenous shock, such as a natural disaster. But if so, then any set of observable root causes would seem to violate the efficient market hypothesis. After all, if we can now see the failures that made a Depression inevitable, then why couldn't the markets? One answer is that the political system is so complex that its workings become apparent only in retrospect.

We may be able to make a little more progress if we focus at the level of policy counterfactuals, which are the causality questions of most interest to economic historians. To begin framing the options, I will briefly digress and consider an even greater disaster that occurred only a few years after the Depression, World War II.

Britain, and later America, entered World War I on the side of the French. As a result of these interventions, the most powerful country in Europe emerged from World War I a defeated, impoverished, and embittered nation. In reaction to the horrors of the war, Britain became somewhat pacifist and the United States moved toward isolationism. The resulting interwar balance of power was highly unstable with no effective counterweight to a resurgent Germany. If this characterization of interwar diplomacy is roughly correct, then what can we say about the policy errors that led to World War II? I would argue that there are two ways to approach this question, which closely parallel the two primary approaches that others have used to explain the Great Depression.

One historical counterfactual would be to assume that the United States stayed out of World War I, and that Germany eventually won the war. (Or, if that weren't sufficient for a German victory, assume that both the United States and Britain stayed out of the war.) In many respects, this outcome might have been undesirable, but it is also hard to see how a German victory would have allowed for the rise of Nazism and the associated horrors of World War II. At the other end of the spectrum, consider a policy counterfactual that had both Britain and America staying heavily involved in post–World War I European affairs through a NATO-type alliance. This might have preserved a stable balance of power where the victorious allies maintained military superiority over the defeated Germans.

This is not to suggest that either of these counterfactuals would have been something that British or America leaders could have easily selected; the domestic political obstacles would have been formidable, if not insurmountable. Rather, I would like to suggest that these two counterfactuals closely parallel the two primary policy alternatives that have been suggested as ways of avoiding the Great Depression.

Both monetarists and Keynesians have argued that American monetary policymakers were too passive during the 1930s and should have moved more aggressively to boost aggregate demand. To be sure, there are important differences in emphasis. Some Keynesians had doubts about how much the Fed could do on its own and suggested that dollar devaluation should have come even earlier. In contrast, Friedman and Schwartz thought the Fed could have done much more, even under the constraints of the international gold standard.

Another two schools of thought attribute the Depression to policy errors that occurred in the decade prior to the stock market crash of 1929. Many French and Austrian economists saw policy as being too interventionist, and more specifically too expansionary, during the 1920s. This raised the price level and lowered the value of gold below its long-run equilibrium value. They argued that the appropriate policy during the 1920s would have been to allow the price level to gradually fall back to its prewar level. Mundell and Johnson took a slightly different approach. While they agreed that the undervaluation of gold was the root cause of the Great Depression, they opposed deflationary monetary policies, instead arguing that a post–World War I adjustment in currency pegs would have been a less painful way of restoring gold to its prewar purchasing power.

At the most basic level, the relatively high price level of 1920–1929 can be seen as resulting from interventionist monetary policies that moved away from the traditions of the classical gold standard. And the gold hoarding and defla-

tion of the early 1930s represents a reversion to those more passive prewar policies. Thus, the monetarist and Keynesian view is essentially that the Depression
was caused by a failure of monetary policymakers to maintain the interventionist policies pursued during the preceding decade, whereas the Austrians
see those very same policies as being the root cause of the Depression. But
the tragedy of the Depression is not necessarily attributable to the failure of
either interventionism or laissez-faire. Instead, it is best viewed as the outcome
of a world moving toward "modern liberalism" but still vacillating between
intervention and passivity.

There are clear analogies between these monetary policy counterfactuals,
and the preceding discussion of British and American foreign policy counterfactuals between the two world wars. Britain, and especially America, needed
to adopt and maintain either an isolationist policy or an interventionist policy,
but at all costs avoid oscillating between the two policies. Similarly, the switch
from the interventionist (high price level) policies of the 1920s to the passive
(low price level) policies of the 1930s led to the deflation of 1929–1933. If there
is a root cause to the Great Depression, it lies somewhere in the painful birth
of the modern world, the difficulty that societies had in letting go of their
emotional attachment to the "barbarous relic," and moving to a more mature,
and interventionist, monetary policy regime.

A sharp deflationary shock at the end of World War I (possibly supple-
mented with currency devaluation) would have caused short-term pain but
would have been vastly superior to a monetary regime that seemed to promise
policy coordination and macroeconomic stabilization to the public, and then
failed to deliver on that promise. Currency devaluation alone might have
worked in 1920, or 1922, but only if accompanied by a policy to prevent short-
term inflation. Otherwise, gold would have quickly become undervalued
again—setting up the disastrous events of the late 1920s, which occurred as
European central banks rebuilt their gold stocks.

Any policy to address gold undervaluation in the early 1920s would have
required either extraordinary activism on the part of the Fed, or international
coordination. Of course, if central banks were capable of such farsighted
behavior in 1920, then they presumably would not have behaved so incom-
petently after 1929. Temin is probably right that even had the interwar gold
standard been relatively well managed, its eventual demise was both inevitable

and desirable. But he may have underestimated the extent to which almost *any* alternative scenario for that collapse would have been vastly superior to the events of 1931–1936. It is difficult to think of any plausible economic policy path for the 1920s that would not have produced a better outcome.

There is also the question of how best to evaluate the decisions made by the relevant political leaders, particularly Presidents Herbert Hoover and Franklin D. Roosevelt (FDR). And this may be even more difficult than policy counterfactuals. Consider my argument that Roosevelt's New Deal policies delayed recovery by as much as seven years. Surely this implies Roosevelt was an ineffective president! But how much of what happened was the result of individual discretion, and how much reflected the powerful currents of history? Capitalism was widely discredited by 1932. During the 1932 campaign, even Hoover was discussing the need for a program like the National Industrial Recovery Act (NIRA)—and without the policy being accompanied by currency depreciation.[1] Indeed, if one were looking for an example of Roosevelt going against the conventional wisdom, the bold move to devalue the dollar would seem a much better bet than the rest of the New Deal. Thus, his most "discretionary" policy also turned out to be his most effective.

It is interesting to speculate how differently things might have turned out had FDR avoided the NIRA and instead relied solely on expansionary monetary (and perhaps fiscal) policy. If the analysis in Chapter 6 is correct, the United States should have almost fully recovered from the Depression by late 1934. This would have been seen as a vindication of the Warren–Fisher approach to macroeconomics, the idea that free market capitalism is fundamentally sound as long as the monetary authority adjusts the price of gold to offset changes in the price level.

In the preceding narrative I had almost nothing good to say about President Hoover.[2] But this raises another important question, would anyone else elected

---

1. Barber (1985, p. 195) showed that much of the New Deal consisted of the implementation of ideas first developed by the Hoover administration.

2. Hoover supported the Federal Reserve's (Fed's) tight money policy aimed at stopping the Wall Street boom, he signed Smoot-Hawley, supported a sharp income tax increase in 1932, encouraged firms to adopt a high wage policy during the deflation of 1929–1932, and he supported agricultural price supports. Glass-Steagall (which solved the problem of free gold) and the debt moratorium were two policies that reflect well on Hoover.

in 1928 have done much better? Coolidge (the most plausible alternative) was less likely to support Hoover's high wage policy, farm price supports, or protectionism, but it's unlikely that this would have been sufficient to prevent the Depression. On the other hand, given the well-known "butterfly effect" in chaotic systems, it isn't really possible to know for certain how even small policy differences would have changed the course of domestic and international financial crises.

Perhaps the greatest advantage of a President Coolidge would have been that his very passivity might have led other actors (both at home and abroad) to become more active. Although historians have often viewed Hoover as a weak, passive, and ineffective president, he was not seen that way in 1929. Indeed, in some ways, Hoover was the most competent crisis-manager ever to assume the presidency of the United States. During the early 1920s, he saved several hundred thousand Europeans from starvation, showing extraordinary skill in delivering food relief to remote areas such as Russia. Roosevelt once said that no one in America was more qualified to be President than Herbert Hoover. Keynes was very impressed by his behavior at the Versailles conference. Even today it is not clear how much of the Depression can be attributed to Hoover's personal failings, and how much was due to forces beyond his control.

The problems associated with presidential counterfactuals are equally applicable to the analysis of any other important historical figure, such as Federal Reserve Governor Benjamin Strong, or leaders of the various European central banks. The fast-moving and extremely complex events of the interwar period simply do not allow us to resolve the age-old dispute between the "great man" and "deep historical forces" views of history, a debate that may tell us more about historians than it does about history.

There has also been much debate over how much responsibility for the Depression should be apportioned to the Federal Reserve (Fed) and the Bank of France. A good argument could be made for blaming both central banks, either individually or collectively. The Bank of France played the biggest overall role in causing the deflation of 1929–1933 and was notably noncooperative toward international initiatives to economize on gold reserves. The Fed was a bit more cooperative and hoarded less gold but was also much more erratic in its policies. Indeed, the initial downturn of 1929–1930 can be attributed to the failure of the Fed to assist the British in their attempt to rebuild their gold stocks in 1930, as they had in 1927. And, of course, the American banking system was a huge engine of deflation after 1930.

Because monetary policies were so interdependent, I have deliberately tried to avoid judging the merits of every policy action leading up to the Depression. In Chapter 2, I argued that *world* monetary policy was reasonably stable during 1928–1929, and that policy only became contractionary in late 1929. Almost everyone else views policy as being either too tight or too easy during 1928–1929. Surprisingly, I don't disagree that either alternative would have been preferable. The Great Depression was by far the worst depression is U.S. history, almost a "perfect storm" of bad luck and bad policy. Given the mistakes made later, almost any alternative policy is likely to have resulted in a better outcome.

The preceding argument may seem odd to economists used to thinking in linear terms. For instance, if the Depression was caused by a bubble in the economy, then surely a tighter monetary policy would have made the bubble smaller and an easier policy would have made it even worse. Yes, but nominal shocks are not like real shocks; in a sense, they are artificial problems. Policymakers can costlessly offset nominal shocks with monetary policy. An even more spectacular bubble bursting would almost surely have led to offsetting actions by policymakers (international policy coordination, currency adjustment, etc.) or the public (greater wage flexibility). Part of the problem in 1929–1932 is that the contraction was never quite severe enough for U.S. and French policymakers to change course. But the contraction of 1929–1932 (in nominal terms) had to be close to the outer limits of what was politically tolerable. Anything more severe would have triggered a more aggressive policy response.

Almost everyone who reads Friedman and Schwartz comes away with the impression that they viewed Fed policy as too tight in the year before the crash. And there is some basis for that interpretation. But they also offer a more nuanced interpretation of alternatives:

> the Board should not have made itself an "arbiter of security speculation or values" and should have paid no direct attention to the stock market boom. . . . At the same time, it seems to us that the final outcome of following an alternative objective single-mindedly would have been preferable to the actual outcome of seeking to serve both objec-

tives. A vigorous restrictive policy in early 1928 might well have broken the stock market boom without its having to be kept in effect long enough to constitute a serious drag on business in general. (p. 291–92)

Even the Austrians could agree with those sentiments.

Because political systems are so chaotic, it is very difficult to know how policy counterfactuals might have changed history—even more difficult than forecasting ten moves ahead in a game of chess. Once again, a World War II analogy might be helpful. Any reasonable observer would have to concede that the Nazi government of 1933 was about as damaging as one could imagine. If so, then virtually *any* policy counterfactual for the Versailles conference that was dramatic enough to change the course of history would have led to a better (i.e., less bad) outcome in Germany.[3]

The preceding argument is not applicable to very many historical situations, because it is rare that an outcome is about the worst imaginable. This leads to another cautionary observation about the "lessons of history." Either of the two policy counterfactuals for 1928–1929 might have led to a smaller "Great Depression," but in retrospect the undervaluation of gold made some sort of downturn almost inevitable. Had either alternative strategy been followed, and a modest depression resulted, that alternative would have almost certainly received historical censure.[4] History is full of tragedy; one must be careful when drawing lessons from policy failures, as even worse outcomes are generally imaginable.

If the policy counterfactuals approach is problematic, another way of establishing the usefulness of the gold market approach is by seeing how much resonance it has for other times and places. Three decades after the Depression, the world saw a much more benign collapse of a commodity price peg, as the dollar price of gold was allowed to float upward beginning in 1968. And once again policymakers had difficulty adapting to, or even understanding, their new powers; the result was the Great Inflation of 1968–1981. And as with

---

3. That is, policy toward Germany might have been either far more punitive or far more conciliatory.

4. This is not to suggest that I view the two alternatives as equally attractive. The interventionist monetary policies of the Fed and ECB during 1982–2007 seem much superior to the (prewar) classical gold standard.

the Depression-era counterfactuals, the root cause of the Great Inflation can be seen as either the decision to abandon Bretton Woods (specifically, the gold price peg), or alternatively, as the failure to implement inflation targeting once floating rates had been adopted.

One can see many aspects of this narrative repeated in recent events in places like Argentina. The country adopted the dollar peg in the early 1990s as a reaction to its experience with hyperinflation (recall 1920s Europe). And Argentina experienced deflation in the late 1990s and early 2000s as the real value of the dollar rose in the foreign exchange markets (recall the real appreciation of gold after 1929). And Argentina hung onto its dollar peg until the economic pain was so great that a new and more left-wing government decided to devalue its currency and tear up promises that debts would be convertible into dollars (recall FDR revoking ending the gold clause). And the left-wing government moved away from the neoliberal policies that they wrongly thought also contributed to Argentina's problems (recall the NIRA). And the powerful expansionary effects of devaluation helped cover up the drag on the economy that normally would have resulted from the adoption of more statist policies (recall the U.S. recovery after 1933). This point is often overlooked; if depressions do encourage statist policy interventions, then deflationary policies may impose costs that are much larger that those predicted by natural rate models of the business cycle.[5] Supply and demand shocks are treated as being independent in our textbooks but are entangled in the real world. Thus, the cost of demand shocks may exceed a temporary decline in output.

If we move back in time we can find other events that can also be illuminated by the gold market approach. In Chapter 2, we saw how the return to the gold standard by France and other countries led to an increase in the demand for monetary gold, which put downward pressure on the world price level during the late 1920s and early 1930s. A similar pattern occurred in the 1870s, when the United States and several European powers adopted the gold standard, and the resulting increase in the demand for gold led to deflation.

---

5. The extraordinarily large and wasteful public works expenditures undertaken during the recent Japanese deflation are another example of this phenomenon. The most dramatic example of nominal shocks leading to harmful public policies is World War II, which might have been avoided had the Great Depression not occurred.

We also saw that fears of dollar devaluation during 1931–1933 and 1937–1938 increased private gold hoarding and reduced prices. Once again, there was a strikingly similar pattern during the early to mid-1890s, when there was agitation in the United States for a bimetallic monetary regime (which would have effectively devalued the dollar). As in the 1930s, the loss of confidence in the U.S. dollar led to gold hoarding and falling price levels. Recovery began only after confidence in the dollar was restored by the defeat of William Jennings Bryan in the election of 1896.[6] But had Bryan won and instituted bimetallism, the Great Depression might never have happened.

Broader Implications for Macroeconomic Analysis

Most debates about economic history are actually debates about current economic theories and policies. If the preceding study is to have lasting value, it will be to the extent that it can illuminate unresolved money/macro issues in other historical periods, including the present.

Today, the overwhelming majority of macroeconomists prefer using interest rates as both an indicator and an instrument of monetary policy. But there have always been dissenters from this Keynesian tradition. Friedman and Schwartz showed that nominal interest rates provided a highly misleading indicator of monetary policy during the Great Depression, and other periods as well.[7] Despite the fact that interest rates fell almost continuously from October 1929 to October 1930, monetary policy was actually contractionary, as the monetary aggregates fell slightly. The news from this study is even worse for the Keynesians. Even Friedman and Schwartz underestimated the extent to which monetary policy tightened after October 1929, which was much more noticeable in the sharp increase in the world gold ratio than in the modest decrease in the growth rate of the broader U.S. monetary aggregates.

If we look at monetary policy during 1933, we see a similar pattern. During the period of dollar depreciation, little change took place in nominal interest

---

6. The discovery of gold in the Traansvale and the cyanide process for mining gold also helped to end the deflation.

7. It is true that *ex post* real interest rates were very high, but in Chapter 6 we saw evidence that *ex ante* rates were also quite low during the 1930s.

rates and the money supply. In contrast, the 69 percent increase in the price of gold shows policy to have been highly expansionary. The devaluation of the dollar almost certainly raised expectations of future monetary growth, and it was this change in expectations that caused such a rapid increase in prices and output. Johnson (1997, pp. 107–08) provided another good example of how nominal interest rates can be a misleading indicator of monetary policy. He noted that France's extraordinarily tight monetary policy of 1928–1931 was accompanied by low interest rates, and then suggested that the French policy of sterilizing reserves "forced other countries to react to France's spontaneous capital inflow as though it were *induced* by high long- or short-term interest rates."

We have seen how the gold market approach to monetary analysis can offer insights that are easily overlooked when utilizing the interest rate indicator, as in modern IS-LM analysis. Some of these problems can be remedied by employing a dynamic IS-LM model featuring rational expectations. But price stickiness is also a central feature of IS-LM analysis, and if the Alchian–Klein conjecture discussed in Chapter 5 is correct, then the price level of interest to macroeconomists is much less sticky than it appears to be.

Mankiw (2000, p. 299) observed that IS-LM analysis cannot account for the first two years of the Great Depression because the real money supply actually increased during this period. He could have made an analogous observation about the early stages of the recovery in 1933. As we have seen, part of this anomaly can be explained in forward-looking models where current policy impacts the expected future money supply. But there is a cost to tacking expectations onto an IS-LM model, as King (1993) pointed out that a contractionary monetary policy could easily shift the IS curve by more than the LM curve, resulting in lower interest rates (real and nominal).

Part of the increase in real money balances during 1929–1931 may also reflect the greater sensitivity of interwar price indices to demand shocks. Indeed, Alchian and Klein's conjecture suggests that real balances may have risen by even more than Mankiw suspected, as the wholesale price index (WPI) and equity prices fell much more rapidly than the cost of living. Here I would like to suggest that perhaps the problem may not lie in the poor quality interwar price indices but rather in poor quality modern indices, and a flawed IS-LM model that assumes more price stickiness than actually exists. A very good example occurred during the recent recession, when almost everyone believes that housing prices were plummeting in America. Yet official statistics show housing costs (which are 39 percent of the core consumer price index (CPI)) actually rose modestly from mid-2008 to mid-2009.

During the interwar years, periods of sharp deflation were invariably associated with falling output, and not surprisingly, there were numerous business cycle models that emphasized the non-neutrality of price level changes. After World War II, these models fell out of favor, probably for the simple reason that inflation became much less procyclical. In Chapter 13, we will see that change reflected two factors. After the war, price indices became much more inertial as their composition shifted away from flexible price commodities and toward services and highly finished goods.[8] And as macroeconomic policy-makers have become more effective at stabilizing demand, supply shocks have become a relatively more important source of output variability. In this environment, models that assumed a money → output → inflation transmission mechanism superseded the interwar models that assumed a money → price level → output mechanism.

Almost anyone who studies the rapid inflation of 1933–1934 will have difficulty maintaining any confidence in the output-inflation transmission mechanism assumed in most NAIRU[9] models.[10] Bernanke and Parkinson note that:

> Theory suggests instead [in contrast to NAIRU] that inflation will be determined by current and expected money supply and demand. Inflation surprises . . . may then have effects on employment. That is, it is inflation rather than employment that should be the independent variable. (1989, p. 212)

This was also Irving Fisher's view.

If I am correct about the superiority of the interwar approach to the monetary transmission mechanism, then as the flaws in the IS-LM approach become more apparent one would expect a revival of interest in models incorporating

---

8. Hanes (1996) shows that this is due to the more comprehensive coverage of modern price indices, as well as a change in the share of highly finished goods in the overall economy.

9. Non Accelerating Inflation Rate of Unemployment

10. Romer (1999) tries to uphold the traditional Keynesian view that the direction of causation runs from output to prices. She argues that although output was low, rapid economic growth caused prices to rise during the recovery of 1933–1941.

asset prices. And this backlash may already be starting. One piece of evidence against the sticky-price IS-LM approach comes from a study of VAR models by Faust, Swanson, and Wright (2004, p. 1107) that rejects "any identification that insists on a monetary shock having exactly zero [price level] effect contemporaneously."

If prices respond strongly to demand shocks, then that also opens up a broad range of price level prediction error models. Gray and Spenser (1990) showed that if one accounts for supply shocks, then this sort of model performs well using postwar data. One type of price prediction error model is the wage-contracting model, which predicts countercyclical real wage movements in response to demand shocks. A recent study by Christiano, Eichenbaum, and Evans (2005, p. 2) suggests that the "critical nominal friction . . . is wage contracts, not price contracts."

The preceding line of analysis also opens the door to those who want to put money back into monetary models. Leeper and Roush (2003) show that in VAR models that include money, inflation is much more responsive to monetary policy shocks than in VAR models that omit money. The fact that money might be superior to interest rates as a policy indicator is good news for monetarists, but the fact that prices seemed to respond quickly to policy shocks also seems to contradict the traditional monetarist focus on policy lags. I say "seems" because we are dealing with a distributed lag, and monetarists have never denied that policy can have *some* effect right away. But I think Mankiw (2000, p. 384) expresses the consensus view when he suggests that "a change in monetary policy is thought not to affect economic activity until about six months after it is made." If one looks at monetarist analyses of specific episodes in American history, it is difficult to reconcile their implicit assumptions about policy lags with the narrative that I have presented in Chapters 2 through 10.[11]

Consider the period from March to July 1933, when price rose briskly and industrial production soared by 57 percent. During the twelve-month pe-

---

11. Schwartz (1981, p. 44n) observed that "a quick adjustment of prices does not preclude a long distributed lag adjustment. A partial adjustment that shows up quickly is not equivalent to the full adjustment of prices." Yes, but this doesn't get Friedman and Schwartz off the hook. There is no explanation for why some shocks (like dollar devaluation and gold hoarding) seem to have huge immediate effects, while others (the tight money policy of 1928, the open market purchases (OMPs) of 1932, and the reserve requirement changes of 1936–1937), do not.

riod preceding that boom, the monetary aggregates had fallen sharply in the United States. Using conventional monetarist analysis, one might have expected a weak economy during the spring and summer of 1933, not the most rapid growth in American history. Here I should emphasize that not just my analysis of 1933, but the entire narrative in Chapters 2 through 10 hinges on monetary policy *strongly* impacting both prices and output almost immediately. If I am wrong, if policy has little or no immediate impact, then this entire narrative is essentially worthless.

I have found repeated links between policy shocks and contemporaneous movements in financial market prices, commodity prices, the WPI, and monthly industrial production. We know that all of these variables (with the possible exception of the policy shocks that I tried to identify) were highly correlated during the Depression. It makes no sense to argue, for instance, that monetary policy shocks had an immediate impact on stock and commodity prices but only impacted the WPI and industrial production with a long and variable lag. The series are simply too closely entangled. I suppose one could argue that the increased gold ratio of 1929–1930 or the gold hoarding of late 1931, early 1932, and late 1937 depressed the economy with a long lag, or that the dishoarding of 1936 and the devaluation of 1933 raised prices and output with a long lag. But then, when was the impact? And why were the stock and commodity price movements that accompanied these shocks so closely linked to movements in broader price and output indices?

One important lesson from this research is that *things happen for a reason*. That is, the capitalist system is fairly stable when not disturbed by monetary shocks or other gross policy errors.[12] If the IS-LM model fails to explain the onset of the Depression, the solution is, not to look for mysterious forces such as "animal spirits" or "consumer sentiment"—rather, the solution is to rethink one's model and look at other policy indicators.

If the gold market approach undercuts some traditional Keynesian and monetarist beliefs, does it then support those researchers who attribute the Great Contraction to flaws in the international gold standard? In some respects, it does. But there are also some important differences between the gold

---

12. The bubble of 2000 might seem to contradict this assumption. But my preferred monetary policy target is nominal GDP, and that indicator showed policy was still excessively procyclical during 1998–2003. And even so, the recession was fairly mild.

market approach developed here and those earlier studies, especially in the way that I view the role of gold. Most fundamentally, the model introduced in Chapter 1 and developed in Chapter 13 is much more than a fixed exchange rate model. For instance, in the paper where Svensson (2003a) argued that currency depreciation offered Japan a foolproof escape from deflation, he also noted that if all major countries were simultaneously mired in a liquidity trap, then a coordinated policy of currency depreciation would not offer an escape. This is true for a fiat regime, but under a gold standard all countries can simultaneously depreciate against gold, and hence can simultaneously increase their expected future money supplies. Recall that the U.S. devaluation of 1933 was able to provide an immediate boost to the U.S. economy, without any "beggar-thy-neighbor" improvement in the U.S. trade balance.

Most open economy models of the Depression view the gold standard as a *constraint*, as something that restricts policy options. While these models see the international gold market as a mechanism for the transmission of monetary shocks, they generally continue to view policy in terms of domestic money supplies and interest rates.[13] The gold market approach takes a much more unified view of the international gold market. Increased demand for gold by any central bank, or by private hoarders, almost immediately increases the real value of gold in all countries. It is not a question of whether or not purchasing power parity holds in the short run; rather, it is a question of policy expectations. It doesn't much matter if the money supply adjusts immediately in country A and six months later in country B. The decisive factor in both countries is what happens to the future expected money supply. Any gold market shock, occurring anywhere in the world, can immediately impact the expected future money supply in all countries, as well as the *current* prices of equities and commodities.

The preceding narrative shows that, when looking at policy under a gold standard, *one needs to take gold seriously*. In our current environment, where Federal Reserve notes are the medium of account, we tend to forget that interwar Americans deliberately choose gold as their medium of account. There

---

13. One notable exception is Glasner (1989, p. 111). Glasner's approach is similar to my own, although he fails to completely reconcile the gold market and monetary approaches to price level determination. Glasner's work is an excellent application of the "new monetary economics" developed in the 1980s.

was widespread discussion of proposals to abandon the gold standard and have the Fed target the price level, but the Goldsborough bill was repeatedly rejected, even during the worst of the Depression. Yet, economic historians often treat gold as merely an unfortunate impediment, which policymakers might or might not have been able to work around when there were adverse demand shocks. This is imposing a modern (fiat money) perspective on a world that looked at things quite differently.[14]

By analogy, consider two ways of forecasting the effects of a severe hurricane that decimates oil rigs in the Gulf of Mexico. One approach would be to first consider whether the U.S. government's emergency crude oil reserve would be sufficient to cover the lost production until repairs are made; and if so, to assume no likely impact on oil prices. A more straightforward approach would be to assume that the government was reluctant to dip into emergency reserves and begin the analysis by assuming that the world supply of crude would decline over the next few months. In most cases, the second approach will yield more accurate price forecasts.

Of course, it is an open question as to whether the preceding analogy is relevant to the interwar gold market. In a sense, answering that question is what this book has been all about. When there were shocks to the interwar supply and demand for gold in one area, should one first examine whether a given country has enough policy flexibility to offset that shock? Or should one begin the analysis with a straightforward examination of the likely impact of the local gold market shock on the worldwide purchasing power of gold? It is now clear that the financial markets took the second view, even in countries (such as the United States) that theoretically had sufficient policy flexibility to offset many of those gold shocks. Financial markets in the United States responded very negatively to increases in the demand for gold, anywhere in the world, and very positively to decreases in gold demand and/or increases in the price of gold.

Policy Implications

The preceding narrative has all sorts of policy implications. One obvious message is that Argentina should not have pegged their currency to a strongly

---

14. Of course, many researchers have taken the gold standard seriously, but more as a policy constraint (Eichengreen) or as an ideology (Temin), rather than as a commodity market.

appreciating dollar, and when this policy collapsed, the new government should not have blamed the subsequent depression on the failures of neoliberalism. Another implication is that artificial attempts to boost the aggregate wage level above equilibrium are a bad idea. Singapore in the early 1980s, East Germany in the early 1990s, and France in the early 2000s all tried to artificially boost wage rates. Now all three policies are widely seen to have failed. Singapore quickly reversed course, France later backed off, whereas in Germany, the political imperatives of reunification virtually mandated the high wage policy. More recently, the 40 percent increase in the U.S. minimum wage (right on the eve of the 2008 recession) was obviously ill timed.

Perhaps the most interesting policy implication relates to the "price of money" approach to monetary policy. Recall my earlier observation that even if all countries simultaneously faced deflation, it would still be possible to employ the policy of currency depreciation against gold, or a basket of commodities, rather than other currencies. An open-ended promise to buy unlimited commodity futures contracts at a high enough price does offer a foolproof method of inflation.

The basic problem with commodity money regimes is that the relative price of gold, or even a basket of commodities, is often quite volatile. Although the equity and commodity markets are especially sensitive to monetary shocks and were often a good policy indicator during the Depression, they are simply too unstable to provide a foundation for a modern monetary regime. Thus, I have some reservations about proposals to have policymakers pay more attention to these markets. But the intuition that simply targeting the price level misses something important (as in the year 2000 tech boom) does reflect a real problem, especially if Alchian and Klein were right about the unreliability of indices dominated by sticky prices. An alternative approach that has been widely discussed would be to target nominal spending, which is much more cyclical than the deflator.

In an earlier paper (1989), I showed that the central bank could offer to buy and sell unlimited quantities of nominal GDP futures at a fixed price (equal to the policy target), which might then be raised at 4 percent per year. Dowd (1994) made a similar proposal for price index futures. Under these policy regimes the medium of account would be a futures contract for a macroeconomic aggregate, rather than gold, otherwise it would operate pretty much like a traditional gold standard.[15] And these policy regimes also meet Svensson's (2003b) definition of policy efficiency, which requires the central bank to target the forecast; that is, to set policy such that its inflation or nominal GDP forecast is equal to its policy goal.

Previous Research on the Depression

If I had written this book ten years ago, I would have spent a lot of time attacking previous accounts of the Depression and discussing why the gold market approach is better. And in the earlier chapters, I have certainly criticized various aspects of some earlier studies. But as the preceding discussion of root causes suggests, there is a certain incommensurability in the various accounts of the Depression. All of the major narratives offer valuable insights into the Depression, and all have deepened my understanding of the issues. Being a bit older (and hopefully, wiser) I'll conclude with a look at how the findings of this study complement earlier research on the Depression.

Although I have criticized many of the specific interpretations offered by Friedman and Schwartz, I do agree with their central hypothesis—that contractionary monetary policy in the United States played a key role in the Great Contraction. And I also believe that they make a plausible argument for the proposition that throughout the Great Contraction the Fed retained enough policy flexibility to turn things around, had it acted more decisively. I was initially skeptical of this view (also held by other monetarists such as Meltzer and Bordo), but have recently become more sympathetic to Timberlake's forceful argument that the U.S. gold stock was enormous, and in an emergency, all gold is "free gold."

---

15. Bernanke and Woodford (1997) argued that targeting the forecast is subject to a "circularity problem." This occurs when central banks are responding to forecasts of inflation, and at the same time, those forecasters know that policymakers will change course if their forecasts stray from the policy target. Sumner (2006) showed that some futures targeting proposals (such as Sumner (1995) are subject to this problem, but that it does not apply to the proposals of Sumner (1989) or Dowd (1994), where the public actually sets the money supply at the level they believe is most likely to result in the policy target being met.

At the risk of seeming to contradict myself, however, I continue to find much merit in Eichengreen and Temin's view that the gold standard constrained U.S. policymakers in the early 1930s. But I would emphasize the psychological aspects of those constraints more than the technical aspects. As Eichengreen noted, tentative policy initiatives might have failed if markets anticipated that the Fed would later become frightened by the gold outflows resulting from those actions. Policymakers imagined themselves confined within a prison of golden bars, even as (in reality) they may have been able to walk out the door at any time. This also highlights the role of the conservative gold standard ideology, which Temin rightly emphasized. Even if the constraints were only psychological, if they reduced policy credibility then they had a real impact on monetary policy effectiveness. I also found evidence (in financial market responses to news) for Eichengreen's view that policy coordination could have been very helpful during the early 1930s, and for Temin's view that dollar depreciation radically shifted policy expectations during 1933.

This study also supports the Johnson/Mundell view that the postwar undervaluation of gold was an important root cause of the Depression. At worst, Johnson may have slightly overestimated the ability of policymakers to address this issue in the early postwar period and underestimated their ability to cooperate in the early 1930s. But Johnson was right in emphasizing that the chronic problems of gold undervaluation and French hoarding helped to create an environment where other policymakers had much less room to maneuver.

I have even developed a grudging new respect for those Austrian and French economists who saw expansionary monetary policies by the Fed during the 1920s as being one of the root causes of the Depression. While I continue to think that it makes no sense to argue that U.S. policy was expansionary during the 1920s or that those policies made the Depression inevitable in a technical sense, given that the world moved away from the gold exchange standard during the early 1930s, it would have been better to allow a gradual deflation during the 1920s, rather than to restore gold's prewar purchasing power by letting the price level fall off a cliff after 1929. When I wrote the first draft of this manuscript, I was skeptical that the Austrian view could make much headway in the modern world. But the current crisis has clearly revived Austrian economics. I don't think the Fed's low interest rate policy of 2002–2004 and/or the housing bubble caused our current recession. But I can't deny that most people do focus on these factors, and this commonsense view of things is very Austrian in spirit.

McCloskey and Zecher were among the first to challenge Friedman and Schwartz's story. They showed how an equilibrium model of the international gold standard could be a useful tool for analyzing issues like policy endogeniety and the link between devaluation and inflation during the Depression. If anything, they pushed the endogeniety issue a bit too far, at least with respect to policymakers in the United States and France, who had enormous influence over the world demand for gold. Nevertheless, my analysis is clearly indebted to their work.

Romer also made a number of useful contributions on issues such as the role of U.S. gold inflows during the recovery period. My differences with Romer (and many other researchers) often relate to my unorthodox views on topics such as wage and price cyclicality, policy lags, and the monetary transmission mechanism. My approach is somewhat closer to that of Bernanke, who made a number of contributions on issues such as gold ratios, real wage cyclicality, and multiple monetary equilibria. Unfortunately, he never fully developed these insights into the sort of integrated and detailed account of the Depression provided by either Eichengreen or Friedman and Schwartz. Glasner's brief narrative of the role of gold market shocks and wage shocks during the Depression offers perhaps the closest parallel to my own account. But rereading his work today one senses that even if he got all the big issues right, he never fully realized the explanatory power of gold shock/wage shock approach. Indeed, to some extent, my work can be seen as fleshing out the implications of ideas suggested by Glasner, and even earlier by Thompson and Hawtrey.

On the question of wage shocks, the most important recent research has been done by Cole and Ohanian, who brought the rigor of neoclassical modeling techniques to the problem of the sluggish recovery. Their findings buttress the conclusions reached in earlier work that I did with Stephen Silver, as well as studies by people like Weinstein (1981) and Vedder and Gallaway (1993). This is now the most exciting frontier of research on the Depression and an area of great relevance for contemporary policymakers.

Conclusion

Previous studies have focused on the debate over the extent to which the international gold standard "constrained" monetary policymakers. This study adds several new perspectives to that analysis. First, policymakers do have some discretion, but only to the extent to which they can impact the world gold reserve ratio in the *long run*. This means that policy constraints must be considered in a dynamic framework. Temporary currency injections that are not seen as plausibly impacting the long-run world gold ratio will not be credible, and will have little or no impact on aggregate demand. Researchers need to consider how gold flows between central banks impacted the expected future path of the money supply, not simply its current level.

Second, the impact of the international gold standard on policy is about much more that simply the size of an economy or the degree to which purchasing power parity does or does not hold. Gold market disturbances (such as gold discoveries or private hoarding) can affect current economic conditions without necessarily impacting the current money supply at all. Once again, it is essential to look at how a specific gold market disturbance affects policy expectations, and no mechanical model can do justice to the variety of complex factors that go into the formation of those expectations.

One reason the gold standard is often viewed as a constraint is that modern economists are used to monetary regimes with a single medium of account—cash. Under that sort of regime it is natural to visualize monetary policy in terms of its impact on the money supply. In contrast, under a gold standard regime both cash and gold are media of account, linked together with a rigid price peg, and changes in the price level can be modeled using either asset. Like Siamese twins, where one goes, the other must follow. What I have tried to do, is to show that when analyzing the Depression, it is often more useful to think of gold as the dominant twin, the one that leads the way. Then the money supply responds endogenously to equilibrate the money market at a world price level that is actually being set in the gold market.

This study also adds new insights to the problem of currency depreciation. While the link between currency depreciation and recovery is well established, I have purposely tried to deemphasize the "foreign exchange rate" aspects of Roosevelt's gold policies. Warren and Pearson were ridiculed for arguing that one could raise the overall price level simply by lowering the value of the dollar in terms of gold—as if international price equalization, and/or higher aggregate demand had nothing to do with the process. Their model *did* oversimplify the problem, but they also saw some things overlooked by more conventional economists (both then and now). By reducing the gold value of the dollar, FDR dramatically changed expectations about the future course of monetary policy. This immediately raised the prices in equity and commodity markets. Changing the *definition* of the currency unit really is a foolproof way out of a liquidity trap.

One of the most important outcomes of my research has been an awareness of the need to integrate gold market analysis with labor market analysis. Most researchers have focused on one problem at a time. But, it is impossible to make any sense out of the events of 1929–1941 without a major focus on *both* the dysfunctional international gold market, and the concurrent labor market interventions arising out of the New Deal. In a sense the "Midas curse" applied to both markets; governments accumulated massive gold holdings, and the resulting deflation drove many close to bankruptcy. Labor sought artificially high wage rates, and the resulting unemployment impoverished many workers.

In the end, this study's most important contribution may be methodological. I hope that my narrative has provided indirect support for using the three tests (for causal factors) discussed in the introduction: theoretical plausibility, correlation with macroeconomic aggregates, and relationship to financial markets. I also hope that I have shown there are no simple econometric shortcuts to the analysis of a complex historical event such as the Great Depression. Any coherent and persuasive account of the Depression must look at a wide variety of variables and use an eclectic set of research methods. The most persuasive explanations will feature a seamless blend of economic theory, economic history, and the history of economic thought.

Postscript

In the twelve months after July 2008, nominal GDP in the United States fell nearly 9 percent below trend. Similar declines occurred in Europe and Japan. According to mainstream new Keynesian theory, it is the responsibility of central banks to prevent this sort of dramatic decline in aggregate demand.

And yet in late 2008, very few economists called on the Fed to adopt a more expansionary monetary policy. Many suggested the Fed could do no more, despite numerous studies showing that central banks have all sorts of policy options once nominal rates hit zero and despite the fact that even Ben Bernanke insists the Fed is not out of "ammunition." Others worried that the bloated monetary base would produce high inflation, despite the contrary evidence from the Great Depression, or more recently Japan. Instead, there was a tendency to blame the recession on imbalances in the economy during the preceding boom. There certainly were imbalances, and a painful period of readjustment was almost certainly necessary. But it is hard to see how a sharp fall in aggregate demand, which cost eight million jobs, would ease the adjustment.

During the 1920s, economists such as Keynes, Fisher, Cassel, and Hawtrey were the most progressive thinkers on monetary affairs. Here is Cassel expressing his frustration in a "Memorandum of Dissent" from the *Report of the Gold Delegation*, written for the League of Nations:

> After having carefully studied the final report of the Gold Delegation, I find it impossible to for me to sign this report. Right and wrong are mixed up in such a bewildering way that it is extremely difficult to state all the reservations to which an endorsement of the report would be subject. . . . Although I very much appreciate much of the research work of the delegation, I strongly feel that the whole matter ought to have presented to a world in the utmost distress in such a way as to let the essential features of the gold problem stand out in full clearness. . . . The way that the Gold Delegation presents the causes of the breakdown of the gold standard seems to me entirely unacceptable. *What we have to explain is essentially a monetary phenomenon, and the explanation must therefore essentially be monetary in character. An enumeration of a series of economic disturbances and maladjustments which existed before 1929 is no explanation of the breakdown of the gold standard.* In fact, in spite of existing economic difficulties, the world enjoyed up to 1929 a remarkable progress. What has to be cleared up is why the progress was suddenly interrupted. . . . It had been made clear during the course of the last decade that the gold standard could be maintained only

by the aid of a systematic gold-economising policy aiming at such a restriction of the monetary demand for gold as would prevent a rise in the value of that metal. To a certain extent, this program had been carried out with the most beneficent result. From 1928 onwards, however, this policy was completely frustrated by extraordinary demands for gold which brought about a rise in the value of gold of unparalleled violence. (June 1932; emphasis added)

One can sympathize with those who disagreed with Cassel. When there is too little money, monetary tightness doesn't seem to be the problem. Interest rates are low and the public may be hoarding lots of cash. It's much easier to argue that depressions are the inevitable hangover from a preceding bout of speculation. Today, most economists agree with Cassel; when nominal GDP falls in half, monetary policy has been far too tight, regardless of the level of interest rates.

So why do we need to keep taking a fresh look at the Great Depression? One reason is that there are still many lessons to be learned. We may think we are far advanced from the primitive economic theory and policymaking of the early 1930s. But we haven't. Many of the debates from the 1930s are being echoed in the recent debate over the eurozone crisis. We have made progress, and our mistakes are now less costly. But there is still much more to be learned. Had I been appointed to a committee studying the economic crisis of 2008–2009, I would have almost certainly ended up writing a dissent very much like the italicized portion of Cassel's. Consider this study as a supporting document to that dissent.

13

Theoretical Issues in Modeling the Great Depression

IN THIS CHAPTER I provide a great deal more detail regarding the "model" employed in the narrative. I put the term model in quotation marks for several reasons. It is actually several models, and it is not a formal (mathematical) general equilibrium model of the sort employed by many younger macroeconomists. It is *ad hoc*, but I hope in the best sense of the term—each component is supposed to address a specific problem. It is low tech in the same sense that Friedman and Schwartz's *Monetary History* is low tech. Some might argue that I don't have the excuse they had; much of modern macro was yet to be developed in the early 1960s. Yet, their study is still the account everyone returns to. If modern techniques are so much better, why hasn't their research been superseded by successive studies?

Despite all our advances in technique, when faced with a severe crisis like the 2008 recession, much of the debate between elite macroeconomists revolves around extremely simple models of the economy, aggregate supply/aggregate demand (AS/AD) debates about whether high unemployment is demand-side or structural, or IS-LM debates about whether monetary stimulus is effective at the zero interest rate bound. If that is how we are going to debate the current crisis, there is no reason why similarly simple but powerful tools cannot illuminate the Great Depression. Indeed, I would argue that Ralph Hawtrey's 1947 account of the Depression, which focused heavily on gold market shocks and nominal wage shocks, is still the most accurate narrative of what went wrong in America during the 1930s. I am greatly indebted to his pioneering analysis.

Figure 13.1 provides a visual description of the basic model used in this study. There are two major tracks: gold market shocks and wage shocks. In the first part of this chapter, I will discuss how the autonomous wage shock

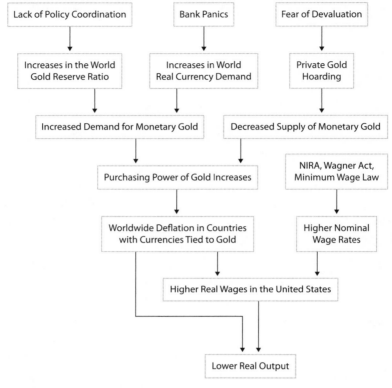

Figure 13.1. Assumed Transmission Mechanisms

hypothesis fits in with previous studies of real wage cyclicality. The bulk of this chapter will focus on the role of gold market shocks, particularly the thorny problem of identifying the impact of monetary policy changes by individual central banks. There are also several appendices that consider issues raised by previous researchers.

The basic AS/AD approach to macro can be modeled in a variety of different ways. There's no reason to needlessly restrict our assumptions unless the data rules out specific mechanisms. For instance, in Figure 13.1 the gold market shocks affect output through two changes: countercyclical real wage movements, and directly. The direct channel represents the impact of AD shocks on output via the "sticky price channel." I focused most of the analysis on the sticky wage assumption for reasons of parsimony, not because I believed all prices to be flexible. Here's a list of the assumptions I used in the narrative, which help define the AS/AD approach that seems most fruitful for the 1930s:

1. Both wages and prices are sticky in the short run and flexible in the long run.
2. Expectations are "rational," although the term "consistent expectations" better describes the concept.
3. Financial and commodity markets are relatively efficient.
4. It is convenient to describe aggregate demand as a given level of nominal expenditure, or GDP.
5. Interest rates are an exceedingly poor indicator of the impact of monetary policy on aggregate demand. During the interwar years the gold/currency ratio and the price of gold were much better policy indicators.
6. Aggregate demand was also impacted by changes in the monetary gold stock, and by currency hoarding.
7. The most important factor influencing the current level of aggregate demand is the expected future path of aggregate demand.

It is not important what name one attaches to this set of theoretical assumptions. Items 1, 2, 3, and 7 are very much in the new Keynesian tradition. The assumptions 4, 5, and 6 are more in the classical/monetarist tradition. I won't defend these assumptions here; instead I hope this study demonstrates their usefulness.

Applying Occam's Razor to the Great Depression

The Great Depression is unavoidably complex, so let's at least see how much we can simplify without losing significant explanatory power. Start with the "monetarist" definition of aggregate demand, which is a given level of nominal spending, or nominal GDP.[1] In that case, a demand shock is simply an unanticipated change in nominal GDP. Of course, the monetarists then go on to model nominal GDP using the famous M*V concept,[2] but we need not

---

1. For the graphically inclined, this is a hyperbola in P-Y space.
2. M*V=P*Y, or the money supply times the velocity of circulation, equals the price level times real GDP.

follow that choice. Indeed, we will see that changes in nominal GDP during the interwar years can be much more easily explained using a model of the world gold market.

There were a variety of supply shocks during the Great Depression, but I will focus on just one type, autonomous wage shocks caused by New Deal legislation. On five different occasions, the aggregate nominal wage rate rose significantly, each time in response to policies enacted by the Roosevelt administration. And each of these five wage shocks aborted promising recoveries that were underway.

Now we have reduced the Great Depression to two major types of shocks: (1) gold market shocks that influence aggregate demand, or nominal GDP, and (2) autonomous wage shocks that impact aggregate supply, or the way NGDP gets split up between prices and real output. Can we simplify any further? Surprisingly, the answer is yes. As we saw in Figure 1.2, the seventeen high frequency output fluctuations discussed in Chapter 1 can be explained with a single variable, real wage rates.

If we apply regression analysis to the data, we will see that the human eye is not deceived; there is an extremely strong correlation between real wages and industrial production during the 1930s. The following table shows the results of regressing the first difference of the log of industrial production on its lagged value, and also the first difference of the log of real wages. Real wages were already strongly countercyclical during the 1920s and became much more so in the 1930s. Why did this happen, and why do economists often fail to find any correlation at all when using post–World War II data sets?

There are many possible explanations for the surprisingly strong correlation between real wages and output. Perhaps modern studies of real wage cyclicality are flawed. Or perhaps real wages were generally more countercyclical before World War II than they are today. The unusual pattern might also reflect the specific nature of the shocks that hit the economy during the 1930s. And of course, there may be flaws in the way I have estimated real wages. In fact, all four of these factors probably play a role in making real wages especially countercyclical during the 1930s.

In the next section, I will show why this diagram holds the key to understanding the Great Depression, *even if real wage changes don't play a causal role in demand shocks*. To explain the path of industrial production between 1929 and 1939, we need to first explain the path of real wages. Because real wage cyclicality is a very complex topic, here I will focus on those factors that I think best explain Figure 1.2. In Appendix 13.c I discuss some alternative theories of wage cyclicality and the implications of those theories for this study.

Real Wages during the 1930s

In earlier research, Stephen Silver and I found that real wages tend to move countercyclically in periods dominated by aggregate demand shocks and procyclically in periods dominated by aggregate supply shocks. We suggested that these findings were consistent with "sticky-wage" versions of the AS/AD model. Thus, an adverse aggregate demand shock would reduce prices and output in the short run. If nominal wages were slow to adjust, this shock would then produce a countercyclical increase in real wage rates. Similarly, supply shocks would generate countercyclical price level movements and procyclical movements in real wage rates.

So can the sticky-wage version of the AS/AD model explain interwar wage cyclicality, and by implication, interwar business cycles? Is the observed countercyclicality of real wages during the Depression simply the result of aggregate demand shocks and sticky wages? Not entirely. Although research is ongoing, many studies now suggest that price stickiness must also play a role in the transmission of aggregate demand shocks. To provide a coherent explanation of real wage movements during the Depression, we need to first separate real wages into their nominal wage and price components and then take a closer look at the cyclical properties of each component.

Christopher Hanes has done some important work on the evolution of U.S. price indices, which have become less volatile in recent decades.[3] Hanes first separated the WPI into two components: the prices of relatively unprocessed goods and the prices of highly processed goods. He found that prior to World War II, the prices of relatively unprocessed goods comprised a much larger share of the WPI than is the case today. Furthermore, the prices of these unprocessed goods (i.e., commodities), are much more volatile than the prices of highly processed goods. Thus, part of the decrease in WPI volatility is illusory,

---

3. See Hanes (1999) and also Hanes (1996).

the result of improved sampling techniques that incorporate a larger number of highly processed goods into the WPI. But Hanes also found that a part of the reduced volatility of the postwar WPI was real. He showed that between 1929 and 1969, the crude goods/GNP ratio declined from 14 percent to 6 percent (and the ratio has certainly declined further since 1969). The interwar economy was much more focused on the production of food, fibers, and metals than is the economy of twenty-first-century America.

To summarize, in terms of comprehensiveness, the interwar WPI lies somewhere in between a broad price index such as the GDP deflator and a narrow price index, including only goods traded in auction-style commodities markets. Despite the "neither fish nor fowl" nature of the WPI, it was a surprising useful indicator of interwar price trends. During the 1930s, the Bureau of Labor Statistics measured the WPI at both weekly and monthly intervals. This makes the WPI particularly useful in studies of high frequency macroeconomic fluctuations. We should keep in mind, however, that the WPI may exaggerate the amount of price level volatility in the overall economy. And if we use the WPI to deflate nominal wages, then any flaws in the index will show up in the corresponding real wage series.

Hanes's research on the WPI can explain at least some of the observed differences between interwar and postwar real wage cyclicality. When aggregate demand fell sharply during 1920–1921, 1929–1933, and 1937–1938, the prices of commodities fell much more sharply than the overall price level (as measured by the GDP deflator). Because the WPI oversampled commodity prices, the WPI also showed an especially sharp decline during those three contractions. And because nominal wages fell much more slowly than wholesale prices, real wages increased sharply, thus explaining much of the countercyclical real wage pattern found in Table 13.1. Hanes's research can also explain why many postwar studies fail to find evidence of countercyclical real wages. These studies typically use a real wage series generated by deflating nominal wages with broader price indices, and these price indices are much less procyclical than the interwar WPI.

To summarize, there are two possible factors that may have contributed to interwar wage cyclicality: a preponderance of aggregate demand shocks relative to supply shocks and a real wage series constructed with a WPI that

Table 13.1. The Monthly Relationship between Industrial Production (IP) and Its Lagged Value and Real Wages, 1920–1939

Independent Variable	Period		
	1920–1939	1920–1929	1930–1939
LaggedIP	.533	.449	.570
	(10.51)	(5.18)	(8.79)
RealWage	−.560	−.348	−.787
	(−6.00)	(−3.00)	(−5.52)
Adj. R2	.453	.335	.520
n	227	107	119

Note: The variables are defined as follows: IP and LaggedIP are the first differences of the natural log of industrial production, and its first lag. RealWage is the first difference of the natural logs of real wage rates of production workers. Nominal wages are deflated by the wholesale price index (WPI). All equations shown in this chapter included a constant term. T-statistics are in parentheses. A regression of the residuals on the lagged residuals, and other independent variables, shows no evidence of serial correlation.

oversampled commodities. Yet Stephen Silver and I found that replacing the WPI with a "cost of living" index didn't change the qualitative results—real wages remained strongly countercyclical during the interwar period.[4] This suggests that the WPI-bias factor cannot fully account for the unusually strong countercyclicality of interwar wages. The next step is to look at the behavior of nominal wages.

During 1933 and 1934, NIRA regulations mandated sharply higher hourly wage rates. After these regulations were declared unconstitutional in 1935, Congress passed the Wagner Act, which made it easier to form labor unions. A series of major unionization drives in late 1936 and 1937 again triggered higher wage rates. And in late 1938 and late 1939, there were increases in the minimum wage.[5] A real wage series that was already somewhat countercyclical

---

4. See Silver and Sumner (1995).

5. There is one additional labor market shock that would not show up in a net wage rate time series. The new payroll tax raised the gross cost of employing workers in 1937.

during the 1920s and early 1930s became even more so after federal labor market policies began to generate countercyclical movements in the nominal wage rate.[6]

To test this hypothesis, I regressed monthly industrial production on its lagged value, the WPI, and nominal wages (see Table 13.2).

Wholesale prices were very strongly procyclical throughout the entire interwar period. This suggests that aggregate demand shocks may have played an important role in the interwar business cycle. For instance, prices fell sharply during the major contractions of 1920–1921, 1929–1933, and 1937–1938. Note that the correlation goes back far earlier than the interwar period and indeed explains the entire Humean tradition in macroeconomics. Because wages are sticky, falling prices push unemployment much higher in the short run. So, there are no big surprises for the price variable. But it does confirm my conjecture that 1970s-style price shocks were not particularly important during the interwar years—we don't observe the sort of inflationary contractions seen during the oil shocks.

In contrast, nominal wages show a very unusual pattern. During the 1920s, there is no significant correlation between nominal wage changes and industrial production. This presumably reflects the fact that there were changes in both the supply and demand for labor, leaving nominal wages almost uncorrelated with industrial production. In contrast, during the 1930s, nominal wages became very countercyclical. Stephen Silver and I showed that the break point occurred not in 1930, but rather in 1933, which is exactly when New Deal policies began to artificially raise the nominal wage rate.[7]

---

6. Bernanke and Carey (1996) looked at wages, prices, and output in twenty-two countries during the Great Depression and found a similar pattern, which they see as supporting sticky-wage business cycle models: "We find that, once we have controlled for lagged output and banking panics, the effects on output of shocks to nominal wages and shocks to prices are roughly equal and opposite. If price effects operating through nonwage channels were important, we would expect to find the effect on output of a change in prices (given wages) to be greater than the effect of a change in nominal wages (given prices). As we find roughly equal effects, our evidence favors the view that sticky wages were the dominant source of nonneutrality" (p. 880).

7. See Silver and Sumner (1995).

Table 13.2. The Monthly Relationship between Industrial Production (IP) and Its Lagged Value, Nominal Wages, Wholesale Prices, 1920–1939

Independent Variable	Period		
	1920–1939	1920–1929	1930–1939
LaggedIP	.509	.345	.543
	(9.09)	(3.73)	(7.43)
Wages	−.459	.124	−.697
	(−3.31)	(0.60)	(−3.84)
Prices	.624	.476	.898
	(5.59)	(3.91)	(4.56)
Adj. R2	.453	.374	.518
N	227	107	119

Note: The variables are defined as follows: IP and LaggedIP are the first differences of the natural log of industrial production, and its first lag. Wages is the first difference of the natural logs of nominal wages of production workers, and Prices is the first difference of the natural log of the wholesale price index. All equations included a constant term. T-statistics are in parentheses. A regression of the residuals on the lagged residuals, and other independent variables, showed no evidence of serial correlation.

The unusual countercyclicality of wages during the 1930s is probably due to a number of special factors. Here are a few that I believe are among the most important:

1. The interwar WPI was biased toward commodities, which tend to have relatively flexible prices. Because the real price of commodities tends to be somewhat cyclical, this made the WPI appear more procyclical than a more comprehensive index would have shown. Thus, the WPI tended to fall more sharply than broader price indices during depressions, which exaggerated the countercyclicality of real wages.

2. The strongly cyclical nature of the WPI also reflects the nature of the interwar economy. Although the index was biased toward commodities, it is also true that commodities comprised a far larger share of the interwar U.S. economy than the twenty-first-century economy. Thus, the

highly cyclical nature of the interwar price level is not just an artifact of measurement error, but also reflects the much more important role of farm products, coal, metals, and other commodities.

3. Because the WPI was very cyclical, and nominal wages tend to be sticky, real wages tended to be procyclical during the interwar period. Note that this was even true during the dramatic 1920–1921 deflation, when wages fell sharply, but (wholesale) prices fell much more rapidly.

4. The fact that postwar studies of wage cyclicality often show no pronounced pattern is partly a reflection of the time periods being examined. Real wages were highly procyclical during the 1970s, when oil shocks depressed both output and real wages. Indeed most supply shocks generate procyclical real wages.[8]

5. The New Deal period was very unusual in that the dominant supply shock was legally mandated wage increases, and this made real wages especially countercyclical. The Orwellian-named National Industrial Recovery Act raised wages and reduced output.

So, there are five special factors that explain why real wages were highly countercyclical during the interwar period, and yet they are almost acyclical in the postwar period. This gives us a simple way to organize the analysis of what went wrong in the 1930s; explain the countercyclicality of real wages in the 1930s, and we've gone a long way to explaining the Great Depression. We don't even need to assume that real wages always played a causal role; aggregate demand shocks might have directly affected output, and the unusually countercyclical real wages might partly reflect the fact that wholesale prices were usually more volatile than nominal wages.

Every factor discussed in this study can be seen as affecting output through either autonomous nominal wage changes or unanticipated price level changes. All that remains is to model the price level, which is our proxy for aggregate demand shocks. What we need is an ad hoc approach in the best sense of the term. We need the monetary model that is best suited to uncovering the specific causal factors behind the Great Deflation of 1929–1933.

---

8. See Sumner and Silver (1989.)

Modeling the Price Level under a Gold Standard

Many economic historians view the gold standard as simply a fixed exchange rate regime that constrained monetary policymakers. Others have focused on how gold flows impacted domestic money supplies and thus transmitted the Depression from one country to another. Although these are important perspectives, this research has often overlooked some even more fundamental issues. The Great Depression was a worldwide phenomenon. By themselves, gold flows tell us nothing about the stance of *world* monetary policy. To develop an explanation for why the real value of gold (i.e., its purchasing power) rose so dramatically during the 1930s, we need to focus on the world gold market.

In Chapter 1, I described a greatly simplified version of the gold standard model presented here. We began with a simple identity showing that the value of gold (the inverse of the price level), is a function of the supply and demand for gold:

$$P = G_s/g \tag{1.1}$$

where P is the price level, G_s is the nominal monetary gold stock, and g is the real demand for monetary gold.

In a 1930 report commissioned by the League of Nations, Gustav Cassel pointed out that the ratio of (annual) gold output to the existing stock of gold had fallen from over 3 percent prior to World War I, to just over 2 percent by the late 1920s. (Because very little gold is lost, this is roughly the rate of increase in gold stocks.) Cassel expressed concern that future gold supplies might be inadequate. On the other hand, he also acknowledged that there were many uncertainties on both the supply and demand side of the gold market, and he certainly did not predict the catastrophic deflation that we now know was already underway. As we will see, while the supply side was an aggravating factor, the demand side of the gold market holds the key to the Great Contraction.

Then, we segmented real monetary gold demand into two components, the gold reserve ratio (r) and the real demand for currency (m_d). The gold reserve ratio was defined as the ratio of the monetary gold stock and the currency stock:

$$P = G_s{}^*(1/r)^*(1/m_d) \qquad\qquad (1.2)$$

Thus, an increase in the price level can be generated by one of three factors: an increase in the monetary gold stock, a decrease in the gold reserve ratio, and/or a decrease in the real demand for currency. During periods when the dollar was floating, the gold supply variable is segmented into the nominal price of gold (P_g) and the physical gold stock (g_s):

$$P = (P_g)^*(g_s)^*(1/r)^*(1/m_d) \qquad\qquad (1.3)$$

The right-hand side of Equation 1.3 features the four primary variables that are used in the gold market analysis of aggregate demand and the price level. A priori, there is no reason to expect this equation to provide useful insights when the dollar is not fixed to gold. It would be equally true today, indeed, not just for gold but any commodity. But in fact it was highly useful during the period of dollar depreciation. This is because the federal government used changes in the dollar price of gold as a signal of future monetary policy. Investors understood that the dollar would eventually be re-pegged to gold, and the price at which that occurred would have a big impact on the future money supply and hence future AD. And new Keynesian models tell us that changes in the future expected level of aggregate demand and prices have a powerful effect on current prices and aggregate demand.

From a Gold Market Identity to a Gold Market Model

It is not difficult to come up with plausible explanatory variables for the terms on the right-hand side in Equation 1.3. Real currency demand is presumably a function of nominal interest rates, real income, risk of bank failures, and tax rates, among other variables.[9] Changes in the physical monetary gold stock will depend on the flow of newly mined gold, as well as industrial demand and private gold hoarding. Both the gold reserve ratio and the price of gold can be viewed as monetary policy indicators. To see which variables were important during the Depression, it will be helpful to first look at some data showing changes in each of the key gold market variables. We will begin

---

9. See Cagan (1965).

Table 13.3. The Impact of Changes in the World Gold Reserve Ratio, Real Demand for Currency, Real Demand for Gold, and Monetary Gold Stock, on the World Price Level, 1926–1932

Time Period	Dec 1926 to Jun 1928	Jun 1928 to Oct 1929	Oct 1929 to Oct 1930	Oct 1930 to Aug 1931	Aug 1931 to Dec 1932	Dec 1926 to Dec 1932
$\Delta(\ln 1/r)$	−3.98	−3.18	−9.62	+1.55	−5.80	−21.86
$\Delta(\ln 1/md)$	−4.05	−2.94	−4.97	−16.18	−13.56	−40.80
$\Delta(\ln 1/g)$	−8.03	−6.12	−14.59	−14.63	−19.36	−62.66
$\Delta(\ln G)$	+5.82	+5.42	+5.25	+3.93	+5.18	+25.61
$\Delta(\ln P)$	−2.21	−0.70	−9.34	−10.70	−14.18	−37.06

$\Delta(\ln 1/r)$ = change in the log of (the inverse of) the gold reserve ratio

$\Delta(\ln 1/md)$ = change in the log of (the inverse of) real money demand

$\Delta(\ln g)$ = change in the log of (the inverse of) the real demand for monetary gold

$\Delta(\ln G)$ = change in the log of the world monetary gold stock

$\Delta(\ln P)$ = change in the log of the world price level

(All of the percentage changes shown above are first differences of logs.)

Notes: Outside the United States, the currency stock was used as a proxy for the monetary base. The change in the real demand for monetary gold is equal to the sum of the changes in the gold reserve ratio and the real demand for currency. The change in P reflects changes in the monetary gold stock and the (inverse of the) real demand for monetary gold. The changes are not seasonally adjusted. The total change in each variable between 1926 and 1932 is the sum of the changes that occurred in each subperiod. See Appendix 2.a for data sources.

by focusing on the period when the dollar was still tied to gold, which allows us to abstract from changes in the price of gold. Table 2.1 (repeated here as Table 13.3, but not annualized this time) showed how variations in each of the variables in Equation 1.2.

The most striking event in Table 13.3 is the sharp break in the world price level after October 1929. In the thirty-four months preceding the stock market crash the world price level had declined by a mere 2.9 percent, whereas over the following thirty-eight months it fell 34.2 percent.[10] In contrast, there is no

---

10. The decrease is 28.9 percent using ordinary percentages. In order to allow changes to be added over categories and across time, the changes in Tables 2.1, 2b.1, 13.3 and 13.5 are

obvious change in the growth rate of world monetary gold stocks after October 1929; the annualized rate of growth was actually slightly higher in the latter period. Thus, in an accounting sense, the Great Deflation of 1929–1932 seems to have been triggered by a sharp increase in the demand for monetary gold.

Most gold standard models assume some relationship between the monetary gold stock and the money supply (usually currency or the monetary base). For instance, a central bank might follow the rules of the game—that is, choose to maintain a proportional relationship between the currency stock and the gold reserve that backs up that money. Thus, when we look for reasons why central banks would have sharply increased their real demand for monetary gold, it is natural to first ask whether that increase represented a departure from the rules of the game. To answer this question, we need to partition the increase in real gold demand into changes in the gold reserve ratio and changes in the real demand for currency. From Table 13.3, we can see that both of these variables increased sharply during the period from 1926 to 1932. Unfortunately, this data does not, by itself, tell us anything about the issue we care most about, which is causality.

Most of the increase in real currency demand occurred between October 1930 and December 1932. Because real income was falling throughout the industrial world during that period, the increase in real currency demand was presumably due to other factors, such as low nominal interest rates and banking instability. Although I briefly discussed these issues in the narrative chapters, the gold standard approach has little to add to traditional monetarist analyses of currency hoarding by Friedman and Schwartz, and others. Instead, I focused on the other three factors in Equation 1.3: gold reserve ratios, the monetary gold stock, and (after 1933) the nominal price of gold.

The world gold reserve ratio rose nearly 22 percent between 1926 and 1932, which is more than one-half the size of the concurrent fall in the world price level. Is there a causal relationship between these two changes? This question is perhaps best posed as a counterfactual: What would have happened had the major central banks adhered to the rules of the game—that is, what

---

reported as first differences of logs. All other changes in this book are expressed as ordinary percentage changes.

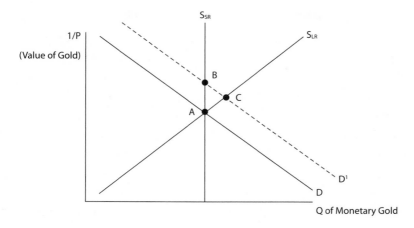

Figure 13.2. The Long-Run Effect of a Higher Gold Reserve Ratio
on the Value of Gold

if they had maintained a stable gold reserve ratio during the late 1920s and
early 1930s? To answer this question, we would need to calculate the impact
of changes in monetary policy (the gold reserve ratio) on the other primary
variables: the world monetary gold stock and real currency demand. This
turns out to be surprisingly difficult, if not impossible. In fact, we can't even
be certain about whether these secondary effects would have tended to offset
or reinforce the direct impact of changes in monetary policy.

At first glance, it would seem that the easiest secondary effect to model
would be the impact of monetary policy on the size of the world monetary
gold stock. If central banks had maintained a stable gold reserve ratio during
this period, then there presumably would have been less deflation and hence, a
smaller increase in the real value of gold.[11] If we assume that the supply of newly
mined gold is positively related to the real value of gold and that industrial
demand is negatively related to the value of gold, then a more expansionary
world monetary policy (which reduced the value of gold) would have led to a
smaller increase in world monetary gold stocks. A reduction in output from
gold mines, as well as increased industrial use of gold, should have partially

---

11. Alternatively, one can think of deflation as reducing the nominal cost of production
for a commodity whose nominal price is fixed.

offset the expansionary impact of the lower gold reserve ratio. Indeed, this represents one of the allegedly stabilizing properties of a gold standard regime.[12]

Figure 13.2 shows the expected short- and long-run impact of a higher gold ratio on the value of gold, and hence the inverse of the price level (1/P). In the short run a higher gold ratio can sharply increase the value of gold, and sharply reduce the price level. If the supply of monetary gold is relatively elastic, then prices will gradually revert back toward the original level as gold output rises and industrial demand falls. Of course, if commodity markets are forward-looking, then the anticipation of this long-run effect can moderate any short-run price level changes.

A slight acceleration in the growth rate of the world monetary gold stock after October 1929 provides some evidence for the traditional gold standard model. Given the sharp fall in the price level after 1929, however, it is surprising that the supply response was not even greater. After all, the output of the world mining industry roughly doubled during the 1930s. And industrial use of gold is believed to have fallen from 20 percent of the total output to roughly 5 percent in 1939, reflecting both the income and substitution effects.[13] In the next section, we will see that one problem was private nonindustrial demand. Beginning in mid-1931, fear of currency devaluation led to private gold hoarding, which slowed the growth of the world monetary gold stock and prevented changes in the supply of monetary gold from having their expected stabilizing impact. In Figure 13.2 private gold hoarding would shift the supply of monetary gold to the left, further increasing its value and reducing the price level.

It is even more difficult to estimate the impact of monetary policy on the real demand for currency. If central banks had maintained a stable gold reserve ratio between 1926 and 1932 (i.e., if they had adopted a much more expansionary monetary policy than what was actually implemented), then real income growth would have been greater, and real currency demand might have increased by even more than 41 percent.

---

12. See Barro (1979).

13. These figures are from Shirras (1940). Barro (1984) cites a study by Mark Rush that estimated the short-run flow elasticity of supply from mines to be 0.31. Subtracting out the private demand for gold implies a higher flow elasticity for the supply of *monetary* gold. However, the short-run stock elasticity of supply during the late 1920s and early 1930s was probably much smaller than the flow elasticity since the annual increase in the monetary gold stock was only about 4 percent per year during that period.

Yet one could make an even stronger argument for the opposite effect, for stronger real growth leading to *less* currency hoarding. Currency hoarding tends to occur during depressions, as nominal interest rates are low and depositors anticipate bank failures. If more central bank gold hoarding (i.e., a higher gold ratio) had depressed the economy and increased currency hoarding, then this would have reinforced the impact of the contractionary monetary policy. This is an important point, as it means that the change in the world gold ratio probably *understates* the impact of central bank gold hoarding. It is well known that tight money can set in motion macroeconomic conditions that reduce velocity. The same is true for central bank gold policies. Central bank gold hoarding can lead to a macroeconomic environment that encourages private gold hoarding, as well as currency hoarding.

If monetary policy had been far more expansionary and the Depression had been significantly milder, it's quite possible that the dramatic increases in real currency demand during the early 1930s would never have occurred. Indeed, without the large increase in central banks' gold ratios during 1929–1930, *it is difficult to see any plausible mechanism by which aggregate demand would have plummeted during the 1930s.*

Figure 13.3 shows the case where a higher gold reserve ratio depresses the economy so much that the public begins hoarding currency. A higher gold reserve ratio, *ceteris paribus,* represents a rightward shift in the demand for monetary gold, and currency hoarding (i.e., higher real currency demand) pushes the demand for monetary gold even further to the right.

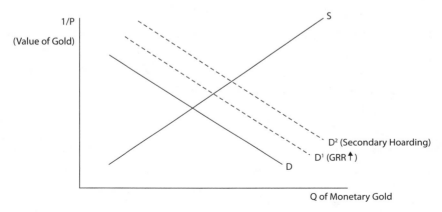

Figure 13.3. The Effect of a Higher Gold Reserve Ratio on the Value of Gold

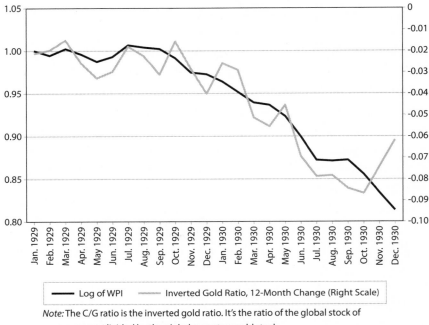

Log of WPI ——— Inverted Gold Ratio, 12-Month Change (Right Scale)

Note: The C/G ratio is the inverted gold ratio. It's the ratio of the global stock of currency divided by the global monetary gold stock.

Figure 13.4. The WPI and 12-Month Change in the C/G Ratio

The preceding discussion is reminiscent of the old Keynesian/monetarist debate over the effectiveness of monetary policy. Keynes (1936 [1964]) argued that an increase in the money supply would reduce interest rates, and that the subsequent increase in the demand for liquidity might produce an offsetting decline in velocity. In contrast, Friedman (1969) argued that increases in the money supply growth rate typically lead to increases in real income and higher inflation expectations. These secondary effects tend to increase the velocity of circulation, thus reinforcing the impact of the original monetary shock.

The various indirect effects are so complex that it is almost impossible to develop reliable estimates of how changes in the world gold ratio affected the world price level. The actual effects would be highly sensitive to expectations and thus the deeper institutional setting that shapes those expectations. What we do know is that the world gold reserve ratio rose sharply after October 1929, and that *ceteris paribus* this action would be expected to sharply depress world prices and output.[14] And as shown in Figure 13.4, the rise in the gold reserve ratio was associated with sharply falling prices in the United States (until the banking crisis at the end of 1930). The gold reserve ratio is inverted to make it easier to see the correlation.

The closest parallel to this analysis is to be found in studies of gold reserve ratios by Bernanke (1995) and Eichengreen (2004). They did show how a higher gold reserve ratio could have a deflationary impact on the world economy, but failed to use this tool to its fullest extent. In a series of earlier papers,[15] I tried to show that gold market indicators could do more than provide a backdrop to the deflation of the early 1930s; they could help us understand month-to-month and quarter-to-quarter changes in the wholesale price level throughout the entire period from 1929–1939 (and indeed the 1920–1921 deflation as well).

Private Gold Hoarding and the Supply of Monetary Gold

The dramatic increase in the world gold reserve ratio between 1926 and 1932 represented gold hoarding by central banks. But private gold hoarding also played a role in the international gold market during the 1930s. Because we lack direct data on private gold holdings, we are forced to infer changes in private gold demand by looking at variations in the world monetary gold stock and the output of gold mines.

The world stock of monetary gold grew at a relatively steady rate during the late 1920s and early 1930s. We also have monthly data showing that the flow supply of newly mined gold was quite stable on a month-to-month basis. Between January 1929 and June 1931, monthly world gold output fluctuated in a narrow range between $31 million and $39 million. And it is widely believed that very little gold is lost each month. Therefore, by comparing the data for newly mined gold with changes in world monetary gold stocks, I was able to

---

14. One should not infer from this discussion that there was ever a golden age when countries adhered to the rules of the game. Nurske (1944) showed that interwar central banks failed to adhere to the rules of the game, and Bloomfield (1959) showed that the rules were not even followed during the classical gold standard era (1879–1914). Rather, the rules of the game provide a useful benchmark to evaluate discretionary monetary policy.

15. See Sumner (1991, 1992, and 1997).

derive a fairly accurate estimate of changes in the private stock of gold. Private gold stocks increase whenever the supply of newly mined gold exceeds the net increase in the world monetary gold stock.

In the thirty months between December 1928 and June 1931, the world private stock of gold rose fifteen times and declined fifteen times. There was only one month during this period when the private stock of gold increased by an amount greater than 0.5 percent of the world monetary gold stock. Then, over the next twelve months, there were five occasions where the stock of privately held gold rose by an amount greater than 0.5 percent of world monetary gold stocks. Note that July 1931 is precisely when the international gold standard began to fall apart. In mid-1931, the public began to hoard gold as a precaution against currency devaluation, just as they had earlier hoarded currency in fear of bank defaults.

Table 3.2 in Chapter 3 clearly showed that growth in the world monetary gold stock slowed sharply during periods when currencies were perceived to be at risk. Gold stocks grew especially fast when fears of devaluation receded, or when there were fears of currency revaluation, as in early 1937. And because monetary gold stock data excludes U.S. gold coins, Table 3.2 modestly understates the amount of private gold hoarding that occurred during currency crises.[16]

In the narrative chapters we saw that periods of gold hoarding were often correlated with (and perhaps caused) economic contractions in the United States. Because this issue is so important, and because some economic historians have expressed doubts about this evidence, it is important to first establish that variations in the growth rate of the world monetary gold stock do, in fact, reflect variations in private gold hoarding.

We have already seen that the output of newly mined gold shows little month-to-month variation. Thus, the fact that growth in world gold reserves became highly erratic after June 1931 provides powerful prima facie evidence that private gold hoarding was having a significant impact on world gold

---

16. For the same reason, Table 2.2 slightly overstates the role of currency hoarding in the Depression. Brown (1940) indicates that Europeans hoarded large quantities of U.S. gold coins during the currency crises of the early 1930s. At that time, the United States was one of the few countries to still mint gold coins, and the stock of those coins was roughly one-thirtieth the size of the world monetary gold stock.

Table 13.4. The Monthly Relationship between Variations in the World
Monetary Gold Stock and Forward Discounts on the Pound,
Dollar, and Franc, January 1931 through December 1936

Independent Variable	GoldGAP	
Dependent Variables	Coefficient	T-statistic
FDPound	−.378	(−1.06)
FDDollar	−.886	(−3.90)
FDFranc	−.213	(−4.11)
GoldGAP$_{-1}$	.681	(10.29)

Adj. R^2 = .772, n = 72

Note: FDPound is the three-month forward discount on the British pound against the U.S.
dollar. FDDollar and FDFranc are the three-month forward discounts on the U.S. dollar and the French franc against the British pound. These forward discounts (which are
set at zero when the forward currency is at a premium) represent proxies for currency
devaluation fears. GoldGAP is the difference between the actual world monetary gold
stock and a four-year moving average of the monetary gold stock. GoldGAP was con-
structing by subtracting a four-year moving average of the world monetary gold stock
from the actual world monetary gold stock. GoldGAP$_{-1}$ is the first lag of GoldGAP.
Diagnostic tests show no evidence of serial correlation.

stocks. But this is not the only evidence we have. In the narrative chapters,
we saw that periods of slow growth in the world monetary gold stock were
associated with currency crises and that major banks reported widespread private gold purchases during those episodes. If this is what caused variations in
private gold hoarding, then one might expect an association between changes
in the growth rate of the world monetary gold stock and the expected rate of
depreciation of major currencies.

Table 13.4 shows the relationship between the world monetary gold stock
and the forward discount for three important currencies during the period
from 1931 through 1936.

A regression of GoldGAP on the three forward discounts and lagged Gold-
GAP suggests that gold hoarding had an important impact on fluctuations in
the world monetary gold stock. The negative coefficients on forward discounts
on the U.S. dollar and French franc indicate that increases in the discount on
the dollar and franc led to reductions in the monetary gold stock, and, by
implication, increases in the (unobservable) nonmonetary gold stock. If these

discounts are good proxies for expectations of devaluation, then these findings suggest that fears of devaluation led to private gold hoarding, which reduced the world monetary gold stock. With the pound not tied to gold for most of this period, it is not surprising that FDPound did not have a significant impact on GoldGAP.

To summarize, there are four pieces of circumstantial evidence to connect private gold hoarding and variations in the world monetary gold stock:

1. Growth in the world monetary gold stock was relatively stable until the onset of currency crises beginning in mid-1931.
2. Between 1931 and 1938, periods of slow growth in the monetary gold stocks were associated with currency crises.
3. Forward exchange rate data for the U.S. dollar and French franc suggests that increased expectations of currency depreciation led to slower growth in the world monetary gold stock.
4. Contemporaneous news reports suggest that private gold hoarders were particularly active during these currency crises.

To these four arguments I would add a (admittedly subjective) fifth argument. There are *no plausible alternative explanations.*

There are a number of obvious parallels between the causes and consequences of currency hoarding and private gold hoarding during the Depression. Both were triggered by fears of what can be loosely termed "default," both led to increases in the demand for a medium of account, and both exerted deflationary pressure on the world economy. And yet, while previous accounts of the Great Depression focused on currency hoarding, gold hoarding has generally been overlooked.

Although private gold hoarding played an important role in the period after mid-1931, the data in Table 13.3 suggests that any explanation for the large decline in prices between October 1929 and December 1932 must focus primarily on the extraordinary increase in the demand for *monetary* gold, a topic to be considered in the next section. But if private hoarding of gold did not cause the Great Depression, it did play an important role in depressing aggregate demand and prices during certain key episodes, particularly during 1931–1932 and 1937–1938. And the gold panics (i.e., the periods of gold dishoarding) also had a significant impact during 1936–1937.

To summarize, there are four gold market variables that can be used to model aggregate demand during the 1930s. It's worth considering just how far the preceding analysis seems to carry us without addressing any of the issues linked to the *international* nature of the gold standard that have so interested economic historians. These issues include Hume's famous price-specie-flow mechanism, McCloskey and Zecher's assertion that domestic money supplies were endogenous under the international gold standard, Eichengreen and Temin's view that the international gold standard constrained the Federal Reserve (Fed) during the early 1930s, and Romer's argument that gold flows to the United States contributed to economic recovery during the late 1930s.

These issues are important and are addressed in the narrative chapters. But it is striking just how much we can do with a model that abstracts from nation states and essentially ignores the "fixed exchange rate" aspect of the gold standard. In the narrative many of the most important applications of this model rely on this simple framework, which is nothing more than a closed economy model of a commodity money regime.

The next step is to add domestic monetary policy to the model. There is a long-standing disagreement among economic historians as to whether countries operating under an international gold standard lose control of their domestic monetary supply, and hence aggregate demand. In the next section, we'll see that the gold market approach can also shed new light on that old policy debate.

Identifying the Stance of Monetary Policy

For readers used to thinking about monetary policy in terms of the Fed tinkering with interest rates, the previous sections may have appeared somewhat mystifying. How do changes in the gold reserve ratio or the price of gold impact interest rates, and thus aggregate demand? Before explaining how monetary policy works under an international gold standard, we first need to clear up a few misconceptions about how monetary policy works under a fiat money regime.

What is monetary policy? This question might seem elementary but in fact is one of the most difficult problems in all of macroeconomics. We have all heard pundits speak confidently of central banks adopting "tight money" or "easy money" policies, and many people have probably assumed that monetary economists must have developed some sort of well-accepted metric, or indicator, for the stance of monetary policy. Nothing could be further from the truth. We don't really know how to measure the stance of monetary policy; and even worse, many of us don't seem to know that we don't know.

The most commonly cited indicator of monetary policy is nominal interest rates, especially short-term rates. When the Fed raises its funds target, most commentators will say that they have tightened monetary policy. But then how can we explain the fact that nominal interest rates are extremely high during hyperinflation? After all, almost no one associates hyperinflation with tight money. In contrast, the most contractionary monetary policy conceivable is likely to lead to rapid deflation, and this can drive nominal rates close to zero.

A slightly more sophisticated argument is that the *real* interest rate is a reliable indicator of monetary policy. But there are all sorts of problems with this claim. Real interest rates on five-year Treasury bonds (T-bonds) soared between July and November 2008, and yet it was difficult to find a single economist who would characterize the Fed's monetary policy as being "tight" during that period. So even if real interest rates are the "correct" indicator, it doesn't seem that economists pay much attention to them. In fact, real interest rates are also an unreliable indicator of policy, as they often reflect changes in credit demand associated with the business cycle. An extremely tight monetary policy can sharply depress aggregate demand and reduce the demand for credit. In this case, real interest rates may decline, despite tight money.[17]

Some monetarists have suggested that changes in the monetary base could be a useful indicator of monetary policy. Unfortunately, changes in the monetary base often reflect changes in the demand for base money (currency held by the public and bank reserves). A good example occurred between 1930 and 1933, when the base increased dramatically during a period where the public and banks hoarded cash out of fear of bank panics. Most economists do not regard an increase in the monetary base as indicating policy ease, if it is undertaken solely to offset a fall in velocity.

---

17. See King (1993).

Because both interest rates and the base have proven unreliable monetary policy indicators, some economists have suggested that the stance of policy should be evaluated in terms of the targets or goals of policy. All sorts of targets have been suggested, including exchange rates, the broader monetary aggregates,[18] commodity price indices, the consumer price index (CPI), and nominal GDP.

According to Lars Svensson, a central bank operating under an unconstrained fiat money regime should adopt a monetary policy that "targets the forecast." Then, the stance of policy would be described relative to the policy target. Under a 2 percent inflation target monetary policy would be considered too "tight" if the inflation was expected to fall short of 2 percent, and policy would be regarded as too "easy" if inflation was expected to exceed 2 percent.

Even if the Svensson approach makes sense for a fiat money regime (and I think it does), it is difficult to see how it could be applied to an international gold standard. Central banks faced important policy constraints and did not have limitless ability to adjust the money supply in order to stabilize inflation expectations. Can we then go back to the traditional policy indicators, such as interest rates and the money supply? No, because those variables are also highly constrained under a gold standard. Indeed, for a small country, it can be argued that both the interest rate and the money supply are endogenous, determined by world monetary policy. And for reasons already discussed, it isn't even clear that the world interest rate and/or monetary base are particularly good indicators of world monetary policy.

---

18. Friedman and Schwartz argued that the broader monetary aggregates were the best indicators of the stance of monetary policy, and indeed M1 and M2 did fall sharply during the early 1930s. But it isn't at all clear that the Fed had control over the broader aggregates once rates fell close to zero and banks began accumulating large stocks of excess reserves. Indeed, this criticism of monetarism resurfaced again in the 1990s and 2000s when both Japan and the United States experienced periods where large increases in the monetary base seemed to have relatively little impact on the broader aggregates.

The point is not to argue that a determined central bank cannot influence the monetary aggregates, or indeed any other nominal aggregate that it wishes to target. Rather, I am suggesting that the aggregates cannot be simply viewed as a "policy tool," under direct control of the central bank. Instead, the monetary aggregates are more like the price level or nominal GDP, variables that are influenced by monetary policy, but not always tightly under the central bank's control.

The truth is that we don't have any reliable and well-accepted indicators of monetary policy under an international gold standard. We will have to make our own way and do so in a pragmatic fashion. In the previous chapter, we saw that changes in the world gold reserve ratio can impact the world price level. At that point there was no obvious reason to choose this policy indicator—after all, we could just as well have used the world interest rate, or the world monetary base. In this section, we will focus on how each *individual* central bank contributes to the stance of world monetary policy. And now the usefulness of the gold reserve ratio will become obvious. Unlike interest rates and the monetary base, which are endogenous under a gold standard regime, each central bank can determine its own gold reserve ratio, and in that way contribute to the stance of world monetary policy.

Recall Equation 1.3, which showed four factors that can influence the price level:

$$P = (P_g)*(g_s)*(1/r)*(1/m_d) \tag{1.3}$$

A higher world price level can result from a decrease in currency demand, a decrease in the gold reserve ratio, an increase in the monetary gold stock, or an increase in the nominal price of gold.

Any model of the world economy is a closed economy model. So let's begin by thinking about how a central bank would operate if it were the only country operating under a gold standard. Indeed this was roughly the situation facing the Fed in 1937, when only the United States and Belgium remained on gold. If a gold standard is in effect then the price of gold is fixed. In that case the gold reserve ratio is the only exogenous policy tool, as real currency demand and the supply of monetary gold are determined by the private sector.

A central bank could increase their gold reserve ratio by increasing their monetary gold stock, decreasing the currency stock, or some combination of the two. If they wished to increase their gold reserve ratio without affecting the monetary base, then they could exchange bonds or other non-gold assets for gold. If they wished to decrease the gold ratio they could swap gold for domestic government bonds or foreign exchange.

Alternatively, the gold ratio might change as a result of ordinary monetary policy operations that impacted the base, such as open market purchases or discount loans. A cut in the discount rate or an open market purchase of government securities would increase the monetary base and currency stock. Because there was no direct impact on the central bank's stock of monetary gold, these expansionary operations also tended to reduce the gold reserve ratio.

So, were there any constraints on a central bank operating in a closed economy gold standard? Yes, but only in one direction—expansionary monetary policies were limited by the need to maintain a positive monetary gold stock. In contrast, the ability of a central bank to engage in contractionary monetary policies was constrained only by the budgetary cost of purchasing a large monetary gold stock. As we saw in Chapters 2 through 4, this asymmetry resulting from the "zero lower bound" on monetary gold stocks had quite similar implications to the zero lower bound on nominal interest rates. Large central banks such as the Federal Reserve and Bank of France had the ability to adopt highly contractionary monetary policies, whereas the policy options of countries favoring a more expansionary policy stance, such as Britain, were much more limited.

Even in a closed economy gold standard, central banks faced *some* constraints. Although they need not fear losing gold to other central banks, a sufficiently inflationary monetary policy would reduce the real price of gold so much that the public would eventually convert currency into gold, exhausting the central banks' gold stocks. In contrast, if a central bank pursued a highly deflationary policy then its stock of monetary gold reserves would eventually exceed the entire monetary base. Any further increases in the gold reserve ratio would require subsidies from the central government, as seignorage becomes negative once the gold reserve ratio exceeds 100 percent. Unlike government bonds, gold earns no interest.

Of course, in the real world there were political constraints on the ability of central banks to adjust their gold reserve ratio, and this meant that even in a closed economy setting central banks had much more limited room for discretionary policies. For instance, in the late 1936 and early 1937 a flood of gold poured into the Fed and prices started rising rapidly. This occurred despite that fact that the Fed partially "sterilized" these gold inflows, and despite the fact that the U.S. government had the resources to do even more sterilization. The public anticipated that much of this gold inflow would eventually be monetized, and this contributed to higher inflation expectations. Thus, even in the absence of hard technical constraints, central banks often had little operating room due to a wide variety of legal and/or informal constraints on policy.

At the other extreme one can envision a scenario where the gold reserve ratio is kept absolutely fixed. In this case discretionary monetary policy is not possible. The value of gold (and the price level) is determined by the supply and demand for gold, and the money supply is completely endogenous. It is still true that part of that demand for gold is derived from the public's demand for real currency balances, and gold backs up those balances. But aside from reserve requirements the central bank has no control over currency demand, and hence gold demand. This scenario most closely approximates the "automatic" or nondiscretionary policy envisioned by both fans and opponents of the gold standard. Here I would like to emphasize two important stylized facts:

1. Gold reserve ratios were not kept constant under the interwar gold standard. Indeed even prior to World War I, under the so-called classical gold standard, there was substantial variation in gold reserve ratios.
2. Although real world gold reserve ratios did vary, central banks considered these ratios to be a very important policy constraint.

The most useful way of thinking about the gold reserve ratio is not to treat it as a constant but also not to dismiss it as being so malleable that it was irrelevant for policymakers. Instead, it makes sense to view a stable gold reserve ratio as a sort of policy benchmark; changes in the gold reserve ratio can then be viewed as an indicator of policy easing or tightening.

Earlier, I suggested that changes in the monetary base are not a particularly reliable indicator of the stance of monetary policy under a fiat money regime. Thus, it might seem odd to argue that the gold ratio is a useful policy indicator, especially as changes in the gold ratio frequently resulted from changes in the monetary base. But there is an important difference between fiat money regimes and gold standards. Under a fiat regime there are almost no technical limits to money creation. Indeed, the only real limit on money creation is the public's willingness to tolerate high inflation rates. In that case, it makes no sense to think of central banks "making a good effort" to stimulate the economy. They can inject as much money as they like; what matters is whether they have hit their targets, whether defined in terms of the broader monetary aggregates or in terms of inflation or nominal GDP.

In contrast, under a gold standard a central bank's resources really are limited. It does make sense to speak of a central bank that dramatically lowered its gold reserve ratio as making a good effort to adopt a more expansionary policy, even if in the end that policy did not succeed. And as we will see, this argument becomes much more powerful in an open economy international gold standard. In that case the constraints on policy are much greater than under a closed economy gold standard, and the gold reserve ratio becomes even more central to policy analysis.

It is generally accepted that under an international gold standard small countries had relatively little policy flexibility, and even larger countries faced important policy constraints. At the same time, almost everyone agrees that policymakers in larger countries had at least *some* flexibility under the interwar gold exchange standard. The questions we need to address are: How much flexibility, in which countries, and over what time frame?

Domestic Monetary Policy under an International Gold Standard

When evaluating domestic monetary policy under an international gold standard, economic historians often gravitate toward one of two perspectives. Some employ an equilibrium model of the gold standard featuring purchasing power parity and view monetary policy as being set in a global context, with domestic monetary policy being mostly endogenous. At the other extreme are those who view the constraints of the international gold standard as little more than a minor nuisance and who model domestic monetary policy using a framework more appropriate to an unconstrained fiat money regime.

Of course, these two extremes oversimplify actual historical studies of the gold standard. Most economic historians have a relatively sophisticated understanding of the various perspectives, and assertions made about monetary policy options are often based on empirical judgments about deviations from purchasing power parity, exchange controls, and/or the size of the domestic economy relative to the world economy. Nevertheless, there is a need for a model that clearly differentiates between exogenous and endogenous changes in monetary policy, and that more clearly specifies what constitutes a "small country" or a "large country" in the context of world monetary policy.

In Chapter 1, we modeled world monetary policy and thus were able to dodge the question of whether to use an equilibrium or disequilibrium gold standard model. As we now shift our focus to the monetary policies of individual central banks, it will no longer be possible to evade the question of whether (or to what extent) purchasing power parity and integrated capital markets constrained the ability of interwar central banks to conduct discretionary monetary policies. For analytical purposes, it will be much easier if we use an equilibrium model with integrated goods and capital markets to evaluate domestic monetary policies.

Under the equilibrium approach to the international gold standard, domestic money supplies and interest rates are at least partially endogenous. For example, the fall in the Canadian money supply during the early 1930s is best seen, not as a discretionary policy action by the Canadian authorities, but rather as an indication of a contractionary world monetary policy. Of course, in the real world there were various "frictions" that inhibited goods and financial market arbitrage. Nevertheless, *none* of the key findings in this book hinge on purchasing power parity working perfectly, only on the weaker assumption that changes in the world price level and interest rates had a powerful effect of domestic monetary conditions.

We normally think of monetary policy as being implemented through central bank actions that change the supply of money. In contrast, under the gold market approach the term "monetary policy" refers to central bank actions that influence the *demand* for gold. In order to evaluate the policy of individual central banks, we first need to partition changes in world gold demand among the major central banks. Under an international gold standard regime, a "large" economy is simply an economy with a large real demand for monetary gold.[19] During the early 1930s the United States and France had far and away the largest monetary gold stocks.

---

19. Here we are using the terms "large" and "small" to refer to the size of a country's impact on the world money stock and price level, not the terms of trade, as in international trade models.

To show the impact of changes in gold demand from individual central banks, Equation 1.1 can be converted from levels to the first difference of logs, and then partitioned by country:

$$\Delta \ln P = \Delta \ln G - \sum_{i=1}^{n} (g_i/g)^*(\Delta \ln g_i) \tag{13.1}$$

where (g_i/g) indicates the "size" of the ith country. Thus, if France holds 20 percent of the world monetary gold stock and the real French monetary gold stock increases by 30 percent, then, *ceteris paribus*, France would have increased its demand for monetary gold by an amount equal to 6 percent of the world gold stock. *Ceteris paribus*, this increase in the demand for monetary gold would have reduced the world price level by 6 percent.

Whether or not it would actually have such an impact would, of course, depend on a much more complex set of secondary effects. We saw that the deflationary impact of increases in the world demand for monetary gold could be partially offset by changes in the supply of monetary gold, but also that this effect would probably be rather small in the short run. As we begin to focus on individual central bank policies, we will also need to keep in mind the possibility of offsetting actions by other central banks, a process termed "sterilization." (These issues are discussed further in "Central Bank Interdependence.") Nevertheless, Equation 13.1 provides a good starting point when thinking about the potential influence of individual central banks on the world price level.

Table 13.5 provides the same data as Table 13.3, as well as gold demand data for some of the more important individual central banks. All percentage changes are expressed as first differences of logs, so that the changes can be added across both time and space. Note that roughly one half of the world increase in real gold demand between 1926 and 1932 occurred in France, and another 20 percent occurred in the United States. To make sense out of these numbers, however, we also need to consider the extent to which changes in the real demand for monetary gold can be viewed as *discretionary* monetary policies.

In Equation 1.2 we partitioned changes in real gold demand into changes in real currency demand and changes in the gold reserve ratio. Now we can do the same for individual central banks:

Table 13.5. The Impact of Changes in the Gold Reserve Ratio, the Real Demand
for Currency, the Real Demand for Gold, and the Total Monetary
Gold Stock, on the World Price Level, 1926–1932

Time Period		Dec 1926 to Jun 1928	Jun 1928 to Oct 1929	Oct 1929 to Oct 1930	Oct 1930 to Aug 1931	Aug 1931 to Dec 1932	Dec 1926 to Dec 1932
United States	1. r	+1.24	−2.59	−4.69	+1.55	+9.46	+5.15
	2. m	+1.55	−0.58	−0.46	−9.85	−9.66	−19.01
	3. g	+2.79	−3.17	−5.15	−8.30	−0.20	−13.86
England	4. r	−1.07	+1.52	−1.38	+1.05	−1.37*	−1.19
	5. m	−0.13	+0.30	−0.55	−0.59	+1.19	+0.29
	6. g	−1.20	+1.82	−1.93	+0.46	−0.18	−0.90
France	7. r	−3.23	−2.73	−2.49	−1.80	−6.53	−17.27
	8. m	−1.47	−1.68	−3.08	−3.02	−5.17	−13.99
	9. g	−4.70	−4.41	−5.57	−4.82	−11.70	−31.26
Rest of World	10. r	−0.92	+0.62	−1.06	+0.75	−7.36	−8.55
	11. m	−4.01	−0.98	−0.89	−2.73	+0.08	−8.09
	12. g	−4.93	−0.36	−1.95	−1.98	−7.28	−16.64
World	13. r	−3.98	−3.18	−9.62	+1.55	−5.80	−21.86
	14. m	−4.05	−2.94	−4.97	−16.18	−13.56	−40.80
	15. g	−8.03	−6.12	−14.59	−14.63	−19.36	−62.66
	16. G	+5.82	+5.42	+5.25	+3.93	+5.18	+25.61
	17. P	−2.21	−0.70	−9.34	−10.70	−14.18	−37.06

r = direct impact of changes in gold-reserve ratio on price level

m = direct impact of changes in real currency demand on price level

g = direct impact of changes in real demand for gold on price level

G = change in the total world monetary gold stock

P = change in the world price level

Note: All numbers represent the first difference in the log of P (times 100); the numbers are
not annualized. The sum of the impact of changes in r and m should equal the impact
of changes in g. For the world as a whole, the change in P reflects changes in G and g.
For more information on rest of world (ROW), see Appendix.

*The decomposition of the British demand for gold has little significance after Britain left
the gold standard in September 1931.

$$\Delta lnP = \Delta lnG_s - \sum_{i=1}^{n}(\Delta ln\ r_i/\Delta ln\ g_i)^*(g_i/g)^*(\Delta ln\ g_i) - \sum_{i=1}^{n}(\Delta ln\ m_i/\Delta ln\ g_i)^*(g_i/g)^*(\Delta ln\ g_i)$$

(13.2)

Equation 13.2 can be simplified as follows:

$$\Delta ln\ P = \Delta ln\ G_s - \sum_{i=1}^{n}(\Delta ln\ r_i)^*(g_i/g) - \sum_{i=1}^{n}(\Delta ln\ m_i)^*(g_i/g)$$

(13.3)

The first summation term in Equation 13.3 shows the sum of the impact of changes in each country's gold reserve ratio on the world price level, while the second summation term shows the sum of the impact of changes in each country's real demand for currency on the world price level. Thus, in the previous example, where we assumed that the French held 20 percent of the world monetary gold stock, a 10 percent increase in the French gold reserve ratio would, *ceteris paribus*, depress the world price level by 2 percent, and a 20 percent increase in French (real) currency demand would depress the world price level 4 percent. All the aforementioned caveats about secondary effects apply here as well.

The data in Table 13.5 does at least dispel one set of misconceptions about the interwar gold standard. Individual central banks may have had little or no effect on world monetary policy, but not for the reasons often cited. If France had limited ability to engage in discretionary monetary policies, it was not because French GDP constituted only a modest share of the world total, nor was it because of the existence of purchasing power parity, nor was it because expansionary monetary policies would have merely led to an outflow of gold. *All of those assumptions are built into the construction of Table 13.5.* Yet even in the context of a frictionless, equilibrium model of the international gold standard, French monetary policy was capable of sharply depressing the world price level during the period from 1926 to 1932 (by roughly 17 percent, if we ignore the secondary effects). Instead, any argument for the impotence of French monetary policy would have to be premised on a completely different set of assumptions.

For instance, changes in the French gold reserve ratio might have led other central banks to move their ratios in the opposite direction. This sort of response was called sterilization. It is also possible that French policy led to offsetting changes in the private supply and demand for gold. As French gold hoarding depressed the world price level, this might have led to an increased supply of newly mined gold and reduced the industrial demand for gold. And finally, if the French policy led to higher nominal interest rates, then it might have reduced the real demand for currency. This is called the liquidity effect, and it would moderate the deflationary impact of a higher French gold ratio.

It would be nearly impossible to estimate stable parameter values in a general equilibrium time series model of the international gold standard, because so many of the secondary effects (private gold hoarding, currency hoarding, sterilization of gold flows, etc.) are extremely sensitive to a wide variety of macroeconomic conditions.[20] Here it might be useful to recall the approach taken by Friedman and Schwartz, whose famous study of U.S. monetary history boils down to three basic elements:

1. Calling attention to the fact that monetary aggregates are closely correlated with U.S. business cycles.
2. A theoretical explanation of how money can influence national income.
3. A long and detailed narrative, which shows that many of the monetary shocks were exogenous.

This book attempts to do something similar for gold market shocks (with the theoretical analysis in this chapter). And the narrative chapters add one new wrinkle to the Friedman–Schwartz method; I link gold market shocks to not just the business cycle, but also to movements in financial asset prices.

One of the most hotly contested issues among economic historians revolves around the question of which central bank (or banks) is most to blame for the Great Depression. Unfortunately, traditional accounts of monetary policy under a gold standard tend to rely on theoretically dubious indicators such as interest rates, the money stock, or gold flows. For open economies, both interest rates and domestic money stocks are at least partially endogenous under an international gold standard. And gold flows between any two countries might reflect either an expansionary policy in the country losing gold or a contrac-

---

20. This parameter instability is perhaps easiest to envision when considering the response of other central banks, which clearly involves game theoretic considerations. But it is just as true for the response of private gold and currency hoarding to policy actions, which will depend on a wide variety of factors including expectations of banking and/or currency crises.

tionary policy in the country receiving gold. Table 13.5 certainly doesn't provide any shortcuts to resolving these issues; there are too many possible secondary effects. But at least with the gold reserve ratio we have a truly exogenous[21] indicator of monetary policy and thus a starting point for the analysis of policy actions of individual central banks under the international gold standard.

Central Bank Interdependence

Until now, we have assumed that one country can change its gold reserve ratio without affecting the ratios in other countries. Keynes disputed the assumption that central bank policies can be treated independently:

> During the latter half of the nineteenth century, the influence of London on credit conditions throughout the world was so predominant that the Bank of England could almost have claimed to be the conductor of the international orchestra. By modifying the terms on which she was prepared to lend, aided by her own readiness to vary the volume of her gold reserves *and the unreadiness of other central banks to vary the volumes of theirs*, she could to a large extent determine the credit conditions prevailing elsewhere (1930 [1953], II, pp. 306–07, emphasis added).

If Keynes were correct, then the Bank of England would have had enormous leverage over the world's money supply.[22] For example, assume the Bank

---

21. In Eichengreen's (1984) gold standard model the problem of the endogeniety of money and interest rates is circumvented by using the discount rate as a policy indicator. Unfortunately, contemporary accounts of the interwar period suggest that even many discount rate changes merely reflected trends in world interest rates. More importantly, even if changes in the discount rate can be considered exogenous, they provide no *quantitative* measure of the effect of a policy action.

22. McCloskey and Zecher (1976) criticized Keynes's assertion by noting that the Bank of England held a gold stock equal to only 0.5 percent of total world reserves. This would seem too small to allow the Bank of England any significant influence over the world money supply (or price level). There are several problems with their criticism. They have assumed that central banks were indifferent between holding gold or Bank of England notes as reserves. Yet, many countries placed great importance on their gold stocks, and in some cases laws specified a minimum gold reserve ratio. Thus, the relevant size variable is the ratio of England's monetary gold stock to the world's monetary gold stock, not the ratio of England's gold stock to total world reserves. More importantly, McCloskey and Zecher ignored Keynes's assump-

of England doubled its gold reserve ratio. This would represent a contractionary policy, which would then lead to a gold inflow to Britain. If other countries
wished to avoid an outflow of gold, they would have had to adopt equally
contractionary monetary policies. In that case, the change in the Bank of
England's gold reserve ratio would have generated a proportional shift in the
world gold reserve ratio.

Although it is unreasonable to assume that foreign gold stocks were not
allowed to change at all, during the interwar period some countries did not allow significant fluctuations in their monetary gold stocks.[23] Other central
banks may have varied their gold holdings but not in response to discretionary
policy decisions taken by the Bank of England. Thus, it is quite possible that
the estimates in Table 13.5 significantly *understate* the ability of central banks
to engage in discretionary monetary policies.

An alternative form of interdependence occurs when countries refuse to
allow gold flows to influence their domestic money supplies. If one country
reduces its gold reserve ratio, other countries can offset or sterilize this policy
by raising their own gold reserve ratios. Complete sterilization would occur
if the other countries raised their gold reserve ratios enough to prevent any
change in the world money supply.

If central bank policies are interdependent, then there are a variety of ways
in which a change in one country's gold reserve ratio might impact the world
gold reserve ratio:

1. $d(\ln r)/d(\ln r_i) = 0$ (the complete sterilization case)

2. $d(\ln r)/d(\ln r_i) = G_i/G$ (the policy independence case)

3. $d(\ln r)/d(\ln r_i) = 1$ (the extreme Keynesian case)

---

tion that other central banks were unwilling to vary their reserves of gold (as the rules of the
game required).

23. There also may have been an asymmetrical response, with central banks being more
reluctant to allow gold outflows than gold inflows. Note that the unwillingness of central
banks to vary their gold holdings does not necessarily imply an unwillingness to freely exchange currency for gold. They could set their discount rate at a level to prevent gold flows.

In Table 13.5 the estimated impact of central bank policy changes was computed under the "policy independence" assumption (i.e., that a change in one country's gold reserve ratio had no impact on gold reserve ratios in other countries).

Given the huge increase in the world gold reserve ratio between 1926 and 1932, and given the large decline in prices and output after 1929, it is natural to wonder why there wasn't more policy coordination among the major central banks. Kindleberger (1973) argued that the interwar gold standard lacked a hegemonic power—a role filled by the Bank of England during the classical gold standard era. Eichengreen suggested that central bank policy *cooperation* was lacking during the early 1930s, when it might have helped to arrest a worldwide decline in prices and output.

Central bank policy coordination (or the lack thereof) is an important theme in the narrative chapters. Instead of looking at what sort of policy coordination was technically feasible or what might have been done under the classical gold standard regime, I focus on financial market expectations about policy coordination: What did the markets expect, and what happened when their expectations went unfulfilled?

Changes in the Price of Gold and Policy Expectations

We have discussed the determinants of three of the variables in Equation 1.3. Now we will consider the fourth variable, the price of gold, which is a constant so long as policymakers adhere to the gold standard. Surprisingly, the gold market approach is especially useful for analyzing monetary policy during periods when a country has temporarily left the gold standard, but only in cases where the price of gold was expected to be re-pegged in the not too distant future.

Because Equation 1.3 is an identity, it is obviously just as true for the U.S. economy in 2010 as in 1933. Why, then, is the gold market approach much more useful when applied to the earlier period? To answer this question, we need to consider the role of *policy expectations*. Today, almost no one expects the United States to return to the gold standard in the near future and hence the price of gold is not a particularly useful indicator of monetary policy expectations.[24] As we saw in Chapters 5 and 7, during 1933 many people (correctly) anticipated that the delinking of the dollar from gold was a temporary expedient and that the United States would soon return to the gold standard. Temin and Wigmore (1990) showed how those expectations allowed policymakers to use the price of gold as a signal of policy intentions. More specifically, dollar depreciation led to expectations of more rapid future money supply growth rates.

In recent decades macroeconomists emphasized the importance of policy expectations. Thus, changes in the current setting of policy tools, whether the fed funds target or the monetary base, have far less impact on aggregate demand than changes in the expected future path of those policy instruments. Policy debates increasingly focus on questions of policy regimes, or rules, such as inflation targeting. To see why, consider the options of a central bank faced with a zero nominal interest rate and a depressed economy. If one thinks about policy merely in terms of the current setting of the fed funds rate, then there doesn't appear to be any way for the central bank to boost aggregate demand. Of course, the central bank could still expand the monetary base, a policy termed "quantitative easing." But even that may be ineffective if banks simply hoard the extra reserves. An alternative strategy would be to commit to a higher inflation target over time. If credible, this policy could allow central banks to reduce real interest rates even when nominal rates are stuck at zero.

Of course, there is much more to be said about liquidity traps, and I examine this issue more closely in Chapter 4. But for now it is enough to recognize two important insights from modern monetary economics:

1. What matters is not the current setting of interest rates (nominal or real), nor current changes in the money supply, however defined. Instead, aggregate demand is most strongly impacted by changes in the expected path of monetary policy over time.

2. The effectiveness of central bank policy will often hinge on whether the policy appears credible to the financial markets. If a policy is perceived as being unsustainable (for either technical or political reasons) it may have little or no impact on aggregate demand.

---

24. It is conceivable that the price of gold plays a minor role in the formation of policy expectations if the Fed uses gold prices as an indicator of private sector inflation expectations.

It is not hard to imagine how important these issues become when we move from a fiat regime to an international gold standard, which imposed important constraints on monetary policy. For example, consider a central bank attempting to adopt an expansionary monetary policy during the early 1930s. If it succeeds in pushing prices above the level of other countries, the policy may lead to a balance of payments deficit and a gold outflow. In the long run, prices would revert back to their original level. This is the classic "price-specie-flow" mechanism described by Hume.

Now let's reexamine this example in light of recent monetary theory. If investors understand the price-specie-flow mechanism, they will expect any monetary injections occurring under a gold standard to be temporary. In that case spot commodity prices may not rise at all, as future expected prices would remain unchanged. If interest rates were already fairly low, then any temporary currency injections might be hoarded by the public or held as excess reserves by banks. In that case monetary policy might not even have the short-term impact assumed in the Humean case; the expectation that policy would be ineffective in the long run would also make it ineffective in the short run.

Now assume that a monetary injection leads investors to worry that the central bank may be forced to devalue its currency. Bernanke (1995) argued that in that case there will be an increase in the private demand for gold, and the value of gold might actually increase—exactly the opposite of what the central bank hoped for when they expanded the money supply. In Chapter 4, we saw that something very much like this happened in the spring of 1932, when open market purchases by the Fed led to a loss of confidence in the dollar and a massive gold outflow.

In contrast, expectations work to assist policymakers when there is a change in the price of gold. In early 1933 President Roosevelt (FDR) devalued the dollar partly because he wished to do an end run around the conservative Federal Reserve. Even if the Fed refused to immediately raise the money supply in response to a higher nominal price of gold (and they did refuse in the short run) the higher price of gold would be expected to raise future price levels in two distinct ways. First, the expected future money supply would rise. And second, even if the Fed tried to avoid increases in the money supply, a higher price of gold would raise domestic prices through international goods arbitrage. And in fact this is exactly what occurred; the price of commodities increased almost immediately after the price of gold was raised and well before the resulting increase in the money supply. Also note that there was no significant change in nominal interest rates. Thus FDR succeeded with a reflationary policy without adjusting either of the two most well-known tools of monetary policy: short-term nominal rates and the monetary base. There is no better example of how the gold market approach to macro can yield insights not seen when using traditional monetary policy indicators.

Concluding Remarks

In this chapter we have looked at the gold market approach to aggregate demand from a variety of perspectives. To better understand the distinctive features of this approach, let's begin with two fundamental questions: How should one think about domestic monetary policy under an international gold standard? And at the level of the world economy, how does the gold market approach differ from other more traditional approaches to monetary theory?

In previous studies of the Depression the international gold standard has been a sort of handmaiden to the analysis of stabilization policy, something that constrained monetary and fiscal policymakers, but didn't really have much direct impact on the price level. In this chapter I've suggested that gold market shocks aren't just important when they affect the money supply, rather they *directly affect aggregate demand and the world price level*. This goes against the common-sense intuition of most macroeconomists, who have generally spent their entire careers focused on fiat money regimes with only a single medium of account—money. But the gold market approach is very much consistent with the most recent trends in both new classical and new Keynesian economic theory, which suggest that the most important influence on aggregate demand is changes in the *expected future path of monetary policy*. Gold market shocks often impacted expected future monetary policy far more strongly than changes in the sort of traditional monetary policy tools studied by Friedman and Schwartz.

It is well known that in an equilibrium model of the gold standard, domestic money supplies and interest rates are at least partly endogenous. Domestic monetary policy can be important, but only to the extent that it impacts the world gold reserve ratio. Of course, we need to keep in mind that these equilibrium models are only an approximation of reality. For instance, because the French franc was significantly undervalued during the late 1920s, the Great Depression hit France somewhat later than most other industrial countries. Deviations from purchasing power parity can certainly give monetary authorities some additional discretion over domestic policy. Nevertheless, the fact that the Depression was a worldwide phenomenon suggests that a useful place to begin is with a *world* model of the gold market.

As soon as we shift our focus to the world gold market we are faced with a second issue: Why is the gold market approach superior to more traditional modes of monetary analysis? The world economy is a closed economy, and thus we can no longer reject monetarist and Keynesian analysis on the basis of the money supply and interest rate being endogenous. Are changes in the monetary gold stock and/or the gold reserve ratio somehow more informative than changes in the world money supply? While there is no simple answer to this question, earlier research on the Gibson paradox provides one example where the gold market approach proved to be an especially useful analytical tool.

The Gibson paradox refers to the positive correlation observed between nominal interest rates and the price level under the classical gold standard. Several studies showed that this correlation reflected the impact of interest rates on the demand for gold.[25] Because the nominal price of gold was fixed, the interest rate was the opportunity cost of holding gold. A decline in interest rates (from an autonomous drop in investment spending) tended to increase the demand for gold (both monetary and nonmonetary). This was because the nominal interest rate was the opportunity cost of holding gold. Thus, low interest rates increased the demand for gold, and as the value of gold increased, prices fell in all countries with currencies pegged to gold.

Readers used to thinking about monetary policy in terms of changes in the money supply may find it useful to consider links between the gold market approach and traditional monetary analysis. For example, during 1930 a reduction in the world monetary base was associated with an increase in central bank demand for gold. Or as another example, on three occasions between

---

25. Most of this research assumed that real and nominal interest rates were similar under the classical gold standard. See Lee and Petruzzi (1986), Barsky and Summers (1988), and Sumner (1993a).

the summer of 1931 and the winter of 1933 a surge in private gold hoarding triggered a reduction in the broader monetary aggregates.

In the narrative chapters, we saw examples where the gold market approach illuminated forces that are almost invisible when viewed through the lens of traditional monetary approaches to the Depression. It is especially well suited to identifying the sort of hidden causal factors that ultimately influenced the money supply and thus aggregate demand during the Great Depression. These insights don't reflect any theoretical superiority of the gold market approach over more traditional monetary analyses but rather the fact that gold market indicators often seemed to be more closely linked to market expectations about the future direction of policy. Disturbances in the world gold market that were expected to impact the future path of the money stock also impacted the current prices of financial assets and commodities.

The gold market model described here looks at four primary factors that affected the world price level. Currency hoarding during the Great Depression has already been exhaustively covered in previous studies, and thus most of the analysis focused on the other three factors: the size of the monetary gold stock, the price of gold, and the gold reserve ratio. The grouping of the nine narrative chapters into three parts reflects changes in the relative importance of these three primary factors. Thus, Part II focuses on the deflationary impact of changes the gold reserve ratio, although private gold hoarding also becomes a significant factor after mid-1931. In Part III changes in the price of gold dominate all other factors. Then in Part IV the emphasis shifts to changes in the supply of monetary gold, caused by variations in private gold hoarding.

Because each of these primary factors raises unique issues, a wide variety of analytical methods are used in Chapters 2 through 10. For instance, the increase in the world gold reserve ratio reflects independent decisions made by a number of important central banks. In order to understand why this occurred, we needed to consider a number of difficult issues. Were the changes in gold reserve ratios intentional? If so, how were they connected to the ordinary tools of central banking, such as discount lending and open market purchases? Were they forecastable? If so, when did markets begin to anticipate this process? Did changes in the world gold reserve ratio reflect policy coordination, policy conflict, or independent decisions taken in isolation?

Why didn't central banks reverse these policies once the Depression became severe?

The analysis in Part II was hampered by the fact that it is often difficult to see exactly which policy changes led to the dramatic increase in the world gold reserve ratio. In contrast, because we have data showing changes in the price of gold during 1933 at daily frequencies, in Part III it is much easier to see the connection between policy shocks and financial market responses. On the other hand, the broader macroeconomic environment becomes much more complex after 1932. Whereas the contraction of 1929–1932 was essentially an aggregate demand phenomenon, after 1933 autonomous wage shocks began to have an important effect on the supply side of the economy. Thus the problem becomes how to disentangle the effects of dollar devaluation from those produced by labor market policies.

After the dollar was again pegged to gold in February 1934, the price of gold no longer played a role in U.S. monetary policy. And as the gold bloc began to disintegrate, central bank hoarding of gold also diminished in importance. In Part IV the gold market analysis focused almost exclusively on the role of private gold hoarding. Once again, the change in subject matter required a corresponding change in analytical methods. Whereas Part II focuses heavily on how international monetary and political shocks affected the prospects of policy coordination and Part III looks at New Deal policies relating to wages and gold prices, Part IV focuses on how news events led to changing expectations of the future value of the dollar. And because the international gold standard had collapsed by 1936, I focus on rumors of impending changes in the value of the dollar against gold, not foreign currencies.

In the beginning of this chapter, I peeled back the first layer of causality by showing how a generic aggregate supply and demand model could explain some of the key stylized facts regarding wages, prices and output during the Depression. Then, I examined the second layer of causation by looking at how the world gold market impacted aggregate demand and prices. Then, I described how individual central banks conducted monetary policy under the constraints of the gold standard. The nine narrative chapters evaluate the most difficult layer of causation, how political and economic turmoil during the 1930s contributed to the policy failures that caused the Great Depression.

Table 13a.1. The Relationship between U.S. Industrial Production, the Gold Ratio, the World Monetary Gold Stock, and the Deposits of Failed U.S. Banks, January 1927 through April 1933, Monthly

Dependent Variable	IP	
Independent Variables	**Coefficient**	**T-stat**
$GRatio_{-1}$	–.242	(–1.50)
$GStock_{-1}$	1.927	(3.60)
FBanks	–.0084	(–3.78)
$IProd_{-1}$	.4104	(3.60)

Notes: The adjusted R^2 = .408 and the Durbin Watson statistic = 1.57. The Cochrane-Orcutt procedure was used to correct for serial correlation. $GRatio_{-1}$, $GStock_{-1}$, and IP_{-1} are the first lags of each variable. Because GStock and GRatio use end of month figures, the actual lag is only about fifteen days. The regressions included a constant term (not shown). The data was derived from various issues of the *Federal Reserve Bulletin*.

Appendix 13.a.
Gold Hoarding and Aggregate Demand

The model discussed in the preceding section implies that exogenous increases in the monetary gold stock should increase aggregate demand and exogenous increases in the gold ratio and/or banking panics should decrease aggregate demand. Unfortunately, monthly nominal expenditure data is unavailable for the early 1930s. If we assume that aggregate demand shocks had a short-run impact on output during the early 1930s, then gold hoarding may also be correlated with monthly changes in industrial production. Table 13a.1 shows the results of a Cochrane-Orcutt regression of the first difference of the log of the U.S. industrial production (IP) on the first difference of the log of the world monetary gold stock (GStock), the log of deposits of failed U.S. banks (FBanks), and the weighted average of the first difference of the log of the gold ratio for seven important industrial countries (GRatio), during the period from January 1927 to April 1933. The weights used to construct GRatio are determined according to each country's share of the world monetary gold stock. This variable represents a crude proxy for world monetary policy.[26]

---

26. These include the United States (1927–1933), Britain (1927–1931), France (1928–1933), Germany (1927–1931), Belgium (1927–1933), Holland (1927–1933), and Switzerland (1927–

The signs on the coefficients of each of the independent variables seem consistent with our gold gold market model, although the coefficient on the gold ratio is not significant at the 5 percent level. It should be emphasized, however, that there is a significant identification problem here, and therefore this regression equation should not be viewed as providing a "test" of the model, but rather merely some useful descriptive statistics, which can augment other types of evidence.

There has been relatively little study of the causes, magnitude, and consequences of changes in the world gold ratio.[27] One problem with estimating the impact of changes in the gold ratio is that aggregate demand would be expected to respond negatively to exogenous changes in that ratio yet might well be positively correlated with changes in the gold ratio induced by central bank attempts to mitigate the impact of shocks to currency demand. For instance, the gold ratio typically declined during banking panics. Because most bank panic–induced increases in currency demand were not fully accommodated, however, these decreases in the gold ratio were associated with falling prices and output. The inclusion of bank failures (FBanks) should pick up some of these shocks, but can hardly be expected to account for all shocks to (world) currency demand. Despite the ambiguous findings in Table 13a.1, it is certainly suggestive that the first year of each of the two major interwar depressions was accompanied by a sharp increase in the world gold ratio, and a relatively low level of bank failures.

The identification problem occurs in any study of the relationship between the world monetary gold stock and aggregate demand. Recall that under a gold standard, aggregate demand can be affected by changes in either gold supply or gold demand. Since there is no theoretical presumption regarding the relative importance of these shocks, it is inappropriate to uncritically accept a quantity theoretic interpretation of a positive correlation between gold stocks and aggregate demand. For example, the deflation of the early 1930s generated a substantial *increase* in the rate of gold production. Thus, a negative correlation between output and gold stocks would not necessarily be inconsistent

---

1933). These countries possessed 70.1 percent of the world monetary gold stock on December 31, 1929, and 76.8 percent on December 31, 1933.

27. See Hamilton (1987), Sumner (1991), Eichengreen (1992), and Bernanke (1995) for some previous studies of this issue.

with models in which *exogenous* increases in monetary gold stocks have an expansionary impact on aggregate demand. Rather, the positive coefficient on monetary gold stocks in Table 13a.1 confirms that during the period from 1927 to 1933 most high frequency variations in the size of the world monetary gold stock reflected fluctuations in private gold hoarding, not disturbances in the flow of newly mined gold.

Appendix 13.b

Data Sources

Currency stock, gold stock, and price index data are from various issues of the *Federal Reserve Bulletin*, U.S. Board of Governors of the Federal Reserve System. Currency data were found for only twenty-nine of the forty-seven members of "rest of world" (ROW) for which gold stock data was available. This currency total was used as a proxy for the total currency stock of ROW. Since most major countries are included in this group of twenty-nine, it is unlikely that the growth rate of real currency demand would have been much different had data from all forty-seven countries been available. Furthermore, errors in estimating the growth rate of the real currency stock of ROW would not affect the estimates of the impact of changes in the real demand for gold in ROW but rather would affect its decomposition into the impact of changes in real currency demand and changes in the gold reserve ratio.

During the late 1930s, some central banks shifted gold holdings from official accounts into other secret exchange equalization funds. I have attempted to adjust the percentage changes to reflect those shifts, but the changes reported in Table 13.5 should be viewed as only a close approximation of actual changes in world monetary gold stocks. The narrative in Chapters 2 through 10 presents evidence that these estimated changes closely correlate with bouts of gold hoarding and dishoarding that were widely discussed in the press.

World cost of living and wholesale price indices were calculated by taking a weighted average of individual country price indices (where the weights were the share of total GNP during 1929). Changes in the world price index reported in Tables 2.1, 2b.1, 13.3 and 13.5 are a simple average of the changes in the world cost of living and world wholesale price indices. This estimate is relatively crude, but for our purposes, we are not concerned with the precise rate of change, but rather with the stylized fact that the world price level declined only slightly during the late 1920s and then fell sharply after October 1929.

Derivation of Table 13.5

Rows 13 through 17 are derived in the same way as in Table 13.3. The impact of changes in the real demand for gold in an individual country on the world price level (rows 3, 6, 9, 12) is derived by first calculating the share of the world real gold demand change that occurs in that country. That share is then multiplied by the (inverse of the) percentage change in the world's real demand for gold (row 15).

The impact of changes in real currency demand and the gold reserve ratios of individual countries are derived by partitioning the real demand for gold into two components. Rows 1, 4, 7, and 10 are derived by multiplying rows 3, 6, 9, and 12, respectively, by $(\Delta \ln r/\Delta \ln g)$. Rows 2, 5, 8, and 11 are derived by multiplying rows 3, 6, 9, and 12, respectively, by $(\Delta \ln m/\Delta \ln g)$. *Note:* By definition, $\Delta \ln g$ is the sum of $\Delta \ln r$ and $\Delta \ln m$.

Appendix 13.c
Other Views on Wage Stickiness in the Great Contraction

The first three narrative chapters focus exclusively on how the world gold market influenced aggregate demand during the Great Contraction; all discussion of autonomous wage shocks was confined to later chapters covering the New Deal period. This does not mean that there were no nonmonetary factors depressing output during the early 1930s. Indeed, Bordo, Erceg, and Evans (2000) estimated that monetary shocks can account for only about 70 percent of the 1929–1933 contraction, and other studies have reached similar conclusions. Thus, it may be useful to discuss some alternative views of the importance of wage stickiness in the Great Contraction.

Today many workers (both union and nonunion) are employed under nominal wage contracts of at least twelve months duration. Because these contracts are rarely indexed, in the short run nominal wages respond strongly to anticipated changes in inflation but hardly at all to unanticipated inflation.[28] One can also observe nominal wage stickiness during the first year of the Depression, when less than 10 percent of workers experienced wage cuts. It is the behavior of wages during the second year of the Depression, however, that presents the greatest challenge to neoclassical labor models. Bordo, Erceg, and Evans noted that as of September 1931 two-thirds of surveyed firms reported that they had made no adjustment in their wage scales since December 1929, by which time wholesale prices had already declined by 23.7 percent.

O'Brien (1989) provides evidence that the unusual wage stickiness of 1929–1931 reflected powerful cultural factors within government and big business. During the 1920s, it was widely believed that sharp wage cuts had worsened the 1921 slump. After taking office in early 1929, President Hoover pressured the business community to maintain a high wage policy during any future downturn. Many business leaders and economists agreed with Hoover, arguing that this sort of policy would help to prop up aggregate demand by preserving workers' purchasing power.

Although one should be skeptical of this sort of ad hoc explanation for anomalous findings, there are good reasons why O'Brien's hypothesis should be taken seriously, at least for the first two years of the Depression. First, there was a striking difference between the rapid response of wages to the depression (and deflation) of 1920–1921, and the much more sluggish response in 1929–1930. Real wages increased sharply during the initial stages of the 1921 depression, as wholesale prices fell even faster than wages. Nevertheless, nominal wages did fall by 20.5 percent between October 1920 and December 1921. In contrast, nominal wages fell by only 2.4 percent between October 1929 and December 1930.[29] And second, in 1933 there would be another cartel-like agreement between government and business to promote high wages, which also seemed to push aggregate wage rates far above the level predicted by neoclassical labor market models. Although cartels are susceptible to cheating, during

---

28. Ghosal and Loungani (1996, p. 665) estimate that the response of nominal wage growth to expected inflation is between 0.6 and 0.8, whereas the response to unexpected inflation is between zero and 0.2.

29. It is true that the WPI fell more sharply during 1921 than 1930, but that can hardly account for all of the difference.

the early 1930s big business was receiving intense pressure to maintain high wages from both above (government) and below (workers).

Our monthly wage series is confined to manufacturing firms, and thus, probably understates the extent of wage cutting during the early 1930s. Cole and Ohanian (1999) show that while real wages in manufacturing increased during the early 1930s, real wages in other sectors actually declined. But this pattern also provides indirect support for the existence of a cartel to maintain high wages. Such collusion would be much more effective among large manufacturing firms than smaller firms in services or agriculture. And Hanes (2000) does find evidence that wage rigidity during the early 1930s was greater in industries that were relatively concentrated and capital intensive.

Simon (2001) showed that during the Depression workers were eager to find jobs, as the reservation wage in "situation wanted" ads placed by clerical workers fell by 58 percent during the early 1930s, a far steeper decline than for actual clerical wages. If one combines Simon's finding with the (sticky) manufacturing wage data, one ends up with a picture of desperate unemployed manufacturing workers drifting into services and agriculture, and then sharply depressing wages in those more competitive sectors. The epicenter of the Great Depression was in industrial sectors such as manufacturing, mining and utilities, as well as transportation sectors such as railroads. Having unemployed industrial workers drift into marginal jobs in agriculture or services was hardly an effective way out of the Depression, and probably helps explain why productivity fell even as the capital/labor ratio increased.[30]

A number of cross-sectional studies also support the hypothesis that sticky wages played a role in transmitting monetary shocks to real output. Eichengreen and Sachs (1985) used the international gold standard as an instrumental variable and found evidence that countries that remained on the gold standard saw larger increases in real wages and larger reductions in industrial production. Bernanke and Carey (1996) used a more sophisticated technique and reached similar conclusions.

---

30. Cole and Ohanian (1999) report that by 1932, manufacturing hours had fallen 45.3 percent below 1929 levels, whereas farm hours had declined by only 1.3 percent. They also report that labor productivity was particularly depressed during 1932–1933, when it had fallen roughly 10–12 percent below 1929 levels.

Cole and Ohanian (2000) countered that wage stickiness could account for only a very small portion of the Great Contraction. Because they deflated manufacturing wages with the GNP deflator, rather than the WPI, their real wage series for workers in manufacturing shows only a modest increase during the early 1930s. And they also noted that with a two-sector general equilibrium model, those workers priced out of the sticky-wage manufacturing sector should have moved to other sectors where real wages did fall, thus partially offsetting the decline in manufacturing output. One has to wonder, however, if other sectors were really capable of rapidly absorbing workers leaving the industrial sector. Demand for food is relatively inelastic, and unemployed factory workers would be unlikely to enter highly skilled service jobs. Some may have entered lower-skilled service sectors such as retailing, but it is difficult to see how more workers selling fewer goods would increase *measured* output in retailing. Many workers presumably drifted into the unmeasured underground economy, becoming peddlers or repairmen.

A more fundamental problem with Cole and Ohanian's (2000) study is that it is difficult to draw any meaningful conclusions from real wage cyclicality in an economy where both wages and prices are sticky. The following thought experiment might help clarify this problem. Consider three hypothetical cases where a monetary contraction causes nominal spending to decline by 50 percent. If wages and prices are completely flexible, then each would also decline by 50 percent, leaving output unchanged. Now assume prices are flexible, but nominal wages are sticky and only fall by 25 percent. In this second case prices might fall 35 or 40 percent, and output might decline by 10 to 15 percent. The exact numbers are not important; the key is that if prices are completely flexible then real wages would rise markedly and thus provide a plausible transmission mechanism for the decline in output. Now consider a third case where prices are *almost* as sticky as wages, and decline by 26 percent (i.e., 1 percent faster than wages). In that case, real wages would rise by only 1 percent, and thus appear completely incapable of explaining the massive 24 percent fall in output. Yet, from the second case, we know that even if prices had been completely flexible, wage stickiness alone was capable of producing a severe recession.

Although the preceding three cases are merely thought experiments, in the third case, I used numbers that are not all that different from the actual changes in nominal GNP, the GNP deflator, real output, and nominal wages during the early 1930s. Thus, while Cole and Ohanian's research contradicts the hypothesis that nominal wage inflexibility is the *only* transmission mechanism for monetary shocks, it does not refute the hypothesis that wage stickiness is the most important transmission mechanism (which is surely the hypothesis that most defenders of the sticky wage transmission mechanism have in mind). Nominal GDP fell by roughly 50 percent between 1929 and 1933. Until new classical theorists are able to come up with a plausible real shock which doesn't require *any important causal role* for this massive drop in nominal spending, it has to be assumed that wage and/or price stickiness played a key role in the Great Contraction.[31] If wage stickiness alone cannot provide a sufficient transmission mechanism, then price stickiness was a contributing factor.

Hawtrey argued that broad price indices are poor indicators of the theoretically relevant price level in business cycle models: "the fall in the prices of manufactured products is checked at the cost of a decline of output. . . . [I]t is the raw materials and farm products, classes which do not meet a shrinkage of demand by a reduction in output, that supply the best measure of the appreciation of gold."[32] He seems to be suggesting that either nominal GDP or commodity price indices are the best proxies for the unobservable equilibrium price level, an interesting hypothesis that I will consider below. Here it is worth noting that when the interwar economy was buffeted by strong aggregate demand shocks, the relatively flexible-price WPI usually tracked demand (i.e., nominal GNP) much more closely than did the GNP deflator.[33] This is probably no coincidence, as the WPI and nominal GNP are each more sensitive to monetary conditions than is the GNP deflator.

Vedder and Gallaway (1993) deflated nominal wages by both wholesale prices and labor productivity and blamed high unemployment on real wages being above the level justified by labor productivity. Although Vedder and

---

31. I don't mean to suggest that Cole and Ohanian take such an extreme position. They seem to view 1920–1921 as a benchmark monetary shock and quite reasonably ask why the 1929–1933 downturn was so much more severe.

32. See Hawtrey (1947, pp. 137–38).

33. Consider the following four periods when there were sharp changes in prices and output: 20:3 to 21:3, 29:3 to 33:1, 33:1 to 34:1, and 37:3 to 38:1. During those four periods the GNP deflator changed (in absolute value) by an average of 15.6 percent. Nominal GNP changed by an average of 30.5 percent. The WPI changed by an average of 27.5 percent.

Gallaway's results are often quite similar to the findings in this study, I think their interpretation of wage cyclicality lumps together two very different events: policy-generated autonomous real wage shocks and the more complex problem of aggregate demand shocks, which (due to wage and price stickiness) leave real wages too high to insure full employment. It is only in the first case that the Vedder–Gallaway data actually shows high real wages to be "the cause" of unemployment. Yet despite this reservation, the Vedder–Gallaway approach provides a unified (albeit, ad hoc) explanation for the Great Depression. Like O'Brien, they emphasized the importance of Hoover's high wage policy in the initial downturn; if they are right about this issue then it is not much of stretch to visualize an explanation for the whole of Figure 1.2 centered on dysfunctional labor markets. After all, when we move on to the New Deal era we will see that Vedder and Gallaway's high wage explanation of unemployment is now almost the consensus view.

Given all of the conflicting evidence, there is no reason to believe that economists will soon be able to reach a consensus on the relative importance of wage and price stickiness in the Great Contraction, or any other business cycle. Thus, in the narrative I took an agnostic position regarding the transmission mechanism for monetary shocks and instead focused on explaining how gold market disturbances generated those shocks. Only where *autonomous* wage shocks were clearly the primary determinant of output fluctuations (as occurred five times during the New Deal) was the focus placed on labor market issues.

To summarize, I began with the hypothesis that aggregate demand shocks produce countercyclical real wages and aggregate supply shocks produce procyclical real wages. Then I saw that this dichotomy is too simple. The higher wages associated with New Deal wage policies almost certainly reduced aggregate supply, even as they made real wages more countercyclical. Instead, the distinction made by Hoehn[34] seems more useful; demand shocks generate countercyclical real wages and productivity shocks (such as the 1970s energy crisis) generate procyclical real wages. During the 1930s, both aggregate demand shocks and autonomous wage shocks contributed to the countercyclicality of real wages. If we combine these various hypotheses we can reach

---

34. See Hoehn (1988).

some tentative conclusions about the striking countercyclicality of real wages apparent in Figure 1.2:

1. The economy was impacted by some unusually strong aggregate demand shocks, which led to countercyclical real wage movements.

2. The WPI oversampled commodity prices, which are especially volatile and often move procyclically. This further increased the (estimated) countercyclicality of real wages in manufacturing.

3. Beginning in 1933, New Deal policies generated a series of autonomous wage shocks, which made real wages even more countercyclical.

4. During the 1930s there were relatively few of the sort of *high frequency*[35] productivity shocks that generate procyclical real wage movements.

Appendix 13.d
Other Factors in the Great Contraction

Falling prices and sticky wages may explain the rapid drop in output during 1930, but it cannot account for the severity of the Depression in 1932–1933. Even nominal manufacturing wages began to decline more sharply once the financial crisis of September 1931 showed that the Depression wasn't ending anytime soon. Unfortunately, any expansionary impact from the wage cuts was negated by tax policy and banking difficulties, which depressed output in 1932, and early 1933.

There has been much debate over the impact of the Smoot-Hawley tariff, with some arguing that it was the single most important cause of the initial contraction, while others argue that it should have boosted domestic output by discouraging imports.[36] Neither view seems likely. The trade surplus did

---

35. This argument applies solely to high frequency productivity shocks. Field (2003) argued that a series of technological innovations led to strong productivity growth throughout the 1930s, which could certainly help explain the surprisingly high *level* of real wages by the end of the decade.

36. See Kindleberger (1984, pp. 366–67). Although I don't agree with Kindleberger's assertion that tariffs would normally have an expansionary impact, I do accept his broader argument that it is unlikely that either the 1929 crash, or the subsequent depression, were caused by U.S. trade policies.

not increase after the tariff was implemented, and by distorting trade, Smoot-Hawley reduced the efficiency of the U.S. economy. So it certainly did not help the economy, but there is also little evidence that an increase in tariff rates could produce anything like the collapse in demand seen after 1929. Indeed, higher tariffs would be expected to raise prices.

Cole and Ohanian represent the consensus view when they suggest that the tariff's impact on employment was relatively minor. But they argue that higher income and payroll taxes did have a significant contractionary effect, reducing labor inputs by roughly 4 percent as of 1939. Although this may seem modest relative to the overall decline in employment, it is hardly insignificant if one is looking for contributing factors, rather than "the" cause of the Depression. The biggest tax increase occurred in 1932, when the top marginal income tax rate was raised from 25 to 63 percent.

Bernanke (1983) argued that financial instability also depressed output during the early 1930s, not just by impacting aggregate demand but also by reducing the economy's efficiency, as credit relationships were disrupted by the widespread bank failures. Cole and Ohanian (1999) estimated that this factor could have depressed output by as much as 4.7 percent (assuming that the financial distress was exogenous). The greatest efficiency losses probably occurred during early 1933, when the economy was buffeted by a severe banking panic, statewide banking holidays, and then a national banking holiday. Higher taxes, tariffs, and disintermediation may help explain why the Bordo, Erceg, and Evans simulations fail to fully explain the depressed level of output during 1932 and 1933. And this problem is not confined to their study; in Chapter 6 we saw that Irving Fisher's famous Phillips curve model exhibited a similar weakness.

References

Ahamed, Liaquat. 2009. *Lords of Finance: The Bankers Who Broke the World*. Penguin Press.

Alchian, Armen A. and Benjamin Klein. 1973. "On a Correct Measure of Inflation." *Journal of Money, Credit and Banking*, 5, 1, pp. 173–91.

Bagehot, Walter. 1873. *Lombard Street*. New York: Scribner, Armstrong.

Barber, William J. 1985. *From New Era to New Deal*. Cambridge: Cambridge University Press.

Barber, William J. 1996. *Designs Within Disorder: Franklin D. Roosevelt, the Economists, and the Shaping of American Economic Policy, 1933–1945*. Cambridge: Cambridge University Press.

Barro, Robert. 1979. "Money and the Price Level Under the Gold Standard." *Economic Journal*, Vol. 89, No. 353, pp. 13–33.

Barro, Robert. 1984. "Some Evidence on the Real Price of Gold, Its Costs of Production, and Commodity Prices—A Comment." from Michael D. Bordo and Anna J. Schwartz, *A Retrospective on the Classical Gold Standard, 1821–1931*, Chicago, The University of Chicago Press, pp. 644–46.

Barsky, Robert B. 1987. "The Fisher Hypothesis and the Forecastability and Persistence of Inflation." *Journal of Monetary Economics*, 19, 1, pp. 3–24.

Barsky, Robert B. and Lawrence H. Summers. 1988. "Gibson's Paradox and the Gold Standard." *Journal of Political Economy*, 96, pp. 528–50.

Beney, M. Ada. 1936. *Wages, Hours, and Employment in the United States, 1914–1936*. New York: National Industrial Conference Board.

Benjamin, Daniel J. and Levis A. Kochin. 1979. "Searching for an Explanation of Unemployment in Interwar Britain." *Journal of Political Economy*, 87: 441–78.

Bernanke, Ben S. 1983. "Nonmonetary Effects of the Financial Crisis in the Propagation of the Great Depression." *American Economic Review*, 73, June, pp. 257–76.

Bernanke, Ben S. 1993. "The World on a Cross of Gold: A Review of *Golden Fetters: The Gold Standard and the Great Depression, 1919–1939*." *Journal of Monetary Economics,* 31 (April): 251–67.

Bernanke, Ben S. 1995. "The Macroeconomics of the Great Depression: A Comparative Approach." *Journal of Money, Credit and Banking,* 27 (February): 1–28.

Bernanke, Ben, S. 1999. Japanese Monetary Policy: A Case of Self-Induced Paralysis? Manuscript: Princeton University.

Bernanke, Ben S. 2003. Some Thoughts on Monetary Policy in Japan. Speech given at the Japan Society, May 31, 2003. http://www.federalreserve.gov/boarddocs/speeches/2003/20030531/default.htm

Bernanke, Ben S., and Kevin Carey. 1996. "Nominal Wage Stickiness and Aggregate Supply in the Great Depression." *Quarterly Journal of Economics,* 111, August, pp. 853–83.

Bernanke, Ben S., and Harold James. 1991. "The Gold Standard, Deflation and Financial Crisis in the Great Depression: An International Comparison." In R. Glenn Hubbard (ed.), *Financial Markets and Financial Crises*, Chicago, University of Chicago Press, pp. 33–68.

Bernanke, Ben S. and Ilian Mihov. 2000. "Deflation and Monetary Contraction in the Great Depression." In *Essays on the Great Depression,* by Ben Bernanke. Princeton: Princeton University Press, pp. 108–60.

Bernanke, Ben S. and Martin Parkinson. 1989. "Unemployment, Inflation and Wages in the American Depression: Are There Lessons for Europe?" *American Economic Review Papers and Proceedings*, 79, May, pp. 210–14.

Bernanke, Ben, and Michael Woodford. 1997. "Inflation Forecasts and Monetary Policy." *Journal of Money, Credit and Banking*, 29, pp. 653–84.

Bils, Mark J. 1985. "Real Wages over the Business Cycle: Evidence from Panel Data." *Journal of Political Economy* 93 (August): 666–89.

Bittlingmayer, George. 1996. "Antitrust and Business Activity: The First Quarter Century." *Business History Review,* 70 (Autumn): 363–401.

Bloomfield, Arthur I. 1959. *Monetary Policy under the International Gold Standard.* New York: Federal Reserve Bank of New York.

Bordo, Michael D. 1994. "Review of *Golden Fetters.*" *Journal of International-Economics*, February, pp. 193–97.

Bordo, Michael D., Ehsan Choudhri, and Anna Schwartz. 2002. "Was Expansionary Monetary Policy Feasible During the Great Contraction? An Examination of the Gold Standard Constraint." *Explorations in Economic History,* 39, pp. 1–28.

Bordo, Michael D., Robert T. Dittmar, and William T. Gavin. 2003. "Gold, Fiat Money, and Price Stability." National Bureau of Economic Research, Working Paper 10171.

Bordo, Michael D. and Barry Eichengreen. 1998. "Implications of the Great Depression for the Development of the International Monetary System." In *The Defining Moment: The Great Depression and the American Economy in the Twentieth Century.* Edited by Michael D. Bordo, Claudia Goldin, and Eugene N. White. Chicago: University of Chicago Press, pp. 403–53.

Bordo, Michael D., Christopher J. Erceg, and Charles L. Evans. 2000. "Money, Sticky Wages, and the Great Depression." *American Economic Review,* 90, 5, pp. 1447–63.

Brown, William A., Jr. 1940. *The International Gold Standard Reinterpreted, 1914–1934.* Volume II, New York: NBER.

Brunner, Karl. 1981. "Understanding the Great Depression." In *The Great Depression Revisited,* edited by Karl Brunner. Boston: Martinus Nijhoff, pp. 316–58.

Burdekin, Richard C.K. and Marc D. Weidenmier. 2005. "'Non-Traditional' Open Market Operations: Lessons from FDR's Silver Purchase Program." Unpublished paper, Claremont McKenna College.

Cagan, Phillip. 1965. *Determinants and Effects of Changes in the Stock of Money, 1857–1960,* New York, National Bureau of Economic Research.

Calomiris, Charles W. 1993. "Financial Factors in the Great Depression." *Journal of Economic Perspectives,* 7 (Spring): 61–85.

Calomiris, Charles W. and Joseph R. Mason. 2001. "Fundamentals, Panics, and Bank Distress During the Depression." *American Economic Review,* 93, 5, pp. 1615–47.

Carr, Edward H. 1947. *International Relations between the Two World Wars.* London: Macmillan & Co. Ltd.

Case, Karl E., John M. Quigley, and Robert J. Shiller. 2005. "Comparing Wealth-Effects: the Stock Market versus the Housing Market." *Advances in Microeconomics,* 5(1): 1–32.

Cassel, Gustav. 1922. *Money and the Foreign Exchange After 1914.* New York: Macmillan.

Cassel, Gustav. 1936. *The Downfall of the Gold Standard.* London: Oxford University Press.

Cecchetti, Stephen G. 1992. "Prices During the Great Depression: Was the Deflation of 1930–32 Really Unanticipated?" *American Economic Review*, 82, 1, pp. 141–56.

Chandler, Lester. 1963. *Benjamin Strong, Central Banker*, Washington D.C., The Brookings Institution.

Chowdhry, Bhagwan, Richard Roll, and Yihong Xia. 2005. "Extracting Inflation from Stock Returns to Test Purchasing Power Parity." *American Economic Review*, 95, 1, pp. 255–76.

Christiano, Lawrence J., Eichenbaum, Martin, and Charles L. Evans. 2005. "Nominal Rigidities and the Dynamic effects of a Shock to Monetary Policy." *Journal of Political Economy*, 113, 1, pp. 1–45.

Cole, Harold L. and Lee E. Ohanian. 1999. "The Great Depression in the United States from a Neoclassical Perspective." Federal Reserve Bank of Minneapolis, *Quarterly Review*, 23, 1, pp. 2–24.

Cole, Harold L. and Lee E. Ohanian. 2000. "Re-Examining the Contributions of Money and Banking Shocks to the U.S. Great Depression." Federal Reserve Bank of Minneapolis: Staff Report 270.

Cole, Harold L. and Lee E. Ohanian. 2004. "New Deal Policies and the Persistence of the Great Depression: A General Equilibrium Analysis." *Journal of Political Economy*, 112, 4, pp. 779–816.

Collery, Arnold. 1971. "International Adjustment, Open Economies, and the Quantity Theory of Money." In *Princeton Studies in International Finance*, No. 28.

Currie, L. [1934] 1935. *The Supply and Control of Money in the United States*. Cambridge, MA: Harvard University Press.

Cutler, David, James M. Poterba, and Lawrence H. Summers. 1989. "What Moves Stock Prices?" *Journal of Portfolio Management*, 15, 3, pp. 4–12.

Dam, Kenneth. 1982. *The Rules of the Game*. Chicago: University of Chicago Press.

Darby, Michael R. 1976. "Three-and-a-Half Million U.S. Employees Have Been Mislaid: Or, an Explanation of Unemployment, 1934–41." *Journal of Political Economy*, 84 (February): 1–16.

Davis, Kenneth S. 1986. *FDR: The New Deal Years, 1933–1937*. New York: Random House.

De Long, J. Bradford. 2000. "The Triumph of Monetarism?" *Journal of Economic Perspectives*, 14, 1, pp. 83–94.

DeLong, J. Bradford and Andre Schleifer. 1991. "The Stock Market Bubble of 1929: Evidence from the Closed-end Mutual Funds." *Journal of Economic History*, 51, 3, pp. 675–700.

DeLong, J. Bradford and Lawrence H. Summers. 1986. "Is Increased Price Flexibility Stabilizing?" *American Economic Review*, 76, 5, pp. 1031–44.

De Vroey, Michel. 2000. "IS-LM a la Hicks versus IS-LM a la Modigliani." *History of Political Economy*, 32, 2, pp. 293–316.

Dimand, Robert W. 2000. "Irving Fisher and the Quantity Theory of Money: The Last Phase." *Journal of the History of Economic Thought*, 22, 3, pp. 329–48.

Dimsdale, N.H., Stephen J. Nickell, and Nicolas Horsewood. 1989. "Real Wages and Unemployment in Britain during the 1930s." *Economic Journal*, 99 (June): 271–92.

Dowd, Kevin. 1994. "A Proposal to End Inflation." *Economic Journal*, 104, pp. 828–40.

Dwyer, Gerald P. and Cesare Robotti. 2004. "The News in Financial Asset Returns." Federal Reserve Bank of Atlanta *Economic Review*. 89, 1, pp. 1–23.

Eggertsson, Gauti B. 2006. "Was the New Deal Contractionary?" Federal Reserve Bank of New York, Staff Report no. 264.

Eggertsson, Gauti B. 2008. "Great Expectations and the End of the Depression." *American Economic Review*, 98, 4, pp. 1476–1516.

Eggertsson, Gauti B. and Michael Woodford. 2003. "The Zero Bound on Interest Rates and Optimal Monetary Policy." *Brookings Papers on Economic Activity*, 1, pp. 139–232.

Eichengreen, Barry. 1984. "Central Bank Cooperation under the Interwar Gold Standard." *Explorations in Economic History*, 21, 1, pp. 64–87.

Eichengreen, Barry. 1985. *The Gold Standard in Theory and History*, New York, Methuen.

Eichengreen, Barry. 1986. "The Bank of France and the Sterilization of Gold, 1926–1932." *Explorations in Economic History*, 23, 1, pp. 56–84.

Eichengreen, Barry. 1988. "Did International Economic Forces Cause the Great Depression?" *Contemporary Policy Issues*, 6, 2, pp. 90–114.

Eichengreen, Barry. 1992. *Golden Fetters: The Gold Standard and the Great Depression, 1919–1939*. New York: Oxford University Press.

Eichengreen, Barry. 2004. "Viewpoint: Understanding the Great Depression." *Canadian Journal of Economics*, 37, 1, pp. 1–27.

Eichengreen, Barry, and Jeffrey Sachs. 1985. "Exchange Rates and Economic Recovery in the 1930s." *Journal of Economic History,* 45 (December): 925–46.

Einzig, Paul. 1933. *The Sterling-Dollar-Franc Tangle.* New York: The MacMillan Co.

Einzig, Paul. 1934. *The Future of Gold.* London: MacMillan and Co. Ltd.

Einzig, Paul. 1937a. *The Theory of Forward Exchange.* London: MacMillan and Co. Ltd.

Einzig, Paul. 1937b. *Will Gold Depreciate?* London: MacMillan and Co. Ltd.

Evans, Martin, and Paul Wachtel. 1993. "Were Price Changes During the Great Depression Anticipated? Evidence from Nominal Interest Rates," *Journal of Monetary Economics,* 32 (August): 3–34.

Faust, Jon, Eric T. Swanson, and Jonathan H. Wright. 2004. "Identifying VARS based on high frequency futures data." *Journal of Monetary Economics,* 51, pp. 1107–31.

Ferderer, J. Peter, and David A. Zalewski. 1994. "Uncertainty as a Propagating Force in the Great Depression." *Journal of Economic History,* 54, 825–49.

Ferguson, Thomas, and Peter Temin. 2001. "Made in Germany: The German Currency Crisis of July 1931." MIT, Working Paper 01–07.

Field, Alexander. 2003. "The Most Technologically Progressive Decade of the Century." *American Economic Review,* 93, 4, pp. 1399–1413.

Fisher, Irving. 1920. *Stabilizing the Dollar: A Plan to Stabilize the Price Level Without Fixing Individual Prices.* New York: Macmillan.

Fisher, Irving. 1923. "The Business Cycle Largely A 'Dance of the Dollar.'" *Journal of the American Statistical Association,* 18, 144, 1024–28.

Fisher, Irving. 1925. "Our Unstable Dollar and the So-Called Business Cycle." *Journal of the American Statistical Association,* 20 (June): 179–202.

Fisher, Irving. 1934. *Stable Money.* New York: Adelphi Company.

Flandreau, Marc. 1997. "Central Bank Cooperation in Historical Perspective: A Skeptical View." *The Economic History Review,* 50, 4, pp. 735–63.

Fleming, Michael J. and Eli M. Remolona. 1997. "What Moves the Bond Market?" Federal Reserve Bank of New York *Economic Policy Review* (December): pp. 31–50.

Freeman, Richard B. 1998. "Spurts in Union Growth: Defining Moments and Social Processes." In *The Defining Moment: The Great Depression and the American*

Economy in the Twentieth Century. Edited by Michael D. Bordo, Claudia Goldin, and Eugene N. White. Chicago: University of Chicago Press, pp. 265–95.

Fremling, Gertrude, M. 1985. "Did the United States Transmit the Great Depression to the Rest of the World?" *American Economic Review*, Vol. 75, No. 5, pp. 1181–85.

Friedman, Milton. 1968. "The Role of Monetary Policy." *American Economic Review*, 58.1: 1–17.

Friedman, Milton. 1969. "The Optimum Quantity of Money." In *The Optimum Quantity of Money and Other Essays.* Chicago: Aldine Publishing Company, pp. 1–50.

Friedman, Milton. 1974. "Comments on the Critics." In *Milton Friedman's Monetary Framework: A Debate with His Critics*, edited by Robert J. Gordon. Chicago: University of Chicago Press.

Friedman, Milton. 1975. "25 Years After the Rediscovery of Money: What Have We Learned? A Discussion." *American Economic Review*, 65.2: 176–79.

Friedman, Milton. 1998. "Reviving Japan." *Hoover Digest.* No. 2. April 30.

Friedman, Milton and Anna J. Schwartz. 1963a [1971]. *A Monetary History of the United States, 1867–1960.* Princeton, Princeton University Press.

Friedman, Milton and Anna J. Schwartz. 1963b. "Money and Business Cycles." In *The Optimum Quantity of Money and Other Essays*. Chicago: Aldine Publishing Company, pp. 189–235.

Friedman, Milton and Anna J. Schwartz. 1991. "Alternative Approaches to Analyzing Economic Data." *American Economic Review*, 81, 1, pp. 39–49.

Ghosal, Vivek, and Prakash Loungani. 1996. "Evidence on Nominal Wage Rigidity from a Panel of U.S. Manufacturing Industries." *Journal of Money, Credit and Banking*, 28, 4, part 1, pp. 650–68.

Glasner, David. 1989. *Free Banking and Monetary Reform.* Cambridge: Cambridge University Press.

Glasner, David. 2011. "The Fisher Effect Under Deflationary Expectations." Social Science Research Network. January, 26, 2011. http://papers.ssrn.com/sol3/papers.cfm?abstract_id=1749062#

Gordon, R. J. and Wilcox, J. A. 1981. "Monetarist Interpretations of the Great Depression." In Karl Brunner (Ed.), *The Great Depression Revisited*, Rochester Studies in Economics and Policy Issues, Vol. 2. Boston: Kluwer-Nijhoff.

Gray, Jo Anna, and David E. Spencer. 1990. "Price Prediction Errors and Real Activity: A Reassessment." *Economic Inquiry*, 28, 4, pp. 658–81.

Greene, Clinton A. 2000. "I Am Not, nor Have I Ever Been a Member of a Data-Mining Discipline." *Journal of Economic Methodology*, 7, 2, pp. 217–30.

Hall, Thomas E. and J. David Ferguson. 1998. *The Great Depression: An International Disaster of Perverse Economic Policies*. Ann Arbor: The University of Michigan Press.

Hamilton, James D. 1987. "Monetary Factors in the Great Depression." *Journal of Monetary Economics*, 19, 145–69.

Hamilton, James D. 1988. "Role of the International Gold Standard in Propagating the Great Depression." *Contemporary Policy Issues*, 6, pp. 67–89.

Hamilton, James D. 1992. "Was the Deflation During the Great Depression Anticipated? Evidence from the Commodity Futures Markets." *American Economic Review*, 82, 1, pp. 157–78.

Hanes, Christopher. 1996. "Changes in the Cyclical Behavior of Real Wage Rates, 1870–1990." *Journal of Economic History*, 54, 4, pp. 317–37.

Hanes, Christopher. 1999. "Degrees of Processing and Changes in the Cyclical Behavior of Prices in the United States, 1869–1990." *Journal of Money, Credit and Banking*, 31, 1, pp. 35–53.

Hanes, Christopher. 2000. "Nominal Wage Rigidity and Industry Characteristics in the Downturns of 1893, 1929, and 1981." *American Economic Review*, 90, 5, pp. 1432–46.

Hanes, Christopher. 2006. "The Liquidity Trap and U.S. Interest Rates in the 1930s." *Journal of Money, Credit and Banking*, 38, 1, pp. 163–94.

Hawtrey, Ralph G. 1923. *Monetary Reconstruction*. London: Longmans, Green and Co.

Hawtrey, Ralph G. 1947. *The Gold Standard in Theory and Practice*, London, Longmans, Green and Co.

Hetzel, Robert L. 2009. "Monetary Policy in the 2008–2009 Recession." Federal Reserve Bank of Richmond, *Economic Quarterly*, 95 (Spring): pp. 201–33.

Hetzel, Robert L. 2012. *The Great Recession: Market Failure or Policy Failure?* Cambridge: Cambridge University Press.

Hicks, John.R. 1937. "Mr. Keynes and the 'Classics'; A Suggested Interpretation." *Econometrica*, 5: 147–59.

Hoehn, James G. 1988. "Procyclical Real Wages under Nominal-Wage Contracts with Productivity Variations." *Federal Reserve Bank of Cleveland Economic Review*, 24, 4, pp. 11–23.

Hsieh, Chang-Tai and Christina D. Romer. 2006. "Was the Federal Reserve Constrained by the Gold Standard During the Great Depression? Evidence from the 1932 Open Market Purchase Program." *Journal of Economic History*, 66, 1, pp. 140–76.

Hume, David. 1752. "Of Money" in *David Hume Writings on Economics*. Edited by Eugene Rotwein (1970). Madison Wisconsin: The University of Wisconsin Press.

Irwin, Douglas A. 2012. "The French Gold Sink and the Great Deflation of 1929–32." *Cato Papers on Public Policy*, Vol. 2, pp. 1–41.

Johnson, H. Clark. 1997. *Gold, France, and the Great Depression*. New Haven: Yale University Press.

Jonung, Lars. 1988. "Knut Wicksell's Unpublished Manuscripts—a First Glance." *European Economic Review*, 32, 2–3, pp. 503–11.

Keynes, John. M. 1911. "Review of Irving Fisher: *The Purchasing Power of Money*." *Economic Journal*, 21, pp. 393–98.

Keynes, John M. 1923. *A Tract on Monetary Reform*. London: Macmillan and Co. Ltd.

Keynes, John M. 1930 [1953]. *A Treatise on Money*. London: Macmillan and Co. Ltd.

Keynes, John M. 1936 [1964]. *The General Theory of Employment, Interest, and Money*. New York: Harcourt, Brace & World, Inc.

Keynes, John M. 1982. *The Collected Writings of John Maynard Keynes*. Volume 9, edited by Donald Moggridge, Cambridge: Cambridge University Press.

Keynes, John M. 1982. *The Collected Writings of John Maynard Keynes*. Volume 13, edited by Donald Moggridge, Cambridge: Cambridge University Press.

Keynes, John M. 1982. *The Collected Writings of John Maynard Keynes*. Volume 21, edited by Donald Moggridge, Cambridge: Cambridge University Press.

Kindleberger, Charles P. 1973. *The World in Depression, 1929–1939*. Berkeley: University of California Press.

Kindleberger, Charles P. 1984. *A Financial History of Western Europe*. London: George, Allen & Unwin Ltd.

King, Robert G. 1993. "Will the New Keynesian Macroeconomics Resurrect the IS-LM Model?" *Journal of Economic Perspectives*, 7, 1, pp. 67–82.

Klein, Benjamin. 1975. "Our New Monetary Standard: The Measurement and Effects of Price Uncertainty, 1880–1973." *Economic Inquiry*, 13: 461–84.

Krugman, Paul. 1998. "It's Baaack! Japan's Slump and the Return of the Liquidity Trap." *Brookings Papers on Economic Activity*, 2, pp. 137–87.

Laidler, David. 1991. *The Golden Age of the Quantity Theory*. Princeton: Princeton University Press.

Laidler, David. 1999. *Fabricating the Keynesian Revolution*. Cambridge: Cambridge University Press.

Lastrapes, William D. and George Selgin. 1997. "Fiscal Folly and the Great Monetary Contraction." *Journal of Economic History*, 57, 4, pp. 859–78.

League of Nations. 1930. *Interim Report of the Gold Delegation*. Financial Committee, League of Nations.

League of Nations. 1932. *Report of the Gold Delegation*. Financial Committee, League of Nations.

Lee, Chi-Wen J., and Christopher R. Petruzzi. 1986. "The Gibson Paradox and the Monetary Standard." *Review of Economics and Statistics*, 68, pp. 189–96.

Leeper, Eric M., and Jennifer E. Roush. 2003. "Putting 'M' Back in Monetary Policy." *Journal of Money, Credit and Banking*, 35, 6, part 2, pp. 1217–56.

Leiderman, Leonardo. 1983. "The Response of Real Wages to Unanticipated Money Growth," *Journal of Monetary Economics,* 11 (January): 73–88.

Leijonhufvud, Axel. 1968. *On Keynesian Economics and the Economics of Keynes: A Study in Monetary Theory*. New York: Oxford University Press.

Leijonhufvud, Axel. 1995. "Review of *Money and the Economy: Issues in Monetary Analysis*" by Karl Brunner and Allan Meltzer, in *Journal of Economic Literature*, September, 1341–43.

Lindert, Peter. 1981. "Comments on 'Understanding 1929–1933'." In Karl Brunner ed., *The Great Depression Revisited*. Boston: Martinus Nijhoff Publishing, pp. 125–33.

Lucas, Robert. 1976. "Econometric Policy Evaluation: A Critique." *Carnegie-Rochester Conference Series*, 1, pp. 19–46.

Lyon, Leverett S., Paul T. Homan, Lewis L. Lorwin, George Terborgh, Charles L. Dearing, and Leon C. Marshall. 1972. *The National Recovery Administration: An Analysis and Appraisal*. New York: Da Capo Press.

MacMillan Committee Report. 1931. *Minutes of Evidence Taken Before the Committee on Finance and Industry*. MacMillan Committee: London: His Majesty's Stationary Office.

Mankiw, N. Gregory. 2000. *Macroeconomics*. 4th edition. New York: Worth Publishing.

Mankiw, N. Gregory and Ricardo Reis. 2006. "Pervasive Stickiness." *American Economic Review*, 96, 2, pp. 164–69.

McCloskey, Deirdre N. 1994. *Knowledge and Persuasion in Economics*. Cambridge: Cambridge University Press.

McCloskey, Donald [Deirdre] N. and J. Richard Zecher. 1976. "How the Gold Standard Worked, 1880–1913." From Jeffrey A. Frenkel, and Harry G. Johnson, *The Monetary Approach to the Balance of Payments*. Toronto, University of Toronto Press, pp. 357–85.

McCloskey, Donald [Deirdre] N. and J. Richard Zecher. 1984. "The Success of Purchasing Power Parity: Historical Evidence and Its Implications for Macroeconomics." In: Michael B. Bordo and Anna J. Schwartz, eds., *A Retrospective on the Classical Gold Standard, 1821–1931*, Chicago: University of Chicago Press.

McGrattan, Ellen R. and Edward C. Prescott. 2004. "The 1929 Stock Market: Irving Fisher was Right." *International Economic Review*, 45, 4, pp. 991–1009.

McKinnon, Ronald I. 2000. "The Foreign Exchange Origins of Japan's Liquidity Trap." *Cato Journal*, 20, 1, pp. 73–84.

McQueen, Grant and V. Vance Roley. 1993. "Stock Prices, News, and Business Conditions." *The Review of Financial Studies*, 6, 3, pp. 683–707.

Meltzer, Allan. 1976. "Monetary and Other Explanations of the Start of the Great Depression." *Journal of Monetary Economics*, 2, pp. 455–471.

Meltzer, Allan. 1988. *Keynes's Monetary Theory: A Different Interpretation*. Cambridge: Cambridge University Press.

Meltzer, Allan. 2003. *A History of the Federal Reserve, Volume 1: 1913–1951*. Chicago: University of Chicago Press.

Miron, Jeffrey A. 1994. "Empirical Methodology in Macroeconomics: Explaining the Success of Friedman and Schwartz's *A Monetary History of the United States, 1867–1960*." *Journal of Monetary Economics*, 34, pp. 17–25.

Mishkin, Frederic. 2007. *The Economics of Money, Banking and the Financial Markets*. Eighth Edition. Prentice Hall.

Modigliani, Franco. 1944. "Liquidity Preference and the Theory of Interest and Money." *Econometrica*, 12, 1, pp. 45–88.

Moggridge, Donald E. and Susan Howson. 1974. "Keynes on Monetary Policy, 1910–1946." *Oxford Economic Papers*, July, 226–47.

Moure, Kenneth. 2002. *The Gold Standard Illusion: France, the Bank of France, and the International Gold Standard 1914–1939*. Oxford: Oxford University Press.

Mundell, Robert A. 1968. "The Collapse of the Gold Standard." *American Journal of Agricultural Economics*, 50, 5, pp. 1123–34.

Mundell, Robert A. 1975. "Inflation from an International Viewpoint." In *The Phenomenon of Worldwide Inflation*. David Meiselman and Arthur Laffer editors. Washington: American Enterprise Institute.

Mundell, Robert A. 2000. "A Reconsideration of the Twentieth Century." *American Economic Review*, 90, 3, pp. 327–40.

Nelson, Daniel B. 1991. "Was the Deflation of 1929–1930 Anticipated? The Monetary Regime as Viewed by the Business Press." *Research in Economic History*, Vol. 13, pp. 1–65.

Nelson, Edward. 2005. "The Great Inflation of the Seventies: What Really Happened?" *Advances in Macroeconomics*, 5, 1, Article 3.

Nurske, Ragnar. 1944. "The Gold Exchange Standard." From *International Currency Experience*. Geneva, League of Nations, pp. 27–46.

O'Brien, Anthony Patrick. 1989. "A Behavioral Explanation for Nominal Wage Rigidity During the Great Depression." *Quarterly Journal of Economics*, 104 (November): 719–36.

Paish, Frank W. 1939. "Twenty Years of Floating Debt." *Economica*, 6, 23, pp. 243–69.

Palyi, Melchior. 1972. *The Twilight of Gold, 1914/1936*. Chicago: Henry Regnery Co.

Patinkin, Don. 1993. "Irving Fisher and His Compensated Dollar Plan." Federal Reserve Bank of Richmond *Economic Quarterly*, 79, Summer, pp. 1–33.

Pearson Frank A., William I. Myers, and Altha R. Gans. 1957. "Warren as Presidential Advisor." *Farm Economics*, New York State College of Agriculture, Cornell University, No. 211, December, pp. 5598–676.

Phelps, Edmund S. 1967. "Phillips Curves, Expectations of Inflation and Optimal Unemployment over Time." *Economica*, Vol. 34, No. 135, August, pp. 254–81.

Phinney, Josiah T. 1933. "Gold Production and the Price Level: The Cassel Three Per Cent Estimate." *Quarterly Journal of Economics*, 47, 4, pp. 647–79.

Pigou, Arthur C. 1927. *Industrial Fluctuations*. London: Macmillan and Co.

Prescott, Edward C. 1999. "Some Observations on the Great Depression." Federal Reserve Bank of Minneapolis, *Quarterly Review*, 23, 1, pp. 25–31.

Rappoport, Peter and Eugene N. White. 1993. "Was There a Bubble in the 1929 Stock Market?" *Journal of Economic History*, 53, 3, pp. 549–74.

Roberts, Mark. 1995. "Keynes, The Liquidity Trap and the Gold Standard: A Possible Application of the Rational Expectations Hypothesis." *The Manchester School of Economic and Social Studies*, 63, 1, pp. 82–92.

Robertson, Dennis H. 1922. *Money*. New York: Harcourt Brace and Co.

Rockoff, Hugh. 2001. "On Monetarist Economics and the Economics of a Monetary History." EH.net, Project 2001.

Romer, Christina. 1990. "The Great Crash and the Onset of the Great Depression." *Quarterly Journal of Economics,* 105 (August): 597–624.

Romer, Christina D. 1992. "What Ended the Great Depression?" *Journal of Economic History,* 52 (December): 757–84.

Romer, Christina D. 1999. "Why Did Prices Rise in the 1930s?" *Journal of Economic History*, 59, 1, pp. 167–99.

Romer, Christina and David Romer. 1989. "Does Monetary Policy Matter? A New Test in the Spirit of Friedman and Schwartz." NBER Macroeconomics Annual, 121–70.

Rooke, John. 1824. *Inquiry into the Principles of National Wealth*. Edinburgh: A. Balfour.

Roos, Charles F. 1937. *National Recovery Administration Economic Planning*.

Rothbard, Murray N. 1963. *America's Great Depression*. Princeton: D Van Nostrand, Inc.

Saint-Etienne, Christian. 1984. *The Great Depression, 1929–1938: Lessons for the 1980s*. Stanford: Stanford University Hoover Institution Press.

Sargent, Thomas, J. 1983. "The Ends of Four Big Inflations." *Inflation: Causes and Effects*, edited by Robert E. Hall. Chicago: University of Chicago Press.

Schuker, Stephen A. 2003. "The Gold-Exchange Standard: A Reinterpretation." In *International Financial History in the Twentieth Century*. Edited by Marc Flandreau, Carl-Ludwig Holtfrerich, and Harold James. Cambridge: Cambridge University Press, pp. 77–93.

Schwartz, Anna, J. 1981. "Understanding 1929–1933." In Karl Brunner ed., *The Great Depression Revisited*. Boston: Martinus Nijhoff Publishing, pp. 5–48.

Schwert, G. William. "Indexes of U.S. Stock Prices from 1802 to 1987." *Journal of Business*, 63, 1990a, 399–425.

Schwert, G. William. 1990b. "Stock Returns and Real Activity: A Century of Evidence." *Journal of Finance*, 45, 4, pp. 1237–57.

Selgin, George. 2012. The Rise and Fall of the Gold Standard in the United States. University of Georgia, unpublished manuscript.

Shirras, G. Findlay. 1940. "The Position and Prospects of Gold." *Economic Journal*. 50, 198/199, pp. 207–23.

Silver, Stephen and Scott Sumner. 1995. "Nominal and Real Wage Cyclicality During the Interwar Period." *Southern Economic Journal* (January): 588–601.

Simon, Curtis J. 2001. "The Supply Price of Labor During the Great Depression." *Journal of Economic History*, 61, 4, pp. 877–903.

Skidelsky, Robert. 2003. "Keynes's Road to Bretton Woods: An Essay in Interpretation." In *International Financial History in the Twentieth Century*. Edited by Marc Flandreau, Carl-Ludwig Holtfrerich, and Harold James. Cambridge: Cambridge University Press, pp. 125–51.

Solow, Robert M. 1985. "Economic History and Economics." *American Economic Review*, 75, 2, pp. 328–31.

Steindl, Frank G. 2000. "Fisher's Last Stand on the Quantity Theory: The Role of Money in the Recovery." *Journal of the History of Economic Thought*, 22, 4, pp. 493–98.

Stigler, George J. and James K. Kindahl. 1970. *The Behavior of Industrial Prices*. New York, NBER.

Sumner, Scott. 1989. "Using Futures Instrument Prices to Target Nominal Income." *Bulletin of Economic Research*, 41, pp. 157–62.

Sumner, Scott. 1990a. "A Note on Price Flexibility and Fisher's Business Cycle Model." *Cato Journal*, 9, 3, pp. 719–27.

Sumner, Scott. 1990b. "The Forerunners of 'New Monetary Economics' Proposals to Stabilize the Unit of Account." *Journal of Money, Credit and Banking*, 22, 1, pp. 109–18.

Sumner, Scott. 1991. "The Equilibrium Approach to Discretionary Monetary Policy under an International Gold Standard: 1926–1932." *The Manchester School of Economic and Social Studies* (December): 378–94.

Sumner, Scott. 1992. "The Role of the International Gold Standard in Commodity Price Deflation: Evidence from the 1929 Stock Market Crash." *Explorations in Economic History*, 29, pp. 290–317.

Sumner, Scott. 1993a. "The Role of the Gold Standard in the Gibson Paradox." *Bulletin of Economic Research*, 45, 3, pp. 215–28.

Sumner, Scott. 1993b. "Colonial Currency and the Quantity Theory of Money: A Critique of Smith's Interpretation." *Journal of Economic History*, 53, 1, pp. 139–45.

Sumner, Scott. 1995. "The Impact of Futures Price Targeting on the Precision and Credibility of Monetary Policy." *Journal of Money, Credit and Banking*, 27, pp. 89–106.

Sumner, Scott. 1997. "News, Financial Markets, and the Collapse of the Gold Standard, 1931–1932." *Research in Economic History,* 17, pp. 39–84.

Sumner, Scott. 1999. "The Role of the Gold Standard in Keynesian Monetary-Theory." *Economic Inquiry,* 37.3: 527–40.

Sumner, Scott. 2001. "Roosevelt, Warren, and the Gold-Buying Program of 1933." *Research in Economic History,* 20: 135–72.

Sumner, Scott. 2002. "Some Observations on the Return of the Liquidity Trap." *Cato Journal,* (Winter): pp. 481-90.

Sumner, Scott. 2003. "Does Monetary Policy Become More Desirable As It Becomes Less Effective?" *Economics Letters* 88.1:125–28.

Sumner, Scott. 2004a. "Exchange Rate Crises and U.S. Financial Markets During the 1930s." In *Exchange Rate Regimes and Economic Policy in the Twentieth Century,* edited by Ross Catterall and Derek H. Aldcroft, Ashgate Publishing Co.

Sumner, Scott. 2004b. "How Have Monetary Regime Changes Affected the Popularity of IS-LM?" *History of Political Economy,* 36, supplement, pp. 240–70.

Sumner, Scott. 2006. "Let a Thousand Models Bloom: The Advantages of Making the FOMC a Truly 'Open Market'." Berkeley Electronic Journals, *Contributions to Macroeconomics,* 6, 1.

Sumner, Scott. 2009. "Comment on Brad DeLong: Can We Generate Controlled Reflation in a Liquidity Trap?" *The Economists' Voice,* Vol. 6, Issue, 4, Article 7.

Sumner, Scott. and Stephen Silver. 1989. "Real Wages, Employment and the Phillips Curve." *Journal of Political Economy,* 97, 3, pp. 706–20.

Svensson, Lars E. O. 2003a. "Escaping from a Liquidity Trap and Deflation: The Foolproof Way and Others." *Journal of Economic Perspectives,* 17, 4, pp. 145–66.

Svensson, Lars E. O. 2003b. "What is Wrong with Taylor Rules? Using Judgment in Monetary Policy Through Targeting Rules." *Journal of Economic Literature,* 41, pp. 426–77.

Sweezy, Alan. 1972. "The Keynesians and Government Policy." *American Economic Review* 62, 1, pp. 116–24.

Tavlas, George S. "Keynesian and Monetarist Theories of the Monetary Transmission Process." *Journal of Monetary Economics,* May 1981, 317–37.

Telser, Lester G. 2002. "Higher Member Bank Reserve Ratios In 1936 And 1937 Did Not Cause the Relapse into Depression." *Journal of Post Keynesian Economics,* 24, 2, pp. 205–16.

Temin, Peter. 1976. *Did Monetary Forces Cause the Great Depression?* New York: Norton.

Temin, Peter. 1989. *Lessons from the Great Depression*, Cambridge Massachusetts: The MIT Press.

Temin, Peter, and Wigmore, Barry. 1990. "The End of One Big Deflation." *Explorations in Economic History*, 27 (October): 483–502.

Timberlake, Richard H. 1993. *Monetary Policy in the United States: An Intellectual and Institutional History*. Chicago: University of Chicago Press.

Vedder, Richard K., and Lowell E. Gallaway. 1993. *Out of Work*. New York: Holmes & Meier Publishers, Inc.

Wanniski, Jude. 1978. *The Way the World Works*. New York: Touchstone.

Warren, George F. and Frank A. Pearson. 1935. *Gold and Prices*. New York: J. Wiley.

Weinstein, Michael M. 1981. "Some Macroeconomic Impacts of the National Industrial Recovery Act, 1933–1935." In Karl Brunner ed., *The Great Depression Revisited*. Boston: Martinus Nijhoff Publishing, pp. 262–81.

Wicker, Elmus R. 1971. "Roosevelt's 1933 Monetary Experiment." *Journal of American History*, 57 (March): 864–79.

Wicker, Elmus, R. 1996. *The Banking Panics of the Great Depression*, Cambridge: Cambridge University Press.

Wicksell, Knut. 1907. "The Influence of the Rate of Interest on Prices." *Economic Journal* 17.66: 213–20.

Wigmore, Barrie. 1985. *The Crash and Its Aftermath: A History of Securities Markets in the United States, 1929–1933*. Westport Connecticut: Greenwood Press.

Wigmore, Barrie. 1987. "Was the Bank Holiday of 1933 Caused by a Run on the Dollar?" *Journal of Economic History*, 47, pp. 739–56.

Williams, Aneurin. 1892. "A 'Fixed Value of Bullion' Standard—A Proposal for Preventing General Fluctuations in Trade." *Economic Journal*, 2, pp. 280–89.

Woodford, Michael. 2003. *Interest and Prices*. Princeton: University of Princeton Press.

Index